Inside the AS/400

BY FRANK G. SOLTIS

A Division of
DUKE COMMUNICATIONS
INTERNATIONAL

Loveland, Colorado

Library of Congress Cataloging-in-Publication Data

Soltis, Frank, 1940-
  Inside the AS/400 : an in-depth look at the AS/400's design, architecture, and history / by Frank Soltis.
    p. cm.
  Includes index.
  ISBN 1-882419-13-8
  1. IBM AS/400 (Computer) I. Title.
QA76.8.I25919S64 1995
004.2'545—dc20
                                    95-33232
                                            CIP

Copyright © 1996 by DUKE PRESS
DUKE COMMUNICATIONS INTERNATIONAL
Loveland, Colorado

All rights reserved. No part of this book may be reproduced in any form by any electronic or mechanical means (including photocopying, recording, or information storage and retrieval) without permission in writing from the publisher.

It is the reader's responsibility to ensure procedures and techniques used from this book are accurate and appropriate for the user's installation. No warranty is implied or expressed.

This book was printed and bound in the United States of America.

ISBN 1-882419-13-8

1 2 3 4 5 KP 9 8 7 6 5

To the love of my life for more than 31 years, my wife, Sandra.

DUKE COMMUNICATIONS EUROPE LIMITED
6 Atlantic Office Park, Caspian Road, Altrincham, Cheshire, England, WA14 5HH.
Telephone: 0161-929 0601 Fax: 0161-929 1609

Acknowledgments

As long as 10 years ago, I considered writing this book. Those were the System/38 days, and people such as Paul Conte were encouraging me to write a book about the System/38 and the people who created it. But it was 1985, and the System/38 had been declared a "non-strategic" product within IBM. It was not obvious this system had any future. With the rebirth of the System/38 as the AS/400 in 1988, I began to write a book about the history, the people, and the development of these two systems. Over the past seven years, I have continued to plug away at that manuscript. Paul and others have encouraged me to finish that history book and share the Rochester story with the rest of the world. *Inside the AS/400* does contain a few historical excerpts from that unpublished manuscript.

Rochester is the most creative site in all of IBM. In the last few years, IBM has received lots of criticism for its inability to capitalize on its own technologies and to recognize the emerging needs of its customers. Yet, year after year, the dedicated men and women in Rochester continue to turn out creative, successful products that delight our customers and bring financial rewards to IBM. Rochester has never been very good at winning the "battle of the foil projectors" at IBM headquarters, but we have always been very good at winning the battle for customers.

Throughout this book, I have tried to name some of those creative, dedicated people who are responsible for the success of the AS/400. It is an impossible task, and I have only been able to name a few. For all of you who are not named, please accept my apologies. Even after 32 years of working for IBM in Rochester, hardly a day goes by that I don't feel inspired by the people around me. Thanks to all of you.

Mike Tomashek managed the development organization in Rochester that rewrote the internals of the AS/400 operating system for the PowerPC processors. It was clear in October 1991 that a massive education effort would be needed for the hundreds of new developers we were going to hire to write the new code. I had just spent the previous six months leading the effort to convince the management and technical leadership in Rochester to adopt the PowerPC technology for the AS/400. Now the project had been funded by IBM, and we were authorized to go out and hire our first 200 people. Mike asked me to organize the education effort (in addition to my role in IBM, I am an adjunct professor and a member of the graduate faculty at the University of Minnesota). His request seemed reasonable, so I agreed.

As part of this education, I developed and taught the first classes on the internals of the AS/400. This undertaking would not have been possible without Jan Schliem working with me. Jan took on the responsibility to organize and manage the entire education project. That freed me to develop the class, and that class material formed the basis for this book. It was also Mike Tomashek who convinced me to turn this material into a book.

I also want to thank the Rochester people who reviewed the various chapters of this book and provided feedback for me. I especially want to thank two of them, Bruce Jawer and Larry Walsh, for being true believers in the AS/400 and for encouraging me to finish this project.

Working with the people at Duke Communications over the past few years has been an enjoyable experience for me. I had my first article published in *NEWS 3X/400* (now *NEWS/400*) magazine in 1992, and I have managed to write something for that magazine every year since then. I have also enjoyed participating in the magazine's annual International Conference in Vail, Colorado, for the past three years. Dave Duke and his staff have done a marvelous job with the magazine and the conference. When it came time to select a publisher for this book, Duke Press was a natural choice. Dave Bernard, the editorial director at Duke Press, worked with me from the beginning to ensure that we produced a high-quality book. Two other people, Sharon Hamm and Richard Rubin, are responsible for the form and content of this book.

Sharon Hamm was the book's editor. The job of an editor is a difficult one. She had to handle the seemingly endless number of changes I kept making to the manuscript and still keep both me and the production staff on schedule. She did a great job of balancing all these responsibilities. Thank you, Sharon; it has been a pleasure to work with you.

The person who shaped the final form of this book more than anyone else was the technical editor, Richard Rubin. Many of you know Richard from his excellent technical articles, especially in the area of database design. I tend to look at the AS/400 from the inside out. Richard provided the customer view of the system. Whenever I began to get carried away with the glorification of some technical aspect of the AS/400, Richard would bring me back to reality by asking, "What does it mean to the customer?" Richard's insistence on examples for just about everything and his attention to detail make this book far more understandable to a wide audience of readers. Thank you, Richard.

Finally, this book would not have been written at all without the most important person in my life, my wife Sandra. I was having all kinds of trouble getting started. When she noted that my desk was beginning to look like the bridge of the Millennium Falcon, she stepped in, organized my material, and transcribed the videotapes of my AS/400 architecture class. Those transcriptions formed the first draft of this book. She then took on the roles of cheerleader, counselor, reviewer, and part-time editor. Thank you for always being there for me.

I also want to thank our three wonderful sons, Mike, Brian, and Steve. In spite of their own busy schedules with work and school, they took on additional responsibilities to give me more free time, and filled in for me on numerous occasions when I needed their help. For example, during the summer months, a couple of them unselfishly volunteered to spend their weekends racing our Porsche at the various racetracks around the Midwest, so I could stay home and dedicate more time to finishing this book. Believe me, I will never be that dedicated, although my time at the track this year is down to almost nothing. I plan to remedy that situation.

— F.S.

Table of Contents

Acknowledgments IV

Foreword XV

Preface XVII
    The Revolution Begins XVIII
    Fort Knox XIX
    The Early AS/400 (aka System/38) XIX
    The AS/400-PowerPC Union XX
    The Technical Development Team XXI
    The Management Team XXIII
    Eleventh-Hour Leadership XXIV
    Why This Book? XXV

How to Read This Book XXVII

Chapter 1: Advanced Application Architecture 1
    Computer Architecture 2
    A Programmer's View 2
    Levels of Abstraction 3
    Software Design 5
    Architecture Classification 7
        Processor-Centric Architecture 8
        Application Programming Interface (API)-Centric Architecture 8
        High-Level Machine Architecture 9
    Historical Background 10
    What's in a Name? 18
    The Rest of the Book 20

Chapter 2: The PowerPC Technology 21
    The PowerPC Alliance 21
    The Evolution of PowerPC 23
    The AS/400 Commercial RISC Processor 29
    PowerPC Technology for the AS/400 31
    The PowerPC Architecture 36

Extensions to the PowerPC Architecture	39
A 65-Bit Processor?	40
PowerPC AS Instructions	41
AS/400 Processor Implementations	42
The A30 (Muskie) Processors	42
The A10 (Cobra) Processors	46
Conclusions	47

Chapter 3: The Technology-Independent Machine Interface ... 49
Overview of the MI Architecture ... 50
A Non-Executable Interface ... 51
AS/400 Language Compilers ... 53
Characteristics of the Machine Interface ... 59
Working with MI Programs ... 60
    Creating a Program ... 61
    Destroying a Program ... 62
    Program Materialization and Observability ... 62
Inside a Program Template ... 65
    The MI Instruction Formats ... 67
    The MI Op-Code ... 68
    The Op-Code Extender ... 68
    MI Instruction Examples ... 70
Conclusions ... 72

Chapter 4: An Integrated System ... 75
The Integrated Operating System ... 77
Microcode ... 79
System Licensed Internal Code ... 81
    SLIC Development Environment ... 83
    SLIC Kernel Technologies ... 84
System/36 Personality ... 85
    Something Old, Something New ... 86
    Advanced 36 ... 88
Conclusions ... 89

Chapter 5: Objects and Object Management ... 91
Object Naming ... 93
OS/400 Objects and MI System Objects ... 94
Finding Objects ... 96
    Libraries ... 96
    Shared Folders ... 98
    Integrated File System ... 98
Accessing Objects ... 101
    Capability-Based Addressing ... 101
    Resolving System Pointers ... 102

Other Pointer Types 102
System Object Characteristics 105
Program Objects 106
Inside a System Object 107
　　Segmented Memory 107
　　System Object Structure 108
　　Multisegment Objects 109
　　Contents of the Headers 110
　　　　Segment Headers 111
　　　　EPA Headers 113
　　Examples of Objects 115
Conclusions 117

Chapter 6: The Integrated Database 119
Relational Database Evolution 120
The Two Faces of Database 123
Overview of Database Operations 124
　　Functions of a Database Management System 125
　　Data Description and File Creation 125
　　　　Creating Physical Files and Tables 125
　　　　Creating Logical Files and Views 126
　　　　Data Dictionary and Catalogs 127
　　Data and Program Independence 128
　　Data Security 130
　　Data Integrity and Recovery 131
　　　　Journaling 131
　　　　System-Managed Access Path Protection 132
　　　　Commitment Control 132
　　　　Triggers 133
　　　　Referential Integrity 134
　　　　High-Availability Disk Systems 134
　　Other Database Functions 136
　　　　Stored Procedures 136
　　　　National Language Support 136
　　　　Predictive Query Governor 137
　　　　Database Performance Enhancements 137
　　　　Distributed Databases 137
　　　　Gateways to Other Databases 138
　　　　DataPropagator for OS/400 138
　　　　OptiConnect for OS/400 139
　　Parallel Databases 140
　　　　Symmetric Multiprocessing (SMP) Parallel Database 140
　　　　Loosely Coupled Parallel Database 141

Implementation of Database Functions 141
    Database Objects 142
        Data Spaces 142
        Data-Space Indexes 143
        Cursors 144
    The User's Path to Data 145
    SLIC Journaling 146
    Commitment Control in SLIC 147
Machine Indexes 147
    Binary Searches 148
    Binary Radix Trees 149
    Internals of a Binary Radix Tree 154
Conclusions 155

Chapter 7: Security and Authorization 157
Integrated Security 157
System Security Levels 158
    Level 10 — No Security 159
    Level 20 — Password Security 159
    Level 30 — Resource Security 160
    Level 40 — Operating System Security 161
    Level 50 — C2 Level Security 162
User Profiles 162
    User Class 163
    Objects Owned and Authorized 164
    Authorization of Objects 164
    Privileged Instructions and Special Authorities 165
Program Adoption of Authority 166
Grouping Authority 166
Authority Search Algorithm 168
Conclusions 169

Chapter 8: Single-Level Store 171
How Many Bytes Does 64 Bits Address? 172
The Single-Level Store in Rochester 173
Virtual Memory 175
    Virtual Memory for Timesharing 176
    A Single-Level Virtual Memory 177
    Persistent Virtual Memory 178
Overview of Single-Level Store 181
Performance Implications of Single-Level Store 186
Pointers and Tags 190
    Hardware Protection for Pointers 191
    Tags-Active Mode 193
    Pointers and Tags on Disk 194

Inside a Pointer 195
   A Tale of Two Address Sizes 196
   Running Out of Addresses 200
Address Translation 202
   Memory Model Characteristics 202
   Machine State Register 202
   Address Translation Overview 204
   Virtual-to-Real Address Translation 207
      Hashing 208
      Page Table Entry 210
      Memory Access Modes 212
      Page Protection 214
Disk Management 215
   Auxiliary Storage Pools (ASPs) 215
   Storage Segments 216
      Disk Extents 217
      Access Group Segments 217
      Auxiliary Storage Directories 218
Conclusions 219

Chapter 9: Process Management 221
  The World's Greatest Tasking Structure 222
   Microkernel Technologies 222
   Starting at the Bottom 224
   Task Dispatching in the AS/400 225
      The States of a Task 226
      Task Dispatching Queue 227
      Send/Receive Queues and Counters 229
   Multiprocessor Considerations 231
      Symmetric Multiprocessing 231
      Asymmetric Multiprocessing 233
  MI Processes 233
   Original Process Model 235
   ILE Process Model 235
   Inside an ILE Process 237
      ILE Process Structure 237
      ILE Activation Group 238
  Exceptions, Events, and Interrupts 241
   Exceptions and Events at the MI 241
   SLIC Exception Management 242
   Hardware Context Switching 245
  Work Management and OS/400 Jobs 247
   Work Management Concepts 247
   Subsystems 249

Original and New Job Structures 250
Processes, Tasks, Jobs, Activation Groups, and Threads 251
Conclusions 252

Chapter 10: The I/O System 253
Historical Perspective 254
The Fort Knox Project 255
The Silverlake Project 257
Hardware I/O Structure 258
I/O Hardware Connections Using Fiber Optics 259
I/O Bus Operations 261
I/O Operations on the AS/400 262
Objects to Support I/O 262
The Components of I/O 263
Putting It All Together 269
Conclusions 275

Chapter 11: Client/Server Computing 277
The Next Generation in Business Computing 278
What Is Client/Server? 279
Models of Client/Server Computing 280
Transformation of the AS/400 284
Client Access for OS/400 286
5250 Emulation 286
Print Serving 287
Mail/Office Offerings 287
Data Serving 288
Client Management 289
Programming Interfaces 291
DB2 for OS/400 Database Interfaces 291
Application Interfaces 292
Program-to-Program Communications 293
Messaging Interfaces 293
Multimedia Enablers 293
File Server I/O Processor 294
AS/400 Advanced Server Models 296
Application Enabling for Client/Server 298
Distributed Objects in a Client/Server Environment 300
Application Development Environments 301
SOM and DSOM 302
Application and System Frameworks 304
Application Environments 304
OpenDoc 304
Taligent 305

WebConnection for OS/400 306
Conclusions 307

Chapter 12: The Future of the AS/400 309
Future Processor Technologies 309
AS/400 RISC Processor Road Map 311
Beyond RISC 313
The Challenge of VLIW Technology 316
History of Long Instruction Word Machines in Rochester 317
VLIW for AS/400 320
The Future of Multiprocessor Systems 321
Multicomputer Clusters 321
Symmetric Multiprocessing 322
Firmly Coupled Multiprocessing 323
The Future of AS/400 I/O 325
Future IOP Technology 325
Disk Arrays 326
Future AS/400 Software Technologies 327
Microkernels 328
Workplace Technologies 329
Application Engines 331
The AS/400 in the 21st Century 332
Technologies 333
Client/Server 334
Application Development 334
Conclusions 335

Index 339

Foreword

IBM's AS/400 is one of the most interesting and effective commercial computer architectures ever introduced. Long before "object-oriented" had become a familiar concept, the AS/400's high-level machine interface (introduced by the System/38, the AS/400's predecessor), presented the application developer with a set of objects, such as queues, indexes, and database files, that could be used as application building blocks. These objects provide a great degree of system functionality in a highly consistent and easily used form. The uniform object interface hides details from the AS/400 programmer so he or she can ignore the often complex control blocks and system routines that comprise the operating system internals. Further, the operating system can limit access of objects to well-defined operations, thus providing additional runtime application protection.

AS/400 objects are implemented with a layer of software over the hardware; this layer lets IBM make substantial changes to the hardware with relatively low impact on applications. For the most part, new hardware can be introduced with only an update of the internal code IBM provides, because the object interfaces, which are used by applications, remain the same. And therein lies another benefit of AS/400 objects: they let applications take advantage of major hardware advances without the need for the programmer to modify the application code. All the implementation details of system objects used by applications are "hidden" in this layer of software.

Programmers become spoiled by the AS/400's architecture — where else will you find such a rational approach to system function? But by nature, programmers ultimately want to know how things work, and AS/400 programmers are no exception. At every conference or user group I attend, I'll find a group of AS/400 programmers sharing lore about what goes on internally when you activate a program object, override a file open, or perform some other operation on a system object. This pursuit of what goes on under the covers of the AS/400 isn't merely to satisfy intellectual curiosity;

in many cases, a deeper understanding of the AS/400 architecture lets a programmer write more functional or faster code. But as any experienced programmer knows, you can't learn everything from the manuals; and this is especially true for the AS/400, since the manuals expressly avoid details about internal structure or operations.

Consequently, despite widespread appreciation for how the AS/400 hides details under its high-level machine interface, many of us have long wanted a book such as *Inside the AS/400*. This book provides clear — and thorough — explanations of all the AS/400 architecture's important components. Any AS/400 programmer will find *Inside the AS/400* essential to his or her technical understanding of the AS/400.

Of course, my curiosity about the AS/400 isn't limited just to its current technical underpinnings — and I suspect the same is true for other AS/400 developers. I'm intrigued by the technical and business *processes* that gave birth to such an advanced system — and curious about the individuals who have been involved behind the scenes. I also have a vested interest in knowing where the AS/400 is headed for the future.

Fortunately, Frank Soltis is just the person to give the real "inside" stories for all three AS/400 areas: its technology, its history, and IBM's future plans. Frank has been one of the central figures in these stories since the first day the S/38 was conceived, and he has played key roles in the evolution of the AS/400 architecture. His experience has spanned several major eras in IBM organization and technology, and his responsibilities have included hardware, software, and business domains. Frank also combines an academic career teaching computer science with his responsibilities as an engineer and system architect. Leaven all this talent and experience with a bit of Minnesotan humor, and you have the perfect guy to make topics like "tagged memory" and "task dispatching queues" an interesting read.

When I first met Frank in 1985, he didn't strike me as the traditional IBMer — but then again, I'd just been introduced to the S/38 after years working with IBM mainframes, and the S/38 itself seemed refreshingly different, too. Frank spent hours filling me in on technical details of the S/38 architecture, as well as much of the personal side of S/38 history. Frank explained technical concepts so clearly — and was such an entertaining story teller as well — that I encouraged him to write a book about the S/38. Only later did I learn that, as far as IBM headquarters was concerned, the future of the S/38 was up in the air at that time. Understandably, Frank waited to tell the story until he was assured it would have a happy ending. With the great success the AS/400 has experienced, and with its ever-widening use and key strategic role for IBM, the time is right for Frank to share his insight and stories with us all. This is truly the best guided tour of the AS/400 around.

Paul Conte
President, Picante Software, Inc.

Preface

"Welcome to Rochester," reads the sign in the airport, "where the winters are cold and the computers are hot." Rochester, Minnesota, is the home of IBM's Application System/400 (AS/400). Since its introduction in 1988, the AS/400 has become the world's most popular multiuser computer system.

I first saw Rochester in 1962 while I was still a university student. IBM had offered me one of the first two summer jobs in its year-old Rochester development laboratory. One of the jobs was working on a joint medical project with the Mayo Clinic. The manager of this project had been the customer engineer who worked on the IBM equipment used in my father's business. At the time, I had no interest in computers and even less interest in living in a small prairie town in southern Minnesota. The lure of the aerospace industry in California tempted me. However, I knew the project manager in Rochester and thought it might be fun to work for him during the summer.

When I arrived in Rochester, I received some bad news. The other summer hire who arrived a week before me had taken over the medical development job. I was going to work on the development of a banking terminal. This was not a good start, and it was too late to go somewhere else. I had already turned down other summer job offers. Besides, I needed the money and still believed that having IBM on my resume would look good to future employers, so I took the job.

The enthusiasm of the people I met in Rochester was contagious. The manager of the bank terminal project must have heard I was disappointed about not getting the medical job. He spent a great deal of time with me that summer talking about Rochester's future. He was convinced computers were a big part of that future, and Rochester would need people with intimate knowledge of computer design. He convinced me, and soon I began to think differently about computers.

I returned to school with a newly discovered interest in these electronic marvels. Most of my studies after that summer focused on digital computer design. The following year, when I graduated and it was time to find a permanent job, I could not resist the draw of this dynamic laboratory in Rochester. I signed on as an IBM employee working for the same project manager I had worked for the year before.

Before long, I again found myself back in school pursuing a doctorate degree. Rochester needed people who understood computer architectures. Most of us were engineers with little experience in the software arena, and my prior training was in electrical engineering. So at Iowa State University I concentrated on studying computer architecture and operating system design.

I returned to Minnesota late in 1968 and began to work on an advanced computer design. I arrived in time for the announcement of Rochester's first computer in June 1969, the IBM System/3. The System/3 was a special-purpose product that looked more like an accounting machine than a computer. I didn't realize it at the time, but the group at Rochester had managed to get into the computer business by telling IBM they were building an accounting machine. That didn't seem to matter much, because the System/3 went on to be the first in a line of successful products that would revolutionize commercial computing. In late 1969, I got a new job assignment. I was to design the architecture for the successor to the System/3.

The Revolution Begins

On a bitterly cold Thursday, January 8, 1970,[1] I presented to Rochester management a proposal for a revolutionary new computer architecture. A high-level machine interface was a fundamental part of that proposal. The addressing structure for the architecture, called single-level store, had evolved from my Ph.D. dissertation work. The driving motivation behind the architecture was to protect the customer's investment in application software by delivering a computer system that was independent of the underlying hardware technologies. This system was very different from a System/3, but it did contain most of the System/3 functions. This capability to have a "System/3 environment" would prove to be valuable years later when we needed to merge the two product lines.

Though many ideas behind the new architecture were truly radical, Rochester's management was willing to accept the proposal and to form a special group in the development laboratory to pursue the new system. Within six months, an organization of nine people formed to make the proposal a reality. My role was to be the architect for this new system. Little did I realize then that I would continue in this role for more than 25 years.

The Advanced Systems organization formed to create the new system stayed separate from the System/3 development effort (the System/3 family continued to grow with the addition of the System/32 in 1975 and the System/34 in 1977). Staffing for the new system did not start in earnest until the middle of the 1970s. Soon, hundreds and then thousands of people

[1] A wonderful trivia question is to ask for the name of two famous celebrities whose birthday is January 8th. The answer is Elvis and the AS/400. Elvis Presley was born in Tupelo, Mississippi, on January 8, 1935 and the AS/400 was born in Rochester, Minnesota, on January 8, 1970.

throughout IBM joined the team. On October 24, 1978, we announced the new system. We called it the System/38.

The System/38 was immediately heralded as an advanced architecture computer. It was easily the most innovative design IBM had announced in many years. Few people either inside or outside IBM fully understood this new system. A cult-like following quickly formed among those customers who did understand its power and potential. User group meetings often took on the appearance of a religious rally.

The System/38, however, never did replace the System/3 family in the way we originally envisioned. It was a new system that did not attract many of our installed customers. The first shipments of the System/38 were delayed until July of 1980, because we said it had performance problems. Actually, the system wouldn't run for any extended period of time before crashing — the ultimate performance problem. This delay scared off some of our existing customers. Also, customers of the smaller System/32 and System/34 found the new system to be too large and too expensive. In May of 1983, the last variant of the System/3, the System/36, was announced to satisfy these customers' needs. Rochester would continue to have two distinct lines of computers.

Fort Knox

In the early 1980s, IBM decided to create a new converged system it called Fort Knox. The intent was to replace five incompatible IBM product lines, including the two from Rochester, with Fort Knox. Customers who owned any of the five machines would be able to move their applications to this single system. The development of Fort Knox started with major investments in four different IBM laboratories.

By 1985, it was clear that Fort Knox was in trouble. Many of us in Rochester believed it was doomed from the beginning, because it was trying to solve an IBM problem rather than a customer problem. Others in IBM saw it as technically too big an undertaking: There was no way to converge five separate systems into one. Still others thought it was impossible to manage the project across the four laboratories. For all these reasons, it failed; and IBM terminated the project.

Fort Knox siphoned off most of the development resources that would otherwise have been put into the System/36 and the System/38. This made it difficult for either system to remain competitive. Further, IBM had gone so far as to declare the System/38 as "non-strategic" and discouraged customers from buying this system. Consequently, Rochester lost an enormous amount of business to competitors.

The Early AS/400 (aka System/38)

Late in 1985, a small group of developers in Rochester demonstrated that software for the System/36 could run as an environment on the System/38.

The cost of hardware technologies had come down so that we could now build small models of the System/38. This meant we could cover the entire Rochester product range. The proposal to combine the two systems into a single machine based on the System/38 quickly followed. We named this new machine Silverlake and convinced IBM management we could build it.

Once again, it was Rochester's turn to show IBM and the whole computer world what it could do. After an unprecedented 28-month development cycle, we were ready to announce the converged system. We told the world it was a new system and called it the AS/400. Insiders, however, knew that under the covers of every AS/400 lurks a System/38.[2]

The AS/400 was an immediate success. Not only did it take back the market share lost to competitors in earlier years, but it also quickly surpassed all of them. There are more than 300,000 AS/400 systems running businesses all over the world, making the AS/400 the best-selling, multiuser computer system ever. The System/38 cult had become a full-fledged religion.

In 1991, Apple Computer, Motorola, and IBM reached an historic agreement to develop a new family of processors. These processors would be used in everything from hand-held devices to supercomputers. Called PowerPC, these new processors were poised to take the computer world by storm. At the time, Rochester was looking at a new processor design for the next generation of AS/400 systems. This was to be the first totally new design since the 1978 processor used in the original System/38. Why not join forces with the PowerPC alliance to create the new AS/400 processor based on this design?

The AS/400-PowerPC Union

I led a team of people from Rochester to identify the requirements for the AS/400 processor. We then worked with the PowerPC architects and designers to create a 64-bit processor based on the PowerPC architecture. Processors built to this new architecture should take the AS/400 well into the next century.

The introduction of these new PowerPC processors, optimized for the AS/400, marks a milestone in the AS/400's history and demonstrates the power of the AS/400 architecture. Other computer system vendors are planning to move their systems to new processor designs with mixed emotions. Those currently making the transition are causing major disruptions to their existing customers. Application software must be recompiled or rewritten. Operating systems also must be rewritten to take advantage of the new processors. The result is that most vendors are reluctant to use the latest processor technologies. In contrast, the AS/400 architecture's technology-independent nature makes it relatively easy for an existing customer to incorporate the new processor technologies.

The use of common hardware technologies is important, but there is greater significance to this announcement. Now the potential exists to have application and operating system software from other IBM and

---

[2] We even changed the name of our operating system for the AS/400 to Operating System/400 (OS/400). To this day, many of our developers still call it XPF. XPF stands for Extended CPF. Control Program Facility (CPF) was the name of the System/38 operating system.

on-IBM systems run on the AS/400. The future benefits to AS/400 customers are enormous.

A question often asked is, "How did the AS/400 come about, and who were the people responsible for this system?" We will cover more of the AS/400 history and identify some of those people who were involved as we go through this book. There are, however, a few key technical and management leaders without whom this system would never have been created.

The Technical Development Team

IBM likes to promote the development of any new product as a team effort with everyone contributing. In truth, a small handful of technical and management leaders with the foresight, creativity, and drive usually make a product successful. Such leaders are responsible for the development and success of both the System/38 and the AS/400.

Rochester has had many good technical and management leaders but only a few true visionaries. A visionary leader not only has a vision of what is possible but also has the ability to convey that vision to others. A visionary leader is able to give away the ownership of that vision to everyone involved. Soon the vision takes on a life of its own as it grows and takes shape. The leader's role becomes one of a cheerleader, encouraging everyone to excel with his or her part of the vision.

In 1972, I was still struggling to sell the radical concepts of the System/38 architecture to our developers. The engineering organization was making progress on the hardware design primarily because most of them thought they were just building System/370 hardware with some new software on top. The format of the internal instructions in the System/38 looked very much like that used in a System/370. This was no coincidence. It was the only way to get the engineers on board and comfortable that they were not doing anything unusual.[3]

Little progress was evident on the software front. Most of our programmers in Rochester were busy building better versions of the System/3 software. They were comfortable with the System/3 design and wanted no part of a revolutionary new architecture.

It was during this time that two individuals stepped forward to help create the total architecture and to help convince the entire development community that we were on the right track. Dick Bains and Roy Hoffman are two of the most creative, truly visionary people I have ever met. They were also true believers. During 1972, the three of us completed the definition of the AS/400 architecture, and though some of the details changed in the following years, none of the concepts have.

Dick's talents were in compiler technology and languages. His expertise was critical to the definition of the high-level machine interface and the internal translator. He had grown up in the neighboring state of Wisconsin. Before joining IBM in Rochester, Dick held several different jobs. At one point he

[3] In later years, people would come to Rochester, see this instruction format, and declare the System/38 was built on a System/370. IBM even funded projects to make the System/38 software run as an operating system on System/370 hardware. These projects all failed.

was a ski instructor in Aspen, Colorado. Whenever things were not going well with our architecture definition, Dick would long for the simpler life of a ski instructor. Thankfully, he never followed through on those longings.

Dick was always one of those individuals who could get so involved in solving a problem he would do something without necessarily thinking about the consequences. For example, a year earlier, Dick was trying to convince management that some of the site's computer systems had a security problem. When no one would listen to him, he decided to demonstrate the problem by going into a system to which he was not authorized and leave a message for those responsible for the system to call him if they wanted to close the security exposure. He managed to unintentionally overwrite some files and almost lost his job. Fortunately for all of us, management recognized his talents and he kept his job. He also made his point.

To this day, Dick still has these same qualities. When he sees something that needs to be done, he doesn't stand on formalities; he just does it. His breadth of knowledge on the AS/400 and his ability to work closely with customers to solve both technical and business problems keeps him in high demand. Dick remains one of the key technical leaders on the AS/400.

Roy at that time was an engineer with expertise in computer architectures and operating system designs. His contributions, especially in the low-level operating system functions, made the System/38 architecture a success. Roy had grown up on a farm just outside of Rochester. Like many young men, he had chosen to leave home to attend college and find a job. He had worked for another computer company for a while; but after finishing his Ph.D., he had returned to Rochester to work for IBM. On weekends, you could find Roy riding through the countryside on his motorcycle. We would have long discussions about the merits of motorcycles versus sports cars, my hobby (I have always preferred to have a roof or a roll bar over my head).

Roy was always very good at solving technical problems. He has a tremendous knowledge of computer systems and can attack a technical problem from a vantage point most of us do not have. His new view often led to the technical solution; helping others with technical advice has always been one of his real strengths. (In fact, Roy didn't stop at technical advice. He often gave those of us around him personal advice as well, whether we wanted it or not. He would take great delight in analyzing and giving advice on subjects for which he had no experience.)

After his work on the System/38, Roy led some of the advanced technology work in Rochester. He also worked on new technologies for all of IBM. Roy was a member of the IBM Academy that was responsible for helping set technical directions in IBM. In 1994, he retired from IBM. Roy is now teaching at a local university and writing a technical book. On a nice day, you will still find him out riding his Harley-Davidson.

Somehow, the combination of a ski instructor, a motorcycle enthusiast, and a car nut worked. By the end of 1972, the design of the architecture was whole. In the following years, Dick, Roy, and I would often get together to discuss changes and new ideas. To this day I am amazed that many of the ideas we collectively put into the system are just now being discovered by others in the computer industry.

Rochester has been blessed with good technical leaders. The many innovations in both hardware and software are testimony to these people. None of the others, however, has had the same vision and foresight for the system as did Dick and Roy. They clearly saw the future. Like so many technical leaders who usually work behind the scenes and are seldom visible outside of their own organizations, these two have never received the recognition they deserve.

The Management Team

No system can be successful with only technical leadership; management leadership is also critical. In my opinion, four management leaders envisioned the System/38 and the AS/400 and then created the environment in which it could be built. One of them, above all others, needs to be recognized: Harry Tashjian saw the need for a small, easy-to-use business system and created a new market for computers. Without his vision, there would be no Rochester-developed computers.

Harry was the management force behind the System/3, System/32, System/34, System/36, and System/38. He was originally the system manager for all of these products and later became the director of the Rochester laboratory. It was Harry's vision that transformed Rochester from an obscure, insignificant little facility in the middle of a Minnesota cornfield to a world leader in the development of business computer systems.

It was also Harry Tashjian, manager of the bank terminal project, who convinced me to pursue computers that first summer many years ago. I still remember our long talks about Rochester's potential for developing new computer systems. Harry encouraged me to return to school to study computer architecture. When I returned to Rochester, he was the one who gave me the assignment and the support to design the architecture of the System/38, which would become the AS/400. Without Harry, there would be no AS/400.

In addition to Harry Tashjian, two other management leaders made the System/38 a success. Ray Klotz was our engineering manager and my boss for most of the project. In 1970, Harry put Ray in charge of the initial development team of nine people. Ray had a strong hardware background, having led a System/360 processor development in Endicott, New York, before coming to Rochester to lead the System/3 hardware effort.

Ray's initial vision for the System/38 was less ambitious than what some of us had in mind. He would sometimes remind us that the entire System/3 hardware only required 3,000 circuits, and he would ask why we needed so many more. He liked to challenge us on our technical decisions until he was convinced we had looked at all of the options. Then he gave us the freedom to take ownership of the design and let us make our own decisions. Whenever we got into trouble, he was always there to support us and help us find the way out.

Ray was very much a father figure for most of us. We all jumped whenever he raised his voice, which he did often. But under his gruff exterior was a tremendously caring individual who demanded perfection from each of us, and he usually got it.

Gaylord Glenn Henry was the most brilliant, and totally outrageous, manager I have ever known in IBM. To say that Glenn did not fit the role of a typical, conservative IBM manager is an understatement. The scruffy beard, the often mismatched clothing, and the six-packs of Tab in the pink cans he carried everywhere identified him as a unique individual. Glenn came from the IBM laboratory in Boca Raton, Florida, in 1972 to be the programming manager for the System/32 and then the System/38. He was an intense individual with tremendous personal drive that inspired everyone around him.

Glenn was a con artist who could convince developers and managers alike to follow him. When seemingly unsurmountable problems arose, Glenn convinced all of us that he had everything under control. Soon, a solution to the problem would appear and Glenn would just smile. Without his talent and vision, the System/38 development likely would have been terminated on numerous occasions.

I miss the shouting matches between Glenn and Ray. When they disagreed, the walls would shake. It was fun to watch the two argue, especially when you knew neither could support the position he was arguing (on occasion, Harry would join in, but more often he would let them settle their own disagreements). They did, however, both agree on one thing: We were going to build the best computer system the world had ever seen. The System/38 was a tribute to these two strong-willed individuals.

After the System/38 was announced, we lost all three of these leaders. Harry Tashjian left Rochester to lead a new start-up company for IBM called Discovision. After Discovision, he directed other activities within IBM before retiring with 38 years of service. Glenn transferred to Austin, Texas, to take over the development effort for the PC-RT. He left IBM in 1988 after 21 years, disgusted with the organization's inability to integrate new ideas. Not surprisingly, some of his ideas are just now being incorporated into IBM products. Glenn's leaving was a major loss for IBM. Ray saw the System/38 announced, but died before seeing the full impact his system would have on the entire computer industry. No one has ever been able to take his place.

Eleventh-Hour Leadership

Without a visionary leader, Rochester's computer systems faltered in the early 1980s. We did, however, have some strong managers who understood the value of the systems we built. Through often devious means, these individuals managed to keep our systems alive. Still, it seemed we did not have much of a future as we continued to lose business to competitors. Fortunately, someone stepped in at the eleventh hour to pull us out from near oblivion. His name was Tom Furey.

Tom has always been a master salesman. He knew how IBM worked internally and managed to convince the corporation that Rochester systems were strategic to IBM's future. He then set about to convince all of us to put in the extraordinary effort required to get a new system out the door in record time.

Tom also understood marketing and customer requirements. He transformed Rochester from a product-driven to a market-driven organization. He first got our customers directly involved with development. Customer councils had a big say in making system trade-off decisions, and the result was a system for which many customers felt personal ownership. Rochester would later win the prestigious Malcolm Baldrige National Quality Award for this market-driven effort.

True leadership is often only recognized in hindsight. Tom was not a technical leader as some of his predecessors had been, and many in the laboratory didn't recognize the leadership he provided. Our technical people didn't think he fully understood what they were doing. He didn't, but it also didn't matter. For example, Tom never understood that the AS/400 was a repackaged System/38; or if he did, he never let on. He told everyone outside of Rochester it was a totally new system from the ground up, and they believed him.

The early commercial success of the AS/400 is clearly due to Tom's leadership. He orchestrated the biggest product launch IBM had seen since the System/360. This launch propelled the AS/400 to the front of the multiuser commercial market. After Rochester, Tom moved to Santa Teresa, California, to be the general manager for the development of IBM's DB/2 database. Later, he became the general manager for client/server computing in IBM.

Why This Book?

The time is ripe for a book on the inner workings of the AS/400. IBM has never before provided an in-depth look at the design, architecture, and history of this remarkable system. Neither has it explained how the AS/400 can do the things it does. My goal in writing this book is to demystify the AS/400 and perhaps shed some light on how this system came to be.

As you might already have sensed, I feel a strong responsibility to include in this book some historical information. A few years back, I informally inherited the position as Rochester's resident historian from its originator, Carl Gebhardt. Carl was our business manager for the early systems and later became the system manager for both the System/34 and the System/38 when Harry Tashjian was the laboratory director. Carl was responsible for the financial success of Rochester's early systems. I worked for Carl in the early 1980s when he was our director of strategy. Carl was a Rochester landmark, having been here for many years. If you ever had a question about something that had happened in Rochester several years earlier, chances are Carl knew the answer. He would often introduce himself as Rochester's resident historian (there was no official resident historian, but both of us thought there should be). When Carl retired, we discussed who should take over this unofficial position, and he passed the title on to me.

This book is written for those who want to know more about the AS/400. It is not a specification written for operating system designers who need far more detail than that documented in these pages. Neither is it a rehash of IBM product announcement material. It is written for customers, application developers, and students who want to understand how the AS/400 works so they can make business decisions, write better applications, or simply see what makes this system tick. Is it magic, or just good design? Perhaps it's a little of both.

I need to point out that the views expressed in this book are my own. I am unashamedly an AS/400 bigot. My views are not necessarily the official views of the IBM Corporation. I hope you enjoy reading this book about the AS/400 as much as I enjoyed creating it.

How to Read This Book

An explanation of how to read this book may seem strange, but there is good reason. The intended audience is reasonably broad, ranging from business executives who want to know how an AS/400 can benefit their business to "bit-head techies" who want to understand minute design details. I wrestled with how to satisfy such diverse interests. I considered splitting the book into two parts, one part giving an executive overview and the other part offering the technical details. But that organization is difficult for someone who needs business benefits and first-level technical details. I also considered putting a road map into the book, recommending which sections should be read by executives, application developers, students, or bit-heads, respectively. I decided against this approach because the classifications are so arbitrary; and whenever I read a book with a road map, I have difficulty keeping track of the sections I should read and those I should skip.

One day while I was discussing my dilemma with Malcolm Haines[1] from London, he came up with a solution. Malcolm, who is one of the most creative people in IBM, suggested I mark the more difficult sections and let the reader decide whether or not to read it. He further suggested using chili peppers to denote the degree of difficulty of a particular section. This idea came from the fact that last year, Malcolm introduced me to an Anglo-Indian restaurant in London named Chutney Mary. This fine restaurant uses small drawings of red chili peppers in its menu to show which dishes are hot

[1] Malcolm Haines is frequently referred to as IBM UK's "propaganda minister," whose duties include promoting IBM via videos and on commercial satellite television networks. Malcolm's AS/400 video, "The World's Greatest Architecture," is classic British humor.

XXVII

— the more peppers, the hotter the seasoning. So, he reasoned, why not use the same approach to identify the "hotter" technical sections in this book?

My chili pepper rating system is as follows:

No chili peppers means the section is relatively mild when it comes to technical content; there will be some, but everyone needs a little spice.

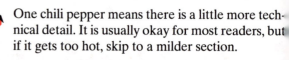

One chili pepper means there is a little more technical detail. It is usually okay for most readers, but if it gets too hot, skip to a milder section.

Two chili peppers means the material is definitely beginning to pick up the technical content. You may want to try just a taste.

Bit-heads are beginning to smile, and sweat may break out on their foreheads when three chili peppers appear. The rest of us may find smoke coming out our ears if we concentrate too hard in these sections. Depending on your tastes, you may want to skip that section altogether.

Happy dining.

Chapter 1
Advanced Application Architecture

The only certainty in computers is change. Technology is changing at such an astonishing rate that last year seems like part of ancient history. This is especially true in the PC world, where the hardware is practically obsolete before you get it out of the store. Hardware technology is as discardable as yesterday's newspaper.

The staying power of any computer system and its ability to protect the investment of its customers is the most important consideration in the purchase of a business computer. Over the years, AS/400 customers have heard about the AS/400's advanced architecture and how new technologies are incorporated into this system in a way that won't have a direct impact on them. They have been told that the architecture is *technology independent,* and that it is this characteristic that protects their investment. While it is true they have not had to change their application programs to take advantage of the new technologies, they often have not really understood — or cared about — how the system worked, as long as it worked.

With IBM's Advanced Series, the AS/400 architecture has once again come into the spotlight. New models incorporate a type of processor architecture called a *reduced instruction set computer* (RISC). For comparison, the processors used in the original AS/400, along with other popular processors such as the Intel Pentium and the Intel P6, are known as *complex instruction set computers* (CISC).

RISC processors generally have simpler instructions than CISC processors, which means that very high-speed processors can be built at reasonable cost. This improvement in cost/performance is an important reason to move to a RISC architecture, but there can be a downside.

For example, other computer vendors moved from CISC to RISC processors, and this move caused disruptions among some of their customers and independent software vendors (ISVs) who wrote application programs. Some application programs or parts of application programs had to be rewritten to move to the new hardware. This happened, for example, when Hewlett Packard (HP) introduced its Precision Architecture (PA) and when Digital Equipment Corporation (Digital) introduced its Alpha architecture.

To appreciate the magnitude of this disruption, consider Digital's move to RISC. Digital estimated that moving its installed base to the Alpha architecture caused from 15 percent to 20 percent of the older VAX architecture applications to be rewritten. For any customer or ISV, application rewrites of this magnitude could be very costly.

In contrast, the AS/400's technology-independent architecture protects the system's customers and ISVs from such disruptions as they move to the new RISC processors. To see how this is possible requires a look at how the AS/400's advanced application architecture differs from all others.

Computer Architecture

A Roman architect in the first century, Vitruvius, defined architecture as the act of designing a structure that had utility, strength, and the power to delight. The architecture of buildings and computers have this, and much more, in common.

Contemporary architecture owes much to the formal orders of classic architecture. Even the most futuristic designs spring from the past. The Egyptian pyramids, the Greek columns, the Roman arch, the Romanesque dome, and the Gothic pointed arch all furnish the foundation for creations we perceive today as the latest thing. In the history of computers, the ancient era starts only a few decades ago. As in building design, the most dynamic and exciting things happening today in computer architecture spring from discoveries and lessons learned from the "classics."

The AS/400 architecture is based on a model developed more than a quarter of a century ago. Because of a flexible design approach at the outset, the AS/400 has been able to adapt quickly and dynamically to modern goals and needs. With its technology-independent architecture, the AS/400 has had, for years, features and capabilities other computer systems still haven't achieved.

[1] S. S. Husson, "Microprogramming Principles and Practices," Prentice-Hall, 1970.

A Programmer's View

In 1970, S. S. Husson[1] defined computer architecture as "the attributes of the (computer) system as seen by the programmer." The architecture includes the set of instructions, data types, input/output (I/O) operations, and other features of the computer. We sometimes separate these and talk about instruction set architectures or I/O architectures. The total architecture includes everything a programmer needs to know to make a program work correctly.

From a hardware perspective, a computer has five main components: input, output, memory, datapath, and control. The last two components are often combined and called the *processor*. The computer architecture defines what operations can be performed by these components. The processor gets instructions and data from the memory. Input hardware writes data to memory, and output hardware reads data from memory. The control hardware provides the signals to cause the operations of the datapath, memory, input, and output.

The processor is sometimes called the CPU, for central processing unit. The CPU name is being used less frequently these days because modern hardware technologies allow us to package entire processors on a single semiconductor chip. Many people use the terms CPU, processor, and processor chip interchangeably. We should, however, keep in mind that not all processors fit onto a single chip. A single processor may require a multi-chip implementation.

If two computers can execute the same instruction set, they are said to have the same instruction set architecture. There can be, and usually are, multiple implementations of a given architecture. Thus, the Intel x86[2] architecture used in many PCs applies to a family of processor chips. These processor chips are realized in different technologies and running at different speeds. The important point here is that the specific technology used to build the computer is not a part of the architecture.

[2] The Intel x86 CISC architecture is used in the family of single-chip processors that includes the 086, 186, 286, 386, 486, Pentium, and P6.

Levels of Abstraction

Most modern computers have hardware and software structures that contain several levels. Lower-level details are hidden to offer simpler models at the higher levels. This principle of *abstraction* is the way hardware and software designers deal with the complexities of computers.

At the lowest level, the electronic circuit, a computer is very simple. The electronic circuit only understands two commands: *on* and *off*. The symbols we use for these commands are the numbers 1 and 0. We communicate with the machine at this level with a string of 1s and 0s. An instruction is a collection of these *binary digits*, or *bits*, that the computer understands. An instruction is, therefore, nothing more than a number in the base 2 number system, or a *binary number*. We call computers *digital computers* because the machine language uses numbers for both instructions and data.

In the early days, programmers communicated with computers using binary numbers. This was not very efficient, so a higher level of abstraction, called the *assembly language,* was invented. The assembly language is a symbolic form for the binary machine language of the computer. An *assembler* is a program that translates the symbolic form of the instruction into the binary form.

Assembly-level programming was still not a very natural notation for most programmers, so an even higher level of abstraction, called a *high-level programming language,* was created. There are hundreds of these languages today; a few of the better known ones are BASIC, C, COBOL, RPG, FORTRAN, and Pascal. The program that accepts one of these high-level programming languages and translates it into assembly language statements is called a *compiler.*

Writing a program in a high-level language (HLL) illustrates how multiple levels of software abstraction work in a computer. The compiler handles the mapping between the high-level language program and the assembly language level. The assembler then translates the assembly language instructions down to the binary machine level that the processor understands. Note that some compilers generate the binary machine language directly, eliminating the assembly level.

The compiler and assembler programs translate the high-level language program into machine language instructions prior to execution. This is a one-time operation, and unless the program is changed, repeating these steps is not necessary to rerun the program. Again, the reason for using these levels is to hide the details of the underlying binary machine language from the programmer to provide a simpler, more productive interface.

The same concept of multiple levels for software can also be true for hardware. Many processors, such as the Intel family, use an implementation technique called *microprogramming.* In a microprogrammed machine, an even lower-level instruction set is used to implement the binary machine language. Instead of using a compiler to map from the higher level to the lower level, microprogramming uses *emulation.* With emulation, machine instructions are fetched and executed one at a time using sequences of the lower-level instructions. There is no separate compile step required to transform the machine instructions into a form acceptable to the microprogram.

Emulation is similar to a software technique known as *interpretation.* Here a program, the interpreter, takes one instruction at a time and executes a sequence of equivalent lower-level instructions. Some high-level languages, such as BASIC, are designed to be easy to interpret. Most computer command languages are also interpretively executed. Type "dir" on the DOS screen of a PC and you will see a listing of the contents in a directory on your PC. A command interpreter in DOS reads the command you typed after you press the Enter key and then executes the sequence of instructions in the computer needed to carry out your command. Most operating systems have such a command interpreter. In a microprogrammed machine, special hardware usually has been added to help the interpretation process. The microprogram is called an emulator to identify this hardware-assisted form of interpretation.

The instruction set architecture of a computer system is usually thought of as the interface between the hardware and the lowest-level software. At the time of Husson's definition of computer architecture, much programming was still done without using high-level languages. A better definition of computer architecture today might be "the attributes of the system as seen by the compiler," because few programmers deal with binary machine language programs.

With multiple levels, it is more accurate to think about a computer having multiple architectures, although the binary instruction set architecture still plays the most important role in most computers. When someone talks about the ability of one computer to execute the programs of another computer with no changes, they often say that the first can execute the *binaries* of the second computer. They mean that the programs can be moved without even requiring a recompile. The binary machine language of one computer is contained in the other computer.

Software Design

Within a computer system, there are generally two types of software: system software and application software. Operating systems, assemblers, and compilers are examples of system software. Application software, on the other hand, is aimed at the end user of the system and is often uniquely tailored for a particular business.

In the past, it was argued that both the system programmer and the application programmer needed access to the lowest-level architecture. This access was usually accomplished through an assembler. There were many reasons for this argument. Precious little memory was available for most programs, the processors were slow and expensive, and the compilers for high-level languages were not very sophisticated. When you needed to get the last ounce of performance out of the machine, "real" programmers used assembly language.

Many believe that assembly-level programming is a relic of the past, something no longer used; but that's not true. Most operating systems in use today incorporate lots of assembler code. This is not only true for the older operating systems, those that have their roots in the 1960s or early 1970s, but also for newer ones. The PC operating systems are good examples. Microsoft's Windows 95 is written mostly in Intel assembler language.

The original PC processors had very limited resources. Memories had a maximum size of 64 kilobytes. One kilobyte is equal to 2^{10}, or 1024 bytes, where a byte is an 8-bit entity in memory used to store a character or digit. Memory was so expensive that the operating system could take no more than 4 kilobytes. The use of assembler language allowed programmers to squeeze the code into the smallest possible space. So much of the operating system was written in assembler that, even when memory sizes increased because of dropping technology costs, it was not practical to go back and rewrite the original code.

Using an assembler to optimize the size and performance of a program does work, but it has at least one major drawback: All programs are tied directly to the hardware. Any change to the hardware can cause some or all of the programs to be rewritten.

To illustrate this, consider a computer that contains eight registers. A register, which is part of the processor datapath, is a high-speed storage area where data and addresses can be kept temporarily while being used by the processor. Registers are generally used to improve the performance of a program. Assume further that each register is 16 bits wide and that the programmer may load and store the registers at will. The existence of these registers and their characteristics show through to the assembly-language programmer. Therefore, every program written at the assembler level for this computer will know about the eight registers and will be dependent on them being there.

Let's now assume that advances in hardware technology make it possible for the engineers to extend the register space to have 16 32-bit registers for the same cost as the original eight smaller ones. The questions is, "What is the impact on the programs written for the original computer?" The answer depends on how the changes were made and how well the original architecture was planned for expansion.

Suppose the original architecture anticipated the change to 16 registers. Enough space could have been reserved in each instruction to address 16 registers, even though only eight were originally implemented. Four-bit fields would be needed in each instruction using registers, because there are 16 unique combinations of 1s and 0s in four bits. Old programs can run unchanged on the new hardware. Note that the old programs would still use only eight registers. New programs could use all 16 registers.

Now instead, suppose that the architecture did not anticipate the change and leave room for future expansion. The new architecture cannot increase the number of registers without causing changes to every instruction that uses registers. It is not possible to stretch a three-bit field in an instruction to four bits without some breakage to existing programs.

One of the many architectures unable to increase the number of user registers is the Intel P6. This architecture is living with the number of registers selected by its Intel x86 predecessors. Although this architecture would benefit from having more registers, the impact on existing assembly-level software would be too great.

What about increasing the size of the registers from 16 to 32 bits? In general, increasing the size has less of an impact than changing the number of registers. If just the size is increased, old programs will still run, but they will only use 16 of the 32 bits in the new registers. Again, this information is embedded in the logic of the program and is difficult to change.

There are countless examples of programs running today that are unable to use the full resources of the hardware. The Intel 386, 486, Pentium, and P6 processors are all 32-bit designs, meaning their hardware registers are 32 bits wide. Yet most of the PC software running on these processors is only 16-bit software. The original programs and the DOS operating system were written at a time when only the 16-bit Intel 286 hardware was available. The effort to rewrite all this software to take advantage of 32-bit hardware will take years.

This problem is not limited to just the PC industry. Hardware technology has advanced to the point that most new processors will be 64 bits wide. To take advantage of the larger hardware, much of today's 32-bit operating system and 32-bit application software will have to be rewritten; and this, too, will take many years.

In the examples we have just used, the hardware changes we examined were the number and size of the processor's registers. Keep in mind that similar impacts on assembly-level software may occur when changes are made to the processor's addressing structure or to the instruction set itself.

The intention of programming only in a high-level language is to minimize the impact on software when the hardware changes described in the preceding paragraphs occur. Unfortunately, the trend for writing system software is to move to a language such as C. Using C helps the portability of the system software because C is available in so many other hardware platforms, but it doesn't eliminate all the difficulties that occur when the hardware changes. Certain hardware characteristics, such as the size of the internal processor, will show through the C language. This capability to see the internals appeals to system programmers and explains the popularity of C. C has been called "today's assembler."

Moving from a 32-bit processor to a 64-bit processor in a conventional computer system will, for example, still require changes to a C program if it is to take advantage of the larger size. This does take away from C's portability. To illustrate the difficulty, consider Digital's experience. Digital has been shipping systems for the past few years with its 64-bit Alpha processor. Yet two of the major operating systems used in these computers, Digital's Open VMS and Microsoft's NT, are both still only 32-bit operating systems, even though they are primarily written in C. Applications running with either of these operating systems are also only using 32 bits. Recompiling doesn't help. Those operating systems and applications will have to be totally rewritten to use the full resources of the processor. Until then, customers can only use half of the processor resources they have already purchased.

Architecture Classification

Many different ways have been devised to classify computer architectures. Probably the oldest is to characterize the formats of the instructions implemented in the processor. Another that we have already seen is to group processors into the CISC or RISC categories. Both of these approaches focus only on the processor's hardware interface. From a customer perspective, the applications are far more important than the type of processor in the system.

Therefore, it is equally appropriate to classify a computer architecture according to how an application deals with the hardware interface.

Processor-Centric Architecture

The vast majority of computer architectures in use today are based on the traditional approach of exposing the hardware interface to the programmer. These are called *processor-centric architectures.* They are called processor-centric because all applications see and directly use the hardware interface. Examples of processor-centric architectures are HP's PA and Digital's Alpha architecture. As we just saw, even a minor change to the processor architecture can cause a major disruption to the software written to the hardware interface. This type of architecture is the original and most common, but it is not the only type.

Application Programming Interface (API)-Centric Architecture

Because of the difficulties caused by processor-centric architectures, many ISVs, hardware vendors, and standards organizations have worked together to create architectures based on application programming interfaces (APIs). These *API-centric architectures* define a communications boundary — an interface — that all applications can use to access the services of the operating system, without getting tied to the specific hardware or software details.

An operating system is a collection of programs that manages the system resources and provides a base for writing application programs. Often, the base for writing the application programs is provided through APIs. An API can take several forms. It might be a call or a command to the operating system to perform some function. A familiar example of an API would be a call by the application program requesting the operating system to perform an I/O operation, such as a disk read. Clearly, the application program does not need to know about the internal workings of the I/O. The operating system programs that perform the I/O functions, often called I/O subsystems, insulate the applications from the hardware and software details. As long as application programs use these APIs to perform their I/O operations, they remain independent of any changes to the underlying I/O structure.

Another benefit occurs if multiple computer vendors implement the same set of APIs. When this happens, an application written only to this set of APIs can be easily moved from one system to another. One of the best known collections of standard APIs is POSIX. POSIX, an acronym loosely defined as "a portable operating system interface based on Unix," is a collection of international standards for Unix-style operating system interfaces. Vendors of Unix-style operating systems are encouraged by government agencies and businesses alike to implement these standards so that an application can be moved from one system to another.

A problem with a standard such as POSIX is that it is never finished, with the definition phase taking many years to complete. Within this context, application developers often take matters into their own hands. In 1993, a group of Unix application developers and Unix system providers got together to define their own APIs. They couldn't wait for POSIX to be defined to a point where it would be usable for real-world applications. Besides, at some time in the future when POSIX would be fully defined, all applications would have to be rewritten to meet the new standard.

Instead, this group looked at the APIs the most popular Unix application programs were currently using. Out of the thousands of Unix applications, they looked at 50 of the most popular and selected 1179 APIs as the basis for a new standard and originally named it SPEC1170. This name was later changed to Single UNIX Specification, and this standard has now become the industry's new definition for Unix. Among the APIs in this standard are some POSIX interfaces, plus several others.

The obvious problem with all the API definition work was best described by someone at the National Institute of Standards and Technology (NIST) who said, "The nice thing about standards is there are so many to choose from." With so many conflicting — and rapidly changing — standards, it is impossible for an application developer to create an application that is portable across all system platforms.

Further, these standards are not complete sets, meaning that in many cases an application may have to "go around" the APIs. Once this happens, the application becomes dependent on the underlying hardware and software. All the problems we saw in the processor-centric architectures reappear the moment the software bypasses the API interface.

High-Level Machine Architecture

If, instead of just randomly defining APIs for various applications, a formal definition of an interface for all applications is made, then true hardware independence can be achieved. Further, if that interface definition is highly expandable, then the APIs defined by standards organizations, such as POSIX or Single UNIX Specification, can be added at any time to achieve application portability. This is the philosophy behind the AS/400 architecture.

The *Technology-Independent Machine Interface,* which is usually just called MI,[3] is the formal definition of the interface for all application and most operating system software. The hardware, along with all the operating system software that must know the details of the hardware, is located below the MI boundary. The exact details of this structure are presented in the following chapters.

The significance of this technology independence is immediately obvious to customers and ISVs alike. Upgrading to 64-bit RISC technology provides more than just a bigger processor. The operating system and all applications are immediately 64-bit software. There is no need to rewrite anything to take advantage of the 64-bit hardware. On day one, the RISC-based

[3] Recently, some have started to abbreviate the name of this interface as TIMI. I am not overly fond of the nickname "Timmy" (with apologies to anyone named Timothy), so we will use the older abbreviation of "MI" to describe the machine interface of the AS/400.

AS/400s have a 64-bit operating system and tens of thousands of 64-bit applications. No other system even comes close.

The architecture of the AS/400 has also been called an Advanced Application Architecture because it has achieved what many other computer systems are still struggling to achieve with API-centric designs. The AS/400 is already independent of its underlying technology. While it is very important to have independence from hardware, it is equally important to have independence from the details of the operating system. Again, the AS/400 has achieved this. The extendability of the architecture means that newly defined APIs from other operating systems, such as those for POSIX or Single UNIX Specification, can be added, providing even more application portability.

In addition to providing new APIs, entire operating systems can potentially reside below the MI boundary. On the surface, it seems strange to want more than one operating system on the same machine; but it isn't. Customers may want applications that are written for different operating systems. The capability of a single system to manage multiple operating systems and provide those applications is valuable. And if those operating systems don't even show through, meaning the customer needs no additional support, the capability is extremely valuable. Once again, the AS/400 does this. In later chapters we will examine how.

Historical Background

Before we go into the details of the AS/400 structure and design, it is worth some time to look a little deeper into the history of computer systems developed by the IBM laboratory in Rochester. Only then can we understand how a system as different as the AS/400 could be developed.

Most of us would like to believe that customer requirements, market opportunities, and competition drive the majority of decisions about new computer architectures. The truth is often very different. New architecture design is more likely to be driven by existing architectures, the current installed base, and internal politics. We can consider these last three factors "history." History influences the design of all new computer architectures more than anything else.

The development location and the previous products from that location also often heavily influence the design of a particular computer system. Computers tend to be re-built. If a development group has had success with a particular product, they will re-invent it during the next development cycle. Rather than build a new system, they generally build a better model of a current system. This is why radical new ideas usually come from an outside organization.

Consider the designs computer companies located on the East Coast have created over the years. They obtained many of their ideas from research done at universities such as the Massachusetts Institute of Technology (MIT). During the 1960s, MIT engineers and computer scientists worked on a Department of Defense project called MULTICS. Companies such as Digital, Data General, and IBM's New York laboratories hired graduates from MIT and other eastern universities. The computers and operating systems designed at these companies borrowed much from projects such as MULTICS. The Unix operating system from Bell Laboratories came out of this environment. Because designs from these companies were variations on the same themes, they pretty much looked alike. It was highly unlikely that a revolutionary new design would ever come from one of these facilities.

The AS/400's history is very different. Because it has always been difficult to get anyone to move from the East Coast to rural Minnesota, Rochester hired almost no graduates from the East Coast schools. As a result, the creators of the AS/400 were midwesterners who did not have strong ties to the same computer designs other companies used.

To illustrate, consider the addressing structure used in the AS/400 versus that of most other systems. Many computers designed in the middle to late 1960s were *time-sharing* systems. Time-sharing was popular because it allowed individual users, often in separate businesses, to rent time on a central computer. Many businesses could not afford their own computer, and time-sharing provided them the resources of a large computer at a fraction of the cost. Each user thought the computer was dedicated to his or her particular task. There was no consideration of directly sharing data between users, because the users generally didn't even know about others on the same system.

MULTICS and others in this time period adopted a hardware addressing structure that isolated one user from another and did not allow sharing. As the cost of computers came down so that a company could buy one of its own, this hardware addressing structure became less useful. When multiple users in the same company wanted to simultaneously access the same data, there was no clean way to accomplish it. Some operating systems were able to make it appear that users were sharing the same data, although this was usually done at a cost of many processor cycles. Other operating systems simply did not allow such sharing. Not surprisingly, most processors today still use the addressing structure designed for time-sharing. The designers are still building variants of the older computers.

The AS/400's single-level store was designed to allow very efficient sharing of data and programs between users. We cover the details and advantages of this design in Chapter 8. The important point is that the AS/400 architecture started with a clean slate. There was no need to carry along the unnecessary baggage from the past, even if that baggage existed only in the minds of the designers.

Rochester didn't always build computers. Starting in 1956 as a manufacturing facility, Rochester initially built punch-card machines, including the IBM 077 Numeric Collator. The 077 was a machine that could read two decks of 80-column IBM punched cards and mechanically collate them. It used relays and vacuum-tube electronics to control the operations. In 1961, a development laboratory was established in Rochester. The first assignment of the new laboratory was to develop the site's first solid-state (transistorized) product, the IBM 188 Collator.

By the mid-1960s, some people in Rochester believed there was a huge market opportunity for a small special-purpose computer for business. IBM didn't share this belief. The System/360 line of computers had just been announced. The philosophy behind the 360 was that a single line of compatible computer systems, where a customer could move effortlessly from one model to another, provided the answer for all customers. The problem IBM had with its special-purpose computers of the 1950s was their incompatible architectures. Customers who outgrew one architecture would have great difficulty moving to another. The 360 line was IBM's answer to this problem.

With this perspective of IBM as background, imagine the following scene. It's the middle of the 1960s. The setting is IBM Headquarters in Armonk, New York. A stranger stands at the entrance to the IBM Headquarters building. He knocks on the large glass door.

"Who's there?" booms a voice from inside the imposing headquarters building.

"I'm a representative from the IBM Development Laboratory in Rochester," responds the stranger meekly. "That's Rochester, Minnesota," he explains, trying to muster a small laugh. "You folks often confuse where we are located."[4]

"What do you want?" growls the voice behind the massive door.

Clearing his throat to conceal his nervousness, the stranger continues, "We thought it might be fun to develop and build some new computers. We don't know much about developing computers, being stuck out in a cornfield in Minnesota like we are, but we're hard workers and we're willing to learn."

"Tell me more," says the voice.

"We've got this great idea for a new business computer," says the stranger. "It will be totally incompatible with the new System/360 mainframe computers, but we're sure our new computer will be just what many small businesses need."

There is a slight pause, then the voice inside says, "That's a wonderful idea! You go ahead and build those computers, and we'll worry about growing your customers into our 360 line after there are a few hundred thousand of them. Who knows," the voice adds pensively, "if you build bigger versions of your new computer, maybe some customers will even buy your systems instead of our 360s."

"That's what we think," responds the stranger. "Our systems will be so simple and inexpensive to use, we even expect some mainframe customers to move to our computers."

Wait a minute! What's wrong with this scene? Would IBM Headquarters really let a group of developers from a cornfield in Minnesota design

[4] IBM executives for many years were not sure where the Rochester facility was located. Some thought it was in Rochester, New York. Others thought it was in Rochester, Michigan, or Rochester, Illinois, or even Rochester, New Hampshire.

and build a new computer system, especially if it was going to be totally incompatible with IBM's mainframe systems and possibly even compete with them? Not likely! A more believable ending to our little scene would be the sound of a gunshot, followed by the voice inside calling, "Next!" The last thing IBM needed was another incompatible line of computer systems. So Rochester didn't bother to tell the corporation it was building a new computer. Instead, Rochester declared it was building a new unit record machine.[5]

The punched-card machines used by businesses in the 1950s had been called unit record machines. A punched card represented a single or a unit record to be processed by the machine, so the name was applied to any machine that processed punched cards. The organization in Rochester that was to design the new machine was appropriately called Advanced Unit Record Systems, or AURS.

The new machine would use a new, smaller, 96-column card in place of the standard 80-column IBM card. Card readers, punches, collators, and sorters are mechanical devices. The cost of such mechanical devices is directly related to the amount of metal used to build them. If you reduce their size, you will reduce their cost. A smaller card meant the size of the devices, and hence the cost, could be reduced.

The design of the processor in the system unit was extremely simple, with an instruction set oriented for commercial processing. It had a total of 28 instructions, most of which operated on data in memory. Decimal, binary, and character were the only data types supported, and the processor operated on one byte of data at a time. Only 3,000 circuits were needed to build the entire processor (by comparison, today's PCs have a few million circuits).

Customers needed some way to program applications on the new system unit. The earlier unit record machines had used wire plugboards, rectangular shaped boards that had hundreds of small holes on the surface. Programming was accomplished by connecting pairs of these holes with wires that had small plugs on each end. These boards, housed in a rugged metal frame with carrying handles, had the appearance of an old-fashioned telephone switchboard. The connections on the board would tell the unit record machine what card columns to use and what operations to perform on the data in those columns. Typically, a single board represented a single application, such as a payroll program. When a different application was to be run, an operator would open a door in the side of the machine, remove the old application board, and insert the new board. Most machine rooms had metal shelving to hold plugboards for the assorted applications required to run a business.

Rochester's new unit record system needed a way to accomplish programming in a manner similar to that provided by the plugboards. A few years earlier, IBM had introduced a software product for the 1401 computer to simulate plugboard wiring. The product was called the Report Program Generator (RPG). RPG was created for the application programmer

[5] **As any child knows, it is easier to ask for forgiveness than to get permission.**

who knew how to wire plugboards, and it incorporated much of the structure and terminology from the unit record machine era. RPG also was later implemented on the lowest model of the System/360. RPG was not terribly successful on either the 1401 or the System/360, because computer hardware was still too expensive to replace most unit record machines. It was, however, recognized as a very easy way to program a business application.

One of the reasons an application was so easy to program in RPG was because RPG was a non-procedural language. Most other programming languages were procedural, which meant the programmer had to direct the flow of the program. A simple way to understand the difference is to imagine you have just landed at the Rochester airport and need to take a taxi to a hotel in downtown Rochester. You get into the taxi and have two choices of how to get to your hotel.

You could give directions to the taxi driver. "Drive to the airport exit, turn right and proceed a quarter of a mile until you cross the highway overpass. Turn left and go eight miles through six stoplights, then turn right into my hotel." This represents a procedural approach, where you direct the "flow" of the taxi. A non-procedural approach would be simply to give the taxi driver the name of the hotel, sit back, relax, and enjoy the ride to your hotel.

RPG allowed the programmer to sit back, relax, and not worry about the characteristics of the system or the flow of the program. The programmer could focus on the file and record definitions and the operations on those records needed to run the business. This was the same level of knowledge needed to wire a plugboard. The original RPG was designed for 80-column cards, so a new version had to be created for the 96-column cards. It was appropriately named RPG II.

Critics claimed RPG was not a real programming language, but that was just fine with Rochester. For years Rochester perpetuated the myth that RPG wasn't a real programming language. After all, only highly paid programmers used real programming languages, and if customers had to go out and hire an expensive programmer for their business, they might not be able to afford a computer. On the other hand, small business owners, accountants, clerks, and secretaries could wire plugboards or program in RPG. Besides, Rochester wanted to sell the new machine as a programmerless system. A tactic we often used to sell to a new customer was to sit the owner and employees of a small business down and let them "program" a simple application for their business. Within an hour, they would see their application running on the system. This was usually all it took to convince them this was truly a programmerless machine, and not something to be afraid of.

In June, 1969, IBM announced the System/3. The original announcement was for a card-only system similar to the unit record machines System/3 was aimed at replacing. The new machine was a batch machine, which meant one job at a time could be read into the machine and processed. Input data was supplied on the punched cards and the output could be either printed or punched into cards. The announcement material stated this configuration "provides most of the functions a punched card accounting installation can perform." Enhancements to the System/3 and new model announcements quickly followed. IBM announced a disk-based system shortly after, and soon terminals could be connected. Rochester was in the computer business.

As expected, the System/3 was extremely successful. The combination of a nearly programmerless environment and low cost made this system very attractive to many small businesses that could not previously afford a computer. This was totally new business for IBM, and approximately 25,000 machines would ultimately be delivered to customers.

The System/3 was the beginning of a family of computers that includes the System/32, the System/34, and the System/36. All these systems were based on the original System/3 architecture. Significant enhancements were added to this architecture over the years, but much of the original low-level design of the System/3 still showed through. An example is the original 16-bit address of the System/3, which limited program sizes to 64 kilobytes.

The System/38 architecture IBM proposed in 1970 was designed to overcome the technology dependencies of the System/3. The idea was to create a new architecture that was totally independent of the underlying hardware technology. As technologies improved, allowing the implementation of larger, more functional computer hardware at a reasonable cost, the internals of a system could be changed with no impact on customer application programs. If those operating system functions that "knew" about the details of the hardware could also be isolated below a technology-independent machine interface, then the remainder of the operating system would not be affected when the hardware was changed.

IBM originally proposed this new technology-independent architecture for a system to be announced in 1975 that was intended to replace the System/3. However, by 1972, the System/3 was so successful that IBM decided to continue this line of computers and to delay the introduction of the replacement system. In 1975, IBM introduced a low-end System/3 for a small business office. With its desk-like packaging, many of us affectionately called it "the bionic desk." This new computer was originally going to be called the System/3 Model 2, but its name was changed to the System/32 before it was announced. The System/34 appeared in 1977 and combined the best of both the System/3 and the System/32. A new technology implementation of the System/34, called the System/36, was announced in 1983 and quickly became a big success with several different models. All of these systems share a common architectural base.

With the decision to continue the System/3 line of computers, a new and totally separate development organization was formed in Rochester to exploit the proposed technology-independent architecture. By being totally independent of the System/3 development organization, this group was free to invent a radically new system. After the announcement of the System/38 in 1978, many people wondered how it was possible two such totally different system designs could come out of the same development location.

The explanation was two separate development organizations that had little contact with one another. They were even housed in separate buildings across town from each other. The System/38 developers had no heritage in the System/3. They were an outside group of people with little incentive to build a better version of the System/3. For all practical purposes, the two organizations could have been in different companies.

Rochester would maintain these two separate development organizations until the System/36 and the System/38 groups merged to build the AS/400. This merger of the two groups was not easy, because each group had strong emotional ties to their own architecture.

The System/36 group could not understand how a big, memory-hungry architecture like the System/38 could ever satisfy the needs of their small customers. They pointed to the fact that the System/38 took megabytes of memory, while the System/36 required only a few hundred kilobytes of memory. With the decision to use the System/38 architecture for the new AS/400, the System/36 group argued that Rochester would not be able to build low-cost machines to attract the System/36 customer base.

The System/36 people were right. The hardware resources to support the System/36 Environment on the AS/400 were greatly underestimated, as was the effort required for a System/36 customer to move to the AS/400. IBM ended up giving an extra 4 megabytes of memory to many customers just to make the System/36 Environment perform at a reasonable level. These early versions of the System/36 Environment gave the AS/400 a bad name among many System/36 customers, and most refused to move to the new platform as Rochester had hoped they would.

Less than a third of the more than 300,000 System/36 systems sold worldwide moved to any other platform in the first six years of the AS/400. The announcement of the Advanced 36 in October of 1994 was an admission that the AS/400 was not for every System/36 customer, even though the Advanced 36 employed the same hardware technology being designed for the AS/400. In fact, the System/36 still is a perfectly viable computer for many businesses. The new Advanced 36 preserves the operating system and applications that these customers have used since 1983.

The System/38 organization, on the other hand, looked down on the System/36. It was old and unsophisticated. In their minds, the architecture of the System/38 was the only one that could take Rochester into the future. Besides, the price of technology had come down to the point where large memory sizes were beginning to appear even in PCs. Rochester systems soon would support gigabytes of main memory, so the System/38 architecture was not too big.

Fortunately, the two organizations were able to work together. The closer they worked, the more alike they found the systems to be. They also found that various features of the two systems complemented each other. For example, the System/36 had a better user interface, while the System/38 had a better application development environment. The System/36 used separate intelligent processors to perform I/O operations, which worked better than the I/O channel used in the System/38. They were thus able to add the best features from each system to the AS/400. Figure 1.1 shows the Rochester system family and how the AS/400 evolved.

The latest models of the AS/400 have been under development since the early 1990s. These models have a totally new internal architecture compared to the original AS/400. History continues to drive these architectures. In the next chapter, we will examine the "new" AS/400 RISC architecture. It should come as no surprise to find that the hardware foundation of this latest RISC architecture has its roots in the early 1960s.

Figure 1.1 Evolution of the AS/400

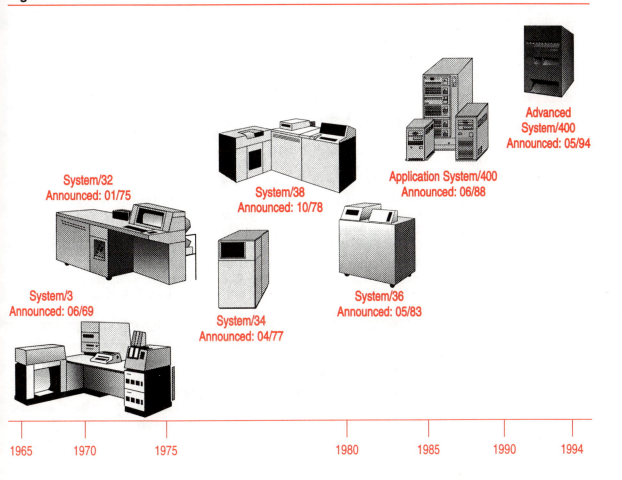

What's in a Name?

Before the AS/400 was announced, it had been given the code name *Silverlake,* after a small body of water in the middle of Rochester called Silver Lake. We modified the name slightly to make it into a single word.[6]

When we began to work on the next generation of the AS/400, we needed a new code name. This time we selected a larger body of water and chose the name *Superior,* after the great lake that borders the northeastern part of Minnesota. Many of us were sure that when we announced the new system, we would also change the AS/400 name.

There is a belief in the computer industry that the life of any computer system is about six years. Since the 1950s, with only a few exceptions, manufacturers have replaced their systems about every six years. Even those systems that did not radically change usually were renamed to give the perception of a new system. Some systems have lasted a little longer and some a little shorter, but six years is a good average. The feeling in the industry is that because technology moves so fast, a six-year-old system is no longer modern. This is probably true for technology-dependent systems.

In 1993, many computer industry pundits were predicting the demise of the AS/400. It would be six years old in 1994. Many speculated the "AS/500" was right around the corner. It seemed logical that we should change the name — we had done so in the past.

In 1988, we could have called the AS/400 a System/38. It was, after all, a repackaged System/38 with lots of new functions. Many System/38 customers called the AS/400 a System/38 with about three releases' worth of functionality added. We elected to rename the system for three main reasons. First, we wanted it to appeal to System/36 customers, and keeping the System/38 name would not have accomplished this goal. Second, a new name means more publicity in the news media. Another release of an existing system does not generate nearly the level of excitement in the press as does a new system. Finally, we changed the name because many in our management chain didn't know it was a System/38. They believed we had created a totally new system in only 28 months. The Silverlake project was a marvelous accomplishment for Rochester, but we didn't start with a clear sheet of paper as some people still believe. We took a System/38, repackaged the hardware, and added lots of new functions.

The odds-on favorite name for our 1988 system was Silverlake. Most of the outside world already knew this code name. Besides, it would have been a refreshing change for IBM. Since the early days of computers, IBM had insisted on using numbers to name its computer systems. The System/360 announcement in 1964 changed that slightly with the addition of the word "System" and a forward slash (/), but that was still a fairly unimaginative naming convention. We were tired of building computers that all had the "System/3X" name, and we wanted a change.

---

[6] Silver Lake is not really a lake. Rather, it is a wide spot in the Zumbro River created by the dam for the municipal power plant. Silver Lake's only notable characteristic is the thousands of Canada geese that spend the winter in Rochester. The power plant heats the water in Silver Lake, so it doesn't freeze over. This makes it possible for the geese to stay rather than fly farther south. Visitors to Rochester who know Silverlake was the name used for the AS/400 often go to visit the lake. They usually come away disappointed, because Silver Lake is a most unimpressive body of water. What they don't realize is that Olmsted County, which contains the city of Rochester, is the only county in the state of Minnesota, "the land of 10,000 lakes," with no natural lakes. Except for a few other wide spots in the river, Silver Lake is all we have.

Before we could select a name, IBM decided on a new naming convention. Because of a project called the System Application Architecture (SAA), there was a desire within the organization to have similar names across IBM products. SAA was IBM's attempt to have common application software run on all its major systems. Similar system names would help enhance this image of commonality. In a bold move, the decision was made to add a descriptive name before the word "System." It was also decided to standardize on the number of digits each system could use.

IBM's mainframe organization quickly picked the name Enterprise System/9000 (ES/9000) for its line of computers. The personal computer division selected Personal System/2 for the name of the new system it announced in April 1987. In Rochester, we debated between two names. Some of us wanted to use the name "Advanced" for our first name, arguing that it described the kind of systems we built. Others wanted the name "Application" to emphasize all the new application software that was being developed for our system. An executive finally picked the latter name. We would eventually use the other name when we introduced the Advanced Series.

We then needed to select a number. Coming from a System/36 and a System/38, we briefly considered "37" and "39," but quickly decided on "40." We were to be the "Application System/40." But before we got too comfortable with this number, the Personal Systems organization asked for all one- and two-digit numbers. They claimed that with only one digit, they could only announce nine different systems. No one would buy a PS/0, they argued. We gave in and added another zero to our name.

Steve Schwartz was the president of our division at the time of the AS/400 announcement. He was concerned that at the announcement a reporter would ask why we chose the number "400." He didn't want to tell them we added another zero to pacify the Personal Systems people. Someone discovered that by coincidence the B60, which was the top model announced in June 1988, could support 400 concurrent users. If asked, Schwartz would cite this as the reason for the name. We were working on systems that would support thousands of users, so most of us didn't think the press would believe such a flimsy explanation. We were wrong — they bought it.

With Superior, we had the chance to rename the AS/400. Many names were proposed (my favorite was AS/6000), but we elected not to change the name. Studies showed that worldwide, the AS/400 name was one of the most recognized names in computers. Brand recognition is not something easily achieved, so when a name is highly recognized, it is foolish to change it.

On May 3, 1994, we proudly announced Superior as the AS/400 Advanced Series. This was a bigger announcement because this system had more features and functions than we had back in 1988 for the original AS/400. Visually, this series of computers was very distinctive in its new black packaging. We also announced that the Advanced Series packages were ready to incorporate the new RISC processors when they were ready in

1995. We also announced a new version of OS/400 that we called Version 3 Release 1 (V3R1).

On June 21, 1995, exactly seven years to the day after we announced the original AS/400, we announced the latest models of the AS/400 with the RISC processors and the latest release of our operating system, which we called V3R6. Doesn't everyone count by fives? What's next — V3R11?

The Rest of the Book

Chapter 2 takes a look at the lowest level in the AS/400 system, the processor architecture. Chapter 3 follows with a description of the high-level MI architecture. Having examined the two main architectural levels in the AS/400, we can then begin to understand the glue that holds them together. Chapter 4 looks at the integration of the system and how the licensed internal code acts as the glue.

Each successive chapter looks at individual system components to help you understand the inner workings of this remarkable system. Examples of topics covered include the structure of objects, the single-level store, the process model, and input/output (I/O). The important characteristics of each component and its interaction with other components are presented. Equally important are the explanations of how these components are designed to enhance the application environment. After all, applications are still what the AS/400 is all about.

Chapter 2

The PowerPC Technology

Shortly after Lou Gerstner took over as IBM's chief executive in early 1993, he set a new course for the organization. Before his arrival, IBM's various business units were moving apart, becoming separate businesses. Gerstner reversed that direction and began to bring IBM's diverse products together. A big part of this process was the sharing of technologies.

IBM is a technology company. Just about every technology that drives the computer industry, from RISC to relational databases, came from IBM. In the past decade, IBM has failed to capitalize on many of the technologies it invented, and Gerstner intends to change that. He has stated that his highest priority is to exploit IBM's technologies by driving certain key technologies throughout its product lines.

The RISC processor in the AS/400 Advanced Series is based on one of those key technologies, the PowerPC. In this chapter we will examine in more detail the evolution of the PowerPC architecture and how the AS/400 uses this technology.

The PowerPC Alliance

Apple Computer in early 1991 was looking for a new processor for its future computers and believed that the future for PC processors was a RISC design. The PC processors that came from Motorola, Intel, and other vendors were still CISC designs. Up until that time, Apple had bought its processors from Motorola; and although Motorola had produced a RISC processor, it was not a big commercial success.

PCs use single-chip processors. The single-chip processor, which is usually called a *microprocessor*, was first developed by Intel in 1971. The original Intel 4004 was a 4-bit processor and had only 2,300 transistors. Technology advances now allow full 64-bit processors with millions of transistors to be put on a single chip.

RISC technology offers fundamental advantages over the CISC designs — a RISC processor provides a performance advantage in a chip that is physically smaller and consumes less power. Apple recognized that the industry would eventually move in this direction, but in 1991 the available microprocessors were still predominantly CISC designs.

At the time, IBM had one of the industry's best RISC processors in its RISC System/6000 (RS/6000). These processors were all multichip, 32-bit designs, but IBM had plans to announce a single-chip version in early 1992 (called RSC for RISC Single Chip). Hearing about Apple's search for a new RISC microprocessor, IBM decided to make a sales call at Apple. Would Apple like to use RISC microprocessors from IBM?

After the shock wore off of having IBM, a competitor in the PC business, try to sell processors to Apple, Apple began to think maybe this was not such a bad idea. The company knew that Motorola also was looking at a new RISC design, and suggested that the three companies get together. IBM agreed and discussions began. In September 1991, the three companies officially announced an alliance to jointly pursue the development of several exciting new technologies, including a broad family of microprocessors. The microprocessor design would be based on the RSC. They named the new family PowerPC.

The three partners recognized that market success depends on selling lots of these chips and having a large installed base of software. Thus, they began recruiting hardware and software vendors to use PowerPC. To further increase the volume of processors sold, they also recruited companies outside the computer field. A good example is Ford Motor Company. Automobiles use multiple computers to control various functions from engine management to braking systems. In the future, Ford vehicles will use PowerPC microprocessors to perform these operations.

The three partners intend to have the best-selling RISC processor in the industry; so far, they are succeeding. PowerPC processors are selling at more than 10 times the rate of their nearest RISC competitor. Intel, the leading producer of microprocessors, still produces CISC designs. But not surprisingly to IBM and its partners, in 1994 Intel announced that it had formed an alliance with HP. The two companies have stated that they will jointly develop a new RISC processor to converge both of their current processor lines — a clear attempt to battle the PowerPC onslaught. Their product will be available near the end of the decade, but some industry analysts have predicted that's too late. The PowerPC will be the dominant RISC processor in the computer industry by that time, and that's just fine with IBM, Apple, and Motorola.

The Evolution of PowerPC

The concepts of RISC were developed by John Cocke at IBM Research. Cocke recognized that compilers had advanced to the point where it was possible to simplify the instruction set of a processor, and to let the compilers absorb much of the complexity that previously had been put into the hardware. His ideas were first embodied in a machine called the IBM 801 minicomputer. The PowerPC processors are direct descendents of the 801.

CISC designs had been primarily motivated by a desire to reduce the semantic gap between the binary machine level of the processor and the high-level languages used by programmers. Instructions were added at the binary machine level to match high-level language instructions. The idea was that the processor would execute fewer of these complex instructions and save memory space. Unfortunately, the instructions at the binary machine level became so complex that microprogramming had to be used for almost every processor design. The overhead of the microprogrammed emulator slowed down the execution of frequently occurring simple instructions. Cocke reasoned that if only simple instructions were used, there would be no need for microprogramming. All instructions could be directly executed by the hardware. Further, if memory cost was not an issue, the compilers could generate the code for the more complex functions directly in-line. Memory sizes would increase, but so should performance.

The 801 processor design came from the world of supercomputers. Supercomputers are the fastest computers available. Although the name supercomputer did not appear until the middle 1970s, there have always been designers willing to push the limits of hardware technology to create the fastest computer of the day. The name synonymous with supercomputers is Seymour Cray. Today's RISC processor designs owe much to the pioneering efforts of this man. A short history will illustrate that this is true.

The single most important invention that enabled greatly improved performance in processors was *pipelining*. Pipelining has been used for many years to implement micros to mainframes. The first general-purpose computer to use pipelining in 1961 was the IBM 7030, which was also called Stretch. Pipelining is an implementation technique whereby portions of multiple sequential instructions are executed concurrently in various stages of the hardware pipeline. Figure 2.1a shows an example of a five-stage instruction pipeline. Each stage performs a specific function in the execution of an instruction. The time required for each stage to complete is called the *processor cycle time.*

Figure 2.1b shows a timing sequence for the five-stage pipeline. Instruction number 1 is fetched from an instruction buffer (during the first processor cycle) by the stage 1 hardware. During the second processor cycle, instruction number 1 is decoded and the contents of any needed registers are fetched by the stage 2 hardware. During this same cycle, instruction number 2 is fetched

Figure 2.1a Pipeline Scaler Processor — Five-Stage Instruction Pipeline

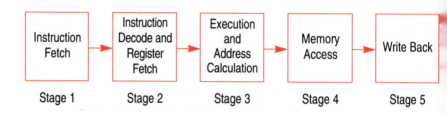

Figure 2.1b Timing Sequence Example

	Stage	1	2	3	4	5
Processor Cycle 1		1				
Processor Cycle 2		2	1			
Processor Cycle 3		3	2	1		
Processor Cycle 4		4	3	2	1	
Processor Cycle 5		5	4	3	2	1
Processor Cycle 6		6	5	4	3	2

from the instruction buffer by the stage 1 hardware. At this moment, we have parts of two separate instructions being worked on concurrently by two separate stages. This is a form of parallelism, and pipelined processors achieve their improved performance because of this parallelism. Note that we are assuming some other hardware in the processor is continuously keeping the instruction buffer full.

The execution continues during the third processor cycle, with the first instruction moving into the execution and effective address calculation stage (stage 3), the second instruction moving into stage 2, and a third instruction entering stage 1. This process continues until after the fifth processor cycle, when the first instruction has completed its execution and has left the pipeline. Thus, any single instruction takes the full five cycles; but after the pipeline is filled, a new instruction completes for every processor cycle. When we say that a processor requires only a single cycle per instruction, we are assuming that the pipeline is full, which clearly is the best case.

During the early 1960s, Seymour Cray at Control Data Corporation was designing the world's first supercomputer, the CDC 6600. He planned to use pipelining and, for simplicity, he wanted to have all instructions execute in the same amount of time. From our example, we can see that the total instruction time is dictated by the longest running instruction. Instructions that fetch or store operands from memory typically take longer than other types of instructions in a processor. If these memory operations also perform logical or arithmetic operations on the data, the instruction time can get very long.

To keep this total instruction time as short as possible, Cray decided the only memory operations in his design would be to *load* a register with the contents of a memory location and to *store* the contents of the registers to a memory location. Any operations on the data would be performed in the registers.

This was a major departure from most other computers that allowed operations on data in memory without using the registers. For example, an S/360 has instructions to allow an operand in memory to be added to another operand in memory and the sum to be put back into memory. This can be a fairly long-running operation, but it is accomplished with a single instruction. This type of instruction is called a memory-to-memory instruction.

Cray's machine would take five instructions to accomplish the same operation. First, two load instructions would put the data into two registers. Then an add instruction would add the two register operands and put the sum back into a register. Finally, a store instruction would move the sum from the register to memory. Cray's machine takes five instructions; but because they can be efficiently pipelined and executed in parallel, the total time required to complete all five is less than an equivalent machine with memory-to-memory instructions requires. The disadvantage to Cray's machine is the larger number of instructions required to perform the operation.

Introduced in 1964, the CDC 6600 was the first general-purpose load/store machine. Cray understood the interaction between pipelining and instruction set design, and he realized the need to simplify the architecture for the sake of efficient pipelining. RISC processors today use Seymour Cray's design; this explains why RISC machines, which only have load-and-store memory instructions, are faster than CISC machines, which have a full set of memory instructions. It also explains why programs compiled for a RISC machine are larger.

Seymore Cray's instruction set design was not the only contribution to high-performance pipelines. Cray introduced hardware in the CDC 6600 to ensure that the pipeline was kept as full as possible. Pipelined machines achieve their maximum performance when the pipeline is full — that is, when every stage in the pipeline is executing part of an instruction. In the real world, there are dependencies between instructions in a program. If an instruction in the pipeline uses data stored by another instruction just ahead of it in the pipeline, the data may not be available in time. This causes a stall in the pipeline. Furthermore, all instructions behind the stalled instruction are also stalled, reducing the processor's performance.

The CDC 6600 introduced hardware that allowed the processor to look at instructions further back in the instruction stream and to determine whether or not they could be started before the instruction that had to wait for another result to be stored. This idea of allowing the hardware to re-arrange instructions in the pipeline greatly improved the performance of the CDC 6600 by keeping the pipeline as busy as possible.

Another idea used by the supercomputers of the 1960s was branch prediction. A branch instruction can create havoc in a pipeline, causing it to stall until the system can decide the next instruction to use. The idea of branch prediction was to guess, based on experience, where the next instruction would come from when a branch was encountered. Sophisticated hardware was used in the IBM 360/91 to do branch prediction with remarkably good results.

All of this specialized hardware to optimize the pipeline performance added to the complexity and hardware costs of these systems. This is not a problem for a cost-is-no-object supercomputer, but it did prevent use of these techniques in ordinary systems.

In the late 1960s, John Cocke was working on the design of a fast scientific computer at the IBM Research Laboratory in San Jose, California. Cocke was concerned with the complexity of the hardware needed to keep the pipelines full. He believed that if much of the responsibility for keeping the pipelines full could be given to the compilers, then the hardware could be greatly simplified. Further, simpler hardware meant lower costs. If it was possible to let the compilers absorb the complexity, then high-performance processing would no longer be the domain of just supercomputers. The idea of RISC was born.

Unfortunately, the research project was canceled before Cocke had the opportunity to prove his ideas. In 1976, at IBM's Yorktown Research Laboratory in New York, he got another chance. He was authorized to design and build a high-speed telecommunications controller. Code-named the 801 after the building in which Cocke worked, it has generally been regarded as the first RISC computer. The 801 showed that compilers could take over the scheduling of a pipelined processor. The combination of a compiler that produced an instruction stream optimized for a specific pipelined processor, and a simplified load/store processor similar to the original Seymour Cray machine, was almost unbeatable.

Today's RISC processors use John Cocke's idea of an optimizing compiler mated to the processor hardware. Advances in hardware and compiler technologies both contribute to the overall performance of a RISC processor. Because so many advances have been made in compilers in the last few years, some in the industry have suggested renaming RISC to "Relegate Interesting Stuff to Compilers."

The first IBM product to use a descendent of the 801 was the PC RT. The office products division in Austin, Texas, needed a new processor and used the 801 as a starting point. A new microprocessor, called ROMP (Research/Office Products Microprocessor), incorporated a subset of the 801 to keep costs down. The chief architect and development manager for the PC RT was Glenn Henry. After we announced and shipped the System/38, Glenn, who was our programming manager, moved to Austin to lead IBM's first RISC effort.

The 801 was also used as a base for RISC processors developed by other vendors. In the early 1980s, research projects were in place at both the University of California at Berkeley under David Patterson and at Stanford University under John Hennessy. Patterson was the one who coined the term "RISC." Both universities had graduate students who had worked at IBM Research and knew about the 801. The SPARC microprocessor used by SUN came out of Patterson's project and the MIPS microprocessor came from Hennessy. Meanwhile, at nearby HP, Joel Birnbaum was leading the effort to design HP's PA-RISC architecture. Birnbaum had managed the 801 group in IBM Research before going to HP. Thus, PA-RISC also had its origin in the 801 project.

These early RISC processors used a single pipeline as did the original 801. Cocke and others in IBM reasoned that it should be possible to dispatch multiple instructions to multiple pipelines each cycle from a conventional linear instruction stream, thereby increasing performance even further. They called this a *superscalar* machine. The first superscalar RISC processor appeared in the IBM RS/6000 in 1990.

To identify this superscalar enhancement to a RISC processor, IBM named the architecture POWER for *Performance Optimization With Enhanced RISC*. The POWER architecture was also based on the 801. The POWER architecture was the starting point for the joint effort between Apple, IBM, and Motorola.

To meet the future needs for all three corporations, certain modifications to the POWER architecture were required. Most POWER processors use multichip implementations. Some simplifications were made to the architecture to enable the building of low-cost, single-chip implementations (i.e., microprocessors). The POWER architecture does not support multiprocessor systems, so these features had to be added. New features were also added to support anticipated future applications. Finally, the 32-bit architecture of POWER was extended to include 64-bit addressing and operations.

The changes resulted in the new PowerPC architecture. Figure 2.2 shows the evolution from the 801.

IBM and Motorola, with help from Apple engineers, created a new design center to develop future PowerPC microprocessors. The Somerset[1] Design Center, located in Austin, Texas, is staffed primarily by Motorola and IBM engineers. Both Motorola and IBM are free to manufacture and market the processors designed at Somerset. Motorola's PowerPC processors are built in its Austin manufacturing facility. IBM manufactures its PowerPC chips in Burlington, Vermont.

Figure 2.2 Evolution of PowerPC

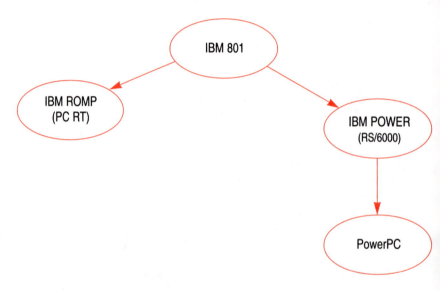

The first four single-chip PowerPC processors are the PowerPC 601, the 603, the 604, and the 620. The 601 is a medium-performance microprocessor for desktop computer systems. Starting with the RSC design, this processor is a transition from the POWER architecture to the PowerPC. Thus, it implements a superset of features from both architectures to allow it to be used in the RS/6000. The 603 is a low-power-consumption microprocessor intended for desktop and portable computers. The 604 is a high-performance microprocessor for uniprocessor and multiprocessor desktop computers and technical workstations. Finally, the 620 is a 64-bit high-performance microprocessor for technical workstations, servers, and multiprocessor systems. In the next sections, we will cover how these PowerPC processors relate to the processors used in the AS/400.

[1] Those readers who remember King Arthur may recognize Somerset as the mythical place warring factions went to make peace.

The AS/400 Commercial RISC Processor

In 1990, a new RISC processor architecture was being defined for future models of the AS/400. The original processor architecture, which had the unwieldy name *Internal Microprogrammed Interface*,[2] or IMPI for short, had been defined in the mid-1970s for the original System/38. This architecture was designed to support interactive transaction-processing commercial applications.

IMPI was primarily a memory-to-memory architecture. Data could be fetched from memory, modified by the processor, and put back into memory, all in one instruction. Interactive, transaction-processing applications typically move lots of data, but modify very little of that data. Consider an inventory update operation.

A customer has just called in and placed an order. As a part of the application, we need to update the inventory record for each item sold. The inventory record for the item is fetched from memory, or more likely, from disk. The quantity field is checked to see if there is a sufficient amount to satisfy the sales request and, if there is, the quantity is decremented by the amount sold. Finally, the updated record is stored back into memory where it can be accessed by another user of the system.

The operation just described can be considered a transaction by itself, or it may be a part of the larger sales transaction. In either case, it is transaction processing. It is also interactive because it is driven by the person at the terminal who received the order. Getting the response back to that person quickly is extremely important. Thus, a processor that can move lots of data and complete the operations in a short time is critical to building a successful interactive transaction-processing system. The AS/400 excels at this type of application.

Over the years, we have examined thousands of applications written for the AS/400 and other Rochester systems. These commercial applications, designed for a multiuser system, share some common characteristics. Some of the common characteristics we have found are

- Hundreds or even thousands of concurrent users can be supported.
- Long instruction path lengths — long strings of sequential instructions — exist with a large percentage of the path length in the operating system rather than in the application. Applications perform lots of calls to the operating system for services, such as I/O.
- Addressing of data structures in an AS/400 is through the use of pointers. This requires integer arithmetic to update the addresses.
- Manipulation of the data structures primarily uses string or integer comparisons, updates, and inserts. There is little need for floating-point arithmetic.

[2] I gave this name to the internal interface of the System/38 in the mid-1970s, assuming that it would be changed before the system was announced. It wasn't and has caused problems ever since. Many people like to talk about the IMPI interface. Of course, the word "interface" is redundant. Note that MI has the same problem. At one point someone decided the last "I" in IMPI should be "instruction." This didn't work either, because we talk about IMPI instructions. Finally, someone dropped the last "I" to solve the redundancy problem. IMP suddenly had no meaning, and conjured up pictures of a small, mischievous demon in the system. That name didn't last long. The move to PowerPC is finally solving our naming problem.

- Fewer loop iterations are found in an AS/400 application, and there are more non-loop branches, than in a scientific application.
- The data to be manipulated is spread over a large amount of disk space. The amount of data fetched in a single disk operation is relatively small and successive disk operations are likely to be spread across multiple disks.

Contrast this type of application with a typical engineering-scientific application performed on a technical workstation. Such applications are often referred to as compute-intensive, because they tend to do lots of computations on relatively small amounts of data. They typically have small instruction working sets with lots of tight loops executing floating-point arithmetic. Even their I/O is often sequential rather than random. As Seymour Cray demonstrated, a processor that works on data only in registers, as does a RISC processor, is the best choice for this type of application.

Although the commercial applications are still the mainstay, more and more compute-intensive applications are finding their way to the AS/400. The move to client/server computing, in particular, has increased the need for the AS/400 to improve its compute-intensive performance. Client/server is a model where the application is split between a PC (the *client*) and an AS/400 (the *server*). A server application tends to require more operations to be performed than does an interactive application. In the future, new applications will likely also require more computing power.

The IMPI architecture has been extended and modified several times since it was originally conceived. Even with those changes, it cannot be considered a high-performance computational architecture. It was obvious to most of us in Rochester that RISC processor characteristics should be added to satisfy the computational performance needs for the future. Thus, in 1990, we began an effort to add RISC features to the IMPI.

We did briefly consider using the processor from the RS/6000, but quickly dismissed the idea. The POWER architecture was originally designed for technical computing. It was lacking some of the characteristics we needed for commercial computing. In addition, it could not handle large amounts of data as efficiently as we needed.

Most RISC processors at the time were 32-bit designs. This means the width of the processor and its registers is only 32 bits. Many of these processors did have 64-bit floating-point registers, but their integer registers were only 32 bits. The integer registers are those used for commercial computing. Because a RISC processor can only move data to and from its registers, the 32-bit size quickly becomes a bottleneck when lots of data needs to be moved through the processor. CISC architectures such as IMPI can perform memory-to-memory instructions, which process data without going through the registers, so they essentially bypass the bottleneck.

Consequently, we decided that we needed a full 64-bit processor for our future design. Another factor that influenced this decision was the AS/400's address width of 48 bits. There was no way to squeeze a 48-bit address into a 32-bit register, and a 64-bit processor would allow us to expand the address used in the IMPI from 48 bits to 64 bits. Our projections showed that at some point in the future, as AS/400 systems got bigger, we would need the larger address.

The decision was made. We would start with the IMPI, expand it to 64 bits, and add RISC computational operations. We would create the first RISC processor designed exclusively for commercial computing. We called it C-RISC for "Commercial-RISC." Another factor that had influenced our decision was the amount of microcode that had to be changed. By starting with the IMPI, we would minimize the microcode changes.

PowerPC Technology for the AS/400

Jack Kuehler was the president of IBM in 1991. Jack led IBM into the agreement with Apple and Motorola to create PowerPC microprocessors. He was also the driving force behind the joint venture with Apple to form Taligent, a company that is developing a comprehensive object-oriented technology environment. This object technology will be used in systems produced by IBM, Apple, and HP, who bought into Taligent in early 1994.

Jack Kuehler believed that by the end of the decade all computers from the smallest hand-held devices to the largest supercomputers would be built using RISC microprocessors. He also believed there would only be a handful of companies building these microprocessors. He was betting that the PowerPC alliance would be one of the few survivors.

Kuehler was perplexed. He couldn't understand why he had two of his major laboratories each developing new RISC processors. His laboratory in Austin, Texas, was working on the definition of the PowerPC, while at the same time his laboratory in Rochester was working on C-RISC. Couldn't these laboratories get together? Convinced that the PowerPC was the right answer for both of us, he began to ask why Rochester could not use the PowerPC.

We dutifully traveled to Armonk to explain to him the differences between processors designed for commercial and technical computing. He didn't dispute our success in building commercial processors, but he also didn't buy our reasons and kept sending us back for more data to prove our position. "Doesn't the RS/6000 do commercial processing?" he would ask.

After about three visits to Armonk, Jack Kuehler was finally convinced. These people from Rochester do know what they are talking about. They know how to build commercial processors, and these processors are different from those used for technical computing. Kuehler sent us back to Rochester one more time. He wanted us to take 90 days and come back to him with the answer to two questions: (1) What changes to the PowerPC architecture are needed to make it suitable for the AS/400? and (2) What would it cost to move the AS/400 to this new architecture? Mr. Kuehler had just opened the door for us to influence the PowerPC design. He also indicated a willingness to fund any additional development costs associated with moving to a new processor based on the PowerPC.

Starting in early April 1991, I led a team of 10 people from Rochester to answer the two questions. Kuehler had also instructed the head of IBM Research, who was responsible for negotiating the PowerPC architecture definition with Apple and Motorola, to work closely with us and make this happen. In addition to working with the PowerPC architects, our engineers worked closely with their counterparts in Austin on processor designs.

The success of this effort was highly dependent on the quality of the technical people on the Rochester team, and we had some of the very best. It was not an easy project. At the outset, it appeared that the requirements for a Rochester system were in contrast with the goals for the PowerPC. Then, there was the feeling that if we converged the processor architectures, Rochester would lose its ability to build processors optimized for our commercial processing. Needless to say, we had some very heated discussions.

We decided to start with the PowerPC architecture as it was defined at the time and add the extensions we needed for the AS/400. We called this new extended PowerPC architecture *Amazon*. This new name allowed us to distinguish between the base PowerPC architecture and the extended architecture.

Although we did have some disagreements in Rochester about whether or not a common RISC architecture was a good idea, we did make rapid progress on the definition. Two individuals on our team, Andy Wottreng and Mike Corrigan, took over the technical ownership of the extended architecture. They did a marvelous job of integrating the AS/400 technical requirements into the new architecture. When they finished, we had the first RISC architecture in the industry that was equally at home with commercial and technical applications.

Darryl Solie was our team member who watched over the processor designs. Darryl worked closely with the processor design teams in both Austin and Rochester to ensure the cooperation we needed. Rochester designers learned a lot from other IBM and Motorola hardware designers. Processor performance levels they originally argued could never be achieved suddenly looked doable. As a result, Rochester now builds some of the highest-performance processors in the industry.

Whenever tensions and emotions flared and some of us became convinced that the whole idea wouldn't work, Bill Berg would step in. His quiet diplomatic style would soon have us convinced that we were doing the right thing and that we were the only ones who could make it happen. Bill was later instrumental in convincing development to use object-oriented programming technologies for our new operating system software.

The PowerPC architecture was defined to run in both a 32-bit and a 64-bit mode. All 64-bit versions of the PowerPC would have the 32-bit subset. We made almost no changes to the 32-bit subset, concentrating only on the 64-bit mode of the architecture. As we defined the various extensions to the architecture, we were able to make the development cost sizings. We worked hard and finished within the 90 days, but it wasn't a pretty picture.

Many of the architecture changes we needed would be difficult to incorporate into the early versions of the PowerPC processors. At the high end of the AS/400 line we needed processors that could handle massive amounts of data, and very wide data buses are needed to accomplish this throughput. We didn't even consider trying to extend the PowerPC 601, 603, or 604 processor designs because they only supported the 32-bit mode. It was doubtful that we could extend the 620, because it was not sufficiently dense to package the size processor we needed at the high end of our line. We would have to build a multichip version of the architecture. Even at the low end of the AS/400 line it was not clear what to use. We briefly proposed an extension to the 620 for our low end that we dubbed the 621, but eventually concluded it would be easier to develop the AS/400 processors within IBM.

At the same time, the RS/6000 developers also concluded they could not use the early PowerPC processors in their high-end systems. The single-chip 601 design was okay at the low end, but a multichip design was required for their high-performance products. Besides, they wanted to incorporate some features, specifically for numerically intensive computing (NIC), that would support the high-performance technical computing marketplace. Many of these NIC features would not be found in the general PowerPC. They created an extension to the original POWER design that they called POWER2. The POWER2 design added more pipelines and new computational instructions. The first POWER2 design appeared in an RS/6000 in 1993.

The POWER2 processors were also used in the RS/6000 Scalable POWERparallel System (RS/6000 SP). The RS/6000 SP is IBM's entry into the parallel processing computer market. The RS/6000 SP can have a large number of these processors (a system with 512 processors has been installed) all operating in parallel. This type of parallel machine is very good for certain kinds of engineering-scientific applications as well as for some commercial applications, such as scanning huge databases.

The AS/400 and RS/6000 architects initially wanted to achieve a common processor design. We decided to include in the Amazon architecture all of the extensions required for both the AS/400 and the RS/6000. In this way, a single processor could be built sometime in the future that would be able to support the special needs of both systems.

The first common PowerPC processor that we planned to use for both the AS/400 and the RS/6000 had several names. The RS/6000 people often called it POWER3. Others called it the PowerPC 630. Internally, we named it *Belatrix*. Belatrix is a star in the constellation Orion. Few people know that this star is also called the Amazon Star. Beletrix was to be the star of the Amazon architecture.

Belatrix was being designed with the help of IBM Research to provide an ultra-high-performance RISC microprocessor. Its design point was 300-400 Mhz, which would boost system performance five to 10 times over current designs. This would certainly be a supercomputer-on-a-chip. This processor was to implement the full Amazon architecture with all the extensions needed for the RS/6000 and the AS/400.

As with many early designs, the Belatrix project was overly ambitious, trying to be everything to everybody, and was terminated. We had decided that it made more sense to have different versions of the PowerPC processors, optimized for various computing environments. Every PowerPC processor would implement a base set of instructions and functions. Beyond this base set would be extensions that could be optionally implemented for each processor. With Belatrix gone, the definition of the PowerPC 630 was changed to be more like a PowerPC 620 with the NIC extensions needed for the RS/6000. Rochester would design the future PowerPC processors with extensions for the commercial environment. Chapter 12 discusses these future processors in more detail.

Even though we couldn't use the standard PowerPC processors in the AS/400, we would be able to share the architecture, experience, and technology. All the PowerPC processors for the AS/400 and the RS/6000 would be manufactured on the same semiconductor line in Burlington. This is the same facility that builds all the PowerPC processors for IBM. We would be able to share the development and manufacturing expenses across IBM.

The software picture using PowerPC looked much worse. All application software and all system software that was above the MI was protected because of the AS/400 architecture's technology independence. However, because PowerPC was so very different from the IMPI, the microcode written below the MI would have to be converted to the new processor. Automated tools could help port some of it to the new hardware. Still, a lot of this low-level operating system code was dependent on the IMPI, and a large amount would have to be rewritten — a major undertaking. Because we needed our existing development programmers to deliver new releases of the AS/400, we estimated that several hundred new system programmers would have to be hired to do the work on the RISC-based systems.

Finally, there was the problem of schedule. We had originally planned to ship the new C-RISC processors in mid-1994. We had already started to work on these processors for Superior. If we used PowerPC, we would have to slip the schedule for the RISC processors into 1995. It would take us that long to build the processors with the extensions we needed and to rewrite the internal code. We would have to ship Superior with the IMPI processors and ensure that they could be upgraded to the PowerPC processors when they were available.

In early July of 1991, we went back to Jack Kuehler with our results. Most in Rochester thought he would thank us for a good job, conclude that moving to the PowerPC processor was just too expensive, and send us back to build C-RISC. He didn't. He gave us the green light and provided the development resources to make it happen. Suddenly, we had to totally change both our hardware and software directions for Superior.

By the end of July we had reorganized the laboratory to concentrate on the new system. The design of our high-end processor, which we called Muskie,[3] was Rochester's responsibility. It was to be a multichip implementation that could satisfy the demanding needs for very large commercial computers. The design for the low end of the AS/400 line went to the IBM laboratory in Endicott, New York. This line was called Cobra and was to be a single-chip, full 64-bit design.

Initially, we decided to build the processors with only the 64-bit mode. After all, the AS/400 wouldn't use the 32-bit mode and no one else would use these early processors, so it didn't make sense to include the full architecture. That decision was reversed about a year later when it became apparent that the AS/400 should be able to run any application software written for PowerPC processors. Because much of that software would be written for 32-bit processors, we needed to include the 32-bit subset in all our processors.

The software effort to port the microcode of the AS/400 to the new processors also started in earnest at this time. Here was the opportunity to redo the internals of the AS/400 operating system, something that hadn't been done since the original System/38 design. As long as we were going to modernize the internals, we decided to go all the way and use the latest object-oriented programming methodologies. We planned to have the most modern operating system in the industry.

Mike Tomashek was given the responsibility to put together the organization to rewrite the operating system internals. Mike knew he didn't have the people or the skills to pull this off in the time he had. Common wisdom said it couldn't be done. Mike worked with key developers such as Bill Berg and Chris Jones to put a plan in place. They needed to hire hundreds of new people, train them in object-oriented technologies, and rewrite the most critical part of the AS/400 operating system in a short period of time. Mike didn't spend too much time on the plan. He just declared it would work, and went full speed ahead. There was no time to look back or debate the topic.

We started our massive hiring campaign for system programmers in late 1991. Ads began to appear in several national newspapers looking for system programmers with C++ programming experience to come to Rochester. Before we were done, we had hired several hundred new programmers. Many industry observers wondered just what we were up to, and now they know.

[3] A Muskie is a large game fish of the pike family. Muskies are found in the lakes of northern Minnesota and Wisconsin. They survive by eating other fish. Catching a big Muskie can be the thrill of a lifetime for a fresh-water fisherman.

The PowerPC Architecture

In most respects, the PowerPC architecture is fairly conventional in that it contains all the characteristics usually associated with a RISC architecture. It has fixed-length instructions, register-to-register architecture, simple addressing modes, and a large set of registers. The PowerPC architecture also has features that set it apart from other architectures.

As already mentioned, the PowerPC architecture was defined as a full 64-bit architecture that has a 32-bit subset. The architecture permits 32-and 64-bit versions of PowerPC processors, but all processors are required to support, at a minimum, the 32-bit subset. The architecture defines a 32/64-bit mode switch that can be set by the operating system to allow a 64-bit processor to run 32-bit programs.

The entire instruction set is designed around the idea of a superscalar implementation. In a superscalar processor, multiple instructions can be dispatched to multiple pipelines during the same clock cycle. The processor hardware examines the instruction stream and dispatches as many independent instructions as it can, typically two to four per cycle. The dispatched instructions can then execute concurrently and even finish out of order. This added parallelism can greatly increase the overall processor performance.

Instructions are dispatched simultaneously to three independent execution units. Conceptually, the PowerPC structure is shown in Figure 2.3. This figure shows a branch unit, a fixed-point unit, and a floating-point unit. Also shown is the instruction cache,[4] the data cache, the memory, and the I/O space, which in the architecture looks like a part of the memory.

The PowerPC architecture defines an independent set of registers for each of the three execution units. Each instruction defined in the architecture can only execute in one type of unit. Thus, each unit has its own set of registers plus its own instruction set. These execution units are often called processors because they have all the characteristics of processors. A PowerPC processor can be thought of as having three separate processors — the execution units. Note also that it is possible to have more than one execution pipeline in each execution unit. If floating-point performance is important for, say, a model optimized for NIC, two or more pipelines may be incorporated into the floating-point unit. In this way, more than one floating-point instruction can be executing in the unit at the same time. The same is true for the other two execution units. PowerPC processor implementations can be built that allow five or more instructions to execute concurrently.

The advantage of this design is not only that multiple instructions can be executing concurrently, but also, because of their separate resources, minimal communications and synchronization are required between units. Execution units can adjust to the changing dynamics of an instruction stream and allow one instruction to slip past another and complete out of order.

Another characteristic of the PowerPC architecture that is different from a conventional RISC processor is the use of several compound instructions.

---

[4] A cache is a small fast memory that acts as a buffer for the main memory. Most RISC processors have separate caches to hold instructions and data. In a single-chip processor, the caches can either be located on the processor chip or on separate chips, while the main memory is always packaged on separate chips.

Figure 2.3 The PowerPC Architecture Model

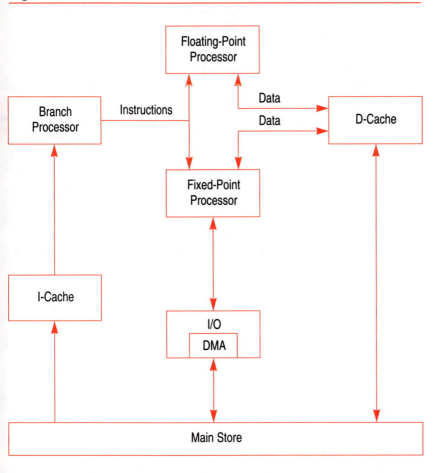

The biggest drawback of RISC relative to CISC is code expansion. A RISC takes more instructions than a CISC to perform the same program. Compound instructions reduce that code expansion. Some compound instructions are fairly simple, such as updating the base register on loads and stores, which eliminates the need for a separate add instruction. Others are more involved, such as load-and-store multiple instructions to allow several registers to be moved with a single instruction. There are also load-and-store string instructions, which load or store arbitrarily aligned byte strings. CISC fans will recognize this last pair of instructions as a not-very-carefully-disguised move-character instruction.

RISC purists objected and accused the PowerPC architects of selling out to the forces of CISC. In fact, the architects were simply recognizing that in the real world certain operations such as moving unaligned byte strings occur frequently enough that they need to be optimized in some way. If a compound instruction does the job, but in doing so violates some unwritten rule of RISC purity, so be it. Compound instructions do not signal a return to CISC architectures. They do, however, show that nothing is ever black and white.

These characteristics of aggressively exploiting superscalar capabilities and using compound instructions show the design philosophy of the PowerPC architecture. Other designs, such as the Sun SuperSPARC and the Motorola 88110, also follow this philosophy. Some in the industry argue that the added complexity makes it difficult to achieve high clock rates, which are usually measured in megahertz (MHz). They believe higher performance can be achieved by exploiting clock rates rather than aggressive instruction-level parallelism.

What is a MHz? In recent years, MHz has become a popular way to specify the performance of the processor chip in a computer. It is used to measure clock rates. An easy way to think of MHz is to relate it to revolutions per minute (RPM) of an automobile engine: It is a measure of how fast the engine is spinning, or just how many revolutions of the crankshaft occur in a minute. A processor's speed can be specified in terms of the number of cycles it can execute in a second. In one cycle, a processor can typically execute one simple instruction, so this is sometimes used as an approximation of the number of instructions that a processor can execute in a second. A hertz (Hz), named after a German physicist, is equal to one cycle per second. One MHz is equal to one million cycles per second.

Some examples that apply this high-clock-rate philosophy are the Digital Alpha, the HP PA-RISC, and the MIPS R4000 architectures. To illustrate the difference, let's look at the PA-RISC. A high-end PA-RISC processor can typically dispatch two instructions per cycle. The smaller PowerPC processors dispatch three instructions per cycle, while the high-end models can dispatch four or more. This added parallelism gives the PowerPC a throughput advantage but at the cost of added complexity, which can slow the clock rate.

The debate over which is the best design philosophy continues. The two camps have been called "Speed Demons" (high clock rates) and "Brainiacs" (complexity). The point here is the clock rate, measured in MHz, does not always indicate the performance of one processor compared to another. A 150 MHz Brainiac may easily outperform a 300 MHz Speed Demon. It all depends on the program being executed and the amount of instruction parallelism the compiler is able to exploit.

Some recent industry announcements may indicate that the scales are tipping in favor of a Brainiac design such as the PowerPC. HP has described its next-generation architecture, which it has dubbed PA-RISC 2.0, and it appears that HP has succumbed to the siren call of complexity. Its PA-8000 will be 64 bits wide and will join the Brainiac camp sometime in 1996.

Extensions to the PowerPC Architecture

We wanted to give our AS/400 processors a new name. Because the processor was to be an extension of PowerPC, some wanted to call it "PowerPC Plus." We didn't like that name because some or all of the extensions could someday become part of the general PowerPC architecture. Besides, no two of the PowerPC processors have the exact same instruction set. The PowerPC architecture defines required and optional instructions for both the 32-bit and the 64-bit instruction sets, and each PowerPC processor implements different sets of the optional instructions.

We wanted to call our processors "PowerPC Optimized for the AS/400 Advanced Series." Because that name was such a mouthful, we decided to give our processors the name PowerPC AS. Most people think "AS" is for "Advanced Series," but many of us prefer to think it is for "Amazon Series." We also decided to identify our processors with new numbers. The previously announced processors were all members of the "6xx" series, where *xx* is two digits, such as 20. We decided to make our new processors members of the "Axx" series. As with the 6xx series, not all the early Axx series processors used in the AS/400 will implement the full architecture. We will discuss the details of what this means later.

The most significant extension to the architecture for the AS/400 is the support for the memory tags. We will also cover the subject of tags in more detail in Chapter 8, but a short description here will show how these architectural extensions were added.

With the System/38, we introduced the concept of a single-level store. Simply put, all memory, including disk, is in a single, large address space. We needed an efficient mechanism to protect areas in memory that a user was not authorized to access. Addressing at the MI is accomplished with the use of 16-byte *pointers*. In Chapter 5, we will see that a pointer contains an address, and a user can modify that address. Because an address can be modified to point anywhere in memory, we had to provide a way to prevent a user's unauthorized modification of addresses.

A special memory protection bit, called a *tag bit*, was associated with every word in the System/38 memory. A word in the System/38 memory had 32 data bits. An MI pointer occupied four of these memory words. Whenever a pointer was stored into four consecutive words in the memory by the operating system, the hardware turned on (set to 1) the four tag bits to indicate that the pointer contained a valid address for the user. If a user changed any part of the pointer in memory, the hardware would turn off (set to 0) the tag bit. If any of the tag bits were off, the address in the pointer was invalid and could not be used to access memory.

For security, a tag bit had to be hidden, kept in a part of the memory where the user could not get at it. A tag bit could not be one of the data bits in the word because a user could see and change that bit. The tag bit had to be a separate bit, but where should it be kept?

The System/38 used separate error-correction code bits for every word in memory. The part of the memory that contained these bits was not visible to programs above the MI. We decided to add another bit to the error-correction code bits and use it as a tag bit. When any user program modified a word in memory, the processor would automatically turn off the hidden tag bit. If that word contained any part of a pointer, it would become invalid. Only the microcode below the MI had instructions to turn the tag bits on.

The AS/400 also uses the tag bits in memory. Because the PowerPC architecture does not recognize tag bits, we had to add a *tags-active mode* to the architecture. In the tags-active mode, the processor recognizes that tag bits exist and it will turn off the tag bit whenever a user modifies a word in memory. All AS/400 processors run in the tags-active mode. Current PowerPC processors use the tags-inactive mode.

A 65-Bit Processor?

The width of the memory word was increased to 64 data bits when the AS/400 was introduced. A tag bit is associated with each eight bytes in memory in an AS/400, and an MI pointer occupies two of these words. For a period of time in 1991, we thought there would be some advantage to keeping the tag bits in the registers of the new RISC processors as well as in the memory. We also wanted to reduce the size of our MI pointers to occupy only eight bytes. The 16-byte pointers had unused space in them, and we thought this was a good time to shrink them.

To keep these tagged pointers in the registers, we had to increase the size of the integer registers to 65 bits. We carried this design for almost a year. In 1992, we threw out the design and went back to having the tags only in the memory. There were three main reasons for this change. First, changing the pointer size had a ripple effect into OS/400, which would require more changes than we wanted. Second, this approach limited our future expansion of address size to only 64 bits. Third, and most important, our processors in the tags-active mode would not be compatible with the PowerPC instruction set.

Originally, we didn't think that not being compatible with PowerPC was important. Future processors that implemented the tags-inactive mode would be fully compatible with PowerPC, where the 65th bit was ignored. In the tags-active mode, we were originally not even planning to implement the 32-bit instructions. We thought the tags-active mode would only be used by the AS/400 operating system, which only cared about 64-bit instructions. We originally didn't plan to run any 32-bit software in the tags-active mode.

When we decided to be compatible with the PowerPC instruction set, we got rid of the 65th bit in the processor. We thought there might be the possibility for some future software convergence among IBM operating systems. Because most PowerPC software will be written for a 32-bit processor, we made sure that all our processors, even in the tags-active mode, implemented the 32-bit instruction set. Future processor designs out of Rochester with the tags-inactive mode enabled will be able to run all PowerPC application and operating system software.

Even though we changed back to a 64-bit processor design years ago, a few people within IBM still talk about the 65-bit design that was never built. The confusion arises because many people don't know why the tag bit is there in the first place. Perhaps if we had originally called the extra bit in the error correction code the "pointer in memory protection" bit, instead of the tag bit, fewer people would be confused. Unfortunately, we would then have had to spend all of our time explaining why we needed a "pimp" bit.

PowerPC AS Instructions

The PowerPC architecture defines privileged operations and instructions that are only used by the operating system. These privileged operations and instructions are not used by the application programs. The tags-active mode enables the extensions that were added for the AS/400 and determines how the privileged operations and instructions are defined.

For example, the address translation mechanism needs to support both a single-level store with a single address space and a conventional store with a separate address space for each process. We use the tags-active mode to tell the processor to use a single-level store. The tags-inactive mode tells the processor to use the conventional PowerPC address translation.

Other extensions for the AS/400 include decimal support instructions, some new load and store instructions, and some enhancements to an internal processor status register to improve branching. Rather than spending time now explaining how these instructions are used in the AS/400, let's hold off that discussion for later chapters. Then we will be able to see exactly how each extended instruction is used.

To summarize the changes to the AS/400 architecture, and to put these changes into perspective with the PowerPC architecture, some numbers are in order.

- The 32-bit PowerPC architecture defines 187 instructions, with 11 of them being optional.
- The 64-bit PowerPC architecture defines 228 instructions (187 from the 32-bit set plus 41 additional), with 21 of them being optional.
- The Amazon architecture defines 253 instructions (228 from the 64-bit PowerPC set plus 25 additional), with 20 of them being optional. Note the 25 additional instructions are only available in the tags-active mode. The tags-inactive mode supports only the 64-bit PowerPC instruction set.

Also note that the definition of any architecture is dynamic and the exact numbers are subject to change.

AS/400 Processor Implementations

The two processor implementations we examine in this section only support the tags-active mode. They also only support the AS/400 I/O structure. This means they can run applications, but not operating systems, written for a standard PowerPC processor. Any other operating system running on one of these processors must use the facilities provided by the AS/400 operating system for such functions as I/O. In later chapters, we will see how this works.

Future AS/400 processors will implement both the tags-active and the tags-inactive modes, in addition to simultaneously supporting other I/O structures. These future processors will then be capable of running any PowerPC operating system. We will discuss this convergence of processor technologies in Chapter 12. For now, we will briefly examine the current implementations of the processors to see how they are designed to support an AS/400 environment.

Before we go into some detail on the implementations of the PowerPC AS processors, we need to bring out our chili pepper rating system. The information in the next two sections is not for everyone. We include it for those readers who want processor hardware details. If you decide to sample some of this information and find it too hot to handle, simply skip over these sections to something a bit milder.

The A30 (Muskie) Processors

Let's examine the implementation of the A30 processor. Designed in Rochester as the Muskie processor, the A30 was announced as the high-end processor for the AS/400 in 1995. At the time it was announced, the A30 was the fastest processor based on PowerPC technology, and the fastest microprocessor in IBM. This high-performance processor has achieved a cycle time of only 6.5 nanoseconds, which equates to a clock rate of 154 MHz. The A30 processor also clearly shows its intended use in a commercial processing system rather than in a technical workstation.

The implementation of the A/30 processor is a single-module, multichip, pipelined, superscalar design intended for the high-end AS/400 models. This processor implementation can dispatch and execute up to four instructions per cycle. From a fixed-point (integer) performance perspective, this implementation has a peak rate of 616 million instructions per second (MIPS). Also included in this processor implementation is a floating-point unit with a peak rate of 308 million floating-point operations per second (MFLOPS), an 8-kilobyte (on-chip) instruction cache, a 256-kilobyte (on-module) cache, and support for up to 64 gigabytes of main memory. This implementation also supports multiprocessor configurations.

With all of its support circuitry, the A30 implementation uses a total of seven chips. These seven chips are packaged on a single multichip module with a total of more than 25 million transistors. One of the chips is an I/O control unit that is technically not a part of the processor. The other six chips that make up the processor complex, along with the interconnections between the chips, is shown in Figure 2.4.

Figure 2.4 A30 Processor Block Diagram

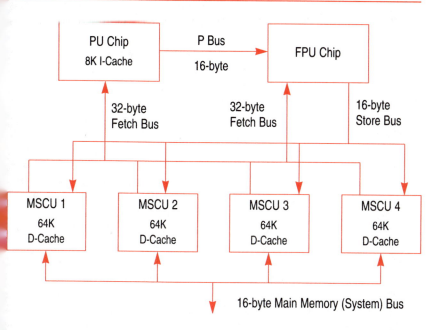

Single-chip processors usually use CMOS (Complementary Metal Oxide Silicon) technology. CMOS consumes less power than other technologies, meaning it dissipates less heat. As a result, more transistors can be packaged on a single chip. As long as all circuits are contained on a single chip, the low-power circuits in CMOS are very fast. Going off the chip is another matter. Performance is reduced when CMOS drivers are used between chips in a multichip processor.

The technology used for all six chips in the A30 is BiCMOS (Bipolar-CMOS). Bipolar is a high-performance, high-power-consuming technology. Bipolar chips cannot be made as dense as CMOS chips because of the heat they dissipate. They have the advantage of being able to maintain their high speed between chips. BiCMOS is a technology that allows both CMOS and bipolar circuits on a single chip. The CMOS is used for the logic that is internal to the chip and the bipolar is used for the off-chip drivers.

BiCMOS is an excellent technology to use for a multichip processor, although at the cost of higher heat. To illustrate, the seven-chip module for the A30 can dissipate approximately 130 watts. You can compare this to the heat given off by a 130-watt light bulb in a package that is just 63.5 mm square. Air cooling is required for this module, which explains why this processor only appears in the high-end model AS/400 physical packages — the 530 and the 53S.

A more detailed look at the processor chips will help to explain why so many transistors are used for this implementation. The six chips that make up a single processor include a Processing Unit (PU) chip, a Floating-Point Unit (FPU) chip, and four copies of a Main Store Control Unit (MSCU) chip.

The PU chip contains the instruction cache, the branch unit, and the fixed-point unit. The instruction cache has 8 kilobytes, organized 32 bytes wide. The cache can fetch 32 bytes (eight instructions[5]) per cycle from memory. The 32-byte data paths are designed to transfer large amounts of data in a single cycle. Even the register stack in the fixed-point unit is designed to load or store four 64-bit registers in a single cycle.

The FPU is contained on a single chip and supports the IEEE standard for floating-point. The design of the FPU is such that it can produce a result every cycle, giving this processor its very high floating-point performance. Four instructions per cycle are passed from the PU chip to the FPU chip on the 16-byte P-bus. All store data from the PU is also passed across the P-bus on its way to the data cache. Data for the FPU is fetched from the data cache at a rate of 32 bytes per cycle. All store data from either the FPU or the PU is passed to the data cache across the 16-byte store bus.

The MSCU provides the data cache as well as the interface to the memory. All four chips work together to provide the 256-kilobyte data cache and the interfaces to the data buses shown in Figure 2.4. The data cache accesses are pipelined so that 32 bytes of data are fetched and 16 bytes of data are stored each cycle. The MSCU supports multiprocessing by providing cache coherency across multiple processors.

In total, there are five pipelines in the PU and FPU, but only four instructions can be dispatched each cycle. The four instructions are

1. A branch instruction (including an operation on the contents of the condition register)
2. A load/store instruction
3. A fixed-point arithmetic instruction
4. A fixed-point logical, or shift, or rotate instruction; *or* a floating-point instruction

The floating-point instructions are executed in the FPU, but they cannot be dispatched at the same time as a fixed-point logical, or shift, or rotate instruction, which executes in the PU. Note that the load/store pipeline does both fixed and floating-point loads and stores. The multiple pipeline implementation allows parts of several instructions to be executing simultaneously.

---

[5] All PowerPC instructions are 32 bits wide for both the 32- and 64-bit processors.

The result of all this hardware is a full 64-bit processor that runs at clock speeds of 125 MHz and 154 MHz. The A30 implementation also supports tightly coupled, shared memory; it also supports symmetric multiprocessing (SMP)[6] configurations. Initially, up to four-way multiprocessing is supported, but larger configurations are possible.

Besides being the fastest IBM RISC processor built to date, the A30 processor is optimized for the needs of a commercial processor. A few of these characteristics will illustrate the point:

- Commercial systems and servers must handle lots and lots of data. The 16-byte (128 bits) and 32-byte (256 bits) wide buses allow this processor to handle massive amounts of data and instructions. Compare this to the typical 8-byte (64-bit) buses used in most high-performance RISC processors. These are designed for use in a workstation whose data requirements are far less demanding.

- Even if a system can move large amounts of data, the cache memory is usually a bottleneck in most RISC designs. The A30 has a 256 kilobyte, single-cycle data cache to overcome this bottleneck. It has a cache bandwidth of up to 4.9 gigabytes per second and a system bus bandwidth of up to 2.2 gigabytes per second. This is double the bandwidth of other very high-performance RISC processors designed for technical computing.

- Because a branch instruction can stall a pipelined processor, RISC processors today implement some form of branch prediction just as the supercomputers have done. Branch prediction used in most RISC processors is typically 80 percent to 90 percent accurate on a technical workload. The reason for these high percentages is that technical computing usually involves a lot of loop processing, where the processor re-executes an instruction loop several times. Branch prediction works well for this kind of processing. For a commercial workload, where there are far fewer loops, branch prediction may be as low as 50 percent accurate (a random guess would be as accurate). For this reason, rather than trying to guess which branch target will be needed, the A30 pre-fetches the instructions at both branch targets and begins to execute them (called speculative execution). This requires a very high bandwidth cache, which the A30 has, but it does achieve essentially 100 percent accuracy for all workloads.

- Another important aspect of commercial processing is the need for high data integrity and high availability. The A30 implements full error-correction codes or parity on all off-chip signals. Various parity schemes are also integrated into most of the control and data-flow logic on each chip. Again, compare this with the typical workstation

---

[6] Recently, a great deal of attention has been focused on new SMP implementations from various computer vendors. In an SMP system, the operating systems can run on any processor in a multiprocessor configuration or on all processors simultaneously. Some SMP implementations have tightly coupled memories, which means all processors share a single memory, while others don't. The AS/400 has had tightly coupled SMP since 1990, four years ahead of most competitors; it is called n-way.

RISC processor, which rarely has anywhere near this level of error detection and correction.

The A10 (Cobra) Processors

Like the A30 processors, the A10 processors implement the 64-bit extended PowerPC architecture. Similarly, they are superscalar designs to take advantage of instruction-level parallelism. Functionally, the two processor families execute the same application-level instruction set. There are slight differences between the two in the optional instructions that are implemented. For example, the A10 is intended for the middle and lower models of the AS/400, so instructions to support characteristics such as multiprocessing are not included.

The A10 processors were developed in Endicott, New York. So far, four versions of the Cobra processors have been built. The two A10 processors announced in the RISC AS/400 systems are the Cobra-4 and Cobra-CR. The CR stands for "cost reduced." The Cobra-CR is a Cobra-4 processor that can only run at 50 MHz, which is the slowest speed of the Cobra-4. The Cobra-4 can also run at higher speeds. We will look at its characteristics shortly.

For the purpose of testing the new operating system software, the Endicott design team designed a special version called Cobra-0. Cobra-0 was used only for testing and was not shipped in any AS/400. A small team in Rochester designed a fourth version for use in the Advanced 36 system announced in 1994. It was called Cobra-Lite because 17 of the required PowerPC instructions were left out.

The design objective for the A10 processors was to integrate the processor and the memory interface on a single chip. The I/O bus interface is on a separate chip. To accomplish this, the A10 uses a CMOS technology instead of BiCMOS. Specifically, the A10 is implemented in a technology IBM calls CMOS-4S. The result is an implementation that dissipates less heat than the A30 and can be used in a smaller package with less cooling required. For this reason, the A10 processors are the only ones packaged in the original physical boxes that were announced for the Advanced Series in 1994.

Like the A30 processor, the A10 has five pipelines, but can only dispatch three instructions in a given cycle. The three instructions are

1. A branch instruction (including a condition register instruction)
2. A load/store instruction
3. A fixed-point arithmetic instruction (including a logical, or shift, or rotate instruction), or a floating-point instruction, or a condition-register instruction

The three pipelines (fixed-point, floating-point, and condition-register instruction execution) share the third dispatch slot.

The initial A10 processors have clock rates of 50 Mhz and 77 Mhz, but the design is capable of higher speeds. At 77 Mhz, an A10 runs at 231 MIPS. To sustain this rate, the A10 has a 4-kilobyte (on-chip) instruction cache and an 8-kilobyte (on-chip) data cache. These caches can be backed up with a 1-megabyte (off-chip — on separate chips) cache.

Conclusions

A 64-bit processor is rapidly becoming the standard in the computer industry.[7] Both the A10 and the A30 are 64-bit "industrial-strength" RISC processors capable of delivering the function and performance demanded by commercial systems and servers. They are the first members of a family of RISC processors that will carry the AS/400 into the next century. In the next chapter we will look at the technology-independent machine interface and see how it allows new hardware such as the PowerPC AS processors to be seamlessly integrated into the AS/400.

[7] Even the video games from companies like Sega and Nintendo now use 64-bit technology. To appreciate how much progress has been made, consider this: These video games have processors that are faster than the original 64-bit Cray-1 supercomputer from Cray Research in 1976.

Chapter 3

The Technology-Independent Machine Interface

In Chapter 1, we saw that because levels of abstraction have been added to most computer systems, we can think about a computer having multiple levels of architecture. The two most significant levels in the AS/400 are the Technology-Independent Machine Interface (MI) architecture and the PowerPC RISC architecture.

The definition of the PowerPC architecture was made with an obvious hardware bias. Like all processor architectures, the hardware chip designers, who had a set of implementations in mind, played an important role in its definition. They left out certain desired functions because those functions would have exceeded the available hardware on a particular chip. They had to redefine other requested functions to ensure that the processor cycle time for one of the designs could be maintained. There is nothing inherently wrong with this approach, because a hardware architecture that cannot be built is of little use. At the same time, a hardware-driven architecture guarantees obsolesence.

In fairness, some hardware-driven architectures have survived for many years. For example, Intel has successfully kept its x86 processor architecture current since the early 1980s. Starting with the Intel 8086, the organization has continued to add functionality as hardware technology allowed more transistors to be packaged on a single chip. And Intel made great strides as it delivered the 186, 286, 386, 486, Pentium, and P6 family of processors. To ensure software compatibility, each of these processors is built on the original architecture. At some point, however, this approach produces a processor that is no longer competitive. For example, the PowerPC 604 running at 100 MHz offers 50 percent more performance than the Pentium running at the same speed, and the PowerPC is less expensive to produce. It seems the x86 family of processors may be nearing its end of life in the next couple years.

Overview of the MI Architecture

The MI architecture definition is not tied to the hardware. It is a logical, not a physical, interface to the system. As described in Chapter 1, the MI architecture provides a complete set of APIs for OS/400 and all application programs. This set of APIs is a complete set by definition; that is, there is no way a system or an application program can go around the MI boundary. The only way to communicate with the hardware and some of the system software below the MI is through the MI boundary. This characteristic distinguishes the MI architecture from an API-centric architecture, which permits applications to go around the APIs and become dependent on the underlying hardware and software.

How were the original designers of the MI architecture so smart they could define a complete set of APIs, to be used by OS/400 and all applications, that would last forever? The answer is, they weren't, and they couldn't. As new applications were added, new APIs to support those applications had to be defined in the MI. The designers made the definition of the MI architecture so expandable that new APIs could be added at any time to support new application or operating-system functions. Today, APIs are constantly being added. This means the MI architecture will never become obsolete because it changes as needs for new functions develop. Because all the older APIs remain intact, previously written applications are also protected by the MI boundary.

At the time the MI architecture was defined, the term API was not in vogue, so the designers simply called these modifications instructions. To show the architected interface was to support both application and system software, the designers chose the name machine interface. Keep in mind that the I in API is the I in MI. The MI instructions are APIs.

The MI architecture has two components: a set of instructions and the operands those instructions act upon. Some of these operands are the traditional bit and byte operands found in conventional computer architectures. Other operands are complex data structures, called *objects*. An object is the only data structure that is supported as part of the MI architecture.

A computer generally represents its information resources, such as directories, database files, and physical device descriptions, as data structures or as blocks in memory with predefined fields. Application and system software directly access and manipulate the fields in these data structures. The knowledge of what that data structure represents and how it can be manipulated remains with the software.

An object at the MI boundary is a container. The container holds the data structure representing an information resource. If, instead of application and operating system software manipulating the data structure directly with bit- and byte-level instructions, only instructions that treat the object as an entity are allowed, a level of independence can be achieved.

With the use of objects, application and system software no longer know about the precise format of a data structure. That knowledge is contained within the object itself and is not visible outside the object. Because it is not visible, any changes to the data structure have no impact on application or system software. The software is independent of the underlying structure. This characteristic of hiding the internal details is called *encapsulation*. We will discuss encapsulation and the internal structure of an object in Chapter 5.

In this chapter, we are going to focus primarily on the set of instructions that are part of the MI architecture. We will see that there are instructions that operate on conventional data (we will look at some examples) and instructions that operate on objects. A detailed discussion of objects and the instructions that operate on them begins in Chapter 5 and continues in subsequent chapters. We begin our discussion here by looking at how compilers use the MI to generate the code that the hardware executes. We will then look at the characteristics of the MI and the MI programs. Finally, we will examine in more detail the structure of the MI instructions.

A Non-Executable Interface

We do not directly execute the MI instructions. They are first compiled to the hardware instruction set before the program can be executed. We call this last step a translation because it performs only a part of the compile function. Earlier, the target of this translation was the IMPI instruction set; now it is the PowerPC instruction set.

The MI instruction set is not a high-level language in the usual sense. It is more accurate to look at MI as the intermediate representation in a modern high-level language compiler. Some like to describe the MI instruction set as being similar to a high-level language that needs to be compiled or translated to a lower level. A short description of optimizing compilers will illustrate why this is a better view.

Figure 3.1 shows the structure of a modern, optimizing compiler. A compiler typically consists of two or more passes. A *pass* in a compiler transforms a high-level, more abstract representation of the program into a lower-level representation. Eventually, this process reaches the hardware instruction set. A pass is simply one phase in which the compiler reads and transforms the entire program. The term "phase" is often used interchangeably with "pass."

This compiler structure was first created in the 1960s to manage the complexities of the many transformations needed to create optimized code. A single-pass compiler is limited in what it can do to optimize the generated

Figure 3.1 Structure of an Optimizing Compiler

Function	Phase	
Transform language to common intermediate form	Front End	Language Dependent
		Machine Independent
Examples include procedure inlining and loop transformations	High-Level Optimizations	
Examples include register allocations and local data assignments	Global Optimizations	Language Independent
		Machine Dependent
Select machine instructions (may include assembler or be followed by an assembler)	Code Generator	

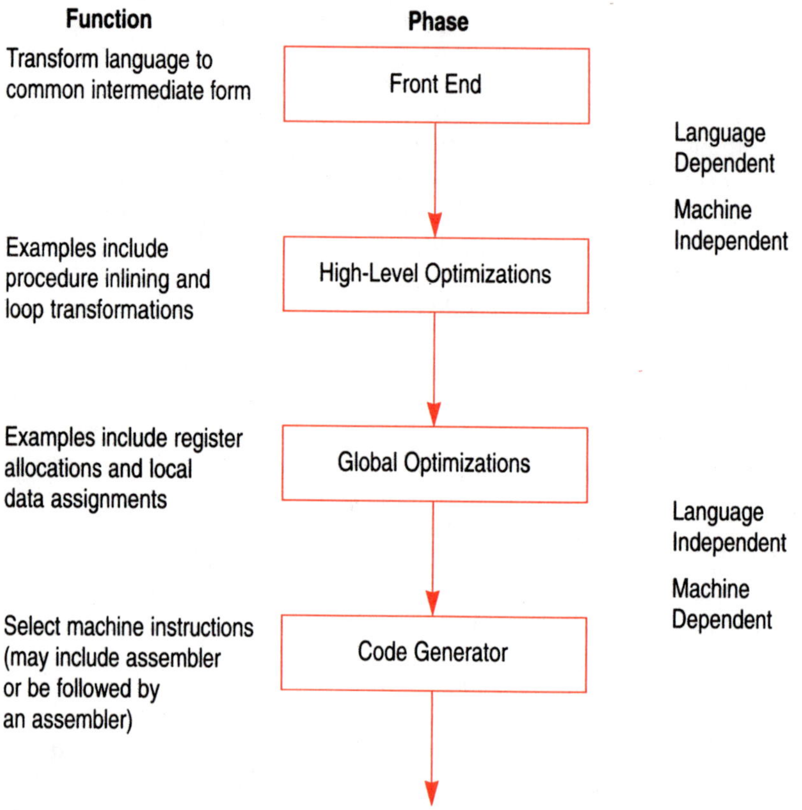

code. Simply put, it cannot look ahead in the instruction stream to see what is going to happen next. A multipass compiler can look ahead and prepare for upcoming computations. Assigning variables to registers based on their interaction with other variables, storing cache contents that are no longer needed, and prefetching operands are but a few of the optimizations that can be accomplished with a multipass compiler.

Compiler optimizations can greatly increase the performance of a program, especially if the program is run on a processor that can run multiple instructions in parallel. A RISC processor has this kind of parallelism and requires an optimizing compiler to achieve high performance. Using multiple passes also makes compiler writing easier.

The first phase of the compiler shown in Figure 3.1 is often called the *front end* of the compiler. Its job is to take the high-level language instructions and transform them into a *common intermediate form*. The *back end* of the compiler consists of the optimization phases and the code generation phase. Front ends are language dependent, while back ends are hardware dependent.

If the common intermediate form is independent of both the language and the hardware, then it can be used in several compilers. Each new language only needs a new front end. Similarily, once a back end has been written for a specific hardware implementation, all front ends will work. This mix-and-match approach makes it easier to put new languages on a computer.

The MI instruction set is similar to the common intermediate form used in a compiler. A high-level language compiler generates the MI form of the program. A *translator* below the MI takes this form, performs the optimizations, and generates the IMPI or PowerPC instructions. The translator is very similar to the back end of a compiler.

The MI instruction set is not always a replacement for the common intermediate form in all AS/400 compilers. Some AS/400 language compilers have their own intermediate form, others do not. The following description of the internals of the AS/400 language compilers will illustrate how the MI fits into the overall compiler operations.

AS/400 Language Compilers

The earliest language compilers on the System/38 and the AS/400 generated the MI instructions in a fairly direct manner. Although they did go through an assembler level, there was no common intermediate form within the compiler itself. The MI instructions were the intermediate form. Examples of this type include the compilers for RPG/400 and for CL, the command language of the AS/400. The program model for these languages, including the form of the program below the MI, is called the Original Program Model (OPM).

Figure 3.2 shows the steps that are taken to create the IMPI code. The language compiler takes the high-level language source statements (along with file descriptions that are not shown) as input and generates IRP code as the output. IRP, which is the acronym for Intermediate Representation of a Program, is essentially the assembler form of the MI instructions. The next step in the process converts the IRP code to the MI instructions. The component that performs this operation is called the Program Resolution Monitor (PRM). The PRM creates a *program template* that contains the MI instruction stream and other data items. Templates are used to create MI objects. The program template is used by the translator below the MI to create the *program object* that contains the IMPI instructions. We will examine the contents of a program template in a later section.

The OPM example shows the classical approach of a compiler generating the assembler form of the program (the IRP) before the assembler (the PRM) generates the binary machine level (the program template). The translator operation is an extra step in the process. Compiles on an AS/400 require extra steps, which also explains why they can take longer to run than some other systems do. Note that the user of the system is not aware

54 Inside the AS/400

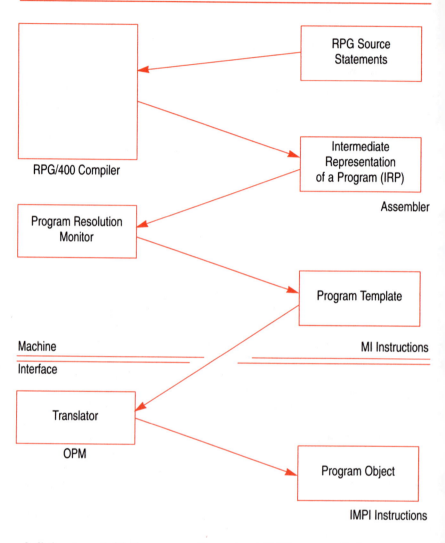

Figure 3.2 Original Program Model Compilers

of all the steps. Initiating a compile on the AS/400 causes all these steps to look like a single operation.

As new languages, such as C/400 and Pascal, were implemented on the AS/400, some extensions had to be added to the OPM to accommodate the new language compilers. The compiler steps for the extended model, aptly called the Extended Program Model (EPM), are shown in Figure 3.3. The compilers for these languages are implemented with separate front and back ends. The common intermediate form inside these compilers is called U-code. A new compiler back end, called the Common Use Back End 1

Figure 3.3 Extended Program Model Compilers

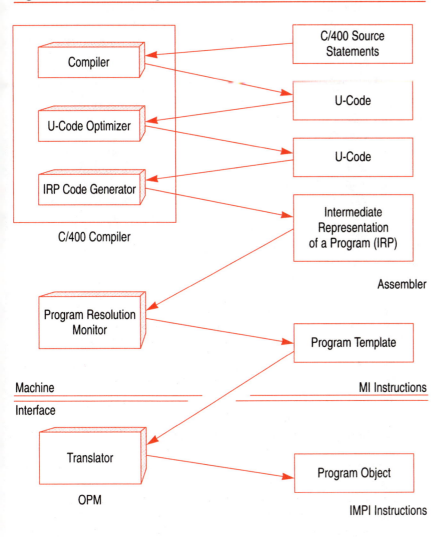

(CUBE-1), was created for the AS/400. EPM did not replace OPM; rather, it was on top of it.

The OPM, based on the System/38 model and designed for RPG and COBOL, had only limited support for block-structured languages such as C and Pascal. Block-structured languages are designed to enable a modular style of programming. Instead of requiring that a program be written as a single unit, these languages allow a program to be written as a series of smaller program blocks that are linked together by call instructions. The EPM enabled the implementation of these languages, but because the EPM was built without changes to the MI to support lots of calls, there was still a performance penalty when users started or called an EPM program.

The only type of call instruction originally supported at the MI was a *call external*. This type of call instruction is dynamic, meaning it resolves all references by name at execution time. This approach is known as *late binding*. Although such calls are the most flexible, they diminish performance. In addition, the OPM only supported a single language source per program object, so external calls were used between program objects when part of a program was written in a different language.

To improve the performance of modular programming and to encourage this style of programming for all languages, an architectural enhancement to the MI and to the objects below the MI was created. Introduced in 1993, this enhancement is called the Integrated Language Environment (ILE). ILE includes new language compilers, a new optimizing translator, and a new binder facility to create packaged programs. ILE changes the way programs are created. Unlike the OPM, the output of the ILE translator is not a program object; instead, it is a new object called a *module*. The ILE binder packages these modules into programs.

In addition to supporting the OPM late-bound calls, ILE introduced the ability to bind at compile time. The benefit of binding at compile time, known as *early binding*, is to reduce the overhead associated with the external dynamic calls. These bound, or static, calls are faster.

Before we look at this further, a few terms need a little more definition:

- Procedure — A procedure is a sequence of source statements that can be called at an entry point with some optional parameters.

- Module — A module is an object that contains code produced as the output of an ILE compiler. Unlike the program object produced by an OPM compiler, a module is nonexecutable. A module can contain one or more procedures. The ILE binder uses modules, possibly from different language compilers, to produce programs and service programs.

- Program — A program is an executable unit of code that consists of one or more modules. These modules may have been generated by different language compilers. A program has only a single entry point and is called with a dynamic call. One of the procedures is designated as the program entry point when the program is created, and control is passed to that procedure when the program is called. Within the same program, procedures are called with a static call.

- Service Program — A service program is an executable unit of code that consists of one or more modules. Again, these modules may have been generated by different language compilers. Although a service program is activated as a unit, it is treated as a collection of procedures.

Each procedure can be called with a static call. As such, a service program can have multiple entry points, one for each procedure.
- Activation Group — An activation group is the working storage within a job that is allocated to run one or more programs. We will discuss activation groups in detail in Chapter 9 when we cover processes.

The purpose for having both programs and service programs is to support two types of static calls. The two types are *bound by copy* and *bound by reference*. Bound-by-copy calls allow multiple modules to be copied together into a single program. As we just saw, the program itself is called with a dynamic call, but then the procedures within any of the modules are called with static calls. Because all procedure names are resolved to addresses at compile time, this type of static call within the program is much faster than a dynamic call. The downside of bound-by-copy calls is that multiple copies of the same module may exist in memory if the module is bound into multiple programs. Memory utilization is traded off for better call performance.

Bound-by-reference calls use a service program to store the modules. Unlike bound-by-copy calls, which copy the modules into the program, bound-by-reference calls store in the program symbolic links to the modules in the service program. With this type of call, there is only a single copy of the service program. When a program is activated, those links are resolved to the address of a table in the service program that contains the addresses of the called procedures. There is some additional overhead when a program is activated, because other functions such as authority resolution (covered in Chapter 7) are also performed. During execution of the program, however, the performance is about the same as a bound-by-copy call.

For both early bound methods, the system uses a new *call bound procedure (CALLB)* instruction. Another new instruction, *call program (CALLPGM)*, supports late binding and replaces the OPM call external instruction. Figure 3.4 shows the structure of the ILE program model compilers.

The ILE compiler front end produces a common intermediate form called W-code. W-code is a more modern intermediate form than is U-code. The back end of these compilers is called CUBE-3. The "3" designates this as the third, and latest, generation of IBM compiler technology. CUBE-3 and W-code are designed to very efficiently support RISC processors. Other IBM systems, most notably the RS/6000, use the same technologies. The back end of the ILE compiler generates the program template directly, eliminating IRP and the PRM step. To provide the necessary optimization for the RISC processors, W-code-like computation and branching instructions were added to the MI.

The ILE program model is an extension to the MI architecture. It is the only program model for the RISC processors. On the IMPI systems, the two program models co-exist, so that compiled code from the earlier compilers, as well as the compilers themselves, can be on the same system. Moving an

Figure 3.4 ILE Program Model Compilers

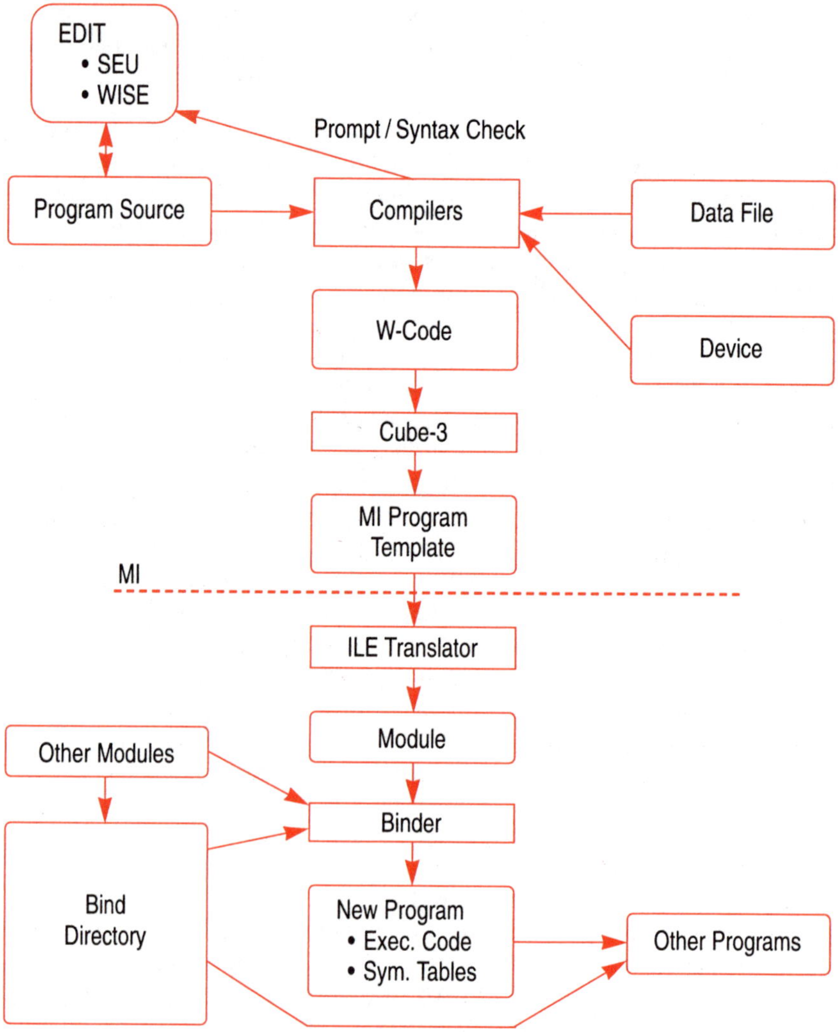

OPM program to a RISC-based system causes the program to be converted internally to the ILE program model. When one of the earlier language compilers is used on the new RISC models, there is an extra step involved. The output of these compilers has to be converted to the ILE program model. This extra step increases the compile time for the original compilers when compared to the ILE compilers.

Characteristics of the Machine Interface

We often describe the MI as a high-level machine interface when we are comparing it with a conventional machine interface. This is because many MI instructions are very high function. For example, not too many conventional machine interfaces have call instructions that support both early and late binding. A conventional interface is more likely to just have branch instructions.

To see the difference, consider an instruction for the conventional machine interface in Figure 3.5. An instruction has both an operation code (op-code) and one or more operand fields. The types of instructions supported are computational (every computer has an add instruction), branching, and data manipulation. More important than the operations performed are the operands that the instructions use.

Conventional machine interfaces work on the contents of registers, memory, or immediate data in the instruction itself. In other words, they do not know about application or operating system data. Take a standard "add register" instruction. The instruction identifies two specific registers in the hardware. The operation performed is to take the bits from one register, add them to the bits in the other register, and put the result someplace. The bits have no meaning to the instruction. The software cares about the meaning of the bits, but the instruction doesn't. The machine does not care what is there; it is just a bit configuration that runs through an algorithm called add. The fact that the two registers contain the names of two employees, so that treating them as operands for an add instruction makes no sense, is of no consequence. Operations at this level are simply working on the contents of the registers or memory.

As discussed earlier, this structure has the problem that it is very hardware-technology dependent. Because the instructions see the address space, the I/O space, and the register space, they are tied to these physical structures. Changes to these physical structures can cause changes to the instructions. Therefore, existing programs could have major conversion problems.

The AS/400 machine interface in Figure 3.6 is different. It has an instruction set with op-codes and operands similar to the conventional machine. It also has various types of operations for computation (add instructions) and branching that work on traditional operands. Unlike the conventional machine, it has instructions similar to the intermediate representations found in a modern high-level language compiler, and data structures (objects) as part of the machine design.

The most important difference here is not the instructions or operations themselves, but the operands that the instructions use. The conventional machine has registers, memory, and immediate data. Here, we still have immediate data but no registers or memory. Instead, there are objects.

Several object types are defined at the MI. Most of these are the complex data structures needed to represent information resources. One of the most

Figure 3.5 Conventional Machine Interface

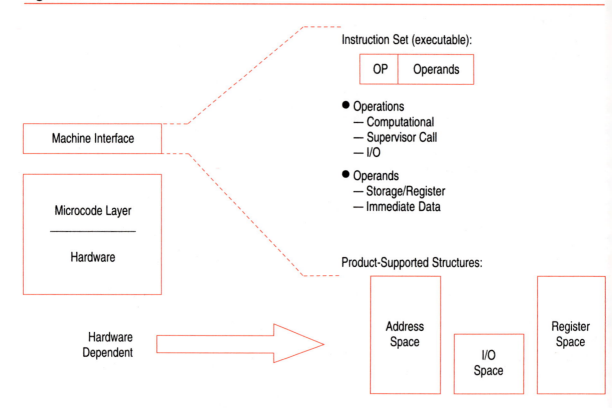

[1] AS/400 people like to talk about the single-level store. As we have just seen, there is no memory at the MI. Therefore, the single-level store is not visible at or above the MI; rather, it is part of the internal implementation of an AS/400.

important object types in the system is a space. A space is simply a chunk of bytes; it has no relationship to the physical hardware. The concept of a flock of bytes floating in the ether is difficult for many people to grasp. They want to tie it to physical hardware. But the MI has no concept of physical memory attached to the space. It is absolutely independent of what is underneath.[1]

When an MI program needs memory, it can use a space. There is no concept of registers, no concept of physical memory, and no memory addresses in the traditional sense. As an example, when an AS/400 compiler creates a program template, it has to put it somewhere; so it puts it into a space.

In addition to spaces, there are several other types of objects that we will discuss in later chapters. So far, the only objects described are the ones in the MI, which are called the *MI system objects*. OS/400 also supports objects.

Working with MI Programs

Several MI instructions work on programs. Because a program is an object, these instructions operate on the program as a complete entity. All of the instructions perform only those operations on a program that make sense.

Figure 3.6 AS/400 Machine Interface

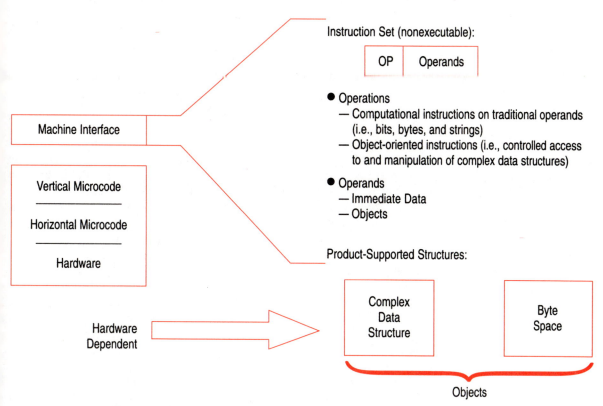

There is a Create Program instruction, but there is no Multiply Program instruction. Creating a program makes sense, but multiplying one program times another does not. The point is, instructions are specific to the type of object being manipulated. Instructions operate on the whole object, not some piece of data within an object. It is not possible to misuse an object, and this provides another major benefit of object orientation: integrity. Programs at the MI do the right thing. In this section we will look at how to create a program, how to destroy a program, and how to *materialize* a program.

Creating a Program

We create a program from a template, which is a predefined structure that describes all the characteristics of a particular MI system object. The code generation part of the AS/400 compilers generates this program template. All MI system objects are created from templates, which are contained in spaces at the MI. Because different types of objects have different characteristics, there is no one generic template; each object has its own unique template.

The Create Program instruction points to a program template. For the purpose of this discussion, there are two types of pointers: a *system pointer* and a *space pointer* (we will see later that other pointer types also are supported). A system pointer points to an MI system object, while a space pointer points to a byte in a space. Each of these pointers is 16 bytes long. Addressing at the MI is accomplished with a pointer. In fact, you can think of a pointer simply as an address at the MI.

The Create Program instruction is implemented by code below the MI. First, the space pointer in the Create Program instruction is used to access the program template. A syntax check of the program template is made to ensure that the template is correct. If it is, the translator is invoked to transform the MI instruction stream contained in the program template to the internal instruction stream. This internal IMPI or PowerPC instruction stream is packaged into an MI system object called a program. Finally, addressability to the newly created program is returned to the requester as a system pointer to the object. If there are problems with any part of this operation, the diagnostics are returned as an exception.

Destroying a Program

Any MI system object that can be created can be destroyed. Just as there are MI instructions to create objects, there are instructions to destroy objects. A user at the MI level provides a system pointer to a program or any other MI system object and says, "Destroy it." Of course, there is a catch: Not just anyone can destroy an object; the user must have the proper authority to be able to do so.

We will discuss object authorization in more detail in Chapter 7; but briefly, for the purposes of this current discussion, it's important to know that a user can have various levels of authority for any particular object. The highest level of authority allows the user to destroy an object. Usually, only the owner is allowed to destroy an object; but there are situations where multiple users may have that authority. Associated with each user in the system is a special MI system object called a *user profile*. The user profile, among other things, identifies the authorizations a user has to the various objects. When a user issues the destroy instruction, the system first checks the user profile to see whether or not that user has the authority to destroy the particular object before it carries out the operation.

Program Materialization and Observability

The program template is the only way the characteristics of a program can be observed above the MI. This template is the output of the high-level language compilers and it is the lowest level at which the components of a program can be seen and manipulated above the MI. Below the MI, the program exists as an MI system object, and all MI instructions that work with this object treat it as an entity.

Inside the object is the IMPI or PowerPC instruction stream. The object is encapsulated, meaning is is not possible to look inside. While this provides technology independence, the instruction stream is not visible, so neither is the final form of the program.

There are times, however, when the application or operating system software would like to look at the characteristics of a program. Fortunately, an MI instruction allows a program to be *materialized*. The instruction for a program to materialize points to an encapsulated program object and re-creates the program template for that program. Materialization is the opposite of encapsulation.

You might find it difficult to imagine how materialization can be done. After all, reverse compiling is not a very well developed technology, and researchers have tried to accomplish it for years.

So how does the AS/400 do it? It cheats. The AS/400 doesn't reverse compile the IMPI or PowerPC instruction stream. Instead, a copy of the program template is kept with the object. When an MI instruction requests that a program be materialized, the copy of the program template is returned to the requester.

Keeping the program template with the MI system object has given both the System/38 and the AS/400 capabilities that other systems do not have. A change to the internal instruction set can be made without having an impact on customer applications. Such changes are first put into a new version of the translator, then each program is retranslated using the program templates. Finally, the new instruction stream is encapsulated back into the object. All of this takes place below the MI, with no customer involvement. A classic example, the introduction of the System/38's Model 7, will illustrate how this has worked in the past.

When the System/38 was first introduced, it was a totally new system. It had an all new instruction set, all new applications, and an all new operating system. As it turned out, no one was sure how the instructions would be used. Programmers typically refer to instruction usage patterns to optimize the hardware implementations to achieve the highest possible system performance, and high-usage instructions need to run fast.

Originally, the IMPI instruction set only had an 8-bit op-code. This meant we could only have 256 instructions ($2^8 = 256$). As time went on and people began to write applications for the System/38, we discovered new functions that could benefit the applications. We continued to invent new instructions (a form of mental illness!) and pretty soon ran out of IMPI op-codes.

There is the tension between keeping the number of operations small, so as not to be unwieldy and redundant, and the desire to simplify complex tasks. It would be nice to say there is a scientific method used to design instruction sets, but there isn't. It is more of an art than a science. It would have taken us a couple years to achieve what we considered an optimum

IMPI instruction set. So we decided to add op-code extenders to the IMPI instruction format to accommodate these new instructions.

By this time, we also knew how the existing IMPI instructions were being used and saw ways to improve performance by remapping the more frequently used instructions into different formats that executed faster. Remapping op-code assignments meant that an instruction that was, say, a load on previous hardware looked like a branch to the new hardware. Such a change would create havoc in any "normal" systems, but not in a System/38, because it was technology independent.

When a customer upgraded to the new hardware, a new version of the translator was also installed. Each program in the system had an object header that, among other things, showed what level of translator was used to create the program. The first time a program ran, the system looked at the header and saw the program was an old version. The program template associated with the object was run against the new translator and the new IMPI code was put back in the object. The program was then executed. This retranslation only happened once. Subsequent calls of the program would use the new code.

This worked very well, but there was one problem. A number of customers called us and said, "I just installed the new system and my main application program ran slower." Of course, we knew why. The first time an application ran, it was retranslated, and that added time. What do you suppose we told them? Obviously, we told them, "Try it again."

This same technique of retranslating programs under-the-covers is used to move to the RISC processors. The difference now is that customers are being told that this will only work if they have not deleted *observability*. What has changed since the System/38 days?

The AS/400 was intended to consolidate both the System/36 and System/38 product lines. The System/38 customers were accustomed to having systems with larger memories and larger amounts of disk space. System/36 customers always got by with smaller capacities. The size of programs, in particular, disturbed many System/36 customers — they were way too big.

The programs in the AS/400 were big because two copies of the program were kept: the encapsulated form and the program template. To minimize the amount of disk needed, an option was given to customers. They could free up disk space by throwing away the program template. It was called Delete Program Observability, because the program could no longer be observed with a materialize instruction.

Customers and ISVs who have deleted observability of some or all of their programs will have to go back to the high-level language source code and recompile the source before they can move to the RISC processors. This is still easier than it is for most other systems, but it is not as automatic as when the program template is still in place.

Inside a Program Template

A program template contains several pieces of information. It has header information, the MI instruction stream, user data, and a structure called the object definition table (ODT).

The examples shown in this section are for the OPM. With the ILE program model compilers, about 35 to 40 new instructions were added to the MI. Some of these new instructions support a structure that is closer to the W-code the ILE compilers use. A better target for the ILE compilers is a stack machine, so the MI was extended to support stacks.

A *stack* consists of data items stored in consecutive order. The first item pushed onto the stack is said to be at the bottom of the stack. The item most recently pushed onto the stack is said to be on the top of the stack. Instructions with no operands are used in conjunction with a stack. The operands for an instruction are found by popping the top two operands from the stack. By contrast, the OPM instructions have the two operands identified in the instruction itself. The ordering for instructions and data for a stack machine has the operator following the operands. This form is called postfix or reverse Polish, after the mathematician who investigated the properties of this notation.[2]

Interestingly enough, the architecture designed in 1972 had this same stack support. At the time, many of us believed that block-structured languages, such as PL/1, would become very popular in commercial computing. But RPG and COBOL were never displaced, and the stack was eliminated. Now languages such as C have brought back the stack.

Figure 3.7 shows the instruction stream and the ODT. The instruction stream in the figure contains a sample MI instruction. The Add Numeric shown is a classic, three-operand OPM instruction. It has an op-code followed by three values in the instruction that are used to locate the three operands. Each of these values is used as an index into the ODT. The specific instruction shown requests that operand 6 be added to operand 2 and the sum be put into operand 3.

The ODT has two components. The first is the ODT Direction Vector (ODV). The ODV contains one entry for each operand in a program. Each entry is fixed in length so the value in the instruction stream can be used as an index into the ODV. The entries in the ODV describe the operands. In our example, operand 6 is a binary number that is 2 bytes long. Operand 3 is another 2-byte binary number, and operand 2 is a constant. Constants and other types of operands can be variable in length, and that is the reason for the second ODT component. The ODT Entry String (OES) has the variable length operands that won't fit in the ODV. The contents of the ODV field point to the beginning of the string in the OES. In our example, operand 2 is a constant having a value of 1253.

The example shows several characteristics of the MI instructions. First, our example is an Add Numeric instruction. It is not an add binary, or an

[2] The Polish mathematician was J. Lukasiewicz. This notation should be called Lukasiewicz notation in his honor. Unfortunately, few Americans could pronounce or spell his name, so it has been called Polish notation instead.

Figure 3.7 Instructions and the ODT

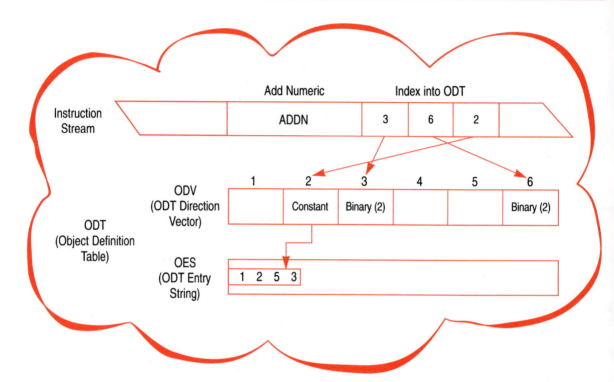

add decimal, or an add floating-point; it is a generic add instruction. The ODT defines the format of the operands to be used. The example shows binary numbers, but they could have been any numeric format. The translator is responsible for generating the data conversions that are required to perform the operation.

A second characteristic shown in the example is that MI is not an executable interface. Notice that neither operand 3 nor operand 6 have associated values. The ODV entry is equivalent to a variable declaration. There is no memory to hold the variable, so the translator has to complete the compile and assign the variables to registers or memory locations.

Finally, note that the example is a fairly conventional computation instruction. An instruction that operates on an object would have a similar format, but the ODT would indicate how to find the object. We will cover the specifics of object addressing in Chapter 5.

The MI Instruction Formats

Figure 3.8 shows the format of an MI instruction in the instruction stream. An instruction has an op-code, an optional op-code extender, and zero or more operands. The MI was designed to be expandable, so the instruction format had to allow for growth in the number of instructions and operands. The op-code is a 16-bit field, as is the op-code extender. Each operand field, which is used to index into the ODV, was originally 16 bits long in the System/38, but was later expanded to 24 bits. This means that a program can have up to 16 million (2^{24}) different operands, and even that number can be extended.

Memory conservation was not a high priority for the program template. The Add Numeric instruction, for example, would take 2 bytes for the op-code, 2 bytes for the op-code extender, and 9 bytes for the operands. That's 13 bytes and we haven't even included the space for operands in the ODT. It's not surprising System/36 customers were upset with the amount of disk space programs used.

Figure 3.8 MI Instruction Format

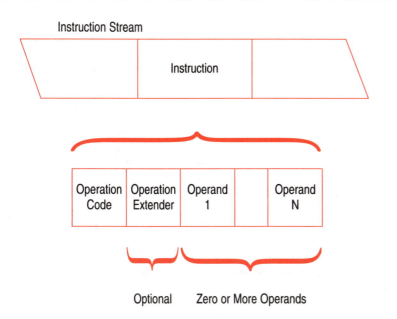

Operation Code Field (2 bytes)
Operation Extender Field (2 bytes)
Operand Field
  — Version 0 Template (2 bytes)
  — Version 1 Template (3 bytes)

The MI Op-Code

Table 3.1 shows the bit assignments for an MI op-code. Bit 3 specifies whether the instruction is a computational format or a non-computational format. If it is a non-computational format, then the function to be performed is encoded in bits 5 through 15 of the op-code. If it is a computational format, like the Add Numeric example, then bits 5 through 7 provide more information about the instruction. The function to be performed for a computational instruction is encoded in bits 8 through 15.

Looking further at the computational format, bit 6 indicates that rounding should be performed. Rounding is a function normally associated with floating-point arithmetic and that is not what the designers of the MI had in mind. The AS/400 is a commercial machine, and the rounding used at the MI is decimal rounding. Decimal data is treated as having a floating decimal point.

Bit 7 says to use the short form of the instruction. It, too, only has meaning for a computational format. In our Add Numeric example, we had three operands. Two of the operands were added together, and the result was put into a third operand. This left the original two operands unchanged. The short form of the instruction would still add the two operands together, but this time the result would be placed back into the first operand. Thus, the short form is a two-operand format with no third result field.

Finally, there are two bits in a computational format that describe the op-code extender. Bits 4 and 5 are used to determine whether or not there is an extender and, if so, how it is to be used. This function requires further explanation.

The Op-Code Extender

The MI op-code extender occupies another 16 bits in the instruction and comes in two forms: branch option and indicator option. The existence of the extender is determined by the setting of bit 4. If there is an extender, the branch or indicator option is selected by bit 5.

For the branch option, the op-code extender is divided into four 4-bit fields. Each of these four fields is used to determine the branching capabilities for this instruction. All MI computational instructions can include conditional branching as a part of their execution. In other words, based on the results of the computation, the next MI instruction can be fetched from some other part of the instruction stream.

Consider the first 4-bit field in the extender. If this field contains a value of 1 (binary bits 0001), it means branch if the result of the computation called for by the instruction is a positive value. If the field contains a value of 2 (binary 0010), it means branch if the result is a negative value. If the field has a value of 4 (binary 0100), it means branch if the result is equal to zero. There are also values for not-zero, not-positive, not-negative, and not non-zero. Also, the same bit combination can have different meanings for various types

Table 3.1 Op-Code Bit Assignments

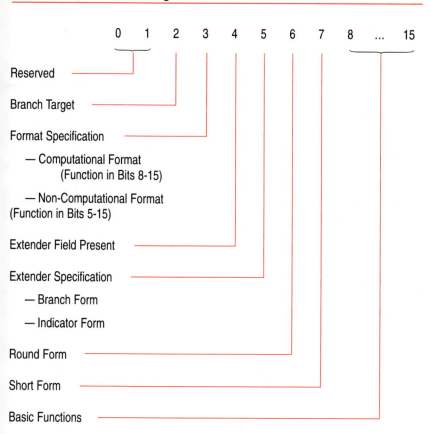

of instructions. For example, a compare instruction interprets the bits differently than an add instruction does.

If the branch condition specified by the first 4-bit field is satisfied, the branch target is found after the last operand in the instruction. If the branch condition is not satisfied, the next sequential instruction is executed. This capability increases, or extends, the length of the instruction.

Because there are four 4-bit fields in the extender, and each of these fields is used to specify a branch condition, each computational instruction can have up to four branch conditions and up to four branch targets. If fewer than four are desired, a value of 0 in the field means no branch.

The ability to do four-way branching on each computational instruction provides a fairly powerful instruction set, but the cost is longer MI instructions. The Add Numeric example can have up to four branch targets, increasing the length by up to 12 more bytes. This instruction can take

25 bytes in memory. This does not create an execution time problem, because MI instructions are not directly executed. It does, however, increase the program size.

The indicator option works in a manner similar to the branch option. The extender has the same four 4-bit fields and the settings are the same. The difference is, rather than branching when the condition is met, an indicator is set. An indicator is a variable in memory that contains a decimal value of one or zero. If, during the execution of a computational instruction, the condition specified in the 4-bit field is satisfied, the indicator is set to a value of 1. If the condition is not satisfied, the indicator is set to a value of 0. Like the branch option, there can be up to four indicators per instruction and the indicator targets follow the last operand.

Many readers will recognize indicators from RPG. The ability to set an indicator, and later perform some action based on that setting, dates back to unit record equipment. RPG indicators are supported directly by the MI instruction set.[3] On the surface, this ability may seem old-fashioned. However, many of today's most modern RISC processors use a very similar approach to set a value of 0 or 1 into a register to indicate the result of a computation. In fact, indicators are alive and well.

[3] A joke that has circulated for years is that a sure-fire way to have a large audience at a user group conference is to include the word "indicator" in the title of any presentation. People supposedly will pack the room.

MI Instruction Examples

The formats for three MI instructions are shown in Figures 3.9a, 3.9b, and 3.9c, respectively. The basic Add Numeric (ADDN) instruction has the hexadecimal[4] op-code 1043. Being a computational instruction, the basic add function is specified by the "43" in the op-code. This instruction also has three operands.

[4] Hexadecimal is a number system to the base 16. The 16 digits used in this number system are 0-9 and A-F. Hexadecimal is often used as a shorthand notation instead of showing bit patterns. Each four-bit field can be represented as a hex digit. Thus, 0001 is a hex digit "1" and 1111 is a hex digit "F."

Figure 3.9a Add Numeric (ADDN) Instruction

Op-Code	Operand 1	Operand 2	Operand 3
1043	Sum	Addend 1	Addend 2

Operation

Operand 1 = Operand 2 + Operand 3

Figure 3.9b Branch (B) Instruction

Op-Code	Operand 1
1011	Branch Target

Operation

Unconditional branch-to-branch target

Branch target can be
- Instruction number
- Relative instruction number
- Branch point
- Instruction pointer
- Instruction definition list element

Figure 3.9c Copy Bytes Left-Adjusted with Pad (CPYBLAP) Instruction

Op-Code	Operand 1	Operand 2	Operand 3
10B3	Receiver	Source	Pad

Operation

The logical string value of the source operand is copied to the logical string value of the receiver operand and padded if needed

Operands are
- Character
- Numeric

Table 3.2 shows the other 11 forms of Add Numeric. The various forms are created by combining the options of short, round, indicator, and branch. Note that the basic function is still "43."

The Branch instruction has only one operand, the branch target. This is an unconditional branch. MI does not have a separate conditional branch. All conditional branching is done in conjunction with a computational instruction. Because Branch is a non-computational instruction, it does not have optional forms like Add Numeric does.

The third instruction shown has the wonderful name Copy Bytes Left-Adjusted with Pad, or CPYBLAP for short. This instruction provides the

Table 3.2 Optional Forms of Add Numeric

ADDNS	1143	Short
ADDNR	1243	Round
ADDNSR	1343	Short, Round
ADDNI	1843	Indicator
ADDNIS	1943	Indicator, Short
ADDNIR	1A43	Indicator, Round
ADDNISR	1B43	Indicator, Short, Round
ADDNB	1C43	Branch
ADDNBS	1D43	Branch, Short
ADDNBR	1E43	Branch, Round
ADDNBSR	1F43	Branch, Short, Round

capability to copy a string of bytes from one field to another. The bytes are left-adjusted in the receiver field, and if the source has fewer bytes than the receiver, the pad is used to fill the remaining bytes. As expected, this is but one of many copy instructions at the MI. Copying data is a function that is heavily used in most commercial applications. Readers might recognize that CPYBLAP is equivalent to the COBOL MOVE statement and the RPG MOVEL with a P in the half-adjust column.

These are but three of the MI instructions; there are hundreds of others. In this section we have only examined the OPM computation and branching types of MI instructions. There are also computational and branching types to support the ILE. Later chapters will show how many of the instructions that operate on objects, which we did not discuss, are used.

Conclusions

The technology independence provided by the MI is extremely important, because it doesn't force changes to user applications or to OS/400. New hardware can be added and fully exploited immediately. But if this was all the benefit the MI provided, it wouldn't be enough. Computing environments change over time — the rise of client/server computing is a prime example. If the AS/400, which was initially designed for interactive processing, could not have adjusted to the role of a server, it would soon have become obsolete.

The MI is a very powerful interface, not just because it is technology independent, but also because it is so expandable. New instructions and functions are added at just about every new release of the system. For example, at V3R1 we added functions to support the Single UNIX Specification APIs so that certain Unix applications could be ported to the AS/400. The MI is an application-centric interface because it supports the APIs applications need. As new applications are desired, their APIs can easily be added. Because it is so expandable, the MI still has a long life ahead.

Now that we have looked at both the PowerPC and MI layers, we can begin to look at how they fit into the total system. In the next chapter, we will see that OS/400 is only part of the operating system in the AS/400. The rest of the operating system function is sandwiched between these two layers.

Chapter 4
An Integrated System

Above all, the AS/400 is an integrated system, and this characteristic sets the AS/400 apart from most other systems. Integration in a computer system means the various parts work together as a whole. The value of integration for a customer is that the system is easier to install, maintain, and use, which usually results in lower operational costs for a business.

If you were to ask a developer from Rochester why the AS/400 is a successful system, (s)he would likely tell you it is because Rochester knows how to build the best multiuser commercial systems. If you press a little harder and ask why, the developer will probably begin to compare specific features, such as the database or the security structure, with other systems. Yes, the AS/400 has a great database and a good security structure, but so do other systems. The value of the AS/400, which many of our developers either miss or take for granted, is that all components are designed to work together to provide a system that is greater than the sum of its parts.

An ISV answering the same question will probably say it is easier to develop and maintain applications for an AS/400 than for some other platform. ISVs who have the same application available on an AS/400 and on some other platform, such as a Unix system, often comment on the differences in the number of people they employ for the two platforms. They generally require far fewer people to develop and maintain their AS/400 applications. Again, the integration is what makes this possible. By ensuring that when any new function is added it works seamlessly with everything else in the system, we preserve the value proposition of the AS/400. All of Rochester's systems up to and including the AS/400 have been integrated solutions, and that is the secret to Rochester's success.

If our own developers miss the integration factor, what ensures that the AS/400 remains an integrated system? The answer is the MI. The MI does two things to guarantee integration. First, it provides a common interface to all application and operating system functions above the MI. Everyone is forced to use the system in the same way. Second, the MI presents a functionally complete interface. Because it is not possible to go around it, the MI must provide all the functions an application or operating system program needs. If some function is missing, that program will not run on an AS/400. MI also is highly extensible to allow new functions to be added as they are needed.

Before someone points out that other Rochester systems, such as the System/36, accomplished integration without a high-level machine interface, I should note that the MI provides two functions: integration and machine independence. While the System/36 did have the equivalent of a machine interface for most of its system functions, it did not for applications. It had two separate processors, one that ran the user application and the other that ran certain operating system functions. To get at these operating system functions in the second processor required the use of a very structured interface between the two processors. This interface, like the MI, ensured that functions were complete and that they worked together. The applications, however, were still dependent on the underlying hardware. For this reason, an emulator is needed to support System/36 applications on other hardware, as we will see shortly.

The negative side of integration is a lack of flexibility. With an integrated solution, the approach is usually all or nothing. A customer cannot choose an operating system from one vendor, a database from another, and a security package from still another, primarily because these components are usually not designed to work with the integrated system.

It seems difficult to believe that any computer system would have components that are not designed to work closely together, but that is often the case. Components such as databases, security, and communications subsystems are routinely developed separately. Their intended use may be with several different operating systems. As a result, the components are usually self-contained, meaning they attempt to use as little of the operating system facilities as possible. This separation leads to duplication of functions between the operating system and the individual components. It also can lead to different interfaces for the user or system operator.

The advantage of having separate components from which to choose is total flexibility. The downside is that the customer must integrate these components into the business' computer systems, and the cost is not just in the integration. There also is the cost of training users and operators on the different interfaces these components present. Then there is the cost of maintenance. Updates and changes made to one component may have an adverse impact on another component in the system. To complicate matters, many systems exist in networks, which themselves require management.

Because many of these costs are not up-front purchase costs, many businesses have difficulty identifying them. The PC world is notorious for having these hidden costs. Businesses often connect their individual PCs into

LANs to better share resources among users, and one study showed that the cost of a PC used in a business over a five-year period can be more than $50,000.[1] The initial purchase price is a small percentage of this total, yet purchase price is regularly the only consideration when a business is making a decision on a particular computer system. In an attempt to eliminate the inconsistencies, some businesses decide to purchase all software components from a single vendor, but that usually doesn't work either.

This reminds me of a recent experience with a home theater system. Each of the four separate electronic components came with its own remote control. Because all the components were from the same manufacturer, the salesman assured me that each remote control was universal, meaning that it could control all the components. Only one would be needed for the whole system. Sure enough, a single remote could control some functions on each component; unfortunately, it couldn't control them all. Total system operation requires the use of all four remote controls. Further, the user interface for each remote control is different. Buttons for the same functions are in different places and often have different sizes and shapes. Even the names for some of the same functions are different. Many business people are using several "remote controls" to run their business computer installations. For both of us, an integrated system would make more sense.

[1] A 1994 Gartner Group survey showed that the total cost of PC ownership over a five-year period can range from nearly $50,000 per client machine in a large business with 5,000 remote PCs and 250 locations, to more than $66,000 per PC for a midsized business with 200 PCs and five sites.

The Integrated Operating System

Earlier, we defined an operating system as a collection of programs that manage the system resources and provide a base for writing application programs. In the last chapter, we looked at the MI, which provides a base for applications. The question then is, "Where are the programs that manage the system resources?"

The obvious answer is OS/400, the operating system of the AS/400. Traditional operating system components handle functions such as memory, process, program, and I/O management. But these low-level functions tend to be hardware dependent, tied closely to the underlying physical structures. For example, the memory-management component must know the exact configuration and characteristics of the memory hierarchy. The MI has no concept of memory, so its management component needs to be below the MI.

None of these hardware-dependent components exist in OS/400. They are part of the operating system of the AS/400, but they must be beneath the MI to preserve technology independence. In this way, the MI protects application programs and OS/400 from hardware changes. The operating system software beneath the MI is called the *licensed internal code (LIC)*. Okay, let's review the structure of the AS/400 as we now see it. By now the distinction should be clear: OS/400 consists of objects and programs above the MI. LIC is the data structures and programs below the MI — it (the LIC) is the link (glue, bridge) between the MI and the hardware. The AS/400's operating system is the combination of OS/400 and the LIC.

In recent years, this part of the operating system in other systems has been called the *kernel*. There are many definitions of just what belongs in the kernel of an operating system. Some purists would argue that the LIC contains far more operating system function than is normally found in a kernel. Regardless, the term "kernel" is a convenient way to describe the operating system functions packaged under the MI.

It is obvious that some operating system components, such as memory management, belong in the LIC. Other system components are not so clearly defined. Look at a database. Parts of a database implementation may need to know about the physical disk drives and how to transfer data in the system. Still other parts of the database implementation can be written to be hardware independent. The designers have to decide where to put the database software — all in OS/400, all in the LIC, or some in each. Note that when I use this two-part division between OS/400 and LIC, I'm thinking of MI system objects as objects that have LIC implementations, as opposed to OS/400 objects, which have MI implementations.

Of course, all OS/400 functions have LIC implementations in the sense that they must go through the MI to communicate with the hardware. But, in many cases, an instruction in a high-level language, after being converted into W Code (or the original MI IRP), is translated directly in PowerPC (or IMPI) instructions without reference to any special LIC data structures or calls to LIC routines. A particular system function may be said to be implemented in OS/400 and not in the LIC if the code that implements it is visible to OS/400 and the data structures required for it are found in OS/400 objects or their visible parts.

Figure 4.1 shows the split of various operating system functions between OS/400 and the LIC. Some functions, such as work management, which schedules jobs in the AS/400, can be predominantly in OS/400, because it has few hardware dependencies. Other functions, such as device support, can be partially in OS/400 and partially in the LIC. The generic characteristics of a device can be in OS/400. For example, knowing that a device is a printer does not tie the application program to a specific printer. However, knowing the details of the printer data stream does tie a program to a specific printer, and this information needs to be in the LIC below the MI.

Some operating system functions that are not hardware dependent are also packaged below the MI. Take security, for example. Security has no hardware dependencies and so it could be totally in OS/400 above the MI. Parts of security, however, should be below the MI to provide a higher degree of protection. In Chapter 7, we will see that system-wide security is in OS/400, while the authorization to system resources is below in the LIC.

Most major operating system functions, like security, have some portions above and some portions below the MI. Even the individual components of an operating system function can be split across this boundary. Figure 4.1 also

Figure 4.1 AS/400 Function Split

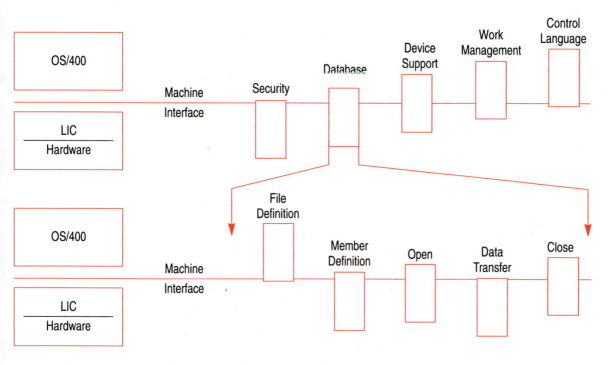

shows a breakout of some components in the database and how they are split across the MI.

Another reason for moving a function or part of a function below the MI is performance. In general, as a function becomes more and more hardware dependent, it can be tuned to achieve higher performance for a given hardware implementation. Moving them below the MI does not guarantee higher performance for all functions, but it does help some. The downside to doing this is that more code in the operating system becomes dependent on the underlying hardware.

Over time, in both the System/38 and the AS/400, more and more functions have moved from OS/400 to the LIC, primarily to improve performance. Additionally, in the LIC below the MI, the opportunity has existed to move functions across another internal boundary — in the microcode.

Microcode

Microprogramming has been described as an implementation technique in which an inner computer was programmed to emulate the operations of an outer computer architecture. The software to accomplish this is often called *microcode*.

The System/38 had two layers of microcode below the MI separated by the IMPI. The two layers were called the *Horizontal Microcode (HMC)* and the *Vertical Microcode (VMC)*.[2] The lowest level was the HMC. This layer contained the microprogrammed emulator that was used to execute the IMPI instructions. HMC also included some of the lowest-level operating system functions. It was written in a special-purpose microinstruction set that was directly manipulated by the processor hardware. This microinstruction set was designed for high performance and supported a lot of parallelism in the processor. Because of this structure, a high-level language to produce this code was not available. The generation of HMC was very difficult and time consuming.

The second layer, which existed below the MI but above the IMPI, was the VMC. VMC contained those operating system functions that were hardware dependent and not already implemented in the HMC. VMC was written in both a proprietary high-level language developed within IBM for system programming and in IMPI assembler. VMC was not microcode in the traditional sense; it was the lowest level of the operating system software.

The kernel of the System/38 operating system was called microcode to avoid the problem of bundling software. Bundling was a practice used by computer companies in the 1960s that required customers to buy the company's hardware to get its system software. In the late 1960s, various companies developed a number of IBM mainframe plug-compatible computers (today we would call them clones). The idea behind these systems was to build hardware that was compatible with IBM's and then sell it at a lower price. The plug-compatible manufacturers could only be successful if their customers could buy the IBM operating systems without having to buy IBM hardware. IBM refused, and lawsuits followed. To settle these lawsuits, IBM agreed not to bundle software with its computers in the future.

We had a problem with the System/38. We wanted a system in which the MI was the only external interface. If we sold just the hardware, we would lose the technology independence the MI provided. We needed to package a complete *Machine Product (MP)* that contained the hardware plus the kernel of the operating system.

Our solution was to call the kernel "microcode," because microcode was considered to be part of the hardware. Therefore, we were not bundling and not violating the agreement. All development costs for VMC had to be charged against the hardware. For accounting purposes, a development organization in the laboratory separate from the programming area had to be created to write the VMC. The existence of these two independent organizations helps to explain why different names are used to describe the similar function or structure in OS/400 and VMC. We will see this in subsequent chapters.

With the introduction of the AS/400, the names of the two layers of microcode were changed. In today's business world, customers can buy the

---

[2] For years, people asked about the significance of the names "horizontal" and "vertical." In fact, there is little significance in the names. We needed names to distinguish the two layers, and since microcode in the early 1970s for some of the System/370 systems was categorized as either horizontal or vertical, we chose those two names. In general, horizontally microcoded machines allowed the processor data flow to perform multiple operations in a single cycle, while vertically microcoded machines performed one operation per cycle. There is some validity to calling the lower level horizontal microcode, but the VMC level does not match the definition for vertical microcode.

computer hardware but not the software. Instead, they purchase a license to use the software. Customers cannot modify, copy, or resell the software unless the license allows it. In some cases, the software license is only good for use on a particular system. Microcode is part of the hardware. Therefore, a customer can own microcode. Because bundling was no longer an issue when the AS/400 was announced, IBM decided to rename the System/38 microcode. Thus, the AS/400 had *Vertical Licensed Internal Code (VLIC)* and *Horizontal Licensed Internal Code (HLIC)*.

The new RISC processors required yet another name change. HLIC contained the microcoded emulator needed to implement the IMPI architecture. But a RISC processor has no microcoded emulator, so there is no HLIC. There is only VLIC. Consequently, the operating system functions in HLIC were rewritten in the VLIC for a RISC processor. Because we now only had a single layer of internal code, we decided it was time to throw away the meaningless names, vertical and horizontal.

System Licensed Internal Code

Question: What has more than one million lines of code, took 200 programmers to produce, and has a name that describes a Minnesota road in winter?
Answer: SLIC (pronounced "slick"). The internal code for the RISC-based systems is called *System Licensed Internal Code (SLIC)*.[3]

When Rochester began working on the RISC processor in 1991, many changes were required to the LIC below the MI. Some components had to be completely redesigned, while others were affected hardly at all. Much of the existing LIC also needed restructuring. This code had had frequent changes and upgrades through the many releases of the System/38 and the AS/400. Programmer productivity had declined, and maintenance had increased in this part of the system because of all the changes. Our programmers' morale was also declining because of the need to continuously patch this old code.

We still had to deliver three major VLIC releases before the RISC processors arrived. There was no way we could stop work on the VLIC and switch all development to SLIC. So we decided to create a totally new organization in the lab to build the new operating system. The new organization would be free to pursue any development means it chose. Mike Tomashek, who headed this organization, met with his key developers to decide how to proceed.

The group considered two ways to approach the changes to the LIC. The first was to redesign and rewrite from scratch the low-level components affected by the processor change. The second was to attempt to move these affected low-level components to the RISC hardware with minimal changes. This type of migration without changing the program logic is often called *porting*. Any other components not affected by the processor change, such as the database, would be ported with as little modification as possible.

Mike and his team decided to redesign and rewrite the affected components from scratch. This was a difficult decision, because much of this

[3] No doubt the developers who named this were thinking of the slang use of the word "slick" — which means wonderful, remarkable, first-rate — rather than a description of Minnesota roads in winter.

low-level code was based on the original System/38 design, and it had been extensively tuned for performance over 15 releases of the system software. Many thought they could not accomplish the task of redesigning this low-level operating system software in the short time they had. All the interfaces to the components being rewritten had to be preserved, while the internals were being completely changed. Changing interfaces would affect the ported components, which the team didn't want to happen. To make matters worse, enhancements to all this software were still being made for planned AS/400 releases. They would be chasing a moving target.

Bill Berg, who was one of the members of the 10-person team that recommended PowerPC for the AS/400, was promoting object-oriented (OO) programming to improve the productivity of this effort. OO languages started to become popular in the late 1980s as a way to deliver programs quickly, and these languages had matured to the point they were usable for such a large project. Bill and others argued this new programming technology would let us invest in our people and update their skills. We also would be able to recruit new people.

Let's briefly review the essential elements and terms related to OO programming. An object is a software entity that combines the data and the operations that can be performed on the data. The operation that an object can perform is sometimes called a *method*. The internal data structure and the methods of an object are hidden from the program. This is called *encapsulation*. The program can only see the interface to the object. OO programming is different from procedural programming because of this combining of operations and data into a single entity. Procedural programming keeps the operations and data separate.

OO programming is an approach that relies on software reuse; the primary mechanism for reuse is a *class*, which is a template that describes all objects that share the same operations and data elements. Thus, multiple objects can be created from one of these classes. This is often called an *instance* of an object.

New subclasses can be derived from an existing class through the use of *inheritance*. Inheritance allows programmers to create new subclasses that reuse the code and data in the base class without having to repeat them. Yet these new subclasses are customized to meet the specific needs of the application. *Polymorphism* is the ability of subclasses of the same class to respond to the same input message and produce different results. Polymorphism combines the concepts of inheritance and dynamic binding.

Sets of objects created from these classes and subclasses can be grouped together to provide the desired operating system services. Once a fairly complete set of classes (called a class library) has been defined, programmers can use the classes to implement their component. There is no need to re-invent functions these classes provide.

For the team, however, there was a downside to using OO technology. The kernel of an operating system is very performance sensitive. Studies of AS/400 applications have shown that they tend to have long instruction path lengths with a large percentage of that path length in the operating system code. This means the performance of the code in the kernel of the operating system has a big impact on the overall system performance in an AS/400. Because OO technology involves reusing lots of small modules to accomplish a given function, the total path length tends to be longer than if the function had been written as a single entity. The team would have to include time in the development schedule to fine-tune these functions to ensure the performance levels the old kernel functions had achieved through years of tuning was maintained.

SLIC Development Environment

The development group had to select a programming language for the project. The VLIC programming language, called PL/MP, and used since the original System/38 development, was based on the PL/1 language. The "MP" in the name stands for Machine Product, a name that was often used to describe the hardware and both levels of microcode. The PL/MP compiler, like the IMPI assembler, generated the IMPI binary machine-level instructions.

The PL/MP language was not usable for OO programming, but the team could still use it for those LIC components that would be migrated and not rewritten. We developed a new PL/MP compiler that produced PowerPC binary machine-level instructions. In addition, we developed a special porting tool that would scan the code looking for any IMPI dependencies before converting it to the new PL/MP.

Over the years, we had looked at other development languages and had tried a few of them in various VLIC components. For example, the ILE translator shown in Figure 3.4 was written in Modula-2. Some other components used the C language. However, we felt none of these was suitable for the OO project we were about to undertake.

Selection of the C++ programming language was reasonably straightforward. We needed to develop some very low-level operating system code. At times it would be necessary to drop into assembly language for optimum performance, and using C++ made this easier. In fact, the C++ language is sometimes thought of as today's version of an assembler language.[4]

The other advantage of C++ was our ability to hire programmers with knowledge of this language. We needed many new programmers for this development project, and we started a massive hiring campaign. Soon we had more than 200 people working on the SLIC project.

Education was critical to our success. New people had to learn about the AS/400's internals.[5] Our existing VLIC programmers had to learn to program in C++. We had people who knew C++, but for the most part they were using

[4] Dick Bains likes to compare programming languages to carving a bar of soap. For example, he says programming in RPG is like carving a bar of soap with a plastic spoon. Programming with C++ is like carving that same bar of soap with a double-edged razor blade; you can make some very precise cuts, but before you are done, you will have lots of blood on the soap.

[5] I originally created much of the contents of this book for that education.

it as a better C language. We needed to educate everyone on how to do OO design. This was a real problem, because we didn't have anyone in Rochester who had done much more than read a few books on the subject.

Chris Jones, who together with Bill Berg and Mike Tomashek put together the original software plan to get to the PowerPC processors, stepped in with a solution: He had found an outside consultant who was an expert in OO technology and C++. We had never before gone outside to find someone to train our people. IBM did its own internal education, and our education people were not too keen on hiring an outsider. Chris persevered and convinced management to hire the consultant, who put all our people through six weeks of intensive training. We even constructed a special classroom, which we used exclusively for teaching this material, right in the middle of our development area.

The ability to iterate the design is a fundamental strength of OO programming, but this also makes it difficult to measure progress. The technique we used to gauge progress was to create Bring up Binds (BUBs). Each BUB was a collection of objects that provided a clearly defined set of operating system functions and interfaced to other components. By creating and testing these BUBs against the other components, we could assure that we were making progress. BUBs allowed the operating system to be staged in an orderly manner (they also gave rise to a take-off on a well-known advertising slogan, "This BUB's for you.").

OO technology held out the promise of greater productivity for our programmers. During the SLIC development, our programmers who used OO saw a gain of four times the productivity over using traditional methods. OO delivered on its promise. The SLIC project, which began in June of 1992, produced more than 1 million lines of C++ code and more than 7,000 classes. Counting all the ported code, we had more than 2-1/2 million lines of operating system code under the MI.

SLIC Kernel Technologies

In the past, every kernel was unique to a particular operating system. There was little desire to build a kernel separate from an operating system, but that attitude began to change in the middle 1980s, when schools such as Carnegie-Mellon University began to study kernels that could be used for more than one operating system. Carnegie-Mellon defined a *microkernel* it called Mach. The Mach microkernel is a subset of a kernel, and it includes the common functions that most operating systems need.

If two or more operating systems are built on top of the same microkernel, it is possible to run those operating systems concurrently on the same processor. Furthermore, the operating systems can share resources and communicate with one another in a very efficient manner. In recent years, multiple operating systems running on a common microkernel have been called *personalities*.

Because SLIC was designed to be a new operating system kernel, it made sense to include some of the technologies needed to support multiple personalities. Actually, much of this was in the original LIC. For example, a microkernel uses a message-based approach to dispatch work for a given operating system in the processor. This same message-based dispatching was used in the original System/38 and was carried forward into the AS/400. In Chapter 9, we will examine this mechanism in detail.

At the time we were developing the SLIC, studies and proposals were being made in IBM to share operating system components across all IBM systems that used the PowerPC processors. One of the leading proposals was to use the IBM microkernel (which was derived from the Mach microkernel) as the basis for this sharing. SLIC already had most of the technologies used in this microkernel, but the question was, "Should we build everything on top of the IBM microkernel?" The answer was pretty obvious. The only implementation being developed at the time was for a 32-bit microkernel. We would have to build a 64-bit version if we wanted to use it in the AS/400. The proposal to share software was also not firm, and there were still questions about scalability of the microkernel (How many users could it support?); so we decided not to build the SLIC on top of this microkernel. We did, however, put a group of people in place in Rochester to develop the 64-bit extensions to the IBM microkernel, so we could use it in the future. We also decided to include in SLIC the ability to support multiple operating system personalities.

Adding support for other operating systems to the SLIC kernel didn't make any sense if we didn't plan to use it. Besides OS/400, what other operating system should we support? To some of us the answer was obvious, but we would need a little subterfuge to demonstrate how this support would work.

System/36 Personality

There has always been a group of developers in Rochester who continue to be committed to the System/36. In 1993, at the height of the SLIC development effort, two of the System/36 group leaders, Dick Mustain and Steve Dahl, had an idea. Why not build a new System/36? With the AS/400 moving to RISC and SLIC being able to incorporate support for other operating systems, it was possible to create a new System/36. These dedicated developers put together a quick prototype and a proposal to put the System/36 operating system on the RISC hardware.

In the preceding few years, various vendors world-wide had started to sell software packages that allowed System/36 customers to move to a RISC-based computer system, either IBM's RS/6000 or a competitor's product. The problem with these "look-alike" products was that they only provided part of the System/36 look and feel. System/36 customers still had to make changes to their applications and operational procedures, and still other

System/36 software products they were using could not be brought over to the new computer.

IBM had decided that the official migration path for System/36 customers was to the AS/400. Some System/36 customers made this migration, but a much larger group had refused to move anywhere. Estimates had more than 200,000 System/36s still running business applications around the world. Many in IBM believed it was only a matter of time before these customers moved to some IBM platform. Needless to say, the developers' proposal for a new System/36 was not met with overwhelming enthusiasm.

Fortunately, some managers in Rochester have always been willing to look at new opportunities, and soon a "skunkworks"[6] was formed to develop a new System/36. A skunkworks is nothing new to Rochester. We have used this approach many times to develop systems that were not thought to be strategic and were, therefore, not given funding to proceed. The AS/400 itself came out of such a skunkworks.

Soon, a small team of System/36 experts began to assemble. Bob Schmidt, who signed up to manage this team and to keep its existence hidden from the watchful eyes of those who approve funding for such projects, had no problem finding volunteers. Within just a couple months, this small band of dedicated developers had the operating system of the System/36 running on the new RISC processor. New life had been breathed into this product line.

Something Old, Something New

The original System/3 announced in 1969 had a processor implemented directly in hardware. It was a very simple design with only 28 instructions. On top of the System/3 hardware was the operating system, along with all applications and utilities. A major change to this implementation structure occurred with the introduction of the System/32 in 1975.

The idea of moving some of the operating system functions into microcode had been well established in the early 1970s in Rochester as a result of the System/38 work. These functions were moved to microcode on the System/38 for purposes of technology independence. The System/32 used a microprogrammed processor to emulate the System/3 instruction set. For performance reasons, several functions were moved out of the System/3 operating system and into the microcode of the System/32. Thus, there were similarities between the System/32 and the System/38. They both had some of their operating system implemented in the microcode, although for different reasons.

The System/32 was designed as an entry system and performed well at that level. The emulation of the System/3 instruction set was slow, however, because the underlying processor was not a very high-performance engine. The System/32 processor did, however, do a very good job of executing the operating system functions. It is notable that the processor used for the

[6] A skunkworks is a small, loosely structured development unit formed to foster innovation, or in some cases, to hide its existence. It is named after Big Barnsmell's "Skonk Works," where the bootleg Kickapoo Joy Juice was brewed, in Al Capp's comic strip "Li'l Abner."

System/32 was a 16-bit, register-based design that looked remarkably like some of the early RISC hardware.

To expand the performance and capacity range of the System/32 required some changes to the implementation. The System/32 processor was good at running parts of the operating system, so the decision was made to keep it. But because this processor was too slow to emulate the System/3 instructions satisfactorily, a second processor similar to the original System/3 was created to directly execute these instructions with the hardware. The bulk of the operating system was written in the System/3 instruction set and would run on this second processor. Because it fetched its instructions from the main memory, it was called the Main Store Processor (MSP). The System/32 processor fetched its instructions from a separate part of the memory, so it was renamed the Control Store Processor (CSP). In 1977, the first system to use this two-processor structure was announced. It was called the System/34.

In 1983, the follow-on to the System/34, the System/36, was announced. The System/36 continued to use the two-processor structure pioneered by the System/34. Just like the AS/400, whose operating system is split into parts, OS/400 and SLIC, the System/36's operating system is split into two parts. The first part, called the System Support Program (SSP), ran on the MSP, while the second part of the operating system ran on the CSP. The larger System/36 models had additional processors to perform I/O operations. These, too, were CSP designs that ran the parts of the operating system for I/O processing. Over the next few years, new models of the System/36 were introduced, all with the two processors.

The System/36 developers in 1993 recognized that the RISC processor to be used for the AS/400 was sufficiently fast to emulate the MSP instruction set without the need for a separate hardware processor. If such an emulator was built into SLIC, along with all the CSP code, then the SSP operating system would run directly on the new RISC processor. The effort they undertook was to create the emulator and to rewrite the CSP code in C++ as a part of SLIC.

The interface between the original MSP and CSP was a Supervisor Call (SVC) interface. An SVC is an instruction that executes in the MSP and requests an action to be taken in the CSP. This is conceptually the same as executing an instruction at the MI level to request SLIC to perform some action. The developers reasoned that if they extended the MI to include this SVC interface, they could run the SSP on top of the MI. This would also make the SSP technology independent. They called this extension to the MI the *Technology Independent Emulation Interface*.[7]

With the decision to use an emulator rather than a separate hardware processor for the MSP instruction set, the developers had decided to create a design that internally looked more like a System/32 than either a System/34 or a System/36. As happens so often, history repeats itself. The bionic desk (aka the System/32) lives again in a new black box!

---

[7] **This name has caused some confusion with the new RISC-based AS/400 systems. The SLIC contains an emulator for the Advanced 36 code (application and SSP) above the MI. There is no emulator for AS/400 code above the MI. Some in the industry believe an emulator was used to move AS/400 code to RISC; but as we have seen in previous chapters, that is not true.**

Advanced 36

We suddenly had a brand new System/36 that ran on the new 64-bit RISC hardware using the SLIC kernel. Furthermore, it was a pure System/36. No modifications were made to the SSP that changed any application interfaces. The new system was totally binary-compatible with the System/36. Recompiling was not even necessary to move an application to the new system.

Clearly, this new System/36 personality could run on the AS/400 when the RISC processors were announced. There was, however, another possibility. We could build an early version of the Cobra processor with everything (the processor, the cache, and the I/O interface) on a single chip. We put a small Rochester team in place and soon they had a single-chip processor based on the Endicott design. This processor ran at 50 Mhz, which was fast enough for any System/36 application. We called the processor Cobra-Lite, because it was missing about 17 instructions from the required 64-bit PowerPC set. These instructions, which were primarily floating-point instructions, were implemented in the software, but that didn't matter. The missing instructions, including a combination floating-point multiply and add instruction used for matrix calculations, were not used by the SLIC and had no effect on the new System/36.

IBM confirmed that its semiconductor facility in Burlington, Vermont, could produce these special chips in sufficient quantity to ship RISC-based System/36s late in 1994. We knew we could package an early version of SLIC along with a new release of SSP for this new product. We also knew we had a major dilemma on our hands.

Here we were, able to ship IBM's first 64-bit RISC computer — but it was a System/36! We had been telling our customers for years to get off the System/36, and now we were ready to ship a new one with the latest technology available. This was going to be a hard sell.

IBM organizations all over the world turned thumbs-down on the idea of a new System/36. Finally, we convinced management to let a few of us talk to customers and Business Partners about the new product and let the market decide whether or not we should announce the new system in 1994. The feedback was overwhelmingly in favor of announcing the system. Many Business Partners offered to write us a check on the spot for the demo machine we showed them. IBM and Business Partner marketing people quickly got behind the idea, realizing the potential of this system. In October 1994, the Advanced 36 was announced, and it became an immediate success.

The initial model of the Advanced 36 ran only the SSP operating system. Later models would run OS/400 and SSP side by side on the same processor. The Advanced 36 showed the power of the AS/400 architecture and its ability to integrate new function, and even whole operating systems, in a totally seamless manner. Every RISC model of the AS/400 has a System/36 inside the SLIC. Perhaps a small label saying "System/36 Inside" would be appropriate for every new AS/400.

Conclusions

Integration creates a unique value proposition for the AS/400. The components are designed to work together in a complementary fashion. Integration also makes it difficult to study the individual components in the same way you can study some other system. For example, we saw earlier that the implementation of a component such as security is split between OS/400 and SLIC. Studying just OS/400 security would not give a complete picture. Contrast this to some other system where security is a separate, self-contained package on top of the operating system.

Examining the AS/400 as a series of horizontal layers does not give a very complete picture of the system. A better way to understand the AS/400 is to look at vertical slices — in other words, to look at the whole function, parts of which are in OS/400, in SLIC, and in the hardware.

In the rest of this book, we will look at the major AS/400 components as a series of vertical slices. Only then can we see that the old adage, "The whole is greater than the sum of its parts," is very true for the AS/400.

Chapter 5

Objects and Object Management

Objects are nothing new. They were first used in the late 1960s in programming languages such as Simula 67, which were used to write simulation programs (modern object-oriented languages such as C++ and Smalltalk are direct descendants of Simula 67). A computer simulation models the behavior of objects in the real world. Operating systems also model and manipulate hardware and software objects, such as I/O devices and programs. Incorporating objects into an operating system seems to be fairly natural. Yet many operating system vendors such as Microsoft, Apple, Taligent, Novell/USL (UNIX Systems Laboratory), and Sun Microsystems are just now building object-oriented operating systems. Next is one of the few vendors already shipping an object-oriented operating system, which it calls NextStep.

There is, of course, another operating system that is object-oriented. Since the introduction of the System/38, we have built operating systems (CPF and OS/400) around an object model.[1] Furthermore, we didn't stop with the operating system; we made objects a fundamental part of the machine design. As we discussed in Chapter 3, the MI is composed of two parts: instructions and objects. In this chapter, we will look at the way the AS/400 uses objects.

The AS/400 is sometimes described as an object-based system rather than an object-oriented system. The two terms have meaning when we are discussing programming languages. For example, there are object-based languages such as Ada and object-oriented languages such as Smalltalk-80. Grady Booch[2] defines the differences between an object-based and an object-oriented programming language. He says an object-based language does not have inheritance. As we introduced briefly in Chapter 3, inheritance defines a hierarchy among classes in which a subclass shares the structure or behavior of one or more base classes. Because AS/400 objects do not inherit

[1] **Some of us were very familiar with computer simulation languages in the late 1960s, which helps to explain why the System/38 was based on an object model. My own Ph.D. research used a computer simulation to model various virtual memory designs.**

[2] **Grady Booch, *Object Oriented Design with Applications*, The Benjamin/Cummings Publishing Company, Inc., 1991.**

from other object types, it is probably still more accurate to describe the AS/400 as an object-based system. No matter what name we choose, keep in mind that the AS/400 doesn't simply use objects or incorporate objects; they are a fundamental part of the design.

An object is just a container. All user and system data structures are packaged within these containers. Further, the object is encapsulated, which, as we discussed earlier, means it is not possible to see inside. A system built around an object model supports machine independence. The reason for putting objects into the System/38 in the first place was to keep the details contained so they could later be changed without affecting user application programs.

Still another reason for using objects was integrity. The original System/3 was a byte machine, which means everything was on a byte boundary. The System/3 instructions had a single-byte op-code. Instructions occupied several consecutive bytes in memory, but there were no enforced boundary alignments for the instructions. This meant that any byte in memory could contain a System/3 op-code. Further, all the bits in the op-code were used to specify the operation to perform and where the operands would be found. Almost any combination of bits in a byte could be interpreted as a valid op-code.

This caused a problem to occur with the System/3 if a program accidentally branched into a data area: The processor would continue to fetch bytes and treat them as instructions. The program might continue executing for a long time, creating all kinds of havoc with the system. Debugging these problems was no fun.

Consequently, we were very sensitive to the System/3's integrity problems, and those of most any other computer system of the time. For example, in a conventional system, a string of bytes can be treated as almost anything. Bytes can be fetched from one part of a program and multiplied by bytes from another part of the program. The processor does not care that such an operation makes no sense. It only looks at bytes, not what the bytes represent.

These things do not happen in the AS/400. Instructions can only work on objects they are supposed to work on. Certain general instructions apply to all objects, such as the Create Object instruction discussed later in this chapter. Other instructions only work on specific types of objects. Thus, it is not possible to misuse an object like it is in a conventional system. The resulting integrity is greatly enhanced.

Another way to look at this is to note that, in most operating systems, anything in permanent storage is a file (in MS-DOS or MVS, a file is called a dataset). Files may have different uses, but the classification is largely conventional. You can read a program object as if it were a file. In OS/400, this is impossible (making one kind of virus impossible, at least above the MI), because the term file applies only to a small set of object types and a program is definitely not a file. By the way, this caused some inconvenience in the System/38, because much of the information about objects was not available to programs. Numerous COMMON (an AS/400 user group) resolutions (now called requirements) were submitted to ask that all display commands (e.g., Display Output Queue (DSPOUTQ), Display Job Queue (DSPJOBQ)) have an option to produce an outfile, so that information buried inside objects could be read in a program. Rochester eventually provided this capability in some commands that did not originally have them (DSPOUTQ and DSPJOBQ still don't). But Rochester's comprehensive answer to the requests came in the form of APIs, extracted information about objects and system into a kind of space object known as a user space, which could then be read in programs more quickly than database files.

Object Naming

The System/38 had objects in both the operating system and in the MI. Two different groups of people in the development organization defined and named these objects. One group defined the CPF objects, which were renamed OS/400 objects with the announcement of the AS/400.[3] The other group defined the MI instruction set and the MI system objects.

The good news is that sometimes there is a one-to-one mapping between an OS/400 object and a system object at the MI. They are the same. The bad news is that sometimes they are not the same. All OS/400 objects are made up of one or more MI system objects. In other words, the relationship between OS/400 object types and MI system object types is one-to-one or one-to-many, never many-to-one or many-to-many. You will see an example of this in the next section. Before continuing, we need to clarify one more point of confusion.

Even when there is a one-to-one mapping of an OS/400 object to an MI system object, the objects may have different names. For example, OS/400 has an object called a library. There is an equivalent system object at the MI, but there it is called a context. How could this happen? The answer goes back to the System/38 days and the two different groups of people with two different naming philosophies.

One of the philosophies said this: If you are going to come up with a new system, you should rename everything. The reason is to force people to go in and understand the new structure. If you are going to implement a library, and you call it a library, someone will say, "I know what a library is; I worked on another system that had a library." Of course, that other system's library may be totally different. If you give the library a new name, such as context, no one will have preconceived ideas about it. Glenn Henry, the System/38 programming manager, advocated this naming philosophy. The group who defined the system objects at the MI used this approach, and they created some very strange names.

The other group was responsible for naming the operating system objects. They followed Thomas Edison's approach to naming: Use a name that

[3] Speaking of names, Rochester systems never used the name "operating system" prior to the AS/400. Operating systems were supposed to be complex and scary to most customers. Names such as Control Program Facility and System Support Program were somehow friendlier and less threatening. To everyone's surprise, when the PC introduced the Disk Operating System (DOS), no one was concerned; hence, the name change to OS/400.

sounds familiar, even if it isn't exactly the same. Back in the days when Edison was selling electricity, he decided to use names familiar to everyone who used natural gas. Thus, he would talk about the electric main coming into the house just like the gas or water mains do, even though a "main" is a pipe or a duct, and electrons don't usually flow through pipes into a house. He also called the heating element on a stove an electric burner, so that people who were familiar with gas burners would accept the electric stove (honest — the electricity in the heating element is not "burning"). Edison would have liked the operating system group.

OS/400 Objects and MI System Objects

Several object types are available in both OS/400 and MI. Table 5.1 lists the types of OS/400 objects. For comparison, Table 5.2 lists the MI system objects. Some of the OS/400 objects map one-to-one with the MI system

Table 5.1 OS/400 Objects

Authorization list	Journal
Chart format	Journal receiver
Class	Library
Class of service description	Line description
Command	Menu definition
Configuration list	Message file
Controller description	Message queue
Data dictionary	Mode description
Device description	Module
Document	Network interface description
Document list	Output queue
Data area	Panel group definition
Data queue	Product definition
Edit description	Program
File	Query definition
Folder	Reference code translate table
Forms control table	S/36 machine description
Graphics symbol set	Service program
Ideographic character table	Session description
Ideographic dictionary	Spelling aid dictionary
Ideographic sort table	Subsystem description
Information search index	Table
Job description	User index
Job queue	User profile

Table 5.2 MI System Objects

Access group	Index
Authorization list	Journal port
Byte string space	Journal space
Class of service description	Logical unit description
Commit block	Mode descriptor
Context	Module
Controller description	Network descriptor
Cursor	Process control space
Data space	Program (3 Subtypes)
Data space index	Queue
Dictionary	Space
Dump space	User profile

objects, but the name of the object in each set may or may not be the same. An example where the names are the same is a program. The library (context) object is an example where the names are different.

Other OS/400 objects have a one-to-many mapping with MI system objects. Figure 5.1 shows an example of this. The OS/400 database file in our example has five MI system objects, and it is composed of four different types of MI system objects (two are spaces in our example). The actual number of objects making up a file can be much greater. A cursor exists for each member, and even a single-membered join file can own or refer to up to 32 dataspace indexes. In the next chapter, we will look at the database and how these various MI system objects are related. For now, we can see the separate pieces.

One of the MI system objects is a data space. The database uses a data space to store the physical data, along with a definition of the fields in the database records. A second system object, called the data space index, contains a description of how the data is to be viewed. In the next chapter, we will see how the data space index provides a logical view of the physical data. The third object is a cursor that essentially accesses the records in the data space and uses the data space index to provide the logical view. The cursor provides the open data path to the data space and also contains the user buffers. The fourth object is a space where the result of the database operation can be placed. This is essentially an I/O buffer. The final object shown in our example, which is also a space, contains the file description. This object's only runtime function is to locate other objects.

Figure 5.1 OS/400 Database File Objects

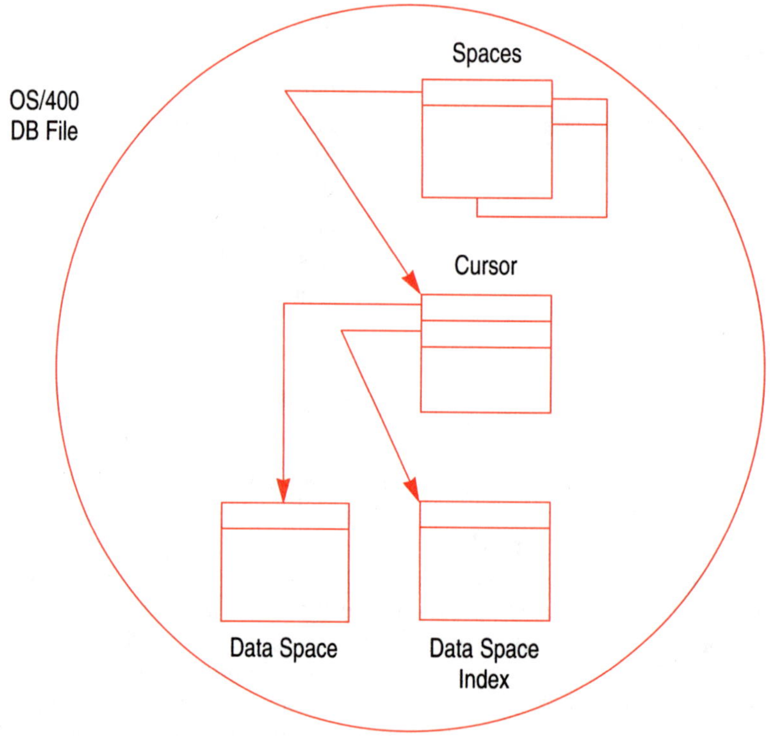

Finding Objects

In the original System/38, it was fairly easy to find an object in the database. Because every object had a name, you simply looked up the name in a library. A library provided a means to organize objects into groups and allowed objects to be found by name. The same library structure was brought forward into the AS/400.

Libraries

A library is an OS/400 object that you use to find other OS/400 objects in the database. The library is organized as a single-level hierarchy, unlike the directory structure found on PCs and in the Unix operating system, which have a multilevel hierarchy. A look at the naming structure for OS/400 objects will illustrate this hierarchy.

To find an OS/400 object requires the name of the library and the name of the object (e.g., LIBRARY/OBJECT). You also need the object type to uniquely identify the object. Two or more objects can have the same name, but they must be different types of objects. In other words, in a library we can have a program named SAM and a data space named SAM, but we can't have two programs named SAM. Also, an object can exist in one and only one library.

With one exception, a library cannot reference other libraries. To do so would violate the single-level hierarchy of LIBRARY/OBJECT. There is, however, a special library called QSYS that can reference other libraries, and it is the only one that can do so. A few other special OS/400 objects can also appear only in QSYS. The user profile objects, which give security authorizations to users, and the I/O configuration objects, which are used for I/O operations, can only appear in QSYS. We will discuss these objects in detail in later chapters.

Figure 5.2 shows the OS/400 library structure. In this example, QSYS contains a user profile (JOHN), a library (LIB1), and a device description (DEVD1). The library (LIB1) contains a database file (DB), a data queue (DQ), and an output queue (OQ).

Later, we will see that there is a list of libraries with each job in the system. This list tells the system which libraries to search when looking for an object and the order in which to search the libraries.

Figure 5.2 OS/400 Library Structure

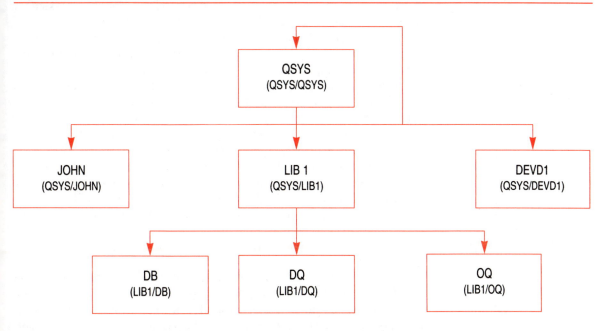

Shared Folders

Shared folders were introduced in the AS/400 primarily to support Office functions. The System/36 was a very good Office system, and many of the ideas about folders on the AS/400 came from this system. An OS/400 folders object was added to support these Office functions. Briefly, the integrated Office support provides a filing system for all Office objects that can contain data for an Office product. Mail, documents, programs, and files are among the traditional items that can be in this filing system.

Document library services allow users to treat the filing system as an electronic filing cabinet complete with folders. Folder management services allow the user to organize objects using these folders. Folders can contain other folders and can be searched interactively.

The desire to efficiently incorporate PCs into this Office environment led to the use of shared folders for the PC Support product on the System/36. This approach was carried forward into the AS/400. Thus, in addition to the traditional Office items mentioned, shared folders can contain spreadsheets, graphs, images, PC programs, and PC files.

PC files stored on the AS/400 can be accessed by the PC as if they were stored locally on the PC. Files can be transferred to and from the PC, with the data conversions automatically performed. Multiple sessions on the PC allow it to interact with multiple AS/400 systems, with multiple tasks on a single AS/400, or with any combination of both.

IBM enhanced PC Support several times, but it was getting old and fell short of what was needed for newer client/server applications. Also, PC Support didn't support all the PC operating systems customers wanted to use. While it provided the ability to attach PC clients that ran DOS, DOS with Extended Memory, and OS/2, it was noticeably lacking Microsoft's Windows 3.1 operating system. PC Support needed major changes.

IBM completely replaced PC Support with a totally new product called Client Access for OS/400. Client Access for OS/400 provides a powerful platform for distributed client/server computing. To support some of the new clients, changes also had to be made to the AS/400's file system. Libraries for database serving, and folders for Office and PC file serving, worked well for their original intended uses, but more was needed. The result was a new file system.

Integrated File System

What if a PC file system, a Unix file system, the OS/400 library system, and OS/400 shared folders were combined into a single structure? This would mean that an application written to use a PC or Unix file system could directly access data stored in an AS/400. Such a file system was announced as a part of V3R1 and was called the integrated file system.

Initially, the major challenge had been to determine how to construct such a file system. After all, the separate file systems were not designed to be compatible with one another, let alone be combined into a single structure. The problem turned out to be easier to solve than we initially had expected.

Notice that the OS/400 library structure is a subset of that used in PC operating systems, such as DOS and OS/2. The names are different in the PC world, but the structure is similar. The PC operating systems have files instead of objects. A library in a PC is called a directory, and files exist in directories. Unlike the OS/400 library structure, directories can exist in directories on the PC; these are usually called subdirectories. This arrangement creates a multiple-level hierarchy for PC file naming as opposed to the single level structure of the OS/400 library. A PC file name can take the form DIR1\DIR2\...\DIRn\FILENAME. Except for the backward slashes (\) this is a superset of the OS/400 library naming structure.

A Unix file structure is, likewise, a superset of the OS/400 library structure. Remember that an OS/400 object can only appear in a single library. That means there is only one *path* to any OS/400 object. A Unix file system allows multiple paths to the same object.

Figure 5.3 shows the integrated file system. Both the shared folders and the library structure are included under the single root node. AS/400 Office and the original PC clients still use the shared folders structure. This structure is fully compatible with the latest version of Client Access for OS/400. The original PC clients still access the folders through QDLS. The original library for database files is also included unchanged. You access this file structure through the QSYS library, just as you did on the System/38.

New for the AS/400 are six other file systems that are all part of the integrated file system. The first is a Unix file system called QOpenSys. It is a fully POSIX-compliant file system. Also new is a file system for LAN server clients called QLANSrv. This is used with the file server I/O processor discussed in Chapter 11. A similar file system, called QFileSvr.400, provides connection to remote file systems. Still another is for Windows clients, called QPWXCWN. A file system optical dataserver called QOPT was added to the integrated file system in 1995. Finally, a separate user-defined file structure is provided. Newly supported clients can access any or all of these file systems through the root directory. The original PC clients still use QDLS (shared folders).

The naming convention IBM uses for the integrated file system is based on the PC standard. A name takes the form DIR1\DIR2\...\DIRn\FILENAME. For those of us who can't remember when to use a forward slash (/) and when to use a backward slash (\), the new naming convention happily accepts either — you can even mix them in the same name.

The lengths of the file and directory names have been increased to match the POSIX standards. In an AS/400, the names in the integrated file system directories are stored in a format called Unicode. Unicode is an international standard that supports multiple languages, including the double-byte

Figure 5.3 Integrated File System

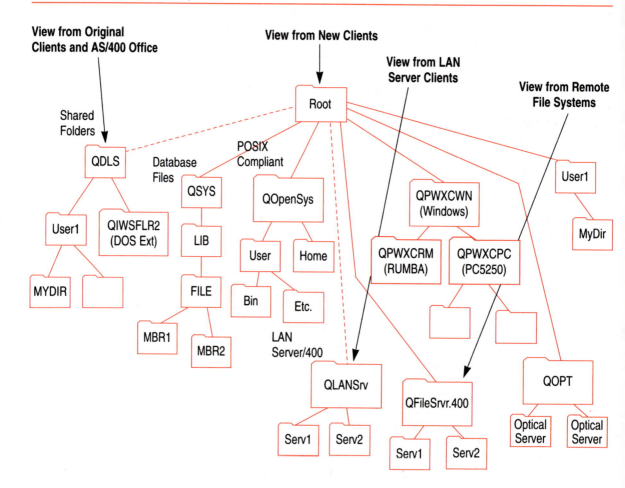

character sets many countries use. New for V3R6 is the capability to store all data in the database in Unicode.

The integrated file system allows any client to look at a file stored in the AS/400 as if it were an extension of its own file system. Unix clients think they are dealing with a Unix file system, while PC clients think they are PC files. The beauty of this is that both clients can be looking at the same data, so there is no need to have separate copies of the data. Original clients and existing AS/400 applications continue to use QDLS and QSYS, respectively. New clients and new applications can use any of the supported file systems. Keep in mind that the integrated file system provides access to the data. The format of the data must be compatible with the application requesting the data, or it must be converted to a compatible format. The introduction of

Unicode support in V3R6 for the database will give application developers the capability to use a universal data format that is being deployed across many platforms in the industry. This capability to use Unicode also means that a single application can be written for use worldwide; a special version of the program is not necessary for countries whose language requires a double-byte representation.

Accessing Objects

It is not enough to just find an object. Some means must be provided to allow a user program or an OS/400 program to access and modify objects. This occurs at the MI for system objects.

OS/400 is responsible for managing its own objects. It keeps track of the separate system objects that make up each OS/400 object. The object management component of SLIC manages the system objects and does not know about OS/400 objects. Again, the goal of the AS/400 design is to keep the two parts of the operating system, above and below the MI, independent. The only common ground between them is the MI, and it is here that access to objects is provided.

A system object is accessed with a *system pointer*. A system pointer occupies 16 bytes in memory and contains the address of the system object. A system pointer also contains information about the type of object to which it points. Chapter 8 describes the format of the system pointer in more detail.

Capability-Based Addressing

A system pointer may also contain information showing the types of operations that can be performed on the object. This is usually called the object *authority*. A pointer that contains the object address and the object authority is called a *capability*. The System/38 had capability-based addressing, because all system pointers contained both the address and the authority. This changed in the AS/400.

The desire to increase the levels of system security for the AS/400 required changes to the way object authority was given to users. By putting the authority in the pointer, any user who has the pointer permanently has the authority to the object. The user may also be able to give the pointer or a copy of the pointer to another user.

Suppose we want to give a user the authority to an object to perform a single operation. The user's program may need to temporarily access or modify data in the object, but the user does not need this authority on a permanent basis. But by giving the user authority in a system pointer, there is no way to take the authority back.

To limit user authority and increase security, IBM added methods to provide temporary authority to the AS/400. At the same time, we removed the authority from the pointers for all user programs. Pointers the operating system uses when in *system state* can still have the authority in the pointer.

I will explain all of this further in the chapter on security and authorization management, Chapter 7.

Many people still talk about the AS/400 as a system having capability-based addressing. However, with the one exception just cited, the AS/400 does not use capability-based addressing.

Resolving System Pointers

A system pointer is said to be *resolved* if it contains direct addressability to the system object. If the pointer contains symbolic addressability to the system object, it is said to be *unresolved.* The symbolic address consists of the object's name, type, and subtype. The subtype is not needed to uniquely identify an MI system object. It is the user-defined field that allows OS/400 to further categorize objects. The symbolic address is used to locate the object in a library.

Figure 5.4 shows how a system pointer is resolved by using the RESOLVE instruction. This instruction uses the name and type of the system object from the unresolved pointer, along with the authority being requested. The libraries in the library list associated with the job that issued the instruction are searched one at a time until the object is located. After the object is found, three checks are performed.

First, the object type is checked to ensure that the instruction is expecting the correct type of object. Next, a check is performed to see if the user has the right to obtain the authority requested in the RESOLVE instruction. This information is kept in the user profile. Finally, a check is made to see if some other user has locked the object so it cannot be accessed.

If all checks are passed, the unresolved system pointer is updated to contain the address of the system object. As previously noted, the authority can only be put in the pointer for a program that operates in the system state. Once the pointer has been resolved, it can be used by the program for all subsequent accesses to the object; it is not necessary to re-resolve the pointer each time it is used.

Other Pointer Types

A system pointer provides the access to a system object, but for some operations, we also need to manipulate the data contained in these objects. We accomplish this with other types of pointers that allow access to the internals of an object. Before I describe these pointers, I need to explain the internal structure of a system object.

A system object internally is divided into two major parts: a functional portion and a space portion. The contents of the functional portion are dependent on the system object type. For example, the functional portion of a program would contain the instruction stream for that program. The space portion of a system object is simply a byte space that is used as a work space. All system objects have a functional and a space portion, with one

Figure 5.4 Resolving a System Pointer

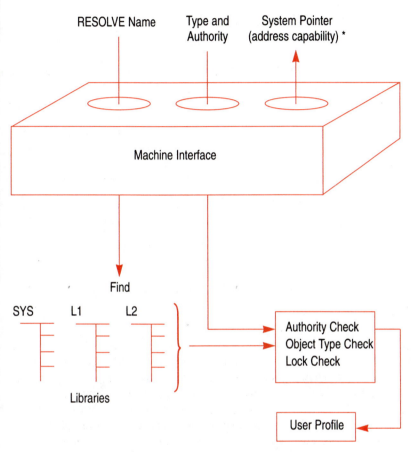

* System pointer authority in system state only

exception. A system object called a space has no functional portion; it only has a space portion.

A separate space portion is needed in an object because of the way the MI views memory. Remember, to be independent of the underlying technology, the MI has no idea of a memory in the traditional sense; it only has objects, and there is nothing outside of these objects. The pointers and the data created by system users need to be kept someplace. The space portion of the system objects provides this place.

Figure 5.5 shows two system objects, each with a functional and a space portion. The space portion can contain both pointers and data. In the figure, the space portion of the second object contains a system pointer that points

Figure 5.5 System Objects

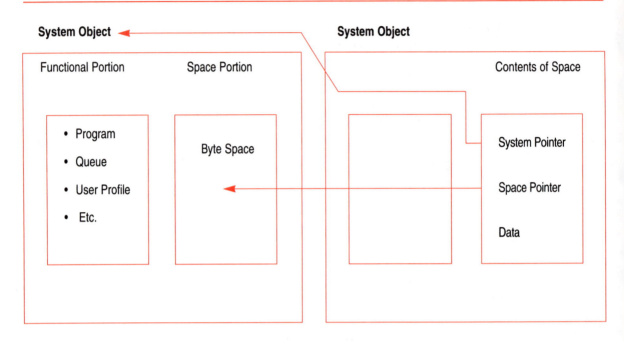

back to the first system object. System pointers always point to system objects. There is very little that can be done to a system pointer, because it can only point to the beginning of a system object. Its primary use is to access the object. But what if we want to get inside the object and manipulate bytes?

Because all system objects are encapsulated, it is not possible to manipulate the bytes inside the functional portion — it is not even possible to look inside this portion. The space portion, on the other hand, is used as a work space. We need some way to access information in this work space, and a *space pointer* provides the mechanism.

A space pointer looks very much like a system pointer. It is 16 bytes long and contains an address. The difference is that the address in a space pointer points to a byte somewhere in the space portion of a system object. So we can use space pointers to access and manipulate the bytes contained in this space.

Another major difference between the two types of pointers has to do with the operations that each can perform on the address. The address in the space pointer can be modified by the MI program to point to other bytes in the same space. The address in a system pointer cannot be modified. It can only point to the beginning of the object. If authorized, a user with a system pointer to an object can get a space pointer for that same object. The second object shown in Figure 5.5 also contains a space pointer that illustrates how this type of pointer provides access to the byte space of the first object.

In addition to system and space pointers, there are four other types of pointers at the MI. A *data pointer* is similar to a space pointer except that it contains the description of the type of data to which it points. This provides the capability to look at a string of bytes in a space and treat that string as any type of data. An analogy to this would be a pointer in the C language. An *instruction pointer* at the MI is used for branching in an MI program. It points to an instruction in the instruction stream of the program.

The four pointer types we have discussed so far (system, space, data, and instruction) were in the original System/38 design. A special version of a space pointer, the *machine space pointer*, was later added to provide access to internal machine storage. When ILE was added to the AS/400, a new *procedure pointer* was added. We use procedure pointers for the call/return operations, described in Chapter 3.

System Object Characteristics

We are now at a point where we can list the main characteristics of all system objects. Some of these characteristics will be covered in later chapters, but they are listed here for completeness.

1. System objects must be explicitly created with a CREATE instruction at the MI.
2. A CREATE instruction references a user-supplied template, which contains the attributes and values for the object. The template is contained in a space object.
3. The attributes of a system object can be materialized.
4. A system object can be explicitly destroyed.
5. All system objects have names if they appear in a context. A system object does not have to be named if it is never referenced in the library or file system. A system object used exclusively by the SLIC is such an example.
6. System pointers provide addressability to system objects.
7. System objects have a space that contains pointers and data.
8. System objects are created as temporary or permanent objects. A permanent object stays in the system forever, unless it is explicitly destroyed. This characteristic is referred to as persistence. A temporary object goes away whenever the initial program load (IPL) operation is performed.
9. Temporary objects can be placed in access groups. An access group is another system object that allows multiple objects of different types to be bundled and accessed together.
10. Authorization to system objects is monitored by the machine.
11. Object use is synchronized through object locks.

The eighth characteristic, object persistence, needs some elaboration, because it sets the AS/400 apart from other systems. As noted, persistence simply means the object continues to exist in the memory system forever. Being in the memory, it can easily be shared among users. This is very different from a conventional system, which requires that information be stored in a separate file system if the information is to be shared or if it is to be retained for a long time. Later, we will see how the AS/400's single-level store enables this object persistence.

Persistence of objects is extremely important for future support for object-oriented databases. Objects need to continue to exist even after their creator goes away. The AS/400 is uniquely positioned to exploit this characteristic of object persistence, whereas other operating systems will have to resort to storing their persistent objects in a separate file system.

Not every object needs to be kept forever. When it is created, an object is identified as either permanent or temporary. Permanent objects last forever; they are more costly because they tie up system resources for as long as they exist. A permanent object only goes away if it is explicitly destroyed. An example of an object that might be created as permanent is a data space, where database records are kept.

Temporary objects disappear at each IPL. In a conventional system, temporary memory areas are associated with user jobs and cannot be shared among users. When the job goes away, so do the temporary areas. In an AS/400, all memory, whether it contains permanent or temporary objects, can be shared among users. Even if the job goes away, the objects remain in the system. When the system was designed, some time, other than job termination, had to be designated when temporary objects would be removed from the system, and IPL time was selected. IPL time was a convenient time to choose to destroy temporary objects, because this resulted in less overhead during execution time. If, for example, we destroyed a job's temporary library when the job ended, there would be some performance impact on the running jobs. So we decided to move that overhead to IPL time.

An example of an object that might be created as temporary is a data space index, which provides a view of the database for some specific job. If this index is created only for a one-time query of the database, there is no sense to making it permanent. Note that a permanent object can ride out a system crash. But if the system has to be IPLed to recover, all temporary objects are lost. Objects sometimes are created as permanent simply to survive such a crash. In a later section, I explain how temporary and permanent objects are handled internal to the system.

Program Objects

So far, we have only described system objects and their characteristics. But at the MI there are other data items also called objects, and these data items have little or no resemblance to an object as it is commonly defined. This creates another terminology problem for us.

In Chapter 3, we examined the contents of an MI program template — the instruction stream and the ODT. The ODT, which is the acronym for object definition table, describes the operands the program uses. In an unfortunate choice of names, the System/38 MI designers called these operands objects. Specifically, they called them *program objects*. Thus, a two-byte binary number is called an object.

These program objects have nothing in common with MI system objects except for the name. But because it is just too easy to confuse a program object with a system object of type program, we will simplify matters and reserve the name object from this point on to describe MI system objects only.

Inside a System Object

Although there is no concept of memory at the MI, all AS/400 processors make use of physical storage, including main memory and disk. System objects below the MI are implemented as well-defined data structures contained in that storage. The object management component of SLIC is responsible for creating and managing these data structures. In this section, we will look at the layout of these data structures and see how they are used to represent MI system objects.

Segmented Memory

The notion of memory and disk space only exists below the MI. Unlike OS/400, the SLIC component of the operating system knows about and deals with this memory. All the main memory and disk space in an AS/400 is contained within a single large address space. This address space is usually called the single-level store of the AS/400, and it consists of the total number of bytes that can be referenced with a 64-bit address.[4]

Single-level store is the AS/400 version of a *virtual memory*. Virtual memory provides a logical view of memory that does not necessarily correspond to the memory's physical structure. In Chapter 8, I describe the differences between a virtual memory found in a conventional system and the single-level store of the AS/400. For now, it is enough to think about the single-level store as a very large address space with everything contained within it.

The entire address space in an AS/400 is logically divided into *segments*. A segment is a block of contiguous bytes in the address space. The System/38 and the original AS/400 had two segment sizes: 64 kilobytes and 16 megabytes. The 16-megabyte segment consisted of 256 of the 64-kilobyte segments and was sometimes called a segment group. With the move to a 64-bit address, the smaller size was dropped and only a 16-megabyte segment size is used.

Segments are nonoverlapping and always start on a segment boundary. This means that the address of the first byte in every 16-megabyte segment has the low-order (right-most) 24 bits set to all zeros. Each 16-megabyte

[4] The number of bytes in a 64-bit address is so large that most people cannot relate it to anything they know in the physical world. When the AS/400 had a 48-bit address, we would often say the number of bytes that could be addressed was equal to the distance from the earth to the sun and back measured in millimeters. Some new analogy is needed for 64 bits.

segment is uniquely identified by the high-order (left-most) 40 bits of the 64-bit address.

The AS/400 address space is mapped onto the physical main memory and the disks by SLIC's storage management component. This logical-to-physical memory mapping uses blocks of memory that are each 4 kilobytes in length, called *pages*.[5] A segment is composed of a multiplicity of these pages that are not necessarily contiguous in physical memory. I cover the details of this mapping in Chapter 8.

[5] The System/38 and the original AS/400 used a 512-byte page size. This was increased to 4 kilobytes for the systems with the 64-bit RISC hardware.

System Object Structure

Figure 5.6 shows the format of a system object in the single-level store. The first 32 bytes contain the segment header. The segment header provides information about the segment itself. Following the segment header is the Encapsulated Program Architecture (EPA) header. The EPA was created

Figure 5.6 System Object Structure

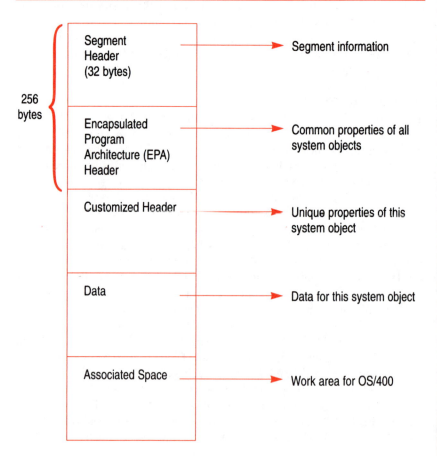

to specify the internal structure of the System/38's encapsulated objects. This same internal structure was carried over into the AS/400. The EPA header contains the attributes (kinds of properties) common to all system objects, regardless of type. Both the segment header and the EPA header occupy the first 256 bytes in every system object and will be described in more detail shortly.

Each type of object has kinds of properties only found in that specific type. A program has unique properties that a data space doesn't have, and vice versa. A customized header, which contains the values of these special properties, follows the EPA header in the object.

Following these three headers are the components that make up the particular object. For example, the instruction stream follows the customized header in a program. Because all system objects have a space portion, a space component is always present. At the MI, this space component is called the *associated space*. The specific components, and the order in which they appear, are dependent on the object type. There are too many types of system objects to describe the customized headers and the object components in any detail. We will, however, look at some examples in a later section.

Multisegment Objects

System objects occupy one or more segments and always start on a segment boundary. The first segment is called the *base segment*, and every object has a base segment. A system pointer always points to the base segment. Depending on the type of object, there may be one or more *secondary segments*. Most objects have an associated space that occupies one of these secondary segments. Further, no segment is ever part of more than one system object.

Figure 5.7 shows a system object that occupies two segments. As shown, the system pointer points to the base segment. Notice that each of the segments has its own segment header. The segment header contains information about the segment, not about the object in the segment. The segment header also contains the addresses that link the segments together. Also note that the EPA header is only contained in the base segment. The EPA header contains information about the total object and only needs to appear in one place. Following the EPA header is the customized header for the object. Again, this header only appears in the base segment.

These multiple segments are allocated at the time the system object is created. This allocation is accomplished through a CREATE xxx instruction, where *xxx* is the type of object being created. Figure 5.8 (on page 111) shows the input and the output for a CREATE instruction at the MI. The CREATE instruction uses a space pointer to point to the object template contained in a space object. Readers should be aware that MI Create xxx instructions are not the same as OS/400 CRTxxx commands. CRTRPGPGM must go through several preliminary passes before reaching the MI CREATE.

Figure 5.7 Multisegment Objects

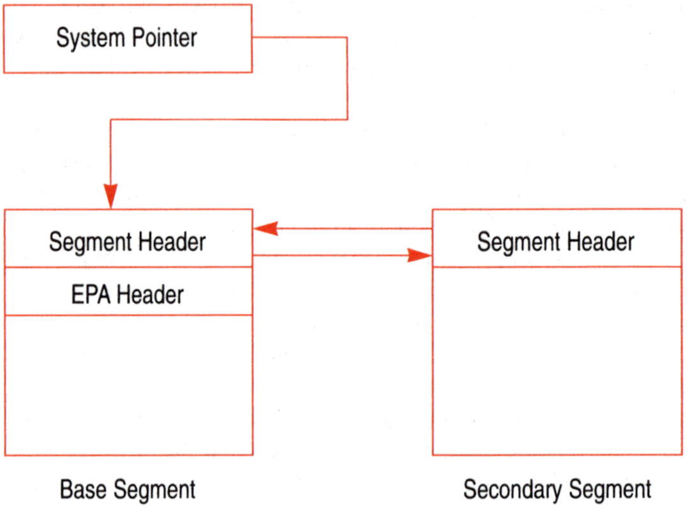

```
                    ┌──────────────────┐
                    │  System Pointer  │
                    └────────┬─────────┘
                             │
                             ▼
          ┌──────────────────┐        ┌──────────────────┐
          │  Segment Header  │◄──────►│  Segment Header  │
          ├──────────────────┤        │                  │
          │   EPA Header     │        │                  │
          ├──────────────────┤        │                  │
          │                  │        │                  │
          │                  │        │                  │
          │                  │        │                  │
          └──────────────────┘        └──────────────────┘
              Base Segment              Secondary Segment
```

The latter is the last pass of a program compile. The execution of the MI CREATE instruction causes the base and secondary segments to be created in the single-level store. Various directories managed by the SLIC are updated to reflect the presence of the new object.

Storage management needs to have access to the segments, and one of its directories is updated. If the object appears in a library, the library (context below the MI) must be updated to contain the name and location of the new object. If no library is specified, the object is placed in the current library of the job that issued the CREATE instruction. One of the libraries in the library list for every job is always identified as the current library. Likewise, the user profile or group profile must be updated to show the ownership of the new object. The final step is to create a system pointer to the object and pass it back to the user who requested the creation of this object.

Contents of the Headers

Now that we have examined the structure of the system objects and how they map to memory segments, we can look at the contents of both the segment and the EPA headers. As we saw, a segment header occupies the first 32 bytes of each segment that makes up a system object. An EPA header appears only in the base segment of a system object.

Figure 5.8 Object Creation

Input

Output

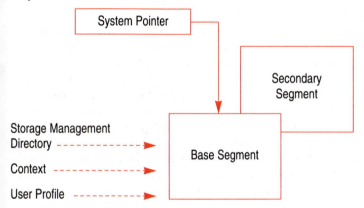

Segment Headers
A segment header provides the following information about a segment:

- Segment type byte
- Flag bits
  — Existence bit (permanent or temporary)
  — Autoextend bit
  — Tags-in-segment bit
  — Others
- Number of pages allocated to the segment
- Address of the base segment for the object
- Address of the associated space for the object

These last two addresses should not be confused with the system pointer and the space pointer to the system object. They are the 64-bit addresses the SLIC uses.

The segment type byte identifies what is in the segment. There are two categories of segment types: those that are part of MI objects and those that are only used by SLIC below the MI. Until now, we have only considered segments that are used for MI objects. There is, however, a whole category of segments for SLIC data structures that are not part of the MI system objects; but they are not treated as entities, as an object would be.

We have already seen two types of segments that are part of a system object. The first segment type was the base segment of a system object. The second was the associated space segment. About a dozen other segment types can be part of the various MI system objects. The system object examples shown in the next section will illustrate a couple more of these MI object segments. We will introduce still others in the following chapters when we cover the topics to which they are related.

Approximately 40 segment types are used only by the SLIC. Everything from storage management tables to the work area used by the translator have their own segment types. Again, it makes sense to delay discussing these segment types until we encounter them in the following chapters. For now, it is only important to understand that they exist, and that they are constructed and managed similarly to the segments used for system objects.

A segment header contains several flag bits that identify characteristics of the segment. Three of the most important flags are the existence, autoextend, and tags-in-segment bits. The existence bit identifies whether the segment is permanent or temporary. Unless it is explicitly destroyed, a permanent segment stays in the system forever, whereas a temporary segment goes away whenever the system is IPLed.

The autoextend bit tells storage management to add disk pages to the segment whenever they are needed. Note that there is a field in the segment header that tells the number of disk pages allocated to the segment. If the autoextend bit is turned off, this means the segment will never grow beyond the size it was when it was created. Whenever this bit is off, storage management attempts to put the entire segment into a contiguous area on disk when the segment is created. If the bit is on, the segment is likely to be composed of non-contiguous pages on disk. Thus, turning the bit off can improve performance at the cost of pre-allocating all the pages.

The tags-in-segment bit identifies whether or not there are any MI pointers in the segment. In Chapter 2, we discussed extensions to the PowerPC architecture and introduced the special bit called the tag bit. To review, a tag bit is associated with every MI address (a 16-byte pointer), and these bits prevent unauthorized modification of addresses. Tag bits are kept in a part of the AS/400 main memory that is not visible to MI programs. When a page is moved to or from disk, these hidden tag bits need to be moved by storage management. The tags-in-segment bit tells storage management whether or not it has to deal with tags in the segment. Chapter 8 goes into more detail about the tag bits.

The two remaining fields in a segment header are addresses. The first is the address of the base segment. The second is the address of the next secondary segment, which for a system object is usually the associated space segment. These two addresses provide the capability to link from one segment to another in a multisegment object.

Note that the addresses below the MI in headers and elsewhere are the 64-bit addresses recognized by the hardware. At the MI, addresses are always contained in a pointer and occupy 128 bits (16 bytes). The pointers protect the addresses contained within them from unauthorized modification and use. They also provide part of the MI's technology independence. Below the MI there is neither that protection nor the technology independence. This is the reason all users of the MI, including OS/400 itself, are not allowed below the MI.

EPA Headers

An EPA header is contained in the base segment of every system object. This header contains the following information about the object:

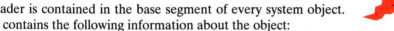

- Attribute byte
  — Permanent object
  — Suspended object
  — Damaged object
  — Access group present
  — Object being traced
  — Object under commitment control
- Object identification
  — Object type
  — Object subtype (user defined)
  — Object name
- Space attributes
  — Fixed/variable size
  — Initial value of space
  — Size of space
- Total object size
- Version number of object
- Creation time stamp
- User profile address
- Context address
- Access group address

- Object-specific header address
- Other information and addresses

The object attributes are contained at the beginning of the EPA header. The bits in the attribute byte are checked at runtime whenever a system pointer is used to reference a system object. The first attribute identifies whether the object is permanent or temporary. This attribute, which is also present as the existence bit in the segment header, is repeated here for ease of checking at runtime.

The suspended and damaged bits describe the condition of the object. A suspended object is one in which only the headers are available. The contents of a suspended object do not exist. Suppose the owner of a system object explicitly destroys the object. What happens if someone else in the system has a pointer to that object and tries to access it after it has been destroyed? The answer is that (s)he will find a suspended object.

With a suspended object, only the headers of the object are left, and the suspended bit in the EPA header is turned on. If someone references the deleted object, (s)he will find just the headers. The system will recognize that the object existed at one time but no longer exists, and it will take the appropriate action.

Further, when a permanent object is destroyed, the address space is not reused. With this approach, there is never a need to look through the system to find all pointers to the destroyed object and invalidate them. The address space will not be reassigned to any other object. There is, therefore, no security or integrity exposures that might result if the address space was reassigned and someone still had a pointer to that address. Other systems have invented elaborate schemes for "garbage collection" to find pointers to the destroyed object. That is not needed in an AS/400.[6] The address space is not reused, but the disk space occupied by the object, except for the headers, is cleared.

Two classes of object damage can be identified: hard and soft. Hard damage means the object has no functional use — it is so badly damaged it can only be destroyed. Soft damage says some data can still be extracted from the object. When damage is detected, OS/400 gets involved in the recovery process.

The damage attribute is used to report problems with the objects across the MI. Storage management is one of the major components in the system that identifies damage. A source of damage is bad disk sectors. Storage management may not be able to read a sector and reports the problem with the damage attribute.

Some other attributes in the EPA header identify that an access group exists for this object, that the object is being traced, and that the object is under commitment control. We will cover more details on these object attributes in Chapter 6.

[6] Computer science research projects at various universities have dealt with the problems of garbage collection for years. Untold numbers of graduate students have worked on solutions to this problem. Sometimes it is smarter to eliminate the problem than to solve it, and that is the AS/400 approach.

The EPA header has three fields reserved for object identification. The object type is contained in one field and the object subtype in another. The object type is defined to be one of the MI system object types. The subtype is the user-defined field. It is user-defined in the sense that OS/400 programmers are users of MI system objects. Only a few object types (such as the User Space) can have their subtypes specified by programmers outside of Rochester development. The object name field contains the name of the object as it would appear in a context.

The space attributes identify whether the space is fixed or variable in size, the initial value of the space (has it been cleared or set to all zeros?), and the size of the space. The total object size field contains the size for all segments in the object. The version number and creation time stamp further identify information about the object when it was created.

Some of the fields in the EPA header are addresses. The more important ones are the address of the user profiles for both the owner and the creator, the address of the context that contains the object name, the address of the access group if the object appears in an access group, and the address of the customized header in the object. Still other information and addresses are in the EPA header for components of the system that have yet to be discussed.

Examples of Objects

Figure 5.9 shows four examples of system objects. The space is the simplest system object, occupying just one segment. It only has a segment header, an EPA header, and a space for user data. An example of an object that occupies two segments is the independent index, usually just called an index. It's primary responsibility is to support the OS/400 user index. The base segment of the index contains a segment header, an EPA header, an index (customized) header, and a binary radix tree. In the next chapter, we will see how a binary radix tree is used to implement indexes in an AS/400. The second segment of the index is an associated space segment, meaning it has a segment header with the type byte set to indicate it is an associated space. This second segment also contains the user data for the index.

Two examples of objects that occupy three segments are shown. The first is a program. The base segment of a program contains a segment header, an EPA header, a program (customized) header, the instruction stream, and the initialization code for the program. The second segment is an associated space segment that contains the user data for the program. The third segment is the materialization definition table (MDT) segment that contains the program template and the object mapping for the program. This third segment contains the information necessary to materialize the program. When a user chooses to delete observability, this third segment is eliminated and the program only occupies two segments.

The last object shown is a data space index. The base segment, like all others, contains a segment header, an EPA header, a data space index

116 Inside the AS/400

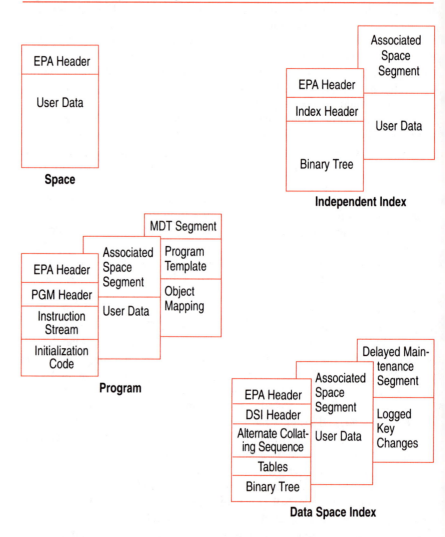

Figure 5.9 Examples of Objects

(customized) header, the alternate collating sequence for this index, the index tables, and the binary radix tree. The second segment is again an associated space segment. Every system object, except the space, has an associated space segment as its second segment. The third segment is a delayed maintenance segment.

One of the options available with a data space index is to delay maintenance of the index. In other words, changes to the index, such as insert or remove a key, are not immediately applied. Instead, they are logged in the delayed maintenance segment until the next time the file member is opened.

Delayed maintenance eliminates the need to wait for the completion of maintenance operations while the index is being used. The updates will, however, have been applied before the index is used the next time.

Conclusions

Objects provide the means to manage and protect the resources of the system. Naming and addressing of nearly everything in the system are tied to objects. So is the system security. Objects are also used to efficiently share information among system users. Through object encapsulation and well-defined operations on these objects, the AS/400 achieves a level of technology independence and integrity unknown in other systems.

Objects are fundamental to the AS/400 design. They were not added on top of an existing design, as is so often the case with other systems. Objects have been a part of the AS/400 from the very beginning.

Many of the objects we have introduced in this chapter are used by the system components described in the rest of this book. In the next chapter, we will look at the AS/400's integrated database. Many of the objects we have already seen are part of that database.

Chapter 6

The Integrated Database

The AS/400's integrated relational database now has a name: It is called DB2 for OS/400. Every System/38 and every AS/400 since the very beginning has had a relational database. Previously, this database never had a name, so why now?

For one thing, many AS/400 customers didn't know they had a database, because the integrated structure of the AS/400 supports internal management of the database. Some surveys showed that as many as 40 percent of our customers were unaware that they had a database and were using it in their business every day. That is both good news and bad news. The good news is these customers don't do anything special to manage their database. They just use it. They certainly don't have anyone identified in their business who has the role of a database administrator, unlike many other databases that require database managers.

The bad news is that many of our customers thought someday they would have to add a database to their AS/400. All modern computers, even PCs, have relational databases, which the user purchases separately and integrates into the system. So surely, the AS/400 should have a relational database. Again, surveys have shown that many AS/400 customers planned to buy a database in the near future. I should note that you should always question survey results; they may say as much about the survey as they do about the AS/400 and its customers.

We at IBM have also had difficulties talking about the AS/400 database, because it is not something we can point to. The AS/400 database is not in only one place; again, the integrated nature of the system makes the database pervasive throughout the system. Conventional databases, on the other hand, are separate software components on top of an operating system. A program has to go through the operating system or use a totally separate interface to get to a conventional database.

By being integrated, partly above the MI and partly in SLIC, the AS/400 database achieves a higher level of efficiency than one built on top of an existing system. It is also tightly integrated with other system components with which it communicates in a manner no conventional database can achieve. Other operating system developers are recognizing the benefits of an integrated database. A prime example is Microsoft's Windows NT. NT includes Microsoft's Structured Query Language (SQL) Server, an integrated relational database.

IBM selected the name DB2 for OS/400 to reflect that it is part of the IBM DB2 family of relational database products.[1] The family resemblance among these database products exists primarily in their external tools and their support for distributed database facilities. The underlying support is quite different in each case, and the AS/400 may well be the best in the group. The DB2 name does help alleviate the perception that the AS/400 does not have as robust a database as other systems. There are still a few areas where the AS/400 database is behind. A good example of this is the AS/400's database tools, which have not kept pace with those available with other databases.

IS managers sometimes ask why they are stuck with one database on the AS/400; why can't they get a database from Oracle or Sybase? What they mean is why can't they get the Oracle or Sybase interface and database tools — not the underlying database manager. The database enhancements IBM announced with V3R1 went a long way to close the gap, but we have more to do. Perhaps even putting the interfaces and tools from these other databases on the AS/400 sometime in the future would be a good idea.

Relational Database Evolution

The first commercial database with relational capabilities appeared in the System/38. It predated other relational databases in the industry by about three years. This unique database helped set the System/38 apart as a very advanced system, and many wondered where it had its origins.

The System/38 database's original developers were looking for a more efficient way to process records than the System/3 used. The first System/3 was designed as a unit record machine. It could only do batch processing, which meant that an application would process all the records in a file, one at a time. The first records were on punched cards, and a deck of punched cards made up a file. Later, files could be stored on disk, although they were still processed the same as the cards had been.

A typical unit record application would first sort the records in the file. The records would have multiple fields containing such things as customer name, account number, part number, and the like. One of these fields, called the *key*, was selected and all records would then be sorted into some sequence based on the value in the key field. The mechanical card sorter in

[1] I was opposed to naming the AS/400 database until I had a meeting with a large manufacturing customer who was moving from another system to the AS/400. In the meeting, the technical people asked me what database I would recommend for the AS/400. I blurted out, "DB2/400," a name being circulated in internal discussions. Immediately, the people in the room began to nod and make comments like, "Oh, that's a very good database." Considering that these people worked for another division in IBM and they didn't know the AS/400 had a database, it was obvious to me that we needed to name it.

most unit record installations was usually kept quite busy. After the file was sorted, it would be processed, one record at a time, until all the records in the file had been exhausted.

Interactive processing was later added to the System/3. The use of disk technology meant individual records could be accessed in random order. An index was used to identify the record to be accessed. An *index* is a small file where each record in the file has only two fields. The first field contains a key value, and the second field contains the disk address of the record that has the matching key value. A sort program was used to sort the index entries according to the key values. The index was then stored on the disk along with the file itself.

To find a record that had a certain key value, the system would first search the index. When it found the key value, the disk address stored with that key value in the index was used to fetch the full record from the file. Because the System/3 had fairly small memory sizes, it was not possible to store much of the index in the memory. This made searching the index fairly inefficient because several disk accesses were required.

The first member of the System/3 family to be designed as an interactive system, rather than a batch system, was the System/34. The System/34 also had relatively small memory sizes, so IBM needed a better way to search for an index entry. The approach it took was to eliminate the requirement to fetch the index from the disk.

Certain tracks on the disk were reserved for the index and special hardware was designed into the disk controller. The desired key value was passed from the processor to the disk controller. The disk controller then began to read the information on the track, looking for the key value. When the controller hardware saw the key value, it read in the next address field and passed this back to the processor. The processor then used this address to fetch the actual record from some other part of the disk.

This type of disk operation was called a *scan*. The scan function greatly improved the efficiency of interactive processing by completely eliminating a disk access to fetch the index. However, a smaller index that could fit into memory did have to be built over the index on the disk. The index in memory identified which track on the disk to search. This same scan operation was later implemented in the System/36 to do file processing.

The System/38, too, needed to do interactive processing very efficiently. The disadvantage of the scan implementation is that it tied file searching very closely to the hardware. There were also other limitations in terms of the number of indexes possible and the ways they could be processed. Because the System/38 was to have a single-level store, the developers decided to put all files and indexes into this large memory.

If we step back and look at the file structure we just described, we see a two-dimensional table, the rows representing records and the columns representing fields in the records. The developers reasoned the most efficient approach would be to build a System/38 file as a simple two-dimensional table in memory. They also thought processing performance would be enhanced if the table could be processed in place without the need to reorder the records with a sort. To accomplish this design, they built an index into the table in such a way that sorting would never be required (see "Machine Indexes" later in this chapter). In fact, they believed there would never be a sort program on the System/38.

But there was — and is — a sort program. Dick Bains wrote the program and named it "Conversion Reformat Utility," probably to disguise what it was and to keep application developers from using it for new projects. This program was, however — and may still today be — the fastest way to sort and select records from large files. Jim Sloan, a developer and planner who helped build the CL compiler, developed a user tool in his set of QUSRTOOLs that used externally defined field names as an interface to the sort.

As the database definition proceeded, Perry Taylor, one of the lead developers, came across an IBM technical report written by E. F. Codd. Codd, who is generally credited with creating the relational database, was working on a project called System/R (R for relational) at IBM's research facility in California. Codd had defined a two-dimensional table, on which four primitive operations could be performed, for his database. The first operation he called *order*, which allowed either rows or columns to be processed in some order using a key field. The second he called *selection*, which allowed rows to be selected based on the value in a key field. The third he called *projection*, which allowed specific fields to be selected from the table. Finally, his fourth operation, which he called *join*, allowed multiple tables to be treated as if they were one large table. A relational database was simply a two-dimensional table with the operations of order, selection, projection, and join.

Perry immediately recognized that the System/38 developers were building a very similar database, with the exception that their database was missing the join. He telephoned Codd to tell him about the work in Rochester and to offer support for Codd's ideas on database. But Codd's reaction was that relational databases are only for large systems; a small system only needs a sort and a merge. According to Perry, the conversation was cordial. Perry likened Codd's tone to that of the police officers in the O. J. Simpson trial when they were being cross-examined by defense attorneys — respectful, but not forthcoming. E. F. Codd and Perry Taylor never spoke again. Three years after the announcement of the System/38, the System/R database was announced as DB2 and was identified as the "first" relational database.[2] Because the System/38 did not originally have the join function, it was recognized as the first commercial database product with relational capabilities.

2 After leaving Rochester, Tom Furey became the general manager of the DB2 organization. At that time, DB2 was about to celebrate its tenth anniversary. The press releases proudly pointed to DB2 as the first relational database. Tom had to remind them that the System/38 database was the first.

The Two Faces of Database

When we talk about a database, we are not referring to just some place to put data. We are talking about a *database management system* (DBMS). A DBMS is a framework for storing and retrieving data that includes definitions of what the data mean, rules of data integrity and the mechanisms for enforcing them, and the operations for storing and retrieving data. A DBMS must have an interface so that users can access and manipulate the data. In this section, we introduce the two interfaces to the AS/400 DBMS: Structured Query Language (SQL) and Data Description Specifications (DDS). In later sections, we discuss the DBMS in detail.

When IBM first introduced the System/38, there were no standard interfaces for a relational database. So the designers had to develop a native interface that was unique to the System/38. Not surprisingly, the native DDS interface looked very much like the file system it was meant to replace. The designers provided several system commands and utility functions to manipulate the database. They also created instructions at the MI to perform operations such as read, write, update, and delete. Programmers could access these instructions directly from languages such as RPG and COBOL. For example, Many AS/400 shops use DDS-RPG: DDS for data definitions, RPG instructions for data access. The native DDS interface from the System/38 was carried forward to the AS/400. System/38 applications continued to use the native interface. In fact, many users still favor this interface. Mainframe customers who have moved to the AS/400 also like the native interface, because it is similar to the one used by IBM's large system database, Information Management System (IMS).

At about the time the AS/400 was being developed, an effort was underway in IBM, and in the industry, to standardize on SQL as the relational database language. SQL came out of System/R. Far from being quickly adopted, it took nearly a decade for SQL to emerge as the standard. Ingres for years used a competing language, QUEL, until it, too, succumbed to the trend. At its introduction in 1988, the AS/400 supported both the native DDS interface and SQL. SQL statements can be embedded directly into RPG, COBOL, and C programs. These SQL statements replace the native instructions such as read, write, and update. DB2 for OS/400 contains precompilers that translate the SQL statements.

If we look more closely at DB2 for OS/400, we find it has two separate parts. The Database Manager and the DDS language both come with OS/400. The Query Manager and SQL Development Kit is a licensed product that must be purchased separately. As its name suggests, this optional product contains Query Manager, the end-user query product for the AS/400 that uses SQL. The kit also contains an interactive user interface to SQL called Interactive SQL, and the language precompilers that are used when SQL statements are embedded in a high-level language. An unfortunate situation that has occurred is IBM's requirement that you pay for SQL, while DDS comes with OS/400. This situation is a key reason why SQL has never been popular in many AS/400 shops, because it sends the message that SQL is a foreign product; but it's not. Most database developers in Rochester these days think primarily in terms of SQL, not DDS. The DDS interface will continue to be supported, but new function will most likely come on the SQL side.

Although there are two distinct database interfaces on an AS/400, it is very important to understand that there is only one database. You can access, define, and manipulate data on the AS/400 through either the DDS interface or the SQL interface. Because the SQL interface was designed to use the same MI instructions that the DDS interface uses, either interface can manipulate data objects that were created through the other interface. This ability to mix and match the two interfaces provides another level of power and flexibility for the AS/400 database.

The biggest problem with having two interfaces is the confusion different terminology causes. As with the naming differences between OS/400 objects and the MI system objects, different groups of people created the names used in the two database interfaces. For example, the native DDS interface has physical files, which contain the actual data in the database. As we saw previously, a physical file is a two-dimensional table. The same physical file in the SQL interface is called a table, which is a more descriptive name for this data structure. A logical file in the native DDS interface does not contain data, but instead points to the actual data; logical files give a program a view of the data. For the SQL interface, a logical file is called a view. Likewise, record and field names in the DDS interface are called row and column names in the SQL interface, to reflect the concept of a table.

Overview of Database Operations

This section will present an overview of various database components found in the AS/400. The purpose here is not to show how to use the AS/400 database. Several good books and articles have already been written to describe the externals of the database and to show how a programmer can use the two database interfaces. Instead, the purpose of this section is to give you an overview of the database characteristics and of the fundamental operations the DBMS performs.

This section is divided into three parts. In the first part, I will describe the fundamental functions any DBMS must provide and show how the AS/400 accomplishes these functions. The second section comprises an overview of some new database features, some of which have to do with database performance and some of which provide support for the AS/400 as a database server. The third part describes support for parallel database operations, a subject of great importance for the future. Following this overview, I will explain the internal implementation of some of the fundamental database functions.

Functions of a Database Management System

There are many ways to implement a relational database; but in general, any database management system is expected to provide seven functions. They are

1. Functions to define and describe the database tables
2. Functions to manage the data (insert, retrieve, update, and delete)
3. Specifications of what the data represent that are independent of program definitions
4. Late bound views of the data to meet changing application program needs
5. Multiple views of the data for different application programs
6. Data security
7. Data integrity

We can now look at how the AS/400 accomplishes these functions.

Data Description and File Creation

The AS/400 database's native DDS language can be used to describe the physical and logical database files. DDS has statements that use keywords and parameters to describe both the attributes of the file itself and the fields in the database records. You can also use DDS to describe the device files used in the AS/400. The format and type of data used with the physical devices attached to the system are contained in these device files.

DDS can define several attributes for the fields in the database records. Some of the attributes include the field's name, its length, and the kind of data (alpha or numeric) the field contains. Depending on the type of data the field contains, you can describe several other specific attributes. For example, if a field contains decimal data, you can define the total number of decimal digits and the number of digits to the right of the decimal point.

DDS statements are stored in source file members, which are then compiled into file objects by the OS/400 commands CRTPF (Create Physical File) and CRTLF (Create Logical File). Likewise, you can use SQL to describe the attributes of the database files. Unlike DDS, which is only a data description language, a single SQL statement both describes and creates the tables and views. In SQL the file definition is not separate from the create instruction. SQL's CREATE TABLE statement, for example, defines the name of the table, the name of the columns (fields), and the attributes of the columns. This statement, when executed, also creates the table.

Creating Physical Files and Tables

The physical files, called tables in SQL, contain the actual data. A physical file record has a fixed set of fields. Each field may be (although is not usually) of variable length. In SQL terminology, a table has fixed-length rows with variable-length columns. To avoid total confusion, I will use the terminology for the native interface whenever possible because it is more familiar to most AS/400 users, unless I need to specifically describe an SQL implementation.

A physical file has two parts. The first part contains the file attributes and the field descriptions. The file attributes include the file's name, its owner, its size, the number of records in the file, the file's key fields, and some other attributes. The field descriptions contain the attributes for each field in the records. The second part of a physical file contains the data.

The data part of a physical file can have one or more members. Members allow a file to be subdivided. All the records in all the members have exactly the same format. Members provide a convenient way to partition these records. We might put this month's information in one member and last month's in another. Each member has its own unique name, and we can access the records in a member by using the member name. We should note that SQL tables can have only one member. SQL's single-member restriction conforms to the relational model's insistence that all data be stored in two-dimensional tables. Multimembered files are three-dimensional.

To create a physical file, we use the CRTPF system command. This command uses the DDS statements in the source physical file as a template to create the physical file. The physical file created with this command contains no data records. We must use a separate program or utility to add the actual data records to the file.

As we saw earlier, the SQL statement to define the data also creates the table. We can execute the CREATE TABLE statement using Query Manager, Interactive SQL, or by embedding it in a high-level language program. The table that is created with this statement is a physical file, and it is identical to the one created through the native interface.

Creating Logical Files and Views

Logical files allow a user to access data in a format that is different from the way it is stored in one or more physical files. Logical files provide the data and program independence we will discuss in the next section. The logical file contains no data records; instead, it contains the relative record number of the data record in the physical file. The logical file contains the index to the physical file. We often say the logical file provides the access path to the data.

A logical file's structure can range from very simple to extremely complex. The four categories of logical files and views are

- Simple logical files or views that map data from a single physical file or table to some other logical record definition.
- Multiple-format logical files that allow access to several physical files, each with its own record format definition. This type of logical file can

only be created through the native interface; it cannot be created through the SQL interface.
- Join logical files that define a single record definition built from fields in any combination of two or more physical files, tables, logical files, or views, as long as the total number of physical files and tables does not exceed 32.
- SQL views are similar to join logical files and provide the same result, but they are implemented quite differently. Join files maintain or share an access path for each join. SQL views find the access paths they need at run time, guided by a Query Definition Template stored with the file.

Like the physical file, the logical file has two parts. The first part looks just like the first part of the physical file. It contains the file attributes and the field descriptions. The second part contains the relative record number of the data record in the physical file. A program using a logical file only sees the data from the physical file presented in the format described in the field descriptions of the logical file.

Not surprisingly, to create a logical file, we use the CRTLF system command. This command uses the DDS statements in a source physical file as a template to create the logical file. DDS statements in this file also identify the names of one or more physical files on which the logical file is based. Once created, the logical file will contain the relative record numbers of the data records in the one or more physical files on which it is based.

The CREATE VIEW statement in SQL identifies the table the view represents, along with the column descriptions for the view. Again, the view created is a logical file, which is identical to one that would be created if the native interface was used. Logical files perform three database operations: formatting (includes projection, joining, and field derivation), record selection, and ordering. A DDS-created file can do all three. An SQL-created file can do either formatting (an SQL View) or ordering (an SQL index), but not both. SQL cannot create views that select a subset of physical file records. An SQL view could be created by DDS, but DDS is not typically used to create files that look only like SQL views.

Data Dictionary and Catalogs
A single place in every AS/400 system contains the descriptions of all components in all the physical and logical files. In the native interface, this entity is called the *data dictionary*. The data dictionary is a special OS/400 object that the database manager maintains and that users can query to find file structure and where-used information. The database manager automatically logs information contained in the data dictionary whenever a new database object is created.

The data dictionary's purpose is to allow users and application developers to see what the database looks like on any system. What record formats are used? What are their attributes? Where is a particular name used in the system? You can find the answers to all these, and other, questions by using the data dictionary. In the SQL interface, the data dictionary is called the *system-wide catalog*. SQL also allows developers to create other catalogs. Each SQL collection (the SQL name for a library in the native interface) can optionally have its own catalog.

Data and Program Independence
The combination of the physical and logical files on the AS/400 provides the independence between the programs and the data those programs use. Separating the description of the data from the program allows application programs to look at the data differently than just the way the data is physically stored. In keeping with the technology independence of the architecture, this concept of separating programs and data was fundamental to the original design of the System/38 and the AS/400.

Let's look at the structure of the physical file, which contains the description of the data along with the data itself. This description is often called the *external file description*, and both the System/38 and the AS/400 are said to have externally described data. The advantage of having externally described data is that the program does not have to contain the data descriptions. This means the program does not dictate how the data is to be physically stored in the system. Also, a single application program can operate on files that contain data in different formats.

The logical file format is as external as that of the physical file, so logical files can be used to redefine the record format for a program. Figure 6.1 shows a very simple example of how a program uses a logical file to give a different view of the data stored in a physical file. This example illustrates some of the functions that are available with the use of logical files.

The example in the figure illustrates field selection. Each record in the physical file contains six fields; yet the program, through the logical file, only sees four of the fields. This ability to exclude fields from the logical file helps to enforce field-level security. Users can access only those fields they are allowed to see. This example only illustrates a small piece of how the AS/400 enforces security. We will cover the topic in detail in Chapter 7.

Another function illustrated in the example is the capability to reorder the fields in the record. The positions of the gross field and the federal income tax (FIT) field in the logical record have been reversed from the way the fields are stored in the physical file. In other words, the program is independent of the order of the fields.

Still another function Figure 6.1 illustrates is the redefining or remapping of the record's fields. The gross field in the physical file is stored as a seven-position, packed-decimal field with two positions to the right of the decimal point. The program is written, however, to expect the gross field as an eight-position, zoned-decimal field with two positions to the right of the decimal

Figure 6.1 Data and Program Independence

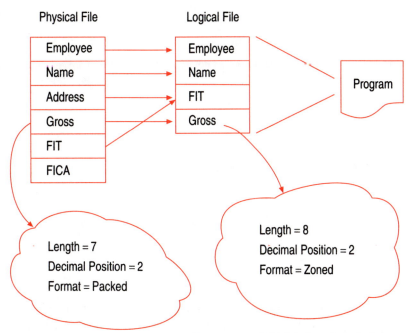

Program uses field definitions in logical view

point. The logical file provides the view the program is expecting. It also provides the conversion between the packed- and the zoned-decimal formats.

The use of multiple logical files over the same physical file enables alternate access paths and data sharing for different programs. Figure 6.2 shows a second logical file for a second program that has been added to our simple example. Each program now has a different view of the records contained in the physical file and each program can only access the fields that program is allowed to see. The fields in the two logical files that are the same allow the programs to share data.

A very important point here is that each program sees the same physical data — there are no copies of the data. An update by one program is immediately seen by the other program. This capability to always have programs working on the current data, and not a copy, has been a characteristic of the System/38 and the AS/400 for more than 15 years.

Figure 6.2 Data Sharing

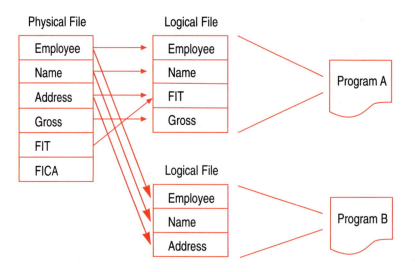

Data Security

Logical files allow data to be secured at the record and field level. In the preceding examples, we saw how the field levels can be secured by omitting the field from the logical file. Not shown in our simple examples is the capability to select records. We can accomplish record-level selection with select and omit logic in the logical file. This lets users access only those records that meet the selection criteria.

If a user is not given access to a particular file, that file is secured. If a user who does not have authority to use the access path that shows gross earnings, for example, tries to run a program that uses that path, the program will fail. All logical and physical files in the AS/400 are system objects, and we need the proper authority before we can access one of these objects. Data security is accomplished with a combination of the logical files and the authorization management component of the operating system.

For a given user who needs to access a particular physical file, we might

- Give authority to the whole file, through authorization management
- Give authority for certain types of file operations (e.g., read, but not update), through authorization management
- Give authority to certain fields, using a logical file
- Give authority to certain records, using a logical file

Data Integrity and Recovery

Integrity of the data in the database is crucial for any business. With multiple users accessing and changing the data simultaneously, it is possible for data to be corrupted. The AS/400 database provides several facilities to ensure data integrity.

Recovery facilities are also necessary in case something does happen either to corrupt the data or to make it unavailable. Several things can happen in a system that will require some form of database recovery. We often think recovery is needed only because the hardware may fail. The AS/400 even has several functions to prevent the need to recover when there is a hardware failure; we usually call these availability functions. While hardware failures may be the most common reason for database recovery, programs can also fail, resulting in the need for recovery.

A complete discussion of data integrity and recovery would fill a book. In this section, we can only introduce and discuss briefly the facilities the AS/400 database provides. Later in the chapter, we will see how some of these facilities are implemented in the machine.

Journaling

A *journal* is a chronological record of changes made to a set of data. The purpose of a journal is to provide a means to reconstruct a previous version of the set of data. Several types of journaling are supported in an AS/400, including database journaling. When a change is made to a record in a database file that is being journaled, a copy of the record is written to the journal, along with information describing the cause of the change.

Two OS/400 objects support journaling. One is a journal, and the other is a journal receiver. The journal identifies which objects are to be journaled. The journal receiver contains the journal entries. Journal receivers can be written immediately to disk for safe keeping.

Each journal entry contains several pieces of information. Some of this information includes the file name, the library name, the program name, the relative record number, the time, and the date. The entry also has the job identification, the user, and the workstation. The copy of the changed record is written to the journal receiver along with this information. As an option, the AS/400 also can write a copy of the record before the change is made.

Database journals are used to recover from both system failures and from database problems caused by programs. If an abnormal system termination occurs because of a hardware or software failure, the journaled database files are automatically recovered when the system is re-IPLed. These database files will be updated to reflect all activity recorded in the journal receivers. If erroneous data is entered by a user program into a physical file that is journaled, the AS/400 provides the ability to do either forward or backward recovery of the file. Forward recovery first restores a backup version of the file. Then the journal entries are applied to the file until the point in time just before the user program entered the erroneous data. Backward recovery removes the erroneous changes from the file. Backward recovery requires that the journaling write the copy of the record both before and after the change.

System-Managed Access Path Protection
One of the difficulties the AS/400 and its users have encountered in the past was long IPL times after an abnormal system termination. When an access path has been opened for the purpose of updating a file, and an abnormal termination occurs, that access path has to be rebuilt when the system is re-IPLed. Recall from the last chapter that we discussed the capability to delay logical file maintenance. This means that the integrity of the logical file is exposed if the system terminates abnormally. Depending on the number and size of the keyed access paths that are open, the time required to rebuild them can be very long — several hours is not uncommon for a larger system.

As we just saw, the AS/400 offers the capability to journal files, including the logical files. If a user journals the access paths, the IPL time can be substantially reduced. The potential problem is that the user must first determine which files to journal, estimate the size of the journal receivers, and issue the commands to start the journaling. Some customers do this, but most do not. IBM designed System-Managed Access Path Protection (SMAPP) to do this journaling automatically. The system calculates the maximum amount of time it will allow for rebuilding access paths during an IPL after an abnormal termination. This maximum allowable time is used by the system to determine how much access-path journaling will be required. The user can always override this system-calculated maximum time with a larger or smaller value. The smaller the value, the more system resources will be required for the journaling. Any journaling requires a trade-off to be made between the system resources used during normal operations and the recovery time.

Once the maximum allowable time is either calculated or set by the user, the system looks at all the keyed access paths that exist in the database. It then calculates the total time required to rebuild all these access paths. If this total time exceeds the maximum allowable time, the system will automatically begin to log selective access paths to guarantee that the maximum allowable time will not be exceeded.

SMAPP uses a special logging area that requires no action on the part of the user. The logging area is circular, meaning it wraps around on itself. The system will always keep enough entries in this logging area to ensure that the maximum time objective is met.

Commitment Control
With multiple users able to access and change the contents of records in a physical file, there are times when data integrity is exposed. Suppose one user fetches a record with the intention of updating a field in that record.

What happens if some other user is also in the process of updating the same field in the record? If the second user changes the field after the first user has fetched it, we could have a data integrity problem. Fortunately, the database provides concurrent update protection so this won't happen. There are, however, more complex situations involving changes to multiple records that the system does not automatically protect against.

Suppose, for example, we have a situation where changes to multiple, related records must be made at the same time. The usual example to describe this situation involves a transaction at a cash machine. A customer at the terminal initiates the transaction by inserting a cash card in the machine, keying in a security code, and selecting the type of transaction. This causes the customer record to be read from the database in the host computer. That database can be in a system across town or across the world. If the customer has requested a cash withdrawal, the record is checked to see if there is a sufficient balance. The balance is then decremented by the amount requested, and a message is sent to the cash machine to dispense the cash. What if there is a failure, and the machine is unable to dispense the cash? Before completing this failed transaction, we would want to roll back the change to the customer's balance. The facility to do this is *commitment control*.

Because it is not normally possible to perform all changes simultaneously, the system must protect the group of related records and not release them until all changes have completed. A COMMIT operation lets the system make the changes to the group of records with what appears to be a single unit of work. If all changes cannot be made, the entire group of changes can be removed through the ROLLBACK operation. Commitment control uses journaling to accomplish these operations.

Triggers

A *trigger* is defined as an action that automatically occurs whenever a change is made to a physical file. Triggers provide a convenient way to tie related database activities together. They are a form of "roll-your-own" database integrity built into the file definition. Situations often occur when a change to the database, such as adding or deleting a record, requires some other action to be taken. A trigger can invoke a program to take the required action. In other situations, a change to an existing record may call for a program to be run to check the value of a field in the record. For example, an update to a record in an inventory file may cause the quantity of items in stock to fall below a predetermined value. A trigger on this file could initiate a program every time an update is made to check the value and to reorder the item from a supplier if the value is too low.

When a trigger is added to a physical file, three attributes need to be defined. The first is the event that will cause the trigger to fire. A trigger event can be either an insert, an update, or a delete of a record from the file. The second attribute to define is when to fire the trigger — before or after the event. Finally, the third attribute to define is the identification of the trigger program to be run. The trigger program is a user-supplied program that can be written in any high-level language supported by the AS/400.

From the above, we can infer that up to six triggers can be defined for each physical file. For each update, insert, and delete, two triggers can be defined — one that runs before the event and one that runs after the event. These triggers are added using the Add Physical File Trigger command and can be removed with the Remove Physical File Trigger command.

Referential Integrity

In the real world, data in one physical file is dependent on data in another file. If a program updates one file without regard to the other, the integrity of the data may be compromised. It is often the responsibility of the application program to ensure that the dependencies are handled. *Referential integrity* is a facility built into the AS/400 database that removes this responsibility from the application programs.

Referential integrity allows data consistency to be maintained across two physical files. It allows rules or constraints to be defined on one physical file to ensure that every record has a corresponding or matching record in the second file. A program will be prevented from modifying a record if doing so would violate the rules.

As a simple example, suppose we have a customer master file that contains a record for each of our customers. The customer ID is used as a key for this file. Within the database, there are other files that also use the customer ID as a key. We might want to add a referential constraint to each of these dependent files to ensure that no application program is allowed to add a customer ID to a file unless the ID already exists in the customer master file. Obviously, we could create far more complex scenarios to ensure database integrity.

High-Availability Disk Systems

Disks are mechanical devices, and mechanical devices can fail. The standard form of protection for any computer system is to periodically save the data on disks to some other media, usually tape. This backup copy contains a snapshot of the database, or part of the database, at some instant in time. In case there is a problem with the data on the disk, the copy of the data on the tape can be used to restore the lost information. Earlier, we discussed forward recovery of the database using a journal. The first step was to restore the backup copy of the data. Then the journal entries from the time the backup was made are applied until the database has been recovered.

The AS/400 provides extensive save/restore facilities. Sometimes, however, the time required to restore lost data if a disk fails is unacceptable for a business. Usually, the system is unavailable to the user during the restore operation. This can be a major problem if the disk has to be physically replaced before the data can be restored. An alternative is to have a disk subsystem that can tolerate a disk failure without causing the system to become unavailable. The AS/400 supports two types of high-availability disk protection. The first uses disk mirroring and the second uses disk arrays.

Disk mirroring requires that disk drives are paired together to provide total redundancy. Whenever the system issues a disk write, the data is written to both disks in the pair. All the data on one disk is duplicated on the second disk. If one of the disks should fail, the data is available from the second disk; the system can continue to run, unless the second disk also fails. To guarantee an even higher level of availability, the disks in the pair can be attached to separate disk controllers, on separate I/O processors, and with separate buses. Chapter 10 describes the details of the AS/400's I/O structure, and how these components interact with one another.

Mirroring provides the highest level of availability; but it is expensive, because it requires total duplication of the disks. Another approach involves the use of disk arrays. With disk arrays, disks are grouped into sets and data is written to all the disks in the set. A sector is a fixed block of data on the disk. A page in memory is usually stored in multiple sectors on the disk, and a write operation spreads the data across the disks in the set.

Adding a redundant disk to the array offers the opportunity to discover a failed disk and automatically recover the lost information. This technology is known as *redundant arrays of inexpensive disks* (RAID). The technique used for RAID technology is to perform an *exclusive or* (XOR) operation on the data in all sectors in the set.

Anyone who has played with this binary operator knows that after two operands are XORed together, either of the operands can be re-created by simply XORing the result and the other operand. Figure 6.3 is an example of such an XOR operation. The XOR operation yields a value of true (i.e., a 1) if — and only if — one of the operands is true (i.e., is a 1) and the other is false (i.e., a 0). Otherwise, if both are true or both are false, this operation yields a value of false (i.e., a 0), as this example illustrates.

The data stored in each sector of a disk is XORed with the data in the corresponding sectors on all the other disks in the set. The result of the XOR operation is stored in a sector on the redundant disk. If a disk failure should occur, the data on a failed sector can be recovered by XORing the data in the corresponding sectors of all the good disks in the set. To prevent any one disk in the set from being overused, a different disk is used as the redundant disk for different sets of sectors. Thus, any given disk in the set will contain some database data and some of the XOR results.

Data integrity, recovery, and availability are major topics for any computer system. We have just touched on some of the facilities the AS/400 provides to ensure database integrity and recovery from failures. Our discussion has not been all-inclusive, but we have covered the highlights of this support.

Figure 6.3 An Example of XOR Operation

```
                Operand 1  = 1101 1010
                Operand 2  = 1000 1100
    Operand 1 XOR Operand 2 = 0101 0110 = Result
```

To Re-Create Operand 1:
```
                Result  = 0101 0110
              Operand 2 = 1000 1100
    Result XOR Operand 2 = 1101 1010 = Operand 1
```

To Re-Create Operand 2:
```
                Result  = 0101 0110
              Operand 1 = 1101 1010
    Result XOR Operand 1 = 1000 1100 = Operand 2
```

Other Database Functions

DB2 for OS/400 includes several additional functions to enhance the AS/400's usefulness in both a client/server and a distributed database environment. Other functions enhance database performance. We will look at some of the more important ones in this section.

Stored Procedures

Stored procedures provide one of the best ways to enhance the AS/400's performance of client/server applications. A CALL statement in SQL allows a client application to call a stored procedure and have it execute on the AS/400 server. In this way, an entire business transaction can be accomplished with a single access to the server. Without stored procedures, numerous database accesses to the server might be required to perform a single business transaction. A stored procedure can, with only a couple of exceptions, be any program in the AS/400. The program can be written in any high-level language and can even contain SQL statements. Access to a stored procedure is only available through the SQL interface using the CALL statement.

National Language Support

In V3R1, the first step was taken toward the implementation of Unicode on the AS/400 by encoding object names in some of the integrated file system components using this multibyte encoding scheme. Unicode allows multiple character sets to co-exist in the same encoding scheme.

With V3R6, this support was expanded to allow database files to store data encoded in Unicode (UCS2, level 1). For example, French, German, English, Hebrew, Chinese, Russian, and other language data can exist in one database file. SQL has the ability to convert to and from Unicode, so that query activities and data manipulation on Unicode data can be done in an application. Also new for V3R6 was locale support, enabling programmers to create applications that adapt themselves to various cultural dependencies, such as currency symbols, date and time formats, numeric formats, collating sequences, and case conversions.

Predictive Query Governor
Most relational databases provide some form of a query governor to ensure that no single query runs too long. After some preset time, the governor in most databases stops the query. DB2 for OS/400 uses a predictive query governor to prevent a query from running if it will run beyond a preset time. In this way, system resources are not wasted on a query that will be stopped anyway.

A query optimizer is used to analyze the way the database is to be accessed to perform a query before it is started. As part of this analysis, the optimizer predicts the amount of time it will take to perform the query. This predicted time is then compared to a query time limit associated with the current user. If the predicted time exceeds the time limit, a message is sent to the user. The user can then choose either to end the query or to run the query even though it exceeds the limit.

Database Performance Enhancements
DB2 for OS/400 provides several mechanisms to allow performance prediction and tuning for various database operations. For example, you can use an EXPLAIN command to predict or review the execution characteristics of a query. This function gathers information about how SQL is used in a program. You can then use the information from EXPLAIN to tune the performance of a query either by making changes to the database or to the query request. Still other functions allow you to block fetch and insert operations, which means you can manipulate arrays of data with a single command.

Also implemented are advanced caching mechanisms for database operations. Users can define both an expert cache and a static cache. The user can define an expert cache in memory that automatically expands and contracts in size. The expert cache uses artificial intelligence (AI) algorithms to dynamically change the cache size based on work load, predictive database activity, and allocated resources. Likewise, the user can define a static cache in memory to allow an entire table or a portion of a table to fit into a memory-resident area.

Distributed Databases
The AS/400 allows an application program to access a database on a remote system as well as the one on the local system; the location of the data is transparent to the application. This means the application can process a database file without knowing where it resides. It also means parts of the

database can be moved to another system without requiring changes to the application programs.

The capability to access a database on a remote system and for other remote systems to access AS/400 data is accomplished through the implementation of two key architectures. One is the Distributed Relational Database Architecture (DRDA), and the other is the Distributed Data Management (DDM) architecture.

The SQL interface uses DRDA to access remote data. An SQL CONNECT statement that includes the name of the remote database is first used to establish the link to the remote database. A directory on the local system is used to look up the remote database name and to identify the specific system where the remote database resides. After the communications link has been made between the systems, SQL requests can be sent to the remote database. The database manager on the remote system performs the SQL request and returns the records that satisfy the request to the local system.

The AS/400's native database interface uses the DDM architecture. A DDM file is used to define the file name on the remote system and the name of the remote system itself. When an application program requires remote data, the DDM file is linked to the program with a command. After the communications link between the systems has been established, the application program can work with the remote file. With the DDM approach, file processing is performed on the local system, as opposed to the DRDA approach, where the processing occurs on the remote system. DDM sends all records in the file back to the local system; whereas with DRDA, only the records that meet the selection criteria are sent back to the local system. If only a few records are involved in a particular database operation, the DRDA approach may result in better application performance because there is less communications overhead.

Gateways to Other Databases

The AS/400 works with databases that support the DRDA and DDM architecture as just described. The AS/400 also provides an integrated approach to support access to other databases. This support allows an AS/400 to work directly with any vendor's database on another system in the network. In addition to a Distributed Database Directory in OS/400, there is a Distributed Database Driver Manager. This driver manager works with the drivers for the target databases or file systems. These drivers for various Unix and PC databases let an AS/400 application work with these databases in the same way it does with any DRDA database.

DataPropagator for OS/400

In a distributed system environment, multiple copies of the same database file can exist on separate systems. A change to one copy is not immediately reflected in another copy. The same file can exist on many systems at a different level of update. DataPropagator for OS/400 provides a mechanism to replicate changes to a file on all systems. At some user-defined time interval, the changes for a particular file are replicated across all systems. Because this approach uses IBM's replicator technology, the changes can be replicated across any DB2 database (DB2 for OS/2, DB/2 for AIX, and DB2 for OS/400) in the network.

OptiConnect for OS/400

With a single system, everything from the processing capabilities to the data itself must be contained on the system. As a single system, the AS/400 supports some very large configurations, including systems with multiple processors, to handle the needs of most large customers. There are, however, customers who have performance requirements beyond what is available with a single AS/400. Even with a network of systems, the overhead of the communications links will limit the amount of performance improvement that can be realized by splitting an application across multiple systems. OptiConnect for OS/400 (hereafter referred to as OptiConnect) may provide the answer to increased performance for such application and database processing.

OptiConnect is a product that allows AS/400s to be coupled together, via fiber optics, to achieve greater transaction processing power. Typically, database processing is separated from application processing and put on a different machine. In this way, the separate systems are configured into a tiered processing cluster, with some machines dedicated to database processing and others dedicated to application processing.

OptiConnect uses DDM, but with an important difference. DDM in a network uses communications protocols across the communications lines or LANs. A communications protocol assumes transmission over a "noisy" line and builds layers of redundancy and checking into the transmission. This tends to reduce the speed at which the useful data is transmitted across the line. An optical bus connection is clean enough that most of this redundancy can be eliminated, thereby greatly enhancing the performance of the link. With OptiConnect, as few as 3 milliseconds are added to the time required to access the database on a remote system compared to the time it takes to access the local database. This is equivalent to increasing the access time of the disk drives on the local system by 3 milliseconds.

The exact performance improvement that will result by splitting application and database operations varies depending on a number of factors, such as percent of database utilization. However, with the ability to include up to 32 machines in an OptiConnect cluster, it is safe to say that a very large configuration can be created. In fact, using clusters, the potential growth from the largest possible configuration in 1994 to the largest possible configuration in 1995 is 50 times! Now that's scalability.

OptiConnect can be used for more than just growth. The fiber-optics-based cabling system can replace existing LAN connections that use DDM to provide faster more reliable network connections. OptiConnect can also be used between duplicate systems to create a high-availability and high-recovery option for critical applications and data.

Parallel Databases

In the future, all large databases will exploit the parallelism that exists in computer systems. In a system such as the AS/400, with multiple processors, database operations can be split among several processors to achieve a higher level of performance. For example, a query could be broken into multiple queries, each of which looks at a part of the total database. By executing all these queries concurrently on separate processors against separate parts of the database, the total query performance could be greatly enhanced. The performance of other database operations, such as a large join, could also be significantly improved by breaking the operation into smaller parts and using parallelism to create the total join file.

In 1994, parallel processing using input/output processors (IOPs) was implemented for queries. The query optimizer can use multiple-disk I/O streams to implement the parallel processing operations across a number of IOPs. New for 1995 is the AS/400's capability to divide the database operations across multiple processors in an n-way system or even across multiple AS/400s. These two approaches are described briefly in the following sections.

Symmetric Multiprocessing (SMP) Parallel Database

This parallel database capability works on any AS/400 SMP models, which we previously called n-way systems. SMP models have multiple main processors; operating system and application programs can run on any or all processors simultaneously. SMP allows multiple processors to share memory and disk space in parallel to resolve queries in a fraction of the time it would take on a single processor. The queries are broken into smaller units of work, which are then divided between the processors, giving an even distribution of the query workload across all processors. The Change Query Attributes (CHGQRYA) command includes an option to allow the user to specify that the query is to take advantage of the multiple processors.

The types of query functions that will benefit from this enhancement are table scan, group-by, index scan, and join. Some functions internal to SLIC, such as index build (discussed in the "Machine Index" sections of this chapter), will also benefit from the SMP parallel database support. All these enhancements will be available on V3R1 and V3R6, except for the parallel index build, which is a function in V3R6 only.

Loosely Coupled Parallel Database

This parallel database support allows multiple AS/400s to be connected together to function as one database. This type of interconnection is often referred to as a *loosely coupled* cluster, because each system (usually called a node) in the cluster runs its own operating system and can only address its own memory. OptiConnect, for example, allows AS/400 nodes to be coupled in this manner. In Chapter 12, we will look at multicomputer clusters and their future in more detail.

Loosely coupled parallel database support allows queries to be broken into smaller units of work that each node can resolve. The difference from the SMP parallel database support is that here each node has its own memory and disk space. Each node in the cluster will have a portion of the physical file or table. The entire query is processed on each node against the portion of the file resident on that node. Because each node is simply an AS/400, a node may contain one or more processors.

An application on any one of the systems in the cluster can access the entire physical file or table by simply opening it as if existed entirely on the local system. DB2 for OS/400 will make this accessibility transparent to both the application and the end user. New CL commands have been added to name all the systems in the node group, and new parameters have been added to the CRTPF and CREATE TABLE commands to allow distribution of files and tables across the nodes. Once distributed across the nodes, a file acts like a local file with respect to insert, update, and delete operations. Initially, referential integrity and triggers are not supported for files that are distributed across nodes.

A major advantage of the loosely coupled parallel database support is that there is no upper limit to the number of nodes that can ultimately be interconnected, which means performance and capacity scalability in the future is essentially unlimited. The largest initial configuration supports a 32-system network. This yields a 16-terabyte database with 128 processors running in parallel (assuming all four-way processor systems). That's not bad for a start.

We are now at a point where we can drop down a level and look at the internal implementation of the database functions. Following that, we will see how we can use a machine index to support many of the database operations we have just discussed.

Implementation of Database Functions

As we saw in Chapter 4, implementation of the AS/400 database functions is split across the MI boundary. Most of the discussion in the previous sections has dealt with the database that is implemented as part of DB2 for OS/400 above the MI. In this section, we will look at some of the MI system objects that are used by DB2 for OS/400. We will also see how some of the operations on these system objects are implemented in the SLIC below the MI. We don't have space to describe in detail the implementation of all the database features and functions that have been covered so far in this chapter, but we will look at some of the more important ones. Following this, we will look at the implementation of the machine index the database and other AS/400 components use. We single out the machine index implementation not only because it is important to many AS/400 components, but also because it is an interesting structure to study.

The size of the database the SLIC supports is very large, as shown in the following list of maximum sizes:

- Up to 240 gigabytes per physical file
- More than 2 billion records per physical file
- Up to 4 gigabytes per index
- Up to 2,048 bytes per key

I should point out that these database size limitations are imposed by the current SLIC implementation. The MI has no inherent limit on the size of the system objects, because it is technology independent. The SLIC is technology dependent, meaning field sizes in certain internal data structures have to be preassigned, which in turn defines certain upper limits. We will see some of these limits as we look at the internal implementations. As with any good design, there is some room built in for expansion should the need arise. Let's start by looking at those MI system objects that support the database.

Database Objects
In the previous chapter, we introduced the three main system objects that support the database. These objects are data spaces, data-space indexes, and cursors. Like all the other system objects, they occupy multiple segments in the single-level store. Each has a base segment containing a segment header, an EPA header, and a customized header for the object. Each also has an associated space segment.

Data Spaces
Data spaces contain the database records. The records in a given data space are homogeneous and fixed in length. In other words, all records in the same data space look alike. The records are stored in arrival sequence, and all records that have been deleted still occupy space.

Three types of segments make up a data-space object. In addition to the base and associated space segments, up to 120 data-space records segments can be part of this object. The data-space records segments, as their name implies, contain the database records. Each entry in a data-space records segment has a status byte and one database record. The status byte provides information about the record, such as its validity, whether or not it has been deleted, and so on.

Each record in a data-space records segment has a number, called the ordinal number. The ordinal number identifies the record position in the segment. Do not confuse ordinal number, which starts again with each segment, with the more familiar relative record number, as it is often referred to at the OS/400 level. The relative record numbers contained in a logical file or a view indicate the location of the data in the physical file or table. These same numbers are sometimes called the data-space entry numbers in the MI.

Starting with zero, the ordinal number identifies whether the record is the first, second, or *n*th one in the segment. Because all records are fixed in length, the ordinal numbers do not have to be stored in the segment. By knowing the ordinal number and the length of each record, we can find the starting byte location of any record in the segment. We will see shortly how the ordinal number is used to locate records in the database.

The base segment does contain information about the data space, but its primary role is to contain the addresses of the many data-space records segments. The base segment also contains the addresses of the data-space indexes that are used with this data space.

The associated space contains the field descriptor table, which provides the description of each field in the record. The associated space also contains a work area that the OS/400 part of the database uses. For example, pointers to logical cursors are kept in the associated space.

Data-Space Indexes

A data-space index provides an alternate ordering for the records in a data space. A binary radix tree is used to provide the alternate ordering. Later in the chapter, in the "Binary Radix Trees" section, we will look at the implementation of such a tree and see how it is used to support several functions on the AS/400, including the data-space index.

Numerous options are available for arranging the data-space index. A data-space index supports variable length keys. The value of the keys can be calculated using a variety of operators such as concatenate, add, subtract, multiply, and so on. You can build a data-space index over as many as 32 data spaces. Options for ordering the index include ascending, descending, numeric, and absolute value. Finally, there are the maintenance options. Updates to the index can be applied immediately or they can be delayed. Delaying updates to an index saves the overhead of maintaining it when a change to the underlying data space occurs and the index is not being used.

In Chapter 5, we briefly looked at examples of objects, including a data-space index. We saw that a data-space index was composed of three segment types: a base segment, an associated space segment, and a delayed maintenance segment. We have already discussed the later two segments, but we need to take a little closer look at the base segment.

The base segment contains the attributes of the alternate collating sequence this index provides. The base segment has a table that describes the way the index views each field in the record of the data space. This is the logical view description. The base segment also contains up to 32 addresses to data spaces that this index can cover. Finally, the base segment contains the binary radix tree.

The binary radix tree may not totally fit into the base segment. To accommodate a very large tree, you can attach a fourth segment type to contain portions of the tree. In fact, up to 64 of these tree segments can be attached to a data-space index.

Each key stored in a tree segment has the byte string containing the actual key value, followed by a pair of fields that serve as a suffix for the key. The pair of fields is generally called the *relative address*. The first field contains the data space number and the identification of the data space records segment. The second field contains the ordinal number of the record in the segment. These two numbers uniquely identify the record associated with the key, and this ID is analogous to the relative record number in the logical file or view.

Cursors

A cursor provides the mechanism to view data in the data space; all data access is via cursors. The cursor we are describing in this section is an MI system object. DB2 for OS/400 supports both scrollable and sequential file cursors as defined in the 1992 SQL standard. This SQL cursor is not the same as the MI system object known as a cursor, although the MI system object is used to support the SQL cursor.

As described earlier in this chapter, records for a physical file are stored in members. A physical file can have one or more members. Members provide a convenient way to partition data in a single physical file. Logical files use this same multimember concept. We also saw that SQL tables and views are limited to a single member per table or view. A cursor is identified with each file member. A cursor can provide access to the data-space records in arrival sequence or in keyed sequence using an index. In other words, a cursor can point directly to a data space, or it can point to a data space through a data-space index. A single cursor can cover multiple data spaces and there can be multiple cursors over the same data space. A cursor keeps track of the position in an access path held by a program (or job or activation group). This function helps explain why a cursor is called a cursor.

A cursor can also provide a mapping to and from a data space. The mapping allows the data to be viewed differently from the way it is stored in the data space. Examples of the kinds of mapping are field renaming, arithmetic and character-string expressions, and data-type conversions.

A cursor also provides the capability to select records. The arithmetic and character-string mapping functions are used to provide this selection. A typical place to specify such record selection is the WHERE clause of an SQL statement (arithmetic expressions are not available in DDS). By restricting a user's authority to cursors (i.e., to access paths) that select only certain records, you can prevent the user from viewing the records not included. This combination of authority and selection is used to enforce database security.

Two segments make up a cursor, a base segment, and an associated space. The base segment contains two sets of addresses to identify the data spaces and the data-space indexes the cursor can use. Up to 32 data spaces and up to 32 data-space indexes can be identified. The only case where more than one data-space index may be required is that of a join-logical file (not an SQL view). The base segment also contains the mapping code and the selection code the cursor uses. The associated space of the cursor contains the member's text and attributes. The member-level links are maintained by the OS/400 component of the database.

Now that we have looked at each of the three main system objects that support the database, we are ready to see how a user accesses database files in the AS/400. We will do just that in the next section.

The User's Path to Data

All user database accesses must come through OS/400 and the MI. Only SLIC has direct access to the data. From a user's perspective, accessing an OS/400 database file is accomplished with an open file operation. We will see that this function is accomplished at the MI with an ACTIVATE CURSOR instruction. Likewise, when a user wants to close a file, there is a DEACTIVATE CURSOR instruction at the MI.

When accessing a data space, the user can specify several open file command options. These include the operation (read, write, update, or delete) and the number of records. When a cursor spans multiple data spaces, the user may define a subset of these data spaces with which to work. This subset definition is specified at file creation time with a CRTLF command, but this definition may be overridden at run time with an Override Database File (OVRDBF) command before a file is opened. How long to wait for a record, if the record is locked, can also be defined by the user. This, too, is specified at file creation time; but it can be overridden before the file is opened.

The user can access the data space in either a random or a sequential mode. In the sequential-access mode, multiple pages can be transferred into main memory from the disk with a single operation, called a *bring*. The user specifies the size of the bring by using the number of records option. This is done in the OVRDBF command or in the Open Query File (OPNQRYF) command. In the random-access mode, usually one page is brought. The random mode is only available if the data space has an index. When a data-space index is used, the database code in SLIC uses a look-ahead scheme to bring in the next logical page in the index.

Because a cursor is needed to access data in a data space, MI instructions exist to provide user access by opening the cursor (ACTIVATE CURSOR) and to close the cursor (DEACTIVATE CURSOR) when the user is finished.

These functions of activating and deactivating a cursor at the MI are equivalent to opening and closing a file in OS/400. The associated space of an activated cursor contains the open data path (ODP) information for the member that is open.

Executing an ACTIVATE CURSOR instruction in the MI causes the cursor to be attached to the process that activated it. Later, we will look at another MI object called the *process control block*. A process is a unit of work in the system, and each process has a process control block. The cursor is attached to this process control block. If the process activates more than one cursor, a doubly linked list of the cursors is chained to the process control block. Further, no other process can now use these cursors. If more than one user wants to share the same cursor, a clone of the cursor has to be created. This cloning operation occurs when a cursor is activated.

This brings us to the subject of permanent and temporary cursors. A permanent cursor is associated with each file member, and every file member can have one and only one permanent cursor. When a clone is created, it is a temporary cursor. If a cursor is activated to provide an open data path to a file member and some other process has already activated the same cursor, a temporary clone of the cursor is created. The mapping code and the selection code are not kept in a temporary cursor. Addresses in the temporary cursor point back to a permanent cursor that contains these codes. The reason for this approach is to save space.

OS/400 has a convention that it always makes a temporary copy of the permanent cursor, using the Create Duplicate Object (CRTDUPOBJ) instruction, and then it only activates the temporary cursors. In this way, a permanent cursor can be a representation of the file member. Other than this convention, no member object exists at the MI. Further, all open data paths are temporary cursors. Again, this arrangement is the result of an OS/400 convention and is not a restriction of the MI.

SLIC Journaling

Earlier in this chapter, we described the database journaling function. The basic functions for logging changes that occur in the database are provided below the MI. Two MI system objects provide this support: *journal ports* and *journal spaces*. A journal port manages the journal definition, and the journal space is the container for the journal entries. These two system objects support the OS/400 journal and journal receiver objects. Notice, once again, the name change at the MI boundary.

A journal port, like so many other system objects, has two segments. The base segment contains addresses to the objects being journaled. It also contains the addresses of the current journal spaces. The OS/400 portion of the database uses the associated space segment.

A *journal space object* is a special MI system object that can have many segments. The base segment contains the address of the journal port. It also contains the addresses of up to 120 journal data segments. A *journal data segment* is another type of segment that can be part of a journal space system object. The journal entries are stored in the journal data segments.

The journal entries themselves are variable in length. Each entry contains a length field; a sequence number; a type field; time and date stamps; user, program and job identifications; and the information being journaled. It is important to note that these entries cannot be updated or deleted. The purpose of journaling is simply to keep copies of changes to the database in case a recovery is required.

Commitment Control in SLIC

The basic functions to commit or roll back changes to the database were discussed earlier in this chapter. The support for these functions exists at the MI and in the SLIC portion of the database. The MI system object that provides this support is the *commit block*. A commit block contains the changes made to an object under commitment control. Commit blocks are associated with processes.

Objects are added to or removed from the commit block. The commit block also holds the record locks. The COMMIT instruction at MI frees the locks. The DECOMMIT instruction, which nearly every high-level language (including the OS/400 command set) calls ROLLBACK, backs out all changes made during the transaction, frees the locks, and repositions the cursor to the position at the start of the transaction.

Machine Indexes

The one final topic on the internal support for the AS/400 database is indexes. We have already seen two forms of an index. In the last chapter, we introduced a system object called the independent index. In this chapter, we have discussed the data-space index. We said both of these system objects contain a binary radix tree.

An index provides a way to rapidly find an entry in a large table. A better definition of an index is an organized set of information to facilitate a fast search over a set of entities. An index is fundamental to many AS/400 components, or to those of any other system, for that matter. Because of this, the decision was made in the original System/38 design to create the most efficient index possible and build it into the part of the machine below the MI. In this way, all system components that need an index can use the one that is built in rather than having to create one of their own. This built-in index is called the *machine index*.

A machine index is useful in table searches, space addressing, and sorting. It is used in several places in the AS/400. In the database, a machine index is used in the data-space index, the journal transaction list, and the commit key list for a data-space index. Storage management makes extensive use of machine indexes for many of its directories. Machine indexes are also used in contexts and in authority searches. OS/400 uses the independent index object for several functions, including message handling, security, and spooling.

Some general characteristics of a machine index are that it

- Allows generic searches to find groups of related entries
- Manages the space used by the index
- Minimizes page faulting through its design
- Supports variable length keys up to 2,048 bytes
- Uses a binary search algorithm
- Stores entries in a partitioned binary radix tree (as described in the "Internals of a Binary Radix Tree" section later in this chapter)

Binary Searches

A simple way to understand a binary search is to think about a number-guessing game that most people have played at one time or another. The idea of the game is for one player to select a number within a range of numbers, say between one and 1,000. A second player attempts to guess the number in as few tries as possible. For each try, the second player is told whether the guess is high, low, or equal to the number.

A technique to quickly guess the number for this game is to use the binary number system. To guess a number between one and 1,000, our first guess would be 512 ($2^9 = 512$). If we are told our first guess is high, we know the number is greater than zero and less than 512, so our second guess would be 256 ($2^8 = 256$), the next lower power of 2. If our first guess was low, we know the number is greater than 512, so we select our second guess by adding 512 and 256 to get 768. The process to determine each guess is to add the next lower power of 2 to our previous guess. If the guess is high, we subtract out that power of 2 and add in the next lower one to form our new guess.

Let's look at an example. Suppose the unknown number selected by the first player was 700. Our sequence of guesses would be 512, 768, 640, 704, 672, 688, 696, and finally 700. We would be told that our first guess was low, the second guess was high, the third guess was low, and so on. We used this information each time to compute our next guess and eventually identified the number in eight tries.

If we look at the sequence of high and low responses from the first player in the example above, we get an interesting pattern. The sequence of responses is low, high, low, high, low, low, low, and equal. If we substitute a zero for every high response and a one for every low or equal response, we have created the value of the number in binary. Recognizing that it takes 10 bits to hold any number between one and 1,000, we can represent 700 as 1010111100. We guessed the number by working from left to right and using the high and low responses to tell us whether the bit positions contain zeros or ones.

We will always find the chosen number with this method in 10 or fewer tries. In our example, it took us only eight tries, because the number was divisible by 4, a power of 2. Notice that any odd number would always take 10 tries, one for each bit. We can calculate the maximum number of tries by computing the logarithm to the base 2 of 1,000. Another way to see this is to realize that $2^{10} = 1024$. To guess a number between one and a million using this technique requires only 20 or fewer tries.

This technique illustrates a binary search algorithm that can be used to find an entry in an index. For a balanced index with N entries, only $\log_2 N$ entries must be compared during a search. A balanced structure is one where all the entries are filled in. Our number-guessing example was balanced, because all numbers are present in the series. Even for grossly unbalanced structures, the average number of comparisons is increased by less than 10 percent. A binary search algorithm works very well for a large number of entries, but it is generally not recommended for fewer than 50 entries.

Binary Radix Trees

We can generalize the binary search method described above as a tree structure. The tree will contain two types of nodes: test nodes and terminal nodes. Each test node in the tree tests one bit in the number. Whether the bit is a zero or a one determines which of two lower-level nodes is selected as the next node. Starting at the top of the tree, the first node tests the first bit in the number (the left-most bit). The second layer in the tree has two test nodes, one of which is selected if the first bit was a zero and the other if it was a one. The third layer has four nodes, the fourth layer has eight nodes, and so on, until the tenth layer has 512 test nodes. The eleventh layer is the last layer in this tree and has 1,024 terminal entries. The terminal node uniquely identifies the value of the unknown number.

To find a number, we start at the top of the tree and test the bits from left to right. Each level in the tree tests one of the bits. After 10 tests, we are at one of the terminal nodes and have uniquely identified the number. We have just described a binary tree. It is a balanced tree, because all nodes are present. In a table search, not all nodes need be present, because not all entities in the table are present. In fact, not all the bits in the number need to be tested, meaning some of the levels need not be present. Such a tree would be called a *binary radix tree* to distinguish it from a binary tree, which has all levels. An example will illustrate how the AS/400 uses binary radix trees to implement the machine indexes.

Figure 6.4 shows a simple file with nine records. The ordering of this file is by arrival sequence. Each record has several fields, only a few of which are shown. One of the fields, the name field, is to be used as the key for this file. An index over this file has been built and is also shown in the figure. Each entry in the index has only two fields: the key field and the logical record address. The nine entries in the index are sorted in key sequence. In this

Figure 6.4 Example of a Simple File and Index

File			Index	
Name	**Birth**	**Rank**	**Name**	**LRO**
JONES	082140	A	BAKER	006
SMITH	122750	K	BARNS	007
WU	041259	Z	CARSON	008
MARKLY	111163	T	JOHNSON	005
PETERS	070457	C	JONES	000
JOHNSON	062753	A	MARKLY	003
BAKER	031747	C	PETERS	004
BARNS	090959	B	SMITH	001
CARSON	013147	B	WU	002

example, the keys are sorted alphabetically, with Baker as the first entry and Wu as the last entry. The logical record address field indicates the relative position of the corresponding record in the original file. The relative position always starts with zero for the first record. The entry for Baker identifies Baker's record as the seventh record in the file.

The exact form of this logical record address varies in an AS/400 depending on how the index is being used. For example, in an earlier discussion we saw that each entry in a data-space index segment has a key and a relative address. That relative address contains the data-space number, the identification of the data-space records segment, and the ordinal number for the entry. This relative address uniquely identifies the record associated with the key. Other uses of an index have other forms of relative addresses.

Let's use this index to create a binary radix tree. Figure 6.5 shows the index from Figure 6.4 with the key field expanded in EBCDIC. It is shown both in hexadecimal and in binary form. For example, the first letter in the name Baker has the hexadecimal representation of C2. C2 in binary is 11000010. The second letter in the name Baker has the hexadecimal representation C1 (11000001 in binary). Each key is laid out in memory as a string of ones and zeros as shown in the figure.

We can now use the binary representations of the keys in memory to create a binary radix tree. The technique used to build the tree is to add one key at a time. We first search the bit string for each new entry from left to right to find the first bit that differs in the new key from other keys currently in the tree. Suppose Baker is the only entry in the tree and we want to add Barns. From Figure 6.5 we can see that the first bit (always scanning from left to right) that differs is the fifth bit of the third byte. If we had only the two entries Baker and Barns in the tree, we could distinguish one from the other by just testing the fifth bit of the third byte. If this bit is a zero, the entry is for

Figure 6.5 Binary Representation of Key Fields

Key	Value	EBCDIC	Key Representation Binary
BAKER	006	C2C1D2 ...	1100 0010 1100 0001 1101 0010 ...
BARNS	007	C2C1D9 ...	1100 0010 1100 0001 1101 1001 ...
CARSON	008	C3 ...	1100 0011 ...
JOHNSON	005	D1D6C8 ...	1101 0001 1101 0110 1100 1000 ...
JONES	000	D1D6D5 ...	1101 0001 1101 0110 1101 0101 ...
MARKLY	003	D4 ...	1101 0100 ...
PETERS	004	D7 ...	1101 0111 ...
SMITH	001	E2 ...	1110 0010 ...
WU	002	E6 ...	1110 0110 ...

Baker. If the bit is a one, the entry is for Barns. In a similar manner, if we now want to add Carson to the tree, the first bit from the left that differs from either Baker or Barns is the eighth bit of the first byte.

Figure 6.6 shows the sequence for building the tree. Step 1 has only a terminal node for Baker in the tree. A terminal node contains some text (BAKER in this case) and the logical record address of 006. Step 2 puts Barns into the tree. Here a test node has been added just above Baker in the tree to test bit 5 of the third byte. A test node contains common text (BA) from the keys and the identification of the bit to test in the next byte. In our example with two bytes of common text (BA), we know the bit to be tested is in the next, or the third, byte, without having to explicitly identify the byte. The pattern for selecting the next node is always to take the left node if the tested bit is a zero and take the right node if the bit is a one. A second terminal node for Barns has been added to the right of the first terminal node with the logical record address 007. Note that with the common text removed, these terminal nodes now contain only the remaining text in the names (KER and RNS for Baker and Barns, respectively).

Step 3 puts Carson into the tree. A new test node has been added to test the eighth bit of the first byte. This new test node has no common text. If the test shows the eighth bit of the first byte is a zero, then the Baker/Barns test node on the left is the next node to be checked. If the eighth bit of the first byte is a one, then the terminal node on the right for Carson is the next node. Again, this terminal node contains text (CARSON) and the logical record address 008.

Figure 6.6 Building a Binary Radix Tree

Step 1: Baker is in the tree

```
BAKER
006
```
"Terminal Node"

Step 2: Add Barnes

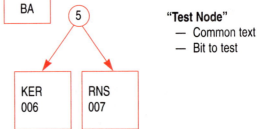

"Test Node"
— Common text
— Bit to test

Step 3: Add Carson

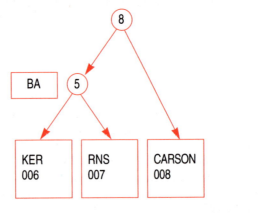

[3] Computer science trees always seem to grow upside down. Who else would put the root at the top with the branches spreading down?

Figure 6.7 shows the whole tree with all nine keys included. The test node at the top of the tree is called the root node.[3] Although this is an example of a relatively small index, it illustrates many of the characteristics of a binary radix tree.

We can find any name that is in the tree by the method we have already described. But what about a name that is not in the tree? Suppose we try to find the name Soltis in the tree. We would test the third bit of the first byte and find it is a one. We then test the sixth bit of the first byte and find it is a zero. This takes us to the terminal node for Smith. The reason for keeping the text in the terminal node is because multiple names can map to the same terminal

Figure 6.7 Binary Radix Tree Example

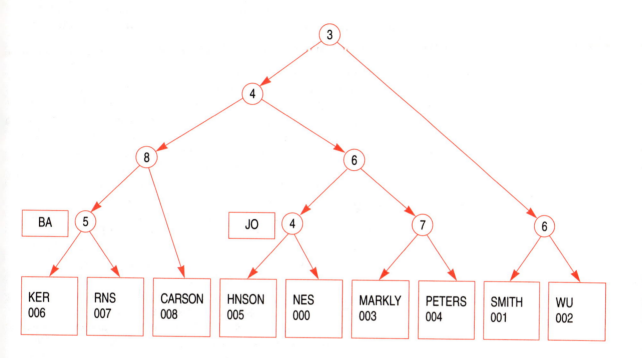

node. When we reach a terminal node, we have to compare the stored text with the rest of the name being searched. If there is a match, we have the correct terminal node. If not, the name being searched is not in the tree.

Another characteristic of the tree comes about because of the way we add entries to the tree. We always search the bit string for each new entry from left to right to find the first bit that differs in the new key from all other keys currently in the tree. By doing so, we assure that any path through the tree always tests bits from left to right. A test node never requires us to back up in the name: We always move forward.

The method used to insert entries also assures the tree will always have the same configuration, no matter what ordering is used to insert the entries. Further, the terminal nodes are always in keyed sequence from left to right. In our example, all the terminal nodes are in alphabetical order by the name in the key field. This is not a coincidence; it is part of the tree structure. The tree itself provides the logical keyed sequence, so the physical entries never have to be sorted.

In addition to finding and inserting entries in a tree, we can also remove an entry. This is an easy operation, because a terminal node can be pointed to by one and only one test node. Specifically, take the name to be removed, search the tree to find the terminal node, delete the terminal node, back up one test node, and delete the test node. The entry now has been removed from the tree.

Internals of a Binary Radix Tree

Internally, a binary radix tree is stored in a form that optimizes both performance and space. Phil Howard, an engineer, originally created the basic structure for the binary radix tree in the 1970s. The design he used had both the left and right child of a test node, along with possible common text packaged together in a cluster. These clusters were arranged sequentially in memory and were referenced by their position number in the string. This eliminated the need to have addresses pointing from one node to the next.

Phil invented a very elegant mechanism to allow movement from node to node in the tree. The cluster does not contain the actual position of either the next or the previous node. Instead, the determination of the next node position or the previous node position uses an XOR operation. This allows bidirectional movement through the tree without requiring the additional space for both forward and backward linkages.

To find the position of the next node in the tree, a value stored in the current node is XORed with the position of the previous node. Obviously, the value stored in the current node is the XOR of the previous and next node positions. In this way, the next position can always be re-created if only this value and the previous node position are known. Suppose we want to move backwards in the tree. By XORing the value in the current node with the position of the next node, we re-create the position of the previous node. Thus, at any point in the tree, by knowing the previous, current, and next positions, along with the contents of the current node, we can move up and down without the need to store forward and backward linkages. A simple three-entry push-down stack can store the three position values as we move through a tree.

The implementation of the binary radix tree minimizes page faults by partitioning the tree into subtrees. Formally, we should call this structure a partitioned binary radix tree. When a page becomes full, a split is made high up in the tree and new subtrees are added to the index.

Suppose, in our example, we wanted to subdivide our tree. Referring to Figure 6.6, we could put all the terminal nodes from Baker through Peters, along with their test nodes, on one page. A second page could contain the terminal nodes for Smith and Wu and the one test node that points to them.

However, we have a problem. None of the nodes contains addresses to link them to other nodes — they use relative position numbers. To go to another page in memory, we need an address. The solution is to create another type of node that contains an address and allows us to reference another page of entries. If we put the top node in our example, the root node, on a third page and let it point to the other two pages, we have partitioned our tree. The top nodes on all three pages are now root nodes for their page, and we have greatly expanded the amount of storage available for this tree.

Another advantage of this partitioning scheme is that once we enter a page while searching for a particular entry, we will stay on that page through all its levels of testing (we do not bounce from page to page while doing a search). We will exhaust the test nodes in our path on the page before falling through to another page. Also, because very large indexes can be searched with relatively few tests (a million-entry index takes, on average, only 20 tests), it is rare to touch more that one or two pages. As a result, this scheme provides better performance than just about any other indexing scheme known.

Conclusions

An integrated database provides many benefits for the AS/400 — there is no other way to provide an equivalent level of efficiency and performance. We have discussed a number of these in this chapter. Because the AS/400 database does not sit on top of the operating system, all system components can use the database facilities. The AS/400 database is not isolated in the same manner that a database is in a conventional system.

The AS/400's database design allows applications written for different interfaces to co-exist and operate using the same data. This characteristic allows the external interfaces and tool sets from other industry standard databases to be implemented directly on the AS/400. Applications written to this other database can then run directly on the AS/400, sharing data with everyone else. This is already happening, and it will become even more important in the future.

The integrated security of the AS/400 protects the database and other components in the system from unauthorized access and possible data corruption. In the next chapter, we will examine this integrated security, as well as SLIC's authorization management component.

Chapter 7

Security and Authorization

Security on computer systems is an afterthought, or so it seems. Most all computers today provide some form of a power-on password protection, but beyond that, the security is left to the software. A separate software security package on top of the operating system is the norm on many computers. Some systems simply leave the matter of security up to the individual application programs: If the application program requires a level of security beyond that provided by the system, the application program should provide it. Recently, however, more and more of the newer operating systems are beginning to recognize the need for better security and to build in security functions; but they still have a long way to go. Security on most PCs used for business, for example, is a joke.

Even systems that are thought to be more sophisticated are often extremely vulnerable. Stories of hackers breaking into systems attached to a network are legion. Think of the number of movies that have used the theme of breaking into a computer. The film *Jurassic Park* has a great scene toward the end where the young girl comes upon the computer that was sabotaged and that allowed the dinosaurs to escape. "It's a UNIX," she squeals and immediately breaks into the system and fixes the problem. This may only happen in the movies, but there is more truth here than many care to admit.

Integrated Security

Like so many other functions on the AS/400, security was built in from the beginning, as a part of the original design; it was not an afterthought. You cannot bypass security in an AS/400 — it is always there and always working.

Obviously, though, not every AS/400 installation needs the same level of security. There are systems locked away in rooms with very limited access.

Such a system probably doesn't require the same level of security as a system connected to a network. Over time, the security needs of a given system installation may also change. The AS/400's integrated security is sufficiently flexible to change as a system's security needs change.

The customer must be able to select and configure the level of security for the system itself. The challenge of a security system design is that the system be able to run without any security, with limited security, or with full security, while the underlying security functions are always active.

AS/400 security is implemented as a combination of OS/400's security component and SLIC's authority component. The levels of system-wide security are implemented in OS/400. OS/400 relies on the object-based security functions provided at the MI to enforce the security level. For example, as we saw in Chapter 5, the MI validates security whenever an object is accessed. SLIC implements these MI functions and provides the ongoing object security. Called authorization, this type of security is designed to protect objects from unauthorized access or modification.

Some parts of the AS/400's security implementation exist entirely above the MI in OS/400. An example is the definition of the system security values. Other parts of security exist entirely below the MI in SLIC. An example of this is object authorization. Still other parts exist partly above and partly below the MI. An example here is the privileged instruction and special authority support. In the following sections we will look at the components both above and below the MI.

System Security Levels

The AS/400 is designed for businesses that require levels of security ranging from nothing at all to full government-certifiable security. By setting a system value, we can configure five increasing levels of security: no security, password security, resource security, operating system security, and certifiable security. When an AS/400 is configured, three system values dealing with security need to be specified. These values are QAUDJRL, QMAXSIGN, and QSECURITY.

The system value that determines the level of security enforcement is QSECURITY. The System/38 and the original AS/400 only had three levels of system security. At V1R3 of OS/400, we added a fourth level of security. An even higher level of security was added at V2R3, to bring the total number of levels to five.

The AS/400 also supports an optional security auditing function. If this function is specified, certain security events are journaled. The specific events that are logged in the security audit journal are determined by the value specified in the QAUDJRL system value and the level of system security specified. Events that can be journaled include authorization failures, deleted objects, the identification of programs that use restricted instructions, and other security-related events. The security auditor in the business can analyze the contents of this journal.

You specify the maximum number of sign-on attempts with the QMAXSIGN system value. If the number of unsuccessful attempts to sign on to the system exceeds this number, the terminal or device that attempted the sign-on is varied off. A device that is varied off no longer has access to the system. This system value effectively disconnects anyone who attempts several different passwords to gain access to the system. The value is reset each time a valid sign-on occurs at the device.

The valid values for QSECURITY are 10, 20, 30, 40, and 50. The following sections describe each of these system security levels, starting with the lowest.

Level 10 — No Security

Level 10 is the lowest level of system security available. Level 10 represents a non-secure system. No password is required to access the system and all users have access to all system resources. This security level does not restrict access to any system object. The users are, however, prevented from affecting the jobs of other users on the system. Level 10 is the default security level and must be changed by the customer if a higher level is desired.

When only physical security, such as a lock on the computer room door, is needed, a system security level of 10 is adequate. Any user that has access to the system can sign on and use the system. That user does not need to be *enrolled*. To be enrolled in a system means there is a user profile for the user somewhere in the system. If a user profile does not exist, one is automatically created when level 10 security is specified.

Level 20 — Password Security

When your situation requires only sign-on security, you should specify level 20. This level requires the AS/400 user to be enrolled and to enter a valid password to gain access to the system. Once access to the system is granted, users are not restricted from using any system resources. This is similar to level 10 security, except a password is initially needed to gain access. We describe both levels 10 and 20 as non-secure systems, because once the user is into the system, almost anything goes.

One special case exists to limit a user's access to the system at level 20. A user profile can indicate the user is a *limited-capability user*. A limited-capability user is limited to selecting options from menus. Most of the system menus have a command entry line, and an installation can restrict the use of commands on these menus.

Suppose, for example, we have a group of system users in our business who are responsible for taking orders for our products and entering those orders into the system. We may elect to create a special menu for these users and only let them perform business functions they can select from this menu. We can accomplish this by enrolling these users as limited-capability users and specifying in their user profile the initial menu for them to use.

But even for a limited-capability user, some commands are necessary. The system allows this user to execute four commands: to send messages, to display messages, to display job status, and to sign off. The user commands and system commands available to the limited-capability user can be individually defined. Limited capability also determines which fields the user can modify at sign-on.

Level 30 — Resource Security

When your situation requires full resource security, level 30 fills the need. At level 30, the AS/400 user must be enrolled and must enter a valid password to gain access to the system — the same as with level 20. Once access to the system is granted, resource security then requires a user to have the authority to access the system resources; unauthorized access is not allowed. Additionally, a user can be enrolled as a limited-capability user under level 30 security.

Individual users can be authorized to use system objects, such as files, programs, and devices. Shortly, we will see how the user profile provides the capability to give users the authority to system objects. We will also look at other ways a user can access system objects using group and public authority.

Level 30 was the highest level of security available on the System/38. This level of security did not distinguish between a user object and one that was only used by the operating system. With the aid of the MI assembler available on the System/38 and some mappings of the internal structure of objects, a major problem began to develop. ISVs were beginning to write application packages that were dependent on the internal object structures, which was beginning to violate the technology independence of the MI.

For the initial version of the AS/400, this same level of security was carried over. Even though there was no MI assembler for the AS/400, and we didn't publish information on the internals, it didn't take too long for people to realize the AS/400 was a System/38. So programs that were dependent on the internal object structures worked on the AS/400.

We knew that we had requirements for even higher levels of security on the AS/400, and that these higher levels had to block access to many of the internal objects. We also knew that we were going to change these internal structures, especially as we moved to RISC. But if we just implemented the higher level of security on the AS/400, those programs that tried to access system object internals would no longer work, causing problems for many of our customers.

We announced that we would implement a new level of security at V1R3, and that the new level would no longer allow access to the internal objects. We also began to seek out the ISVs who were using the internal objects. We wanted to provide them with standard system APIs they could use to get the information they needed for their programs.

Most of these programs were utilities that used the information in some field inside a system object. A tape management system, for example, may have needed some additional information about the tape header. The only way to get this information was to go into a system object. We created hundreds of APIs to provide this needed information across the MI, and we guaranteed these APIs would always work in future releases of the operating system. Essentially, these APIs were new MI instructions. We were then free to make changes under the covers.

There was a larger issue involved here: the issue of AS/400 openness. For years, many ISVs had not only been using internal objects but also insisting that IBM make the operating system internals public, because this was holding back software development. IBM argued that there was a danger of software failure caused by mishandling of MI instructions for which IBM could be held responsible. IBM's compromise (the managed openness exhibited in the APIs) came, in part, out of a series a meetings at COMMON, which were initiated by ISVs and other users. Ron Fess, one of our lead software developers with a long history of accomplishments in both CPF and OS/400, took the lead to work with ISVs and to define the new APIs. Ron's work led to additional openness for the AS/400 with the incorporation of the Single UNIX Specification and other industry-standard APIs in later years.

Level 40 — Operating System Security

At V1R3 of OS/400, we introduced level 40 security. Again, at this level the AS/400 user must be enrolled and must enter a valid password to gain access to the system. A limited-capability user also is still supported at this level. As with level 30, the user must have the authority to access the system resources. New for level 40 is that access to nonstandard interfaces is blocked.

With level 40 security, all the MI instructions are no longer available to the user. Many of these instructions are blocked, meaning the system will not execute them in a user program. A user program can only use the approved set of MI instructions, including the hundreds of APIs we created for the ISVs.

The set of blocked MI instructions are, however, still available to OS/400 with level 40 security. To distinguish between an OS/400 program and a user program, we created the notion of a *system state* and a *user state*. Each process in the AS/400 runs in one of these states. The use of blocked instructions and, therefore, access to certain objects in the system are only allowed in the system state. Not all of OS/400 needs to have access to everything, so parts of the operating system can run in user state.

To support the higher level of security at V1R3, we also eliminated capability-based addressing by taking the authority out of the system pointers for everyone except the operating system.

Level 40 provides a very secure system for most businesses. Some businesses, however, require that their systems have a level of security that is certified by a government body. There are several levels of government-certifiable security, including the so-called Class C2 level.

The U.S. government specifies computer security guidelines for government applications. Achieving a government-approved security rating allows a computer system to participate in government bids. The government security guidelines specify certain required capabilities, such as protecting one user's resource from another and preventing one user from taking all the system resources, such as memory. Many businesses are now requiring these same guidelines.

We recognized that with a couple of additions, our level 40 security on the AS/400 could meet the government C2 level. An extensive government audit of a computer system's security must be conducted before the system is certified to meet the C2 standard, and we decided to go for the certification.

Level 50 — C2 Level Security

We announced level 50 security for V2R3 of OS/400. Level 50 security on the AS/400 has now been certified by a government audit to meet the federal government's C2 certification standard. All the level 40 security attributes are included at level 50, although some of the interfaces were modified to meet the C2 standards. We also added the security auditing capability to meet this standard.

The U.S. Department of Defense defines the Class C2 level of security as providing "discretionary (need-to-know) protection and, through the inclusion of audit capabilities, for accountability of subjects and the actions they initiate."[1] This requires that the owner of a computer system resource has the right to decide who can access the resource, and that the system can detect when the resource is accessed and by whom. The auditing capabilities specified by the QAUDJRL system value allow the security auditor to analyze the information the system detected.

The U.S. government defines security levels that range from A through D, where A is the highest level of security and D is the lowest. Classes B and C have several sub-levels. The C2 security level is the highest level commonly specified for business computing. In the future, we could include even higher levels of security in the AS/400 should the need arise.

User Profiles

The user profile is an OS/400 object and an MI system object. This is the object that identifies the user to the system. Every user in the system must have a user profile; although, as we will shortly see, user profiles can be shared — they do not have to be unique for each user. Even in a system with no security (level 10), if a user profile was not available for some user, the system would create one. User profiles contain the information related to

[1] Department of Defense Trusted Computer System Evaluation Criteria, DoD 5200.28-STD, December 1985.

security. They are used by both the OS/400 security component and the SLIC object authority component.

The authority component controls the use of objects, resources, certain instructions, and machine attributes in the system via the user profile. The user profile defines the following capabilities for a particular user:

- User Class — Each user class has special authorities based on the system security.
- Objects Owned and Authorized — A list of the objects owned and authorized to the user is contained in the user profile.
- Authorization of Objects — The authority to the above list of objects is in the user profile.
- Privileged Instructions and Special Authorities — Any privileged instructions and special authorities for the user are contained in the user profile.
- Password — This password is required for all security levels except level 10 to sign on to the system.
- Current Library — When the user creates a new object, the object is put into the user's current library.
- Initial Program and Menu — After the user signs on to the system, this field identifies the first program and the first menu the user will see.
- Limited-Capability User — When this option is enabled, the commands are restricted and the user is limited to menu selections.
- Limit Device Session — The user is limited to one session per device.
- Maximum Storage Allowed — This field gives the total disk space allowed for objects this user owns.
- Priority Limit — This field gives the highest scheduling priority a user can have. We will discuss priorities in more detail in Chapter 9.
- Special Environment — This field specifies the environment in which the user will execute (e.g., System/36 Environment).

Most of these fields are self-explanatory, but the first four need some elaboration.

User Class

The AS/400 has five user classes that determine the level of system access a user is permitted. The class defines the functions a user can perform, the menu options available to the user, and the privileged instructions, if any, the user can execute. The five user classes, starting with the highest level of access, are

- Security Officer. This is the highest level of user in the system. The security officer performs all security functions, including the creation of other user classes.
- Security Administrator. The security administrator has the responsibility to enroll users and to secure the system resources.
- System Programmer. This user develops applications for the system.
- System Operator. This user performs the system operation functions, such as backing up the system.
- Workstation User. This is the user of the application programs. The workstation user has the lowest level of access in the system.

When the AS/400 is initially shipped, one user profile exists for each user class. It is then up to the customer to decide who in each installation fills each of the roles. Obviously, for a given installation, a single person can fill more than one role.

Objects Owned and Authorized

The user profile contains two lists. The first is a list of all the objects owned by the user, and the second is a list of all the objects authorized to the user. A user who creates an object is the owner of that object. If a user profile is a member of a group file, which we discuss later in this chapter, you can specify in the user profile that all objects created by the user belong to the group. Object ownership can be transferred. The owner of an object or anyone with object management authority (see next section) has the authority to grant other users private authority to the object. These individuals can also grant public authority to the object. Thus, every user in the system has access to his or her owned objects, the objects to which (s)he has been granted private authority, and any objects that have public authority. Only the objects with owner and private authority are listed in the user profile.

Authorization of Objects

For each object on the AS/400, eight authorities can be granted. These are

- Object operational authority — Allows the user to look at the description of the object and use the object as determined by the data authorities the user has to the object.
- Object management authority — Allows the user to specify the security for the object, move or rename the object, and add members to the database files. Object existence rights are needed to remove members from database files.
- Object existence authority — Allows the user to delete the object, free the storage of the object, perform save/restore operations, and transfer ownership of the object.

- Authorization list management authority — Allows a user to add, remove, and change users and their authorities on an authorization list.
- Read authority — Allows the user to access the object.
- Add authority — Allows the user to add records to the object.
- Delete authority — Allows the user to delete records from the object.
- Update authority — Allows the user to change records in the object.

OS/400 groups these eight authorities into four combinations to make it easier for the end user to understand the capabilities allowed. End users are not prevented from creating other combinations, but most use these combinations of authorities. The four groupings are

- ALL — Combines all eight authorities.
- CHANGE — Combines object operation, read, add, delete, and update.
- USE — Combines object operation and read.
- EXCLUDE — Has no authority to the object. EXCLUDE overrides any authority granted to the public or group profile, because of the order in which authorities are searched. We will see this search order later in this chapter.

Privileged Instructions and Special Authorities

Each user profile contains information indicating privileged instruction and special authority for the user. Several MI privileged instructions can only be executed by users who are authorized to do so in their user profiles. For example, the profile for the security officer is created with the capability to execute the instruction that terminates the machine processing. The instruction that does this is accessed through the Power Down System (PWRDWNSYS) command. This privileged instruction is, for obvious reasons, not available to all users. Likewise, a series of special authorities exist that can be granted to selected users. These special authorities deal with such functions as suspending objects, controlling processes, performing load/dump operations, and using low-level service tools.

Although all the privileged instructions and all the special authorities can be individually specified in the user profile, OS/400 combines instructions and authorities into six groups. These are

- All object special authority — Allows access to any system resource, whether or not the user has any private authority to the resource.
- Security administrator special authority — Allows the user to create and change user profiles if authorized to the commands to create and change the user profile.

- Save system special authority — Allows the user to save, restore, and free storage for all objects on the system, whether or not the user has object existence authority for the objects.
- Job control special authority — Allows the user to change, display, hold, release, cancel, and clear all jobs that are executing on the system or are on job queues or output queues.
- Service special authority — Allows the user to perform Display/Alter/Dump service operations.
- Spool control special authority — Allows the user to delete, display, hold and release spool files owned by other users.

The user profile is the heart of the security system on an AS/400, controlling access to just about every resource in the system. Even though a user's profile may not provide the authority to some resource or object in the system, there may be other ways the user can obtain the authority. In the following sections, we will look at the two ways to gain additional authority: program adoption of authority and group authorities.

Program Adoption of Authority

While a program is executing, the user profile that owns the program can serve as another source of authority. This capability to adopt authority allows a program to perform operations that require an authority the user does not have directly. Rather than granting additional authority to a user, the user's application program calls another program whose owner has the authority to perform the operation. Thus, program adoption of authority requires the concept of a call stack. When a program adopts the authority of the called program's owner, it is always additive; adoption will never decrease authority.

Adoption is a program attribute specified at the time a program is created. If a called program is identified as one that allows adoption of authority, any calling program can use the owner's authority while the called program is running. A program can specify no adoption, but only if it executes in system state. A program can also specify no propagation. This indicates that the calling program will adopt while executing, but programs further down the call chain will not keep the authority.

So far we have only discussed a single user having authority to a single object. There are times, however, when we want to give the same authorities to a group of users. And there are other times when we want to give a user authority to a group of objects. We will next look at grouping authority.

Grouping Authority

Three methods for grouping authorities are available on the AS/400. Authorization lists and group profiles simplify the administration of AS/400 security. These two approaches are used to eliminate the need to separately grant authorities when several objects or several users have the same authorities. IBM introduced authority holders for the System/36 Environment.

An authorization list enables the authorization of multiple objects to multiple users. In addition, each user can have a different level of authority for all the objects in the list. Figure 7.1 shows an authorization list with three users and three objects. Each of the three users has authority to all the objects on the list, but in our example, each user has a different authority. To add, remove, or change users and their authority on the list requires the authority list management previously described. At the MI, the authorization list is implemented as a system object.

Group profiles allow users to share a common profile in addition to having their own user profile. Users who are members of a group, such as a department in a business, can share common objects. The authorization of all members in the group can be managed by authorizing the group profile.

Access to the group profile is through the individual user's profile. If an individual user profile has authorization to an object, that private authority overrides the authority of the group profile. This characteristic allows specific group members to be given either more or less authority than other members of the group.

System/36 applications have the ability to authorize users to a non-existent file. Authorization can be given before the file is created. The application in the System/36 can even continue to have authority to the file even after the

Figure 7.1 Authority List Example

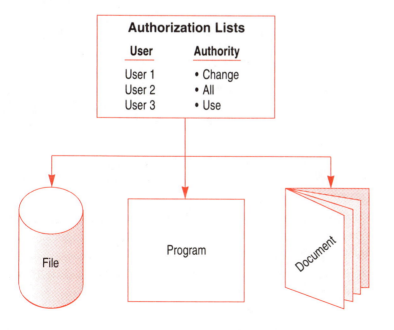

file has been deleted. Within a System/38, there was no such concept. Authorization could not be granted until the object had been created. Also, if an object in a System/38 was deleted, all records of authority to the object were removed from the system.

For the System/36 Environment on the AS/400, authority holders were added to support authorization to non-existent files. The use of authority holders, which is only required for migration, is limited to certain types of program-described files; authority holders are not supported for other types of files and objects. Because of this, neither OS/400 nor the MI has an authority holder object.

Authority Search Algorithm

Now that we have defined all the types of authorities and the various ways a user can gain these authorities, we need to look at the search algorithm to see how authority is actually granted. As we will see, a very specific search order is always used. The reason for this specific order is to allow users to be granted more or less authority for an object than the public, group profile, or authorization list authority.

The authority search algorithm is implemented in SLIC when the user first accesses the object. This was part of the resolve pointer operation we looked at in Chapter 5. The search algorithm stops when any authority to the object is found. The first authority found is used, unless there is program adoption. In this case, the adopted authority is added to the first authority found in the search. The search order is as follows:

1. Individual User Profile
   - All-object special authority
   - Object authority (owner and private authority)
   - Authorization list if object is on an authorization list (private authority)

2. Group Profile — Searched only when there is a group profile and no authority was found in the user profile
   - All-object special authority
   - Object authority (private authority)
   - Authorization list if object is on an authorization list (private authority)

3. Public Authority — Searched only when no authority was found in user or group profiles
   - Object authority (public authority)
   - Authorization list if object is on an authorization list (public authority)

By searching the individual user profile first, and always taking the first authority found, the user can be granted more or less authority for an object than the public, group profile, or authorization list authority. If we put the EXCLUDE authority in the individual user profile, direct access to the object by the user is blocked. The user can still perform operations on the object with the adopted authority the user acquires while running an adopted program. This is the most common way to restrict access to a system object.

Conclusions

Security is one of the most important functions in any multiuser system. With so many systems being connected to the "information highway," the need to guarantee a secure system will only increase. OS/400's security component and SLIC's object-based authorization component provide a mechanism that satisfies today's requirements and yet is flexible enough to provide for future expansion. As requirements for even higher levels of security evolve, they can be added in a non-disruptive manner to the AS/400.

In addition to the overall system security of an AS/400, we have described in this chapter the ways a user's authority is commonly managed. These include

- Menu access
- Adopted authority
- Group authority
- Private authority

In Chapter 6 we discussed how the database can be accessed through the use of logical files. Data access can thus be restricted by managing logical file authority with any of the methods just listed.

As a part of pointer resolution, the authority search algorithm described above is performed. But the authority to an object is not much good if you can't address it. In the next chapter, we will look at addressing and the management of the single-level store. Though not usually considered a part of security, the single-level store on the AS/400 plays a major role in protecting users and user data.

Chapter 8
Single-Level Store

Probably the best known characteristic of the AS/400 is the single-level store. In IBM terminology, this subject would be referred to as storage management. Many IBM documents do not use the term "memory," because it seems to give a computer human qualities. These documents often refer to the names main storage instead of memory and secondary storage instead of disk. Another common name for disk within IBM is DASD (pronounced daz-dee), the abbreviation for direct access storage device. This name comes from the mid-1950s to describe how data on a disk can be directly accessed, as opposed to a tape, which is sequentially accessed. But in this chapter, we will try to avoid using some of these strange names.

Rarely is the single-level store not prominently mentioned in a presentation about the AS/400. Those who are new to the AS/400 are told that the system treats all storage as a single large memory. For years, AS/400 supporters have proudly pointed to the 48-bit address and the 256 terabytes of memory this approach supports. Now they are attempting to describe the number of bytes that can be addressed with 64 bits. Newcomers are told the single-level store frees programmers and other users from having to manage disks, thereby increasing their productivity.

Single-level store has also taken some flack over the years and has been blamed for some AS/400 problems. Detractors believe single-level store is the cause of long IPL times that can occur after an abnormal system termination. They point out that objects are often spread across multiple disks. When a single disk fails, parts of many objects are lost, so the system cannot continue. They say the single-level store is the cause of this problem.

What is so unusual about all these positive and negative claims is that none are true. Nobody and nothing above MI sees the single-level store. OS/400 doesn't see it, application programs don't see it — even the compilers don't see the single-level store. The AS/400's single-level store is only seen by the SLIC. The MI works with objects, and objects are referenced by name, never by address. The closest thing to a memory at MI is a space, and a space is a far cry from a single-level store.

It is true that no application programmers above the MI ever manage disks, but then they don't in any system. Programmers generally deal with disks when they work with a file system, and as we have already seen, the AS/400 has an integrated file system that looks very much like one on a PC or a Unix system.

Long IPL times are caused by the system's need to rebuild access paths, which has nothing to do with the single-level store. Objects are spread across multiple disks for performance reasons. Parts of an object can be fetched from several disks in parallel, thereby improving system performance. This spreading of an object also has nothing to do with single-level store.

The single-level store is invisible to most AS/400 users. About the only one who sees some information on the single-level store is the person responsible for performance. For example, the Work with System Status (WRKSYSSTS) display and the performance tools can be used to show various characteristics of single-level store, such as page faulting rates. But even though single-level store is invisible to most users, its benefits are not.

Shortly, we will show that the major benefit of the single-level store is that it reduces the number of instructions that are executed for many operating-system functions. This means improved performance for all the software above and below the MI. We will also show the other benefits this design brings to AS/400 users. Single-level store is much more than just a large 64-bit address. "But," you ask, "just how big is it?"

How Many Bytes Does 64 Bits Address?

The answer is 16 exabytes, which is about 18.4 quintillion bytes (or to be more exact, 18,446,744,073,709,551,616 bytes). This number is too big for most of us to comprehend. In Chapter 5, I said we often talked about the number of bytes that could be addressed with 48 bits was equal to the distance from the earth to the sun and back measured in millimeters. I also said we needed a new analogy for 64 bits.

Richard Rubin, who helped immensely with the review of this book, offered an analogy for 64 bits. Richard notes that George Gamow, in his book *One, Two, Three, Infinity*, tells a story about King Shirham of India, who wanted to reward his grand vizier Sissa Ben Dahir for inventing the game of chess. The vizier asked that the king put one grain of wheat on the first square of the chessboard, two on the second, four on the third, eight on the fourth, and so on, doubling the amount on each square until he reached the 64th square. The total number of grains would be $2^{64}-1$. Gamow estimates that at 5 million grains of wheat per bushel, it would take 4,000 billion bushels to cover the chessboard. World production in 1946 (when Gamow's book was written) was 2 billion bushels a year. At that rate, it would take the world two thousand years to produce enough wheat.

For those of you who like the millimeter analogy, 18 quintillion is about twice the number of millimeters in a light year. That's just less than half the distance to Alpha Centauri (the closest star to the solar system) in millimeters. Obviously, if we want to start measuring astronomical distances in millimeters, we will need more than 64 bits. Let's see, 128 bits in a pointer will give us ... No matter how you look at it, 64-bit addressability gives a mighty big store. Speaking of big stores, there is another famous one in Rochester. Before we get into more details and benefits of the AS/400's single-level store, let's digress a bit and take a brief historical tour of the other famous single-level store that brings back fond memories for many of us in Rochester.

The Single-Level Store in Rochester

By 1973, the decision had finally been made to build the System/38 (we had had a development organization in place since 1970, but the decision to fully staff this organization had taken three years). The System/38 was, after all, a very radical departure from conventional computer systems, and several alternates had been considered before the decision was made to proceed. The U.S. economy also went through a recession in the early 1970s, and companies such as IBM were reluctant to invest in major new development programs that required lots of new people. At last, all of that was behind us. Now the effort to hire development personnel began in earnest, and most of this staffing took place over the next two years.

The System/38's engineering organization was well established by 1973, with new processor and I/O hardware already under development. A problem we had at the time was where to put all the new people we were bringing into Rochester. The System/3 development organization had grown to the point where the development laboratory buildings were just about full, and to construct a new laboratory building would take a long time.

The proposal for new laboratory buildings would first have to be sold to the IBM Real Estate Division. That group would study the proposal to determine whether or not such a building was really needed. They would look at the impact of a new building on the community, consider whether or not it would fit aesthetically with other IBM buildings, determine how to pay for it, and on and on — the bureaucracy would take years. And when the decision to build *was* finally made, the actual construction would take a couple more years. At best, our new buildings would be ready for occupancy starting in 1977 or 1978.

Rochester's winters are harsh, so the idea of pitching some tents in the parking lot until our new buildings were ready was quickly dismissed. We did, however, consider doing something similar. IBM had a collection of portable, modular buildings that we could use until permanent buildings were erected. These modular buildings were large trailers that could be towed to a site and then bolted together to form temporary buildings — but these temporary buildings had a habit of becoming permanent (one of the IBM Rochester south parking lots has had "the trailers" in place for more than 20 years). We concluded that trailers would not be big enough to hold the System/38 development organization, so we needed an alternative.

Rochester has had a history of outgrowing the space available for our development organizations. Since it was founded in 1961, much of the development laboratory has been located off-site. IBM would lease a building somewhere in Rochester for use as a development facility. Eventually, a new building would be added at the main site, and the people would move back. The growth in Rochester, however, has been so great that until 1995 we have always had off-site, leased facilities for development.[1]

We ultimately found our new building for the System/38 development group across town in the former Wells Department Store. The building was not desirable for a development laboratory, but it was big and it was available, so we moved in. Originally, IBM had leased half the building as a storage warehouse. We decided to lease the other half, remodel it for offices and laboratories, and move the engineering group into the building. Eventually, we would remodel the warehouse half of the building and move in the programming group. For the next few years, many of us would call this home.

Discount department stores "took off" during the 1960s. Kmarts and Wal-Marts sprang up in many towns across middle America. Others tried to copy the success of these organizations, including a chain of stores in Minnesota called Wells Department Stores. The Rochester store, along with other stores across the state, was built in the early 1970s. The parent company of Wells overextended itself and went out of business, so the two-year-old department store in Rochester was forced to close.

Discount department stores then and now all seem to be built using the same pattern. Located at the back of a large parking lot, this department store was housed in a one-story, cement block building. There were no windows other than at the entrance and a few along the top front of the building. The inside of this giant warehouse had a ceiling open to the metal struts that held the roof on the building.

Because IBM was only leasing the building, the remodeling effort was a classic example of temporary design. Eight-foot-high partitions were erected as office walls. An 18-foot-high ceiling meant that the offices were open and very noisy. You could easily overhear conversations several offices away. Only the hallways and a few conference rooms were covered.

The heating and cooling system for the building was designed for a large, open, warehouse-like store. Putting up partitions totally disrupted the building's airflow. To solve the problem, large fans were placed on top of the covered hallways to move more air. The fans were so loud that any conversations were drowned out, ensuring total privacy. If you were unfortunate enough to be too close to one of these fans, you also discovered that you couldn't keep papers on your desk — they all blew away.

---

[1] Over the years we have leased several facilities. We have been located over shopping centers, in bank buildings, and in standard office buildings. One of the more unusual facilities was a Howard Johnson Hotel. During the late 1970s, the System/38 planning organization occupied rooms in this hotel. The beds were removed from the hotel rooms and office furniture was installed to create offices for our planners. The most desirable of these rooms overlooked the pool, but that's another story.

With hundreds of offices created using these partitions, the view from the top was that of a maze. Because there were no windows, it was very difficult to locate someone's office in this maze. One hallway looked like another as we wandered from place to place. We fully expected some day to have the roof open and a giant look down on us to see how the rats were doing in their maze.

In the early days, to identify the location of an office in the building, we used the names of the department locations in the old Wells store. A performance group was in the toy department and an I/O group was in automotive. As it turned out, the architecture group was in ladies' lingerie. But these original locations were quickly forgotten as new people, who had never been in the Wells store, moved in and IBM numbered all the offices.

The Wells building was not an ideal physical facility, but it did contribute greatly to the System/38's success. The entire development organization was housed in this building, isolated from the rest of IBM. We were our own computer company and we built our own computer. Most of us are convinced that never would have happened if we had been located at the main site with the System/3 developers. IBM liked to number all leased buildings and arbitrarily called the former department store building 648; but many of us affectionately called this one-story, cement block, former department store the *single-level store*.

Virtual Memory

The AS/400's single-level store was not named after a department store, although it certainly could have been. It was named after the original work the virtual memory pioneers had done. To understand where the term single-level store came from requires a look at its intended design and the evolution of virtual memory.

Virtual memory first appeared on a computer called Atlas, designed in Manchester, England, in 1961. The core memory technology used for the main memory of computers in those days was very expensive. Large programs needed lots of memory space, often more than the computer had available. To make these large programs fit into the limited memory size, the programmer would have to break his or her program up into pieces, each small enough to fit into the existing memory. Those pieces of the program that didn't fit would be stored on a magnetic disk or drum.

Drums were popular in the early 1960s. A drum is similar to a hard disk, except that it has one read/write head per track. Drums generally provided higher performance than disks because with drums it was not necessary to wait for the head to seek to the desired track. As disk seek times improved, however, drums disappeared.

The problem with having to break large programs into smaller pieces was the increased programmer effort required to manage the memory. When a piece of the program to be executed was not in memory, the programmer had to issue the commands to read that piece from the disk or drum and write it into the memory. These pieces were called *overlays*, and much of a programmer's time was spent creating and managing overlays. Virtual memory attacked this problem by letting the programmer think there was such a large memory that the entire program would always fit. The operating system would manage the movement of data and programs in this large virtual memory, relieving the programmer from the effort.

Kilburn, et al., wrote in their 1962 paper that described the memory system of the Atlas computer, "… a system has been devised to make the core drum combination appear to the programmer as a **single-level store**, the requisite transfers taking place automatically."[2]

[2] T.D. Kilburn, B.G. Edwards, M.J. Lanigan, F.H. Sumner, "One-level Storage System," *IRE Transactions on Electronic Computers*, April, 1962.

Virtual Memory for Timesharing

Virtual memory was adopted by many computer vendors in the late 1960s because of the advent of timesharing systems. Timesharing was an evolution of the earlier multiprogramming operating systems. Multiprogramming partitioned the system's memory into several pieces, with a different program in each partition. When one program was waiting for an I/O operation to complete, another program could be using the processor. If enough programs could be kept in memory, the processor could be kept busy all the time. Multiprogramming operating systems then were still basically batch systems.

Timesharing was a variant of multiprogramming, in which each user had an on-line terminal. Because these were interactive users (meaning the program was driven by the user at the terminal), there was less demand for long periods of processor time and more think time involved. This type of computer can handle more users, so many more pieces of programs must exist in the memory at the same time. Interactive users wanted fast response time, so the need to efficiently manage these multiple pieces was critical. Virtual memory held the hope for doing just that.

The original idea behind a timesharing system was that individual users in various businesses could rent time on a central computer. This was a popular approach, because many smaller businesses could not afford their own computer. Timesharing provided them with the resources of a large computer at a fraction of the cost. Because the computer users were from nonrelated businesses, there was never a need to share information between them.

Virtual memory evolved to support timesharing by giving a separate address space to each user. The memory space of one user was isolated from the memory space of another user, thereby providing a degree of protection between them. When the resources of the computer were switched to operate on the program for another user, a new address space was used. This operation is usually called a *process switch*, where a process can be thought of as a unit of work for a user in the system.

In the past, a process switch required lots of overhead. Memory tables had to be changed, registers had to be purged, and new data had to be loaded. To accomplish all this work required that many instructions be executed in the processor. The time required to do this became excessive in many of the computers of the mid-1960s, and many were looking for ways to simplify this process and make it more efficient.[3]

Worse yet, the designers of these timesharing systems decided to keep the file system outside of virtual memory. They created two places to store data and programs: the virtual memory and the file system. With this design, the data and programs can only be used or changed if they are in virtual memory. This means that anything in the file system must be moved into virtual memory before it can be used or changed.

In a conventional system, the file manager keeps a directory that relates the name of a file to the location on the disk where the data for the file is stored. The file manager provides an interface to allow programs to "open" a file. The data is then copied into memory buffers, which are usually part of the virtual memory. There, the data can be used and manipulated. When the program is finished with the data, a "close" operation is performed, which causes the data to be moved from the virtual memory back to the file system.

A simple example for this process that most of us can relate to is using a word processor on a PC. We first open the file, which contains the document we want to use, and we watch the hard disk light blink as the document is read into memory. Actually, it is first being read into our virtual memory, and then part of the document is read into memory. At some time in the past, when we configured our PC operating system, we told it how much disk space should be reserved for virtual memory. In the PC world, this space is sometimes called the application swap file. As we are scrolling through the document, we notice the hard drive light again blinking. As needed, new parts of the document are being read into memory from this reserved disk space.

The act of opening the file has created a second copy of our document. The original copy of the document still exists unchanged on our hard drive. The second copy is in the disk space we reserved for virtual memory. The virtual memory manager in the operating system will automatically bring pieces of the document from the reserved disk area into memory as we need them, and put them back when they are no longer needed. There are actually three copies of some parts of our document, if we count the copy in memory.

When we are finished making changes and close the document, we are asked if we want to save the changes we made. In other words, do we want to take the updated copy in virtual memory and write it back to the permanent location of the file on the disk? If we do, the copy in virtual memory replaces the permanent copy.

A Single-Level Virtual Memory

The programmer in the virtual memory implementation just described sees and manages two levels of storage; the file system and the virtual memory are separate. This two-level store also creates overhead in the system. Opening a

[3] I was fascinated with the whole subject of virtual memory and decided to pursue this as my research topic at Iowa State University. I was perplexed at how the major computer vendors, including IBM, had taken this simple, elegant idea and twisted it into an overly complex structure. My research effort to find a virtual memory mechanism that required less processor overhead, and therefore better performance, led to the System/38's single-level store.

file causes a disk write to the swap area, and closing a file requires a disk write back to the permanent location. An alternate approach is to have only one copy of the file.

By not having two separate copies, we would not need to reserve disk space for a swap file. With this approach, the entire file system would become part of virtual memory. The file manager still keeps a directory, but now it relates the name of a file to the location in virtual memory where the data for the file is stored. The open and close operations no longer need to physically copy the entire file from its permanent location on the disk. Just the portion (or record) you are reading or working on is copied to a memory buffer. We often describe this by saying the files are always used "in place," thereby improving overall system performance.

This one-level storage is exactly what the original inventors of virtual memory had intended, and it is the model of virtual memory we implemented on the System/38. In honor of the original inventors, we decided to call our virtual memory "single-level store."

Like a two-level virtual memory, the memory is still used as a buffer. Processors can only operate directly on data in memory, not on the disk. The difference with only one level is that memory is now a cache for all the disk storage, rather than just for a reserved area on the disk. Also, when one user makes a change to a file, the change is instantly available to any other user who is sharing the file.

The downside of single-level store is the requirement for a large address in the computer. The address has to be large enough to cover all the disk storage attached to the system. Consider the 32-bit address used in many of today's systems. A total of 4 gigabytes can be addressed with a 32-bit address. This is nowhere near enough to address all the disk storage that can be attached to even a large PC. So these conventional systems are forced to copy disk data into and out of their relatively small virtual memories.

The System/38 and earlier AS/400 used a 48-bit address to eliminate this restriction. Now the AS/400 uses a 64-bit address, with even more address bits available for future expansion. There is a hardware cost for the additional bits, but this cost is far outweighed by the sharing capabilities and the performance advantages of single-level store.

Persistent Virtual Memory

The AS/400's address size is much larger than necessary to cover the total disk storage. The reason behind this large address is another characteristic of the single-level store that we call persistence. In Chapter 5, about objects, we introduced this characteristic. An object that has persistence continues to exist in the memory system forever, even after the object has been destroyed. We said this type of object is called a permanent object on the AS/400, and we described how the virtual address space for a permanent object is never reused. When a permanent object is destroyed, we free up all the disk space the object occupied, except for the headers. This disk space is then reused for other objects.

The reason we don't reuse the virtual address space is to eliminate security and integrity exposures. If a permanent object is destroyed and the address space is reused for another object, someone who had addressability to the original object through a resolved pointer could address the new object. Because pointers can be stored anywhere in the memory system, most garbage collection schemes to find all the pointers become overly complex. By using a sufficiently large address and not reusing the address space for permanent objects, the AS/400 eliminates the need for garbage collection.

Most conventional virtual memories have no garbage collection problem, but for different reasons. In an early virtual memory scheme (still used for some PC operating systems), each user is given a separate virtual address space. When the user process goes away, so does its virtual memory. There is no way to keep an address to anything in the system. The only place for sharing is the file system, and virtual addressing is not used in the file system.

This early virtual memory implementation of not sharing anything is not acceptable for most multiuser operating systems, such as Unix, and so a variation was defined for these operating systems. Instead of giving the user program direct addressability to the virtual memory, these systems give the program an address that must be translated by the hardware into the virtual address before it can be used. In the PowerPC architecture, we call this address the *effective address*. As we will see, the use of an effective address does enable some level of memory sharing at the cost of more processor overhead.

The virtual memory in these systems is logically divided into segments, where a segment is a block of contiguous bytes in memory. An effective address identifies one of these segments. A typical implementation of the translation from effective to virtual address uses a few registers (four to 16) on the processor hardware chip, called *segment registers*. Each segment register contains the virtual address of one segment in the virtual memory. Some high-order bits in the effective address are used to identify one of the segment registers. The remaining bits in the effective address identify the byte within the segment (called the *offset* into the segment). Because an effective address contains the offset into a virtual address segment, this type of addressing is sometimes called *segment-relative addressing*.

A simple way to think about an effective address is to recognize that it is a subset of the larger virtual address. A user program can directly access only a few of the segments in the virtual memory — those whose addresses are loaded into the segment registers. The program can request that the operating system reload the registers, giving the program access to other segments, but the program is still only working with a small piece of the virtual memory. For example, some Intel processors have only four segment registers, which allows access to only four segments at a time, while some RS/6000 processors use 16 of these registers, which still allows access to only a small part of the total virtual memory.

For the PowerPC architecture, we got rid of the segment registers and replaced them with a special table in memory called a *segment table*. This gives a user program access to far more segments than does a register implementation. Each entry in the segment table still contains the virtual address of one segment in the virtual memory. The effective address used by a program now identifies an entry in the segment table and the byte offset into the segment. Two programs can share the same virtual address if they use the same segment table entry, or if the same virtual address is stored in more than one segment table entry.

With segment-relative addressing, the user program only sees the effective address and, therefore, cannot store away a virtual address. The effective-to-virtual translation process requires additional overhead, but the virtual addresses are protected and there is no garbage collection problem. Because only the operating system can reload the segment registers, a level of control also exists over which segments a user program can address and share with another program.

Note that because the effective address only contains the identifier of an entry in the segment table and the offset portion of the address, the effective address can have fewer bits than the virtual address. This is exactly how a 32-bit processor with a 32-bit effective address can have a larger virtual address — the virtual address is not restricted to the size of the processor's registers. Even in this case, the effective address still can reference only a subset of the virtual address space without having the operating system reload the segment registers. Also note that, even though the virtual address may be larger than 32 bits, any single operation can still use only the 32 bits of addressability the processor provides. This means the 4-gigabyte limitation is still there, no matter how many bits are in the virtual address — which explains why even systems that claim large virtual addresses are moving from 32-bit to 64-bit processors.

Now let's contrast the segment-relative addressing we have been discussing in the last several paragraphs with the single-level store in the AS/400. The single-level store and the virtual address exist below the MI and are not visible to the user. There is, therefore, no need to force addresses through another level of translation (effective-to-virtual) to protect them. The protection is accomplished through the pointers we introduced in Chapter 5. We need to protect the pointers (with the tag bits), but we don't have to add the additional processing overhead to load and store the segment tables for every program.

In an AS/400, the single-level store is also divided into segments, as we saw in Chapter 5 when we looked at the structure of objects. A major difference is that with the single-level store the large address in the AS/400 (either 48 bits or 64 bits) lets a program below the MI address any segment in the entire virtual address space, not just a subset of the segments, as is the case with the segment-relative addressing model. A program can access the entire virtual memory, and all the virtual memory can be shared with no additional processing overhead. Another way to look at this for the PowerPC hardware versions of the AS/400 is to see that, with one exception, there is no difference between an effective and a virtual address — they are one and the same; so the segment table supported by the PowerPC hardware is not used.

The exception is that for security auditing purposes with C2-level security, addresses from AS/400 programs operating in the user state use the segment table supported by the PowerPC processor hardware to create the virtual address. Because the hardware was already in every PowerPC processor to support a segment table, we decided to use this table for our C2-level security implementation. The use of the segment table provides an easy way to prevent a user program from accessing a virtual address without involving the operating system to load a segment table entry. This accomplishes the C2-level security goal of being able to monitor and log which objects each user is accessing. The additional overhead is only incurred for programs operating in the user state. In the IMPI processors, we had to accomplish this same C2-level security function in the microcode.

Overview of Single-Level Store

Before we jump head-first into the single-level store implementation, we need to look at an overview of the concepts and components to see how they all fit into the big picture. Then we can get into a discussion about why single-level store is so important to the AS/400 and look at some of the low-level details on exactly how it works. To help us picture what is happening as we go through these sections, let's define a simple running example. Suppose we have a program doing a sequential read to an indexed database file (this could be a high-level language READ or an SQL FETCH). For this example, we would need to assemble a few objects (program, index, cursor, data space, and possibly a space or two) — some would be found in memory and some not.

Let's start with a brief review of how these or any other objects are addressed. No distinction is made between memory and disk storage (or other auxiliary storage) above the MI. OS/400 thinks only of objects, their names, and their public contents. MI sees its objects (which are decompositions of OS/400 objects) by their identifiers (pointers). Objects are not otherwise located at the MI level.

Programs, cursors, data spaces, and other objects can be found simply by specifying the object's name. An executing program need only know an object's name and type (library is optional, because the library list will be searched if the library is not specified) to use it as a resource. The name, however, is quickly mapped into a virtual address. The virtual address of each named object is stored in the library that contains it. This address is loaded into a pointer as part of the resolve operation we described in Chapter 5. A system pointer, therefore, contains the virtual address of the object header (which may in turn contain pointers to other parts of the OS/400 object or to other associated MI objects).

Although the answer may be obvious to most readers, a question often asked is, "Why does the virtual address have to get down to the byte level? Why can't it just address objects like instructions at the MI do?" To fully answer this, we need to realize that the processor hardware in the AS/400 (either the CISC or RISC models) is fairly conventional. The processor hardware knows nothing about objects. As we saw in Chapter 1, a processor gets instructions and data from memory. The MI system objects are located in memory and the processor uses byte addressability to get at the information contained in these objects: records in a file, instructions in a program, and so on. An IMPI processor uses the original 48-bit virtual address, which it translates to a real address to access the memory. To access the memory, a PowerPC processor uses the effective addresses we have discussed and translates these addresses first to virtual and then to real. Hardware registers in both of these processors keep track of the next instruction in the program to execute and the addresses of data being used.

For the contents of an object to be changed or referenced, or for instructions in a program to execute, they must be brought into memory. In our sequential database read example, the portion of the program that contains the actual instructions to perform the database read would have to first be brought into memory from disk before the instructions can be executed. This movement between disk and memory occurs below the MI, because the MI does not distinguish between memory and disk.

You can picture this movement in two different ways. One view is that all objects appear to be in memory. That the physical memory is too small to hold all objects is a limitation of current hardware technology. When a part of an object is needed but not found in memory, the missing part is brought in and replaces some unused portion of memory. Another picture is that memory is a set of screens used to view the vast space that holds all objects. The process of bringing pages in and out of memory can be thought of as changing the view in one or more screens.

Memory is composed of page frames (the screens in the preceding analogy), which on IMPI machines are 512 bytes, but are now 4 kilobytes (4,096 bytes) on PowerPC machines. These screens are called "page frames" because they hold pages. The object on disk is divided into pages. Pages on disk are the same size as page frames in memory. A virtual address of an object implies a page on disk. This virtual address can designate any byte in the object space, so it could point to the middle of a page. A large object can occupy many pages, and by design, a single page can never contain parts of more than one object.

A page previously brought into memory by one process (job) is available to any other process. Program instructions can be shared by any number of jobs. Recently read records from the database are likely to be in memory. Disk I/O is greatly reduced if the same records are read many times. Suppose, in our database read example, we are using an index that is shared with other users in the system. If that index has recently been used by one of those other users, part or all of the index is likely to still be in memory and we will not have to wait while index pages are fetched from disk. In a conventional system with more limited sharing, a new copy of the index would have to be brought into memory even though one might already exist.

Given a virtual address, the hardware looks first to see if the corresponding page is already in memory. If it's there, the hardware uses the page in memory. If not, a page fault has occurred, which means the missing page must be retrieved from disk.

The translation of a virtual address into a real address is to find the page frame in memory corresponding to the virtual address. This virtual-to-real translation uses a page table that is located in memory. The hardware's search of the page table uses a hashing algorithm (which we will describe later in this chapter) to locate a page table entry group (PTEG). Each PTEG contains eight page table entries, and these are searched individually to see if the sought-for page has a match. If not, a page fault occurs — a hardware interrupt that signals the SLIC to find the disk address corresponding to the virtual address and to instruct an I/O processor to go out to disk and retrieve the page.

To speed the search for recently used pages, a set of registers exists on the processor chip, called the *translation lookaside buffer* (TLB), that holds the most recently used entries in the page table. Because the TLB registers are built into the processor, a load from memory (where the page table is located) is not required if the virtual address points to a recently used page. If the virtual address is not there, a second stage of the translation process has the hardware look in the page table located in memory.

If C2 security is in effect for a user program, the hardware first looks at the *segment lookaside buffer* (SLB), another set of registers on the processor hardware chip that hold the most recently used parts of the segment table. If there is no match in the SLB registers, the hardware looks at the segment table in memory before going to the TLB registers and the page table. In other words, with C2-level security, a three-step translation process occurs — effective-to-virtual-to-real.

In the event of a page fault, to send the message to the I/O processor, the SLIC uses another kind of address called a *direct store address*. Such addresses are used to communicate with any external device. These addresses begin with the hexadecimal value 801. Part of the direct store address is passed directly to the process managing the external device.

When a page is brought from disk, it replaces a page not recently used. Special reference bits associated with each page are set whenever the page is referenced. Pages that have been changed are also marked, so that when they are replaced they are written back to disk.

Memory contains program instructions, data, and pointers. Data in this case means anything that's not an executable instruction and not a pointer. This would include all non-program OS/400 objects, as well as parts of program objects that are not executable. Contrast this with the distinction made on the Work System Status (WRSYSSTS) display between database and non-database page faults. Database means strictly physical and logical files. Non-database faults refer to all other objects. In our sequential read example, any page faults for the program, cursor, or any space would be considered non-database page faults.

In the preceding paragraphs we have looked at page faults. It is not necessary to wait for a page fault to read a page in from disk. Any SLIC component or any translated MI program can request the memory-management component of SLIC to explicitly *bring* (read) a range of virtual pages (one or more) into memory. Functionally, it is never necessary to explicitly bring pages into memory, because the required pages will always be brought in as the result of page faults. When a page fault occurs, the process incurring the fault will wait for the disk read to complete. Requesting a bring operation before the pages are needed allows the disk read operations, which may take a long time, to occur overlapped with other processing. Brings can improve performance.

It is also possible to explicitly create clear page frames in memory. A *clear* request to memory management results in one or more page frames in memory set to binary zeros. This is a useful operation when, for example, a buffer is going to be filled with new data and you don't care about its current contents on disk. Rather than reading in the pages of the buffer with individual page faults or even with a single bring, the clear operation gives page frames set to binary zero without performing a single disk read operation.

An option called an *exchange* may be requested as part of a bring or a clear request. This option specifies a range of virtual pages that the memory-management component of SLIC can use for replacement instead of the normal page replacement algorithm. The intent of the exchange operation is to avoid flushing memory of pages that are being referenced and replacing them with pages that are not likely to be referenced more than once. The exchange option is good to use when a large number of pages is to be brought into a small memory or a small memory pool. In Chapter 9, we will see how memory is often divided into several smaller pools, and how all paging for a given process operates in a single pool.

A bring or a clear request can also optionally specify that the page or pages be "pinned" in memory. A pinned page is made resident in memory and will not be removed or written back to disk while it remains pinned.

Certain SLIC data structures, such as the dispatching elements used by process management, which we will discuss in the next chapter, need to be resident. To perform I/O to or from a virtual page, the page must be pinned, because the real address of the frame in which the page resides is used to move the data from the I/O bus. A separate request can be made to memory management to unpin a single page or a range of pages.

In addition to bringing and clearing pages, it is possible to *purge* (write) one or more page frames to disk. A purge operation makes sense only when a page frame in memory has been changed so that the copy of the page on disk is not up to date. Unlike bring and clear operations, which are never functionally necessary (page faulting will perform the functions), a purge is sometimes required. For example, if we are doing database journaling, the SLIC component of the database must guarantee that the journal entries in the journal space object have been written to disk. This component can't wait until page faults occur that force the pages in the journal space to be written to disk; it must use the purge function. A purge operation may also specify that the page or range of pages in memory be unpinned.

Finally, page frames can be *removed* from memory without writing the pages back to disk. There is no functional reason to remove pages, but doing so does eliminate later disk write operations. This function is useful when, for example, a buffer in memory has been emptied and there is no further use for the data in the buffer.

Data and instructions have separate caches in the PowerPC processors. A cache acts as a buffer between the main memory and the processor. These are essentially registers on the processor chip that enable fast access to recently used instructions and data in the memory. In the AS/400, the virtual address is used to access these caches.

Pointers must be protected from corruption. It is possible for user-written MI instructions to deliberately change a pointer because pointers are stored in the associated space of MI objects (along with other structures that user-written code needs to access). Physical changes, such as fluctuations in current, can also corrupt pointer values. If a pointer is changed by anything other than an SLIC routine that has the right to change it (using an instruction not directly accessible from the MI), the pointer's tag bit is turned off by the hardware. This makes the pointer invalid.

All temporary and permanent objects are pageable (i.e., can be moved to disk and back into memory as needed). Some SLIC structures (such as the page table) and some SLIC routines are not pageable; they are loaded during IPL and must be in memory at all times. Their addresses do not have to be translated. The virtual address of such a structure or instructions is the real memory address. Such virtual addresses always begin with hexadecimal 800.

With this brief overview, we are ready to get into a detailed examination of these same topics. Let's first look at the performance implications of the single-level store, then we'll get into the details of the pointers; finally, we will be able to examine the specifics of address translation. We will finish up the chapter with a discussion of disk management. As appropriate, we will use our peppers to identify the hot stuff.

Performance Implications of Single-Level Store

Earlier, we stated that a major benefit of the single-level store was to reduce the number of instructions needed to perform certain operating-system functions. We saw that the file system was greatly simplified by not having to move files into the single-level store. Because the database is contained in the single-level store, it, too, sees benefits. We could look at many examples of operating system functions to see performance benefits, but there is one that all AS/400 users see. This is the AS/400's interactive performance, which is directly affected by the time it takes to perform a process switch. Let's continue to look at the example of a process switch and see how it influences overall AS/400 performance.

A conventional operating system that uses segment-relative addressing requires that the contents of the segment registers be changed on a process switch. If these were not changed in such a system, the smaller effective addresses in the new program would mistakenly translate into virtual addresses that belonged to a program in the previous process. The problem occurs because each process in this type of system has its own effective memory, which starts over with address zero. Most modern Unix operating systems, such as IBM's own AIX, use this type of addressing.

The role of the segment registers in this kind of system is to map the effective addresses into the larger virtual memory. To make this work, the contents of these segment registers must be saved somewhere in memory every time a process is switched out, and restored when the process is brought back in. The use of the segment table, instead of segment registers, in the PowerPC processors eliminates the need to save the register contents in memory — the segment table is already in memory. The SLB registers, however, must be purged on a process switch because they contain the mappings for the previous process.

As the new effective addresses are translated to virtual addresses using the segment table in memory for the new process, the contents of the SLB registers are updated one at a time. Using the memory table until the SLB registers are reloaded can add many processor cycles to every memory access. As a result, the performance of the process is degraded until some number of SLB registers have been loaded. If, for example, the new process switched in was our sequential database read, we would have to translate at least four addresses — one each for the program, index, cursor, and data space — just to get started. In reality, since each of these objects has multiple segments (each with its own virtual address), we would probably have to translate eight to 12 addresses using the memory tables before the SLB registers would be of much use to speed up the translation process.

We just saw that with the one exception for C2-level security, the AS/400's single-level store does not use the segment table. The effective address is the same as the virtual address — no mapping is required. All the virtual memory can be directly addressed from the program. The PowerPC processor hardware bypasses both the segment table and the SLB registers for AS/400 programs. This means there is no performance degradation due to the segment table on a process switch. Even with C2-level security enabled in the AS/400, the segment table and the SLB registers are only used by a process that has programs running in the user state — operating system processes don't use them. Bypassing the segment table and the SLB registers can be a significant performance improvement for the AS/400, but it is only the beginning.

Later in this chapter, we will see in detail how a virtual address is translated into a real address using a page table. Depending upon the specific operating system design, each user process in a conventional system may have its own private virtual memory with its own unique page table. An example of an operating system like this is Microsoft's Windows NT. The memory management component in Windows NT provides a large, private, virtual address space for each process. This means a process switch not only has to change the page table to correctly map the new process' private address space, but it also has to purge all the TLB registers. After the process switch, addresses are translated from virtual to real using the new page table, and the contents of the TLB registers get reloaded one at a time. Just like reloading the SLB registers, reloading the TLB registers after a process switch degrades performance.

Only one virtual memory exists in the AS/400, so only one page table exists that everyone uses. Consequently, there is no need to purge the TLB in an AS/400 on a process switch. Because the TLB registers are not purged, an AS/400 also can make more efficient use of a larger TLB than some other system can. The TLB registers hold the most recently used entries in the page table. As time goes on, older entries are displaced by more recently used entries. With more registers, the likelihood that a virtual address that was translated in the distant past is still in the TLB is higher. When a process that ran in the past is again switched in, the larger TLB means some or all of its addresses may still be available. This would not be the case if the TLB registers had to be purged on each process switch. Once again, the single virtual memory of the AS/400 saves a great deal of processing time.

Finally, modern processors don't fetch and store information directly to or from the memory. They use cache memories. A cache memory contains portions of the main memory and has its own directory. Depending again on the design of the cache memory a particular computer uses and whether or not bits from the virtual address are used in the cache directory, the cache may have to be purged on a process switch. Again, however, this is not a problem for a single-level store.

Operating systems designed to work with conventional virtual memories usually try to avoid doing too many process switches, because such a large overhead is required. When these systems are faced with a situation that requires lots of process switches, they have to rely on high-performance processors to achieve acceptable system performance.

Process switching in an AS/400 is extremely fast compared to other systems, because there is so much less to do. The performance degradation when a new process starts is also less in an AS/400. As a result, the parts of the operating system, both OS/400 and SLIC, are designed to do lots of process switches. A few years back, the IBM Research Division did a study of the AS/400. This group found that, in a typical AS/400 user environment, a process switch took place about every 1,200 instructions. This was unbelievable to them, because some operating systems can take 1,000 instructions or more just to perform the process switch. Not so for an AS/400.

Because of this ability to rapidly switch between processes, the AS/400 excels in interactive performance. The System/38 and the original AS/400 were optimized for interactive, transaction-based applications. This optimization means many terminals can be attached to an AS/400. A single large AS/400 can easily support more than 2,000 concurrent users, something many of its competitors such as Unix and Windows NT have difficulty doing. In an application environment that requires many process switches, an AS/400 can outperform systems with faster processors, because it executes fewer instructions.

If we look at an application environment that does not require many process switches, we see a big performance difference. Consider, for example, a batch environment, where a single process keeps executing for a long period of time. Here, the speed of a process switch does not play a significant role. Early AS/400 systems were not strong batch performers, because the processor performance showed through. In the past, the AS/400 never had high-performance processors.[4]

Even in quoting performance for various models of the AS/400, in the past Rochester never wanted to quote processor ratings such as millions of instructions per second (MIPS) or MHz (just as MIPS measures how many instructions a processor can execute in a second, MHz measures the number of cycles per second the processor can execute). If two different processors have to execute the same number of instructions or cycles to get a particular job done, and everything else is equal, then MIPS or MHz might give some indication of how the two processors perform. But if the processor doesn't have to execute as many instructions to do the same job, then neither MIPS nor MHz has any value.

Rochester has always insisted on using ratings such as transactions per second to show the amount of work an AS/400 can perform. IBM Rochester has been a leader in helping to establish industry standard benchmarks for transaction processing and has worked closely with the Transaction

---

4 Before some of my performance friends, such as Rick Turner, point it out, batch performance depends on more than just processor performance. Such things as memory sizes and disk I/O capabilities play major roles in batch performance.

Processing Council to create the TPC ratings for computer systems. These ratings also factor in the cost per transaction, based on the hardware and software prices for a given configuration. This allows a customer to compare computer systems from various vendors on the basis of both cost and performance. Needless to say, the AS/400 has been one of the leaders both in cost/performance and raw performance using these benchmarks, because it is designed to do this type of processing well.

Interactive processing assumes terminals, such as the 5250, are attached to the AS/400. Functions such as updating the fields on a screen require many process switches, especially if there are hundreds or even thousands of these terminals attached. With the move to client/server computing, much of this screen handling is processed in the PC (client), reducing the number of process switches needed in the AS/400 (server). But in client/server computing many features still resemble interactive processing. With hundreds or thousands of users pressing keys or clicking mouses at the same time, each requesting some database I/O and then waiting for the response, rapid process switching is still needed in the AS/400. The AS/400 is able to leverage its strength in handling numerous simultaneous users (processes) with the data-transfer requirements of the client/server environment.

Other server applications are more compute-intensive. An example is a decision-support application where a large amount of data can be analyzed to create reports. Users are able to construct elaborate queries, answer "what if" questions, search for correlations in the data, and so on. The type of processing required for such an application looks more like a batch environment than an interactive environment.

Higher-performance processors were needed in an AS/400 for some of these server applications. For this reason, when we introduced special models of the AS/400 designed especially for server performance, we put higher-performance processors and lots of memory into them. On various client/server benchmarks, the Advanced Server models introduced in 1994 have demonstrated that they are very competitive in the industry, both in price and performance. Not surprisingly, many customers find these models are better batch machines because of the higher-performance processors.

A big reason for IBM's move to RISC processors was to get even higher performance for server applications. Consider, for example, the highest performance processors available before and after the RISC models were introduced. The fastest processor available in 1994 had a cycle time of approximately 20 nanoseconds (50 MHz). In 1995, that cycle time is down to 6.5 nanoseconds (154 MHz). This is not exactly a fair comparison, because the 1994 processor was a CISC design, and these usually require fewer cycles to perform a given operation than does a RISC design. On the other hand, the 1995 RISC design does far more of these cycles in parallel.

Process switching is a heavily used function in either interactive or client/server applications, and a fast process switch is always better than a slow one. The single-level store not only improves process switching performance, it also improves the performance of many functions by eliminating instructions to execute. Consider, for example, the file operations we discussed. A conventional server does many file opens and closes, causing extra disk activity. This reduces overall system performance. The AS/400 processes these files in place, eliminating the extra overhead. High-performance processors are important, but keep in mind that every instruction that does not need to be executed is equivalent to having an infinite-speed processor for that instruction. RISC processors are fast, but not that fast.

Pointers and Tags

Aside from performance, the biggest advantage of a single-level store is that everything can be shared; its biggest disadvantage is that everything can be shared. When every user in the system has access to the same single, large address space, some way has to be found to guarantee that users cannot access or change something to which they are not authorized. In Chapter 5, we saw that pointers provide this protection in an AS/400. In this section, we will look at pointers in more detail and see how they provide the protection.

The act of resolving a system pointer provides access to an object at MI, as we saw earlier. Pointers are 16 bytes (128 bits) long. A resolved system pointer contains direct addressability to a system object. This means the 64-bit virtual address is contained in the pointer. Similarly, the other types of pointers (space, data, instruction, and procedure) each also contain a virtual address.

Pointers are contained in the associated space of a system object. Also contained in this space are data that an MI program can access and modify. The accessing and modifying of the data in an associated space is legitimate; modifying a pointer is not. If an MI program could modify the contents of a pointer, we would have a potential security exposure. The address in the pointer could be changed to point to someone else's object or to some other structure in the system where the program was not allowed to go. Of course, I am speaking here about a user-written program that directly specifies MI instructions; I am not talking about programs written in high-level languages such as RPG or COBOL.

When we originally designed the pointer structure, we knew of ways to reduce this potential security exposure by eliminating the MI assembler, making certain instructions privileged, and taking the authority out of the pointer. As we saw in Chapter 7, these actions have been taken over time as we tightened the security levels of the AS/400. But even with these actions, a need still exists to protect the contents of a pointer from illegitimate modification.

We saw, again back in Chapter 5, that the associated space containing pointers occupies a separate segment in a system object. For the original

System/38 design, we decided to use two segments, one for the data and one for the pointers. We were not happy about this approach, because it had an impact on system performance. Pages from both the data and the pointer segments had to be fetched when an object was used, and this increased our system overhead. Two segments also meant a slight increase in memory size requirements. The only reason we had planned to add the associated pointer segment was because we thought it could protect pointers from being modified by users. But we were wrong.

We soon discovered we could not protect the associated pointer segment from being modified. With the system security levels we had planned for the System/38 (up through level 30), a user who had authorization to an object could get into the object with the use of the MI assembler. Putting the pointers somewhere else in the object provided no additional protection, so we had to find another solution.

Hardware Protection for Pointers

We realized we needed some form of hardware memory protection for pointers. Many of the larger systems at the time, such as the System/370, used special bits in the hardware to provide memory protection. These bits were used by the hardware to allow or inhibit user access to some block of bytes in the memory. These protection bits were usually kept in a separate hardware memory array, where the user could not get at them. With every access to memory, this special hardware array was checked to determine whether or not the user was allowed to access the block in memory. This type of memory protection was usually on a page-sized physical block of memory.

We originally hadn't planned to implement this type of memory protection in the System/38 hardware, because we didn't think we needed it. Our protection was at the object level. But when we realized we needed some form of hardware protection, we briefly considered protection on a page-sized block; but that was expensive and not exactly what we wanted. Ideally, we would have protection for every 16 bytes in memory, because a pointer occupies 16 bytes. But for performance reasons, we wanted to put pointers anywhere, and the expense of putting in a separate hardware array with protection bits for every 16 bytes in memory was prohibitive. Then we found the answer. We had extra bits in our memory for our error-correcting code (ECC). We would use an ECC bit for memory protection.

Computer memories occasionally make errors because of voltage spikes on power lines or other causes. To guard against errors, most memories use error-detecting or error-correcting codes. When these codes are used, extra bits are added to each memory word. A memory word contains the number of bits that can be read from or written to memory in a single operation. When data is read out of memory, the extra bits are checked to see whether or not an error occurred in memory.

The simplest form of error detection is to add a single *parity* bit to the memory word. The value of the parity bit is chosen so the number of 1 bits in the memory word, including the parity bit, is always an even number. If an error occurs in memory that causes any bit to change from 1 to 0 or from 0 to 1, that error will be detected when the memory word is read out, and the number of 1 bits is no longer even. Parity provides single-bit error detection, but it doesn't tell which bit failed. Parity can detect whether or not an odd number of bit errors occurred, but it tells nothing if an even number of bit errors occurred in the memory word. Parity is usually used for PC memories.

Most computers that are used for commercial processing, such as the AS/400, use additional bits in their codes to provide both error detection and correction. These additional bits can detect all single- and multiple-bit errors, and they can even identify which bit failed on a single-bit error. Thus, the hardware can correct errors and continue processing. The value of error correction is obvious to anyone who has powered-on a PC and received the message "memory parity error." Nothing happens with that PC until the bad memory module is replaced.

The original System/38 hardware had a 32-bit (4-byte) memory word. The ECC for this word size required an additional 7 bits. For every memory word, we needed 39 bits — 32 for data and 7 for ECC. Our memory technology in those days was always packaged in 8-bit increments, meaning our memory word was actually 40 bits wide. We had an extra bit for every 4-byte word in memory, and that bit was to become our memory protection bit. We called it a tag bit.

A pointer occupies 16 bytes in memory. We decided to always store pointers on 16-byte memory boundaries (the low-order 4 bits of the memory address are all zeros). From a terminology standpoint, we usually call this a quadword, which means it is a 16-byte field aligned on a 16-byte boundary. Likewise, we have doublewords and words, each aligned on 8- and 4-byte boundaries, respectively. Within the computer industry, the name "word" is generally accepted to mean 4 bytes.

A pointer in the original System/38 occupied four consecutive 4-byte words in memory, each with its own tag bit. We decided to have the tag bit for every memory word set to 1 if that word contained any of the four parts of a pointer. If there was no part of a pointer in the word, the tag bit was set to 0. The pointer itself only needed one tag, so we said if all 4 bits in the consecutive four memory words were set to 1, then the pointer had a logical tag of 1. If any of the 4 bits was 0, then the pointer had a logical tag of 0.

Later implementations of the AS/400 have a 64-bit (8-byte) memory word. A 64-bit memory word requires 8 ECC bits; so with the tag bit, the AS/400 memories are packaged 73 bits wide. We still keep pointers on 16-byte boundaries and each pointer has one logical tag bit. For the AS/400 with the 64-bit memory word, the two tag bits in the consecutive two words that hold the pointer must both be 1 for the pointer to have a logical tag of 1. If either tag bit is 0, then the pointer has a logical tag of 0. To keep with the industry terminology, we call the 64-bit memory word a doubleword.

Whenever a write to memory occurs in an AS/400, the memory control hardware creates the ECC and stores it with the memory word. As part of this write operation, the memory control hardware also turns off the tag bit in the memory word (sets it to 0). Any standard instruction that writes to memory will always result in the tag bits for the words written being set to 0.

Tags-Active Mode

In Chapter 2, we talked about extensions to the PowerPC architecture. One of the extensions we discussed was a tags-active mode. When a PowerPC processor is configured in this mode, additional instructions are available that do not appear in the tags-inactive mode. We said there were 25 instructions added for the AS/400 and they are only available in the tags-active mode. These include instructions to allow loading and storing multiple quadwords to and from the registers. There are also instructions for decimal arithmetic, system call/return functions, and select instructions to test bit settings in control registers. Six of the new instructions support tags.

A couple of these special tag instructions can be used to set or test the tag bits. One of them, called Store Quadword (stq), stores 16 bytes of data from two 64-bit registers into memory and turns on the two tag bits. Another, called Load Quadword (lq), loads 16 bytes of data from memory into two 64-bit registers and sets a bit in a control register to 1 if both tag bits in the memory words fetched are 1; otherwise, the bit is set to 0. Still another instruction allows the tags to be fetched from memory and put into a special register in the processor. We will describe the use of this last instruction in the next section.

The tag instructions are only used by SLIC. These instructions are not generated by the translator for MI programs. This means that any store to memory that is generated for an MI program uses the standard instructions and always turns off the tag bits. When a pointer is created as part of a resolve operation, SLIC builds the pointer in two 64-bit registers and uses the stq instruction to turn the tag bits on in memory. Whenever an MI program attempts to use a pointer, SLIC uses the lq instruction to load the contents of the pointer into registers and then tests to see whether or not the tag bits are still on. If the tag bits are found to be off, this means someone modified the pointer and, therefore, it is invalid.

Tag bits in the AS/400 do not prevent the modification of pointers. They are used to detect the modification when the pointer is used. This approach is different from the one most memory protection schemes use. Typically, memory protection prevents the modification. This is also important, and later we will see that the AS/400 has this type of protection on a page basis. For pointers, however, the modification is detected after the fact. This approach reduced the amount of hardware needed in the early implementations of the system and still provided the needed level of protection.

Pointers cannot be counterfeited. Tags ensure that a pointer was created by the operating system (SLIC) and that it has not been modified by anyone other than SLIC. Anyone else who creates a pointer, copies a pointer, or modifies a pointer has no way to turn the tag bits on and will end up with a useless 16-byte entity.

Pointers and Tags on Disk

When we wanted to move a page from memory to disk on a System/38, we had another problem. Memory has extra bits for ECC and tags; the disk does not. Disks use a different form of error-detection coding, called a cyclic redundancy check (CRC), which does not add extra bits to each memory word. We needed to find a way to keep the tag bits with the pointers when we moved the page containing the pointers to the disk. In short, we had to find some extra space on the disk.

A magnetic disk is a collection of platters, each of which has two recordable surfaces. Each disk surface is divided into concentric circles, called tracks. Each track in turn is divided into *sectors* that contain the information. The sector size for the System/38 and the AS/400 is 520 bytes. Each sector has an 8-byte sector header and a 512-byte data area. This sector size was selected to match the 512-byte page size of the System/38 — a page fits into a sector.

We defined some special IMPI instructions in the System/38 to manipulate tags. One of these instructions, called Extract Tags, was used to gather the tags from a page in memory. As part of the operation to write the page to disk, these tags were also written to disk. Another IMPI instruction, called Insert Tags, was used to put the tags back in memory when a page was read from disk.

Many ISVs and customers who knew about the tag bits in the System/38 assumed they were stored in the 8-byte sector headers on the disks. That was not the case. The information in the page itself was stored in the 512-byte data area of the sector. The sector header contained information about the page, but its most important function was to contain the virtual address of the page. This address was needed for recovery purposes. If we ever lost the table in memory that related the virtual addresses to the disk locations, we could recreate it by reading each sector header to see which virtual address was associated with each sector. With most of the space in the sector headers taken by the virtual address of the page, there was no room for the tags.

A quick calculation will show this. A single page can contain 32 pointers (16 bytes x 32 = 512 bytes), which means there are 32 tag bits per page. A virtual address for the System/38 was 48 bits, but we didn't need all those bits to identify a page. The low-order 9 bits in the virtual address identify the byte in a 512-byte page ($2^9 = 512$). Therefore, we only needed to store the high-order 39 bits of the virtual address (48 bits − 9 bits = 39 bits) to uniquely identify the page. Even without any status bits, however, we would need a minimum of 71 bits to store both the virtual address of the page and all the tag bits (39 bits + 32 bits = 71 bits), and the sector headers each had only 64 bits. There was no way to store the tag bits in the sector headers.

We became very creative with the System/38 and found space inside the page for the tags. In the next section, we will see that a pointer contains some unused space. If a page contains at least one pointer, we have some unused space where we can store the tag bits. If there were no pointers on a page, all the tag bits for the page would be 0s, so there is no need to store any tags. The sector header in the System/38 contained information about whether or not there were tags on the page and, if so, where on the page they were located.

We continued to use the 512-byte page size in the AS/400 until the introduction of the RISC processors, and the method for storing tag bits was as we just described. But we had wanted to increase the page size for several years.

The 512-byte page size had been selected for the System/38 because the main memory sizes were constrained.[5] But a 512-byte page was too small for the AS/400's larger main memory sizes. There were too many pages, and our page tables were getting too large. Besides, for years we have been blocking these small pages into larger "logical" pages to reduce disk activity. For the new processors, we decided to increase the size of the pages to 4 kilobytes (4,096 bytes).

We retained the 520-byte sector size on disk for the new models. A 4-kilobyte page is now stored on eight consecutive sectors. With eight 8-byte headers for each page, there is more than enough room to store the 256 tag bits that a 4-kilobyte page can contain.

We also added a special tag register to the PowerPC processor architecture to be used for extracting tags from memory. When the processor executes another of the special tag instructions, called Load Multiple Doubleword (lmd), up to 16 doublewords (eight quadwords) from memory can be read into 16 registers. The eight tag bits from the memory quadwords are stored in the tag register as part of this instruction. Note that the logical eight bits are stored in the tag register, not the 16 physical tag bits that would be found in memory. Recall that a quadword is two 64-bit (8-byte) memory words; therefore, there are two physical tag bits in a quadword, which is how we get 16 physical tag bits in eight quadwords. The tag bits for the page can be collected using this instruction, so they can be written to disk with the data. Again, this instruction is only available in the tags-active mode.

[5] An IBM "expert" came to Rochester before the System/38 was announced and declared that our planned memory sizes were too large. Over the protests of those of us who knew better, we were forced to reduce our memory sizes. The original Model 5 was a poor performer because it was constrained to 2 megabytes of memory. When memory sizes increased, so did performance. When the same expert came back to help us with the AS/400, we threw him out.

Inside a Pointer

We use a pointer to access objects on the AS/400. In this section, we will concentrate only on the format of a resolved pointer, which provides two functions. It describes the object and the authority the user has to the object; it also provides the address of the object in the single-level store. If we look inside one of these 16-byte pointers, we find it divided into two 8-byte parts. The first part contains the description of the object and the second part contains the virtual address.

The first part of a resolved pointer contains status bits that, among other things, identify whether this is a system, space, data, instruction, or procedure pointer. There is also information in this first part about the object or data accessed by the pointer. For example, a system pointer identifies the MI system object type and the OS/400-defined subtype for the object. A data pointer describes the type of data to which it points. The final piece of information contained in the first part of the pointer is the authority to the object. As previously noted, the authority field is only used when the pointer is owned by the operating system in the system state. Pointers created by user programs in the user state do not have the authority field filled in.

The information in the first part of the pointer (just described) does not occupy all 8 bytes; it only occupies 4 bytes. This means there are 4 bytes in the pointer that are unused. We have reserved this space for future expansion of the address. This extra 32 bits, together with the 64 address bits in the pointer, gives us the opportunity to expand the AS/400 address to 96 bits (12 bytes) without affecting any program above the MI. If we wanted more space, we could even move the type and authority information out of the pointer and go beyond 96 bits.

The second part of a resolved pointer contains a 64-bit address. What's more, it has always contained a 64-bit address, and this has caused confusion for years over the size of the virtual address in a System/38 and an AS/400. Is it 48 bits or 64 bits? Today, with the new RISC models of the AS/400, the answer is simple: It is a 64-bit address. For the System/38 and earlier models of the AS/400, it was both. The MI always had a 64-bit address, and the hardware always had a 48-bit address. How these worked together is our next topic.

A Tale of Two Address Sizes

The introduction of the new AS/400 RISC models with their full 64-bit hardware addresses has eliminated most of the problems and a lot of the confusion that existed with the mixed 64-bit and 48-bit addressing structure of the previous models. To appreciate why the 64-bit hardware address is so significant, we need to look at the original 48-bit implementation.

The 48-bit address came about as a compromise. The System/38 operating system designers decided they wanted a 64-bit address. Once the size of a pointer had been set to 16 bytes, there was plenty of room for the 64-bit address. At the hardware level, we had a different problem. The more bits we had in the address, the larger the size of the registers in the processor. Larger registers meant more circuits and more hardware costs.

Ray Klotz was our engineering manager for the System/38. Ray wasn't convinced we needed such a large address. We had many conversations on this topic, but he wasn't buying the arguments for a persistent, 64-bit address that would last forever. In the mid-1970s, the IBM mainframe division was about to announce a new larger address for the System/370, called extended addressing (XA). The System/370 address was about to grow from 24 to 31 bits with XA. Ray accused us of trying to build a system architecture that was larger than the System/370 — he argued that 32 bits was bigger than 31. We could beat them by 1 bit. "You don't need to beat them by 33 bits," he would say.

We argued a 32-bit address would not work for the single-level store of the System/38. We needed 64 bits. When it became obvious we were making no progress in reaching a decision, we did what anyone who has ever haggled over the price of a used car has done. We split the difference between 32 and 64 bits. From that point on we would have a 48-bit address.

To support the segmented memory, the 48-bit address is divided in two. The high-order bits of the address identify the segment. This high part of the address is called the segment identifier (SID). The low-order bits identify the byte in the segment, which is called the offset. In the hardware, we decided to use the high-order 32 bits for the SID and the low-order 16 bits for the offset. For notation purposes, we will call this the 32/16 view of the address. The 16 bits in the offset means a segment size of 64 kilobytes (2^{16} = 64 kilobytes).

The original System/38 processor hardware had a 16-bit data path and a 16-bit adder for computation. The idea behind the 32/16 view of the address was to keep the 16-bit offset portion of the address in this data path, because it gets updated very frequently. We decided to keep the 32-bit SID outside of the processor data path in a separate set of SID registers. These SID registers could be accessed by the processor, but they could not be updated in place.

The programmers responsible for the operating system software beneath MI, originally called the VMC, did not agree with the 32/16 view of the address. They felt the 64-kilobyte segment size was too small. An initial thought was that they would create segment groups, each containing one or more of these 64-kilobyte segments. In the end, however, they decided the segment group should always have 256 of the 64-kilobyte segments. Whenever a new segment was assigned as part of a newly created object, the segment size was always 16 megabytes (256 x 64 kilobytes = 16 megabytes). In effect, the VMC programmers created a second segment size of 16 megabytes. From that point on, we talked about 64-kilobyte and 16-megabyte segments, although sometimes we would call this latter size a segment group. This ambiguity in the definition of a segment and a segment group would continue until we introduced the PowerPC processors with SLIC. If you want to get out your calculator or your powers-of-2 table, you will see that with the 16-megabyte segment size, the VMC programmers began to look at the 48-bit address as having a 24-bit SID and a 24-bit offset, since 2^{24} = 16 megabytes.

This 24/24 view of the address used by the VMC did not match the 32/16 view used by the hardware. This was a problem because of the way an overflow out of the offset portion of the address was handled. From our previous look at objects, we saw they are made from one or more noncontiguous segments, and no segment can contain parts of more than one object. It should be clear that we do not want to have an address offset incremented beyond the end of one segment into the next segment. That next segment may be part of a different object. For example, we do not want to have the address in a space pointer incremented beyond the end of the associated space in an object. The way to detect this address overflow is to watch the offset portion of the address whenever it is incremented to see whether or not there is a carry out of the offset into the SID. Such a carry would indicate that we are trying to address something in the next segment.

Hardware is very good at detecting and reporting these overflows. The mechanism used to report such an occurrence in the hardware is an *exception*. We discuss exceptions in Chapter 9, but one is of interest to us now: the effective address overflow (EAO) exception. This exception was defined for the System/38 to report whenever an overflow occurred out of the 16-bit offset. When this EAO exception occurred, the hardware did not increment the 32-bit SID portion of address. Instead, it reported the exception to the VMC.

The VMC had to look at every EAO exception to see whether or not it was a problem. Because the VMC considered the segment to be 16 megabytes long, made up of 256 of the smaller hardware segments, an overflow out of a 64-kilobyte segment in the middle of the 16-megabyte segment was not a problem. With its 24/24 view of the address, the VMC only recognized an overflow out of the low 24 bits into the high 24 bits. For each EAO exception, the VMC had to increment the 32-bit hardware SID, check to see whether or not there was an overflow into the high 24 bits, and if not, pass control back to the hardware. The VMC software had to constantly deal with this 32/16 versus 24/24 mismatch.

As time went on and the processor data path width grew from the original 16 bits to 32 bits and then to 48 bits, the separation of the SID and offset registers in the hardware became less important. For the AS/400, instructions were added to the IMPI to support the 24/24 view of the address, so the AS/400 did not have to handle this in the software. For compatibility with the original VMC, however, the 32/16 view had to be retained at the IMPI.

The original VMC had another problem with addresses. It had to support the 64-bit address in the MI pointer with a 48-bit hardware address. We could have tried to treat the 64-bit address as a larger virtual address, which somehow got mapped into a smaller 48-bit virtual address, but we chose not to do this. Instead, we decided to treat the high-order 16 bits of the 64-bit address as a separate value. We called this 16-bit field the SID extender. For the value in the SID extender, we chose the IPL number. Every time the system was IPLed, we incremented the IPL number by one. This gave us a new

48-bit address space at each IPL. Figure 8.1 shows the fields that make up the 64-bit address in the original MI pointer.

Figure 8.1 Original Format of an MI Pointer Address

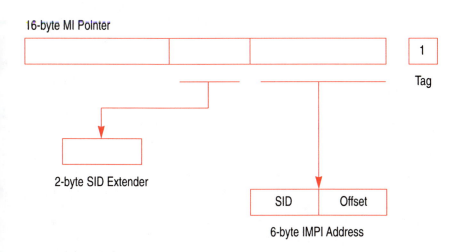

Originally, the segment header described back in Chapter 5 had another field that contained the 16-bit SID extender for the segment. When an MI program attempted to use a pointer in the System/38 and the early AS/400 models, a special IMPI instruction was used to check the tag bits and to load the 48-bit address into a processor register. This instruction was called Load and Verify Tags (lvt). The lvt instruction was analogous to the lq instruction in the RISC processors, but the lvt instruction had an additional responsibility. It had to compare the high-order 16 bits of the address in the pointer to the SID extender field in the segment header. This compare would guarantee that the high bits in the pointer address matched the address of the segment. After that first access, only the 48-bit address was used to access the segment.

Every time we incremented the IPL number, we got a new address space for temporary objects. Temporary objects are destroyed at IPL time — not so for permanent objects. Permanent objects exist across IPLs. Because the hardware only used 48 bits, the same 48-bit address could not be used for two permanent objects. The 48-bit address can be reused only if the permanent object that previously had the address was explicitly destroyed in an earlier IPL. Only the headers are kept when a permanent object is destroyed. The headers were found when the full 64-bit address (which has the IPL number in the first 16 bits) in the pointer was first used. There is no conflict with reusing the 48-bit address as long as only the headers exist for the previous permanent object and the IPL numbers are different. Note that only headers for destroyed permanent objects are kept — nothing is kept when a temporary object is destroyed.

Running Out of Addresses

Because we had decided not to reuse the 48-bit address except at IPL boundaries in the System/38, there was a question of whether or not we could run out of addresses. Some original calculations were done to see if we had a problem. According to these figures, with one IPL per day, 365 days per year, it would be 180 years before we reused the IPL number. Running out of SID extenders was not a problem. By knowing the projected performance of our future processors, it was possible to calculate the maximum number of 64-kilobyte segments we could generate between daily IPLs. These calculations also showed there would be no problem. But all these calculations were wrong, and some large AS/400 systems started to run out of addresses.[6]

What happened? First, one IPL per day may have been a good assumption for the early System/38, but as businesses began to need their computers 24 hours a day, there was no time for IPLs. Also, the size of our systems had grown to the point that the IPL time was too long. We have made major changes to the AS/400 in the last few releases to significantly reduce IPL time. We have already discussed some of these changes. But even with the changes, one IPL per day is still an unreasonable assumption. The second problem with the calculation was the assumption of a 64-kilobyte segment. With the 24/24 view of the address, the original VMC always created 16-megabyte segments.

To further aggravate the problem, the memory management component of the original VMC had divided the entire 48-bit virtual address space into quadrants. The top two bits of the 48-bit address were used to identify the quadrant. Addresses were assigned from one of these quadrants based on their intended use. One quadrant was reserved for addresses of permanent objects, so all permanent addresses had the same setting in the first two bits. Another quadrant was reserved for temporary object addresses. A third was reserved for addresses of temporary objects in an access group. In Chapter 5 we introduced an access group, which is another system object that allows multiple temporary objects of different types to be bundled and accessed together. Readers may be familiar with a process access group (PAG). Because permanent objects cannot be in an access group, the fourth quadrant was not used. This original decision was based on the assumption that a 48-bit address space was so big, one quarter of it could be thrown away with no loss. Of the 256 terabytes (2^{48} bytes) of virtual memory we liked to brag about, 64 terabytes were never used in the System/38 and the early AS/400 models.

The problem that occurred with some large AS/400 systems was that they were running out of temporary addresses. This was called SID wrap, because

[6] As the one who made those original calculations and reached the conclusion that there would not be a problem, I have taken a lot of heat in recent years. I have also been highly motivated to move the AS/400 to a 64-bit hardware address.

all the SIDs available during an IPL were used up. By dividing the address space into quadrants, there were only 4 million 16-megabyte temporary segments per IPL. Consequently, large systems with applications that used lots of temporary objects could run out of temporary SIDs if they were not IPLed for several days. The fix from a customer viewpoint was to re-IPL the system. This solved the immediate problem but was not a long-term solution.

During the first few operating system releases of the AS/400, changes were made to the system software to reduce the SID wrap problem. Components began to use 64-kilobyte segments, whenever possible, instead of 16-megabyte segments. The quarter of the address space that had been thrown away was also reclaimed. These system software changes did not fix the problem, however; they only gave us some breathing room until the 64-bit RISC processors arrived.

We have not discussed permanent addresses. Their maximum number is limited by the amount of disk space attached to the system, because we always keep some physical disk storage even for deleted objects. We limited the total amount of disk space that could be attached to an AS/400, so that a customer would not run out of permanent addresses. Running out of permanent addresses cannot be fixed with an IPL. The solution requires the entire system to be reloaded, and that is totally unacceptable for anyone. We therefore limited the disk sizes in previous AS/400 models.

The reason we've spent the last several paragraphs describing the addressing structure of the System/38 and the early models of the AS/400 has been to show the real reason why IBM chose to move to the RISC processors. We knew even before the introduction of the original AS/400 that the 48-bit address would limit the future growth of the system. As systems got larger and faster, they were going to use more temporary addresses. Customers also wanted to attach more disks to these systems.

There was no way the 48-bit address was going take us far into the future, though it did take some time to convince management this was the case. Rochester has always followed the old adage, "If it ain't broke, don't fix it"; but we finally convinced them it was broken. The good news was that the breakage was inside the system. The AS/400's technology independence protected our customers.

When you break the address in a computer architecture, you might as well change everything. We now had the chance to get rid of the IMPI and move to a RISC design. Our original RISC processor that we started to design in 1990, which we called C-RISC (the "C" was for commercial), had a 96-bit address. We had the room for this large address in the pointers and decided to go all the way. When we decided to use the PowerPC architecture in 1991, we scaled the address back to 64 bits.

Address Translation

The virtual address in a computer system must be translated into a real address before the memory can be accessed. Earlier, we saw that the Power-PC architecture has another level of address, called the effective address, which programs generate. These effective addresses must first be translated into virtual addresses before the virtual addresses can be translated to real addresses. In this section, we will discuss how these translations are accomplished. Some of the details may get a little spicy.

Memory Model Characteristics

We have already introduced some characteristics of the AS/400's memory model in this chapter. Let's review a list of these characteristics, together with some we have not seen before (we will discuss all these characteristics in more detail in the next couple of sections):

- The page size is 2^{12} bytes (4 kilobytes).
- The effective address range is 2^{64} bytes.
  — The number of effective segments is 2^{40}.
  — The effective segment size is 2^{24} bytes (16 megabytes).
- There are two types of address translation:
  — Translation through segment table when in C2 mode.
  — Direct translation (bypass segment table) when not in C2 mode.
- There are two special types of effective addresses that override address translation. These special addresses are identified by the 12 high-order bits (3 hex digits) of the effective address.

  hex 800   Effective = Real (E=R) addresses map all of real memory. There are 2^{28} effective segments for E = R addresses.

  hex 801   Effective = Direct-Store (E=DS) addresses map the I/O space. There are 2^{28} effective segments for E=DS addresses.

- The virtual address range is 2^{64} bytes.
  — The number of virtual segments is $2^{40} - 2^{29}$.
  — The size of virtual segments is 2^{24} bytes (16 megabytes).
- The real address range is 2^{52} bytes.

Again, the characteristics listed are for the tags-active, 64-bit processor implementations the AS/400 uses.

Machine State Register

The address translation process is controlled by the tags-active or tags-inactive mode and by the *state* of the processor. A special register in the processor, called the Machine State Register (MSR), defines the state of the processor. The bits in this register tell the processor how to perform certain operations, such as address translation. In the next chapter, we will look at this register and see how the bits in the register can be altered. A few words about some of these bits in the MSR and their settings are needed to help you understand address translation. The bits are

- 64-bit mode bit (MSR_{SF})
  0   The processor runs in 32-bit mode.
  1   The processor runs in 64-bit mode.
- Instruction relocate bit (MSR_{IR})
  0   The instruction address translation is off.
  1   The instruction address translation is on.
- Data relocate bit (MSR_{DR})
  0   The data address translation is off.
  1   The data address translation is on.
- C2 security (MSR_{C2})
  0   The C2 security is off.
  1   The C2 security is on.
- Problem state (MSR_{PR})
  0   The processor is privileged to execute any instruction.
  1   The processor can only execute the non-privileged instructions.
- User state (MSR_{US})
  0   The operating system code is executing.
  1   The user code is executing.

The address translation process uses the 64-bit mode bit (MSR_{SF}) to determine the size of the addresses. For example, in the 32-bit mode the effective address is defined in the PowerPC architecture to be only 32 bits long. With the tags-active mode in the AS/400 processors, only the 64-bit mode setting is recognized by the hardware. Thus, SLIC, which controls the settings of the MSR bits, will only set the 64-bit mode.

The instruction relocate bit (MSR_{IR}) and the data relocate bit (MSR_{DR}) allow the processor to operate in the real addressing mode. When relocate is turned off by SLIC, the address translation mechanism is bypassed, and the low-order 52 bits of the effective address are passed directly to the memory subsystem as a real address. The memory subsystem is defined as the cache memories and the main memory. The PowerPC architecture supports a cache model in which there are separate caches for instructions and data. For this reason, separate relocate bits are provided for instructions and data. This model is called a Harvard-style cache.[7]

The C2 security bit (MSR_{C2}) setting is used to bypass or not bypass the segment registers during the translation process. This bit is only in the tags-active mode. The problem state bit (MSR_{PR}) is used in the address translation process and for memory protection. The problem state bit defines whether or not the processor can execute the privileged instructions in the

[7] In the early 1940s, Harvard University, with funding from IBM, developed a series of computers, called Mark. The Mark-III and Mark-IV had separate memories for instructions and data. The term Harvard architecture is used to describe machines with separate memories.

PowerPC instruction set. These privileged instructions should not be confused with MI privileged instructions (like the PWRDWNSYS instruction we saw in Chapter 7) — only SLIC executes privileged PowerPC instructions. An example of a PowerPC privileged instruction is one of the tag instructions such as the lq we discussed in an earlier section.

The user state bit (MSR_{US}) supports the AS/400's security level 40 and up. This bit is used to distinguish system state versus user state for an AS/400 process. The user state bit determines whether or not the authority can be put into a pointer, and whether or not MI privileged instructions can be executed by the process. The user state bit is also used for memory protection. Note that the user state bit is also only used in the tags-active mode.

Address Translation Overview

Figure 8.2 shows the PowerPC address translation with tags active. The hardware checks the 64-bit effective address generated by a program to determine whether or not it is a translated address, an E=R address, or an E=DS address. The high-order 12 bits (3 hex digits) of the effective address are used to make this determination.

If the high-order 3 hex digits of an effective address are 800, the address is an E=R address. Parts of SLIC must work with real addresses and be able to address anything in memory. Much of the memory management code also must operate with these addresses. A part of the effective address space is set aside for these E=R addresses. Not coincidentally, there are 2^{52} of these addresses (64 bits minus the 12 high-order bits for 800) to match the real address range.

When the hardware detects an E=R address, it checks the problem state bit to see whether or not the process that generated this address can execute privileged PowerPC instructions ($MSR_{PR} = 0$). If so, the remaining 52 bits in the E=R address are passed directly to the main memory as a real address. If $MSR_{PR} = 1$, a given processor implementation will either generate an exception or treat the address as a translated address — different PowerPC processors react differently. With a valid E=R address, there is no translation overhead. We like to say that using an 800 number is a toll-free way to access the memory.

The PowerPC architecture uses a range of addresses, called the direct-store addresses, to access the I/O space, which we briefly introduced in Chapter 2. An external address space is defined, which to the processor looks like a part of the memory. Of course, this address space is not part of the memory; rather, the address is used to identify a particular I/O device attached to the system. Typically, devices in any system are attached to an I/O bus. In Chapter 10, we will see that AS/400 devices are attached to I/O processors, which in turn are attached to I/O buses. This direct-store address is used in the AS/400 to identify both an I/O bus and an I/O processor attached to the bus.

Figure 8.2 Address Translation with Tags Active

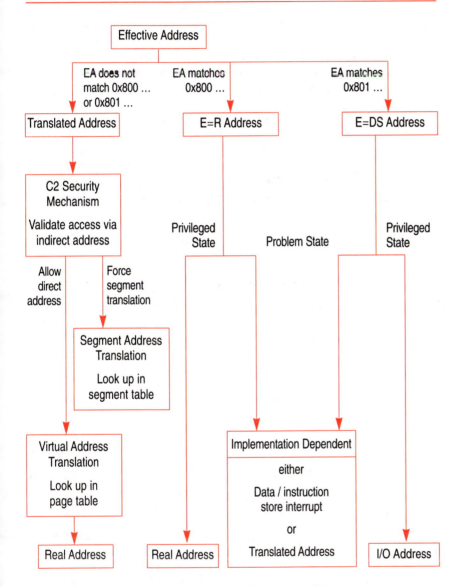

With this type of architecture, which is often called memory-mapped I/O, a special set of instructions exclusively used by the processor to communicate with the I/O devices is not needed. Instead, any load or store instruction can be used to pass commands and data to the devices using this external address space. A direct-store address is a mapping of an effective address to this external address space.

If the high-order 3 hex digits of an effective address are 801, the address is an E=DS address. When the hardware detects an E=DS address, it checks the problem state bit to see whether or not the process that generated this address can execute privileged PowerPC instructions ($MSR_{PR} = 0$). If so, the remaining 52 bits in the E=DS address are passed directly to the I/O space. Like the E=R addresses, E=DS addresses have 2^{28} effective segments. If $MSR_{PR} = 1$, a given processor implementation will either generate an exception or treat the address as a translated address.

If the high-order 3 hex digits of an effective address are neither 800 nor 801, the address is a translated address. The system first converts this type of effective address to a virtual address. The C2 security mechanism determines whether or not the segment table is used to create the virtual address. After the virtual address is created, it is translated into a real address using the page table. Figure 8.3 shows the steps involved in the address translation. The

Figure 8.3 Steps Involved in Address Translation

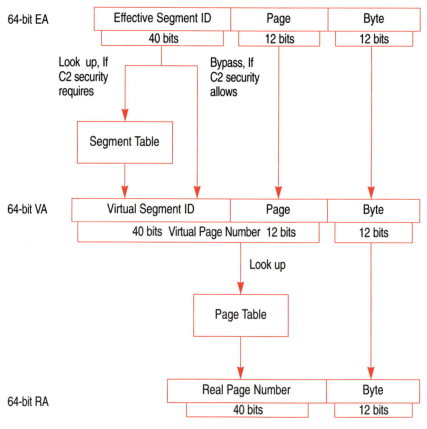

high-order 40 bits of the effective address are called the *effective segment identifier* (ESID) and the low-order 24 address bits are called the *offset*. As shown in the figure, the offset is further divided into a page offset and a byte offset. Each of these offset fields is 12 bits long. The page offset identifies the page in a segment, while the byte offset identifies the byte in the page.

The first step in the process is to create the virtual segment identifier (VSID). The method used to calculate the VSID is determined by the C2 Mode. The value of the C2 Mode is computed as follows:

$$\text{C2 Mode} = \text{MSR}_{C2} \,\&\, \text{MSR}_{PR} \,\&\, \text{MSR}_{US}$$

If C2 Mode = 1, then a segment table look-up is required. If C2 Mode = 0, then the segment table look-up is bypassed. In other words, the segment table look-up is only used if C2 security is on, the process is running in the problem state (non-privileged), and operating system code is not executing. All three conditions must be met before the segment table is used.

The virtual address, like the effective address, is 64 bits long and has a 24-bit offset. Notice that no matter how the VSID is formed, the total offset portion of the effective address is passed directly to the virtual address. The VSID and the page offset portions of the virtual address make up the virtual page number (VPN). From Figure 8.3 we can see that the VPN is 52 bits long. The VPN is used to look up the real page number (RPN) in the page table. The RPN is the number of a page frame in memory, not the number of a page on disk. The byte offset is always passed from the effective address to the virtual address to the real address. The byte offset identifies the byte in a 4-kilobyte page and never participates in any of the translation process.

We are going to skip an in-depth look at the segment table and focus our attention on the page table. Suffice it to say the implementation of the segment table is very similar to the page table. The general approach used to look up an entry in the segment table is the same as the one used to look up an entry in the page table. In an AS/400, the virtual-to-real address translation that uses the page table is more important than the segment translation, because most effective addresses bypass the segment table.

Virtual-to-Real Address Translation

The data structure in memory that contains the RPN is the page table. The approach to building a page table in most non-AS/400 virtual memory implementations is to have one entry in the table for every page in virtual memory. The VPN is used as an index into the page table to select one of the entries. The selected entry contains the RPN, which then becomes part of the real address.

Many systems, such as the System/370, use this page-table structure. Suppose we have a computer system with a 32-bit virtual address and a 4-kilobyte page. The VPN size for this address is 20 bits. If we further assume 4 bytes per page-table entry, the size of the page table would be 4 megabytes. A memory table that occupies 4 megabytes is fairly large, but is still workable for a system with large memory sizes. This is not the case when the virtual address is larger than 32 bits. The size of a conventional page table is prohibitively large when the virtual address is 48 bits or 64 bits long.

The System/38 was the first major computer system in the industry to use an *inverted page table*. An inverted page table has one entry for every real page (page frame) in memory, rather than one entry for every virtual page on disk. The total size of this table is directly related to the memory size. The bigger the memory, the larger the page table, but the percent of memory the table uses is always the same.

The difficult part of an inverted page table is determining how to locate the correct page-table entry. You can no longer use the VPN to directly index into the page table, because there is no longer a one-to-one mapping of the VPN to a page-table entry. So you must use some other method. The technique used in the AS/400 is to apply a *hashing* function to the VPN to identify a page-table entry.

Hashing

Hashing has always been a difficult concept to explain. The hash function on an AS/400 takes some high-order bits out of the VPN and XORs them with some low-order bits from the VPN. This value is ANDed with mask bits from a special register that contains the size of the page table. Finally, this result is ORed with the real address of the page table. The result of this is a 52-bit real address into the page table. Only a handful of people really understand (or care) about this hashing function and how it works; yet many people want to understand *why* it works.

Several years ago, while pondering how to explain hashing to System/38 developers, I was walking through a Sears store in Rochester. A few days earlier, I had placed an order with the catalog sales department and was curious about whether or not my order had been received. When I inquired about my order at the catalog sales desk, I was asked for the last two digits of my telephone number. I said it was 83. On the wall behind the desk were 100 pockets numbered from 00 to 99. The person behind the desk pulled a stack of orders out of the pocket numbered 83 and began searching for my order. When the paperwork for my order was not found, I was told my order had not been received. I immediately blurted out, "You just had a page fault." The somewhat surprised Sears employee had no idea what I was talking about, but I suddenly realized how to explain hashing. Sears was using a hashing function to track the orders that had been received, similar to the way we track which pages are in memory.

Sears had determined it could uniquely identify a customer by name and telephone number. Rather than keep a record on every customer who could place an order with its catalog sales department, the company decided to keep records only on those customers whose order had been received but not yet picked up. To speed the search for an order, the employee would select a portion of the total identity — the last two digits of the telephone number. So all orders received were sorted according to these two digits. When an inquiry about an order was made, only one of the 100 pockets had to be searched to find a match for the name of the person who placed the order.

The hash function Sears used (selecting the last two digits of the telephone number) ensured a relatively uniform distribution of orders across the 100 pockets, which meant it would take about the same amount of time to search through any of the pockets. If, for example, Sears had selected the first two digits of the phone number, a few of the pockets would be very full and others would be empty (most communities only use a few telephone prefixes, so selecting the first two digits would give a poor distribution). Similarly, the combination of XORs, ANDs, and ORs to create the hash code in an AS/400 ensures a uniform distribution of accesses across the "pockets" in the page table.

On the AS/400, the equivalent of the Sears pocket is called the page table entry group (PTEG). Each PTEG contains eight page table entries (PTEs). The hash algorithm identifies one of the PTEGs. The eight entries in this group must then be searched to find the one with a VPN that matches the VPN of the virtual address being translated. This search is necessary because many virtual addresses map to the same PTEG. This is analogous to the Sears example — more than one customer can have the same last two digits of a telephone number. The pocket identification just says all the orders in that pocket belong to people with telephone numbers having the same last digits. The orders must be individually searched to find a particular customer's.

Because the number of orders received but not picked up by the customer could fluctuate during the day, Sears needed to accommodate this variability. Sears used a fixed number of pockets with a variable number of entries per pocket. The AS/400 also uses a fixed number of pockets; but as we just saw, it also has a fixed number of entries per pocket. The particular VPN we are looking for may or may not be in one of the eight PTEs. If there are more entries than can fit into a PTEG, a secondary page table is used and this table can have a variable number of entries.

In most AS/400 implementations, the number of PTEGs is at least one-half the number of real pages in the memory. With eight entries per PTEG, this means a table this size can map four times the number of pages that can be held in memory. Put another way, the average number of PTEs used per PTEG is only two. This average assumes the hashing function provides a uniform distribution across all PTEGs. There are situations when this will not be true, and one or more PTEGs will have more than eight entries. In those cases, the extra entries will have to be kept in the secondary page table. Suppose one of the pockets used by Sears got too full to hold all the paperwork.

Some of the orders would have to be removed from the pocket and put somewhere else. This would be equivalent to having a secondary page table.

On the AS/400, if a PTE is not found in either the primary or the secondary page tables, we have a page fault. Remember: We have a PTE in one of these tables for every page in memory. Not finding the PTE means the page is not in memory, which we define as a page fault. The memory-management component of SLIC must go to the disk and bring in the requested page. As part of this operation, it also must update the page table to reflect the fact that the new page is in memory. Of course, to make room for the new page, the memory-management component may have to bump some other page.

The following three sections are really hot, so we are giving them three peppers. The first of these sections deals with the virtual-to-real address-translation process, which uses the page-table entries. I have included this section for completeness and for those readers who love to play with bits. The next section describes how either the SLIC or the translator can control the memory access to every page. This type of control is needed in a multi-pipelined, multilevel memory RISC processor because the memory operations can be performed in a different order by the processor than they appear in the instruction stream. The PowerPC architecture provides four mode-control bits for the software to use, and I briefly describe them here. This can become a very complex topic. Finally, the last of these sections describes how an access to a page is protected. Each page can be treated as a read/write, read only, or no-access page, depending on the settings of the processor state and the protection keys in both the segment table and the page table. This, too, can be a very complex topic. If you need something with more spice than the previous few sections, try one or all of the next three.

Page Table Entry

Each PTE is 16 bytes long, as shown in Figure 8.4. The first field in each entry is 57 bits long and is called the *abbreviated virtual page number* (AVPN). Astute readers will remember from Figure 8.3 that the full VPN has only 52 bits. So how can an abbreviated form be longer? The PowerPC architecture is designed to support virtual addresses up to 80 bits long. The VPN for an 80-bit virtual address is 68 bits long, so 57 bits is indeed an abbreviated form. The AVPN can be used rather than the complete VPN, because at least 11 low-order bits of the VPN are used in the hash function and do not need to be repeated. Similarly, Sears would not have to include the last two digits of the customer's telephone number on the order form, because these digits are used in the hash function and do not need to be repeated in the search process. The AVPN for the 64-bit virtual address used in the AS/400 is only 41 bits long. The high-order 16 bits of the AVPN are set to 0.

Each of the PTEs in the PTEG are searched in turn for a match with the VPN of the virtual address. If the AVPN matches during the search of a PTE

Figure 8.4 Page Table Entry Format

AVPN	SW	/	H	V	/	TS	0..0	RPN	//	AC	R	C	WIMG	/	PP
0	57		60	62 63	0	1		12	51	54	55	56	57	60	62 63

DWORD	BIT	Name	Description
0	0:56	AVPN	Abbreviated virtual page number
	57:60	SW	Reserved for software use
	62	H	Hash function identifier
	63	V	Entry valid (V = 1) or invalid (V = 0)

DWORD	BIT	Name	Description
1	1	TS	Tag set bit
	2:11		Must be zero
	12:51	RPN	Real page number
	54	AC	Address compare
	55	R	Reference bit
	56	C	Change bit
	57:60	WIMG	Storage access controls
	62:63	PP	Page protection bits

All other fields are reserved.

and the valid bit is on (V = 1), then the 40-bit RPN in the entry is passed to the memory-addressing hardware where it is joined with the 12-bit byte offset to form the real address.

The other bits in the PTE provide additional information about the page. The SW bits are reserved for use by the memory-management component of SLIC. The H bit identifies whether or not this entry is in the primary or secondary page table, each of which uses a slightly different hash function. The TS bit tells whether or not this page contains pointers and therefore has some tag bits set to 1. The AC bit, if it is on, invokes the data address compare mechanism, which provides a means to detect loads and stores to a block of memory. The hardware sets the R and C bits to a value of 1 every time this page is referenced (R bit) or changed (C bit). The remaining bits deal with access modes and page protection. We will discuss these topics shortly.

A few more words are in order about the R and C bits. Memory management uses the settings of the R and C bits to determine which page to bump from the memory when a page fault occurs and a new page must be fetched into memory. Memory management also uses these bits whenever a bring, clear, or purge operation is requested by another SLIC component or by a translated MI program.

To speed the search for a page frame to replace, memory management maintains a "search list" of all the page frames that are eligible to be replaced. On a page fault (or a bring or a clear), memory management first searches this list for a page frame that has both the R and C bits set to 0. This combination means the page in the frame has not been recently accessed and has not been changed — it is the best candidate to replace. After a page replacement, all the R bits are reset to a value of 0. In this way, the R bits identify which page frames have been referenced since the last page replacement. The least recently used pages have R values set to 0.

While the page replacement algorithm is looking for a page to replace on the search list, if it encounters a page frame that has been changed but not recently referenced (R=0, C=1), it places the page on the "change list." When the change list accumulates a sufficient number of pages, one or more page-out tasks are started. The pages are written to disk and then returned to the search list (with C=0), where they are eligible for replacement, assuming they are not referenced or changed again. The reason for these page-out tasks is to prevent memory from being filled with changed pages that have not recently been referenced.

From our discussion so far, it should be obvious that searching the page tables takes a long time — so long that it would be intolerable if we had to do it for every memory access. Fortunately, once a page has been accessed for the first time, there is a very high likelihood that page will be referenced again in the near future. This is the principle behind using lookaside buffers — if you are likely to reuse the page table entry again, keep it around in a register that can be accessed quickly. For performance reasons, the hardware keeps a translation lookaside buffer (TLB) that holds PTEs that have been recently used. The TLB is searched prior to searching the page table. The time required to search the TLB is very short compared to that needed to search the page table. The size of the TLB is usually selected to be large enough to have 95 percent or more of the translations performed in the TLB without having to go to the page table. For example, the A30 processor has 512 entries in its TLB. Therefore, the use of TLBs significantly reduces the performance impact of virtual address translation.

Memory Access Modes

All memory accesses on the AS/400 are performed under the control of four mode-control bits: Write Through (W), Caching Inhibited (I), Memory Coherence (M), and Guarded Storage (G). One of the characteristics of a

RISC processor is the ability of the software to control the hardware. These four bits are set by the SLIC to provide some of that control on a page basis. For all translated accesses, these bits come from the PTE. For all real addresses (E = R or relocate turned off), these bits are assumed to have values 0, 0, 1, and 1. The W and I bits control how a processor uses its data cache. The M bit specifies whether or not the processor must ensure memory consistency. This usually applies to multiprocessor systems. The G bit controls whether or not out-of-order fetching of data and instructions is permitted. Following is more detail about each of these bits:

W Write Through
If W = 1, any update to the data cache must also be written to the main memory. If the data in a main memory page must always be current because, for example, it is shared by multiple processors, this bit will be set on. A load instruction will use the copy in the cache if it is there. A store will update the copy in the cache and in the main memory.

I Caching Inhibited
If I = 1, the memory access is made to the location in main memory. During the access, neither the accessed location nor the block in memory containing the location are copied to the cache. This is useful for large blocks of data that are only read sequentially and would flush the contents of the cache if not inhibited.

M Memory Coherence
If M = 1, the processor must enforce data coherence. Coherence refers to the ordering of writes to a single memory location. For improved performance, the memory control hardware sometimes can write data to memory in a different order than the processor issued the store instructions. But this can be a problem if multiple processors are sharing a location in memory and the ordering of stores to that location is important. By setting this bit on for the page, the stores by all processors to the same location are serialized.

G Guarded Storage
If G = 1, out-of-order fetching of data and instructions from the page is not allowed. To achieve higher performance, some processors can execute an instruction before it is known that the sequential execution model requires it. Suppose, for example, that a particular processor has an instruction pipeline that is not being used during a given cycle. If there is an instruction farther ahead in the instruction stream that could execute in this pipeline, the processor can start the execution. This is called out-of-order execution. Of course, the machine must appear to follow the sequential execution model. If a branch or an exception occurs before the processor would normally get to the out-of-order instruction, the state of the processor must be

rolled back to appear as if it never executed the instruction. Sometimes a memory area may not be well-behaved with regard to speculative operations. For example, an I/O device may be using a memory area and a speculative load to this device may cause the device to perform unexpected or incorrect operations. If the SLIC wants to ensure that this does not occur, the G bit for the page can be turned on.

Page Protection

Our final topic within address translation is memory protection. The memory protection mechanism in an AS/400 provides protection on a page-size block. This is different from the tag bits, which protect pointers on 16-byte memory blocks. Another big difference is that tags do not prevent access to a pointer — they detect modification after the fact. The page-protection mechanism can prevent the page from being read or written.

The PTE contains two page-protection (PP) bits. These two bits together with bits from the MSR are used to determine the type of access allowed to the page. Some of the MSR bits are first used to compute the value of a key.

If not in C2 mode: $Key = MSR_{US}$

If in C2 mode: $Key = (K_p \,\&\, MSR_{PR}) \text{ OR } (KS \,\&\, \neg MSR_{PR})$

where K_P is the problem state storage key and K_S is the system state storage key. Both of these keys are only found in the segment table. The key has a value of 1 if the processor is executing in the problem state and the problem state key for the segment is on, or if the processor is executing in the supervisor state and the supervisor state key for the segment is on.

You can use Table 8.1 to determine the types of accesses that are allowed to the page based on the value of the key and the settings of the PP bits.

Table 8.1 Protection Key Processing

Key	PP	Page Type	Load Access Permitted	Store Access Permitted
0	00	read/write	yes	yes
0	01	read/write	yes	yes
0	10	read/write	yes	yes
0	11	read only	yes	no
1	00	no access	no	no
1	01	read only	yes	no
1	10	read/write	yes	yes
1	11	read only	yes	no

Wow! it's great to get out of those spicy sections! Let's look at disk management and how it fits into single-level store. This topic should be a lot milder for most of our tastes. Is it hot in here?

Disk Management

The component in the SLIC responsible for managing AS/400 disks is called *auxiliary storage management*. This disk management component has several responsibilities. These include

- Managing auxiliary storage pools (ASPs). An ASP is a set of one or more disk units.
- Creation, extension, truncation, and destruction of segments on disk.
- Managing the free space on each disk unit.
- Maintaining the directories that relate virtual addresses to disk locations.

Auxiliary Storage Pools (ASPs)

The original idea for the System/38 was to keep any knowledge of disk drives totally below the MI. No application or operating system code above the MI was ever to know there were disks attached to the system. Technology independence means no software should ever be dependent on the specifics of an I/O device. However, the software certainly needs to know about devices such as terminals and printers. So why doesn't it know about disks?

The answer relates to the fact that some of us in the System/38 community held a strong belief that disks did not have much of a future. After all, how long can a technology that depends on a coating of rust on a platter last? We believed disk technology would be replaced by one of the upcoming semiconductor technologies. Two new semiconductor devices in the mid-1970s showed some promise of replacing disks: Perhaps magnetic bubbles or charge-coupled devices would be the ultimate answer. Or maybe main memory technologies would become so inexpensive that no other form of storage would be needed.

To ensure that when these new technologies were ready we could slip them into the System/38 with no disruption, we kept all knowledge of disks below the MI.[8] But the requirement that software not know about disks above the MI caused problems for us. (Be aware that when the disk management component writes an object to disk, it usually tries to spread the object across multiple disk drives. This is especially true for large objects. The idea behind this spreading is to improve performance and disk utilization. By spreading the object across several disk arms, the time required to read or write the object can be reduced because the disk operations can take place in parallel. Even today, disks on an AS/400 are not treated as I/O devices. They are treated as memory.)

If a disk drive on the System/38 failed and could not be recovered, no one above the MI knew what was on a specific disk. After the failed disk had been repaired or replaced, the entire disk subsystem had to be reloaded from the last tape backup — not a good situation. So we decided some knowledge and control of disks had to exist in OS/400, and we created auxiliary storage pools (ASPs).

An ASP is a collection of disk devices. All the disk storage in a pool appears to be a single, contiguous area in memory. Individual devices are not visible. The minimum size to an ASP is one disk arm, and the total disk storage on an AS/400 can be divided into a maximum of 16 ASPs.

The first ASP is always the system ASP. OS/400 and certain types of system objects controlled by OS/400 must be in the system ASP. Up to 15 user ASPs can be defined. Any object that does not have to be in the system ASP can be put into any user ASP, but the entire object must fit. Objects cannot cross an ASP boundary.

By dividing disk storage in this way, any disk failure is isolated within a single ASP. This can greatly reduce the recovery time by minimizing the amount of disk that has to be reloaded. Certain types of objects, such as journal receivers, can also be isolated from other parts of the system, thereby improving recovery options. The disk management component of SLIC handles ASP management.

Storage Segments

All objects are composed of one or more nonoverlapping segments. When a segment is created, several characteristics of the segment must be specified. One of these is the segment's initial size. Disk management allocates the number of pages for the segment based on this initial size. As we saw in Chapter 5, the autoextend bit in the segment header indicates whether or

[8] Obviously, however, the "new" technologies never lived up to their expectations and disk storage will likely be with us for a long time.

not the segment can be extended. If it can, the segment can grow up to the 16-megabyte limit for a segment.

Disk Extents

When a new segment is created, disk space is allocated as one or more disk extents. A disk extent is a set of contiguous 520-byte sectors on a disk device. The minimum number of sectors in an extent is eight, because the smallest memory size that can be allocated is a 4-kilobyte page. The number of pages in an extent is always a power of two. Thus, the individual extent sizes available are 4, 8, 16, 32, and 64 kilobytes, continuing up to 16 megabytes.

Using extents simplifies the management of free space on the disk, because extents limit the number of fragment sizes. Storage management uses a machine index to keep track of the free extents on each disk and combines contiguous smaller extents into larger extents.

A virtual segment can be made up of several physically discontiguous extents on disk. This is especially true if a segment is extended. When a segment needs to be extended, storage management finds a combination of extents large enough to hold the requested number of pages. These extents may even be on different disk devices, although they will always be in the same ASP.

To net all this out:

An object is made up of one or more segments.

A segment is made up of one or more extents.

An extent is made up of one or more pages (some power of 2).

A page is made up of eight disk sectors.

A sector is made up of 520 bytes on disk (512 bytes of data and 8 bytes of header).

Access Group Segments

Earlier, we saw that segments are created as permanent or temporary. A temporary segment can also be created as part of an access group. A few additional words are in order for access groups. The purpose of an access group is to enhance the performance of reading into and writing out of memory the temporary segments associated with a user job in the system. A typical user job may have dozens of temporary objects associated with it. If these were treated as ordinary objects, they would each occupy one or more temporary segments. Each segment would have at least one extent. If we wanted to move all a job's pages from memory to disk, it would take at least one I/O operation per extent. The same would be true when we wanted to read the job's pages back into memory.

An access group is a system object that was defined to eliminate most of this performance overhead. An access group consists of two segments. The first segment, the base segment, contains a table of contents (TOC). The second segment is a data segment. Each TOC entry contains the effective address of a unique data page in the data segment.

When a temporary object is created within an access group, its segments will be assigned the next available spaces in the access group data segment and the TOC will be updated. In this way, several physically small temporary segments can be packaged within the same data segment extent on disk, and all can be read or written with a single I/O operation.

Note that an access group only works for physically small objects and their small segments. All segments have 16 megabytes of address space, but most temporary segments for a job only occupy a few pages of physical memory. Access groups work very well for these types of small temporary segments. There are no access groups for permanent objects, because permanent objects tend to be larger in size, which defeats the advantage of an access group.

Auxiliary Storage Directories

We are now at a point where we can look at the directories that are maintained and used by auxiliary storage management to keep track of the disk space.

- Free Space Directory — This directory is a machine index (as described in Chapter 6) in which each entry contains the disk location of a single extent of free space.
- Static Directory — This directory is a list of extents that have been allocated to pre-assigned permanent segments. The static directory is used to locate virtual segments that are essential for machine execution when the normal (permanent and temporary) directories may be unusable.
- Permanent Directory — This directory is a machine index in which each entry contains the disk location of one to four extents that have been allocated to a permanent virtual segment.
- Temporary Directory — This directory is a machine index in which each entry contains the disk location of one to four extents that have been allocated to a temporary virtual segment.
- Lookaside Directory — This directory is a list of recently referenced extents from the permanent and temporary directories. The lookaside directory is essentially a "cache" for the permanent and temporary directories. Its purpose is to avoid the relatively lengthy index operations on these directories.
- Access Group Member Directory —This directory is a machine index in which each entry contains the address of the access group to which a specific member (segment) of an access group belongs.
- Access Group Table of Contents — Each access group, as we saw, has a table of contents (TOC). The TOC is a list where each entry contains

the disk location of a specific page of a member (segment) of the access group.

Because the free space directory and the permanent directory are machine indexes, they may become unusable as the result of a system crash. At each IPL, auxiliary storage management checks to see if these directories are good. If they are not, a directory recovery procedure is run. This procedure scans the contents of all the disks and uses the information stored in the sector headers and segment headers to rebuild the free space directory and the permanent directory. Because temporary objects, including access groups, go away at IPL time, the other directories do not have to be rebuilt.

Conclusions

In their 1976 paper, Bell and Strecker reflected on the Digital PDP-11 and what they had learned. As they put it, "There is only one mistake that can be made in a computer design that is difficult to recover from — not providing enough address bits."[9] They were describing some of the reasons Digital had to abandon the PDP architecture with only a 16-bit address and move to the VAX architecture with a 32-bit address. In recent years, Digital has moved to the Alpha architecture with its 64-bit address.

The System/38 and AS/400 architects vowed that their architecture would never break because there were not enough address bits. They defined a 128-bit pointer in which to store their address and made sure there was plenty of space for expansion. From an addressing perspective, the AS/400 has staying power.

The AS/400's large, single-level store will be even more important in the future. Many computer vendors are just discovering the importance of persistence. As more operating systems become object oriented, we are increasingly aware that objects need to exist outside of a process so they can be shared. Virtual memory systems that destroy all the objects owned by a process when that process goes away have limited usefulness in an object-oriented world. Permanent objects in an AS/400 provide an elegant solution to this problem.

In the next chapter, we will look at processes in an AS/400 to see how they tie together many of the topics we have already discussed.

[9] G. Bell and W.D. Strecker, "Computer Structures: What Have We Learned From the PDP-11?" *Proc. Third Annual Symposium on Computer Architecture,* January 1976, pp. 1-14.

Chapter 9

Process Management

Time is Mother Nature's way to keep everything from happening at once. Processes are a computer's way of doing the same thing. A process is a program in execution, which consists of the executable program, the program's data, and any state information (defined below) needed to continue running the program. Every operating system provides the facilities to support a process. Earlier, we said a process could be thought of as a unit of work in the system, and this is still a good definition.

Perhaps the easiest way to get an intuitive feel for a process is to think about timesharing systems. Timesharing, as we saw in Chapter 8, means sharing the processor and memory with several users at the same time to give the appearance that every user has his or her own machine. With a single processor, only one user process can be executing a program at any instant in time. Process management is the SLIC component that keeps everything from happening at once by switching the resources of that single processor between processes.

Periodically, the operating system decides to stop running one process and start running another because, for example, the first one has used its current share of processor time as of the last second. When a process is temporarily suspended like this, it must later be restarted in exactly the same state it had when it was stopped. This means all information about the process — called the state information — must be saved somewhere during the suspension. How and where this state information is stored varies from one operating system to another. In this chapter, we will see how the AS/400 does it.

OS/400's work-management component deals with these same topics at a higher level. The need to efficiently manage the flow of work through and within the system is important to achieve high performance for a wide range of application environments. Later in this chapter, we will see how work management interrelates with process management. First we will look at the foundation on which process management is based.

The World's Greatest Tasking Structure

In any computer system, often only a small number of basic ideas give the system a competitive edge. The technology independence of the AS/400 the MI provides is one such idea, as is the performance advantage the single-level store provides. Some of these ideas are known to everyone; others are not. One of the most important ideas in the AS/400 is the tasking structure, yet it is not widely known.

Before the AS/400's announcement, a study of the patents covering the new system was undertaken. The intent of this study was to select the most important of these patents. IBM and other companies always want to be sure the important ideas in any new product are protected by patents, so others cannot copy them. Patents give a company exclusive rights to specific new ideas, which can give the owning company an advantage over its competitors if the new idea is significant enough. These key patents are also valuable in the respect that the rights to use the patent can be sold to other companies.

The most important patent on the AS/400 was U.S. Patent Number 4,177,513,[1] which covered the tasking structure of the System/38 and the AS/400. (The patents covering single-level store were not selected, nor were any patents on technology independence.)

The tasking structure of the AS/400 is the foundation on which the operating system is built. SLIC's process management component and OS/400's work management component are based on this tasking structure. For most of the operating system topics covered so far, we have started at the highest level in the system and progressively worked our way down to the lowest level of support. In this chapter, we want to start at the bottom, because it is so fundamental to the AS/400. Before we do so, a few words are in order about future directions for operating systems. Only then will the importance of the tasking structure become obvious.

Microkernel Technologies

A microkernel is a small operating system core and one of the most hotly debated topics in computer science today. Proponents of microkernels claim that they provide the foundation for modular, portable operating systems. Opponents of microkernels claim they create a bottleneck in the operating system that limits the size of a multiuser system. Almost no one agrees how to organize the operating system services relative to the microkernel. The one thing experts seem to agree on is the message-passing communications structure a microkernel uses. Most believe this is the direction for all future operating systems.

In Chapter 12, we will look at microkernels and see how they are influencing the future design of the AS/400. For now, let's look briefly at how operating system components have traditionally communicated and interacted. A Unix operating system provides us with a prime example. The original

---

[1] Roy L. Hoffman, William G. Kempke, John W. McCullough, Frank G. Soltis, and Richard T. Turner, "Task Handling Apparatus for a Computer System," United States Patent 4,177,513, filed July 8, 1977, issued December 4, 1979.

Unix, and most of the versions currently available, use a layered approach to operating system design.

Groups of operating system functions in Unix, such as the file subsystem, the process control subsystem, and the I/O subsystem, are divided into layers. This layering approach is not unusual. Most operating systems, including the one in the AS/400, are built using layers of software. The differences in design among different operating systems relate to the way the layers communicate and work with one another. In a Unix system, each layer communicates only with the layer directly above it or that below it. This is an advantage because each layer only needs to know about the ones immediately above or below it. Requests and responses move from layer to layer as if they are climbing up and down a ladder. Applications and the operating system itself communicate with other functions using this ladder.

This structured approach works well, as evidenced by the number of successful Unix operating systems in use today. It is, however, difficult to add features or change existing features using this approach, because of its monolithic design. The entire operating system is bound together in the hierarchy of layers. It is not easy to pull out one layer and replace it with a new layer, because the interfaces between layers are many and varied. An intimate knowledge of the operating system and lots of time are usually required to make changes to any of these layers. In addition, many of the APIs between layers are undocumented, making it even more difficult to guarantee code correctness when a change is made. This is a real problem when new functions need to be added or moved from one layer to another.

A microkernel replaces this vertical communication hierarchy with a horizontal structure. All operating system components above the microkernel communicate directly with one another, using messages that pass through the microkernel. The microkernel validates the messages, passes them between components, and grants access to the hardware resources. An operating system designed around a microkernel is very extensible. Operating system components become quite modular with this design. New components, which were never even envisioned when the operating system was created, can be plugged in without tearing up other parts of the design.

But there is a cost for all of this. Message passing is not as fast as the function calls a typical Unix system uses, so care must be taken to optimize the performance of message passing in the microkernel. But even though message passing is not as fast as a function call, it can still improve the system performance if it eliminates the need to go through unnecessary levels.

Thus far, everything we have said about communications in a microkernel design applies to the AS/400. The tasking structure of both the System/38 and the AS/400 is message-based, exactly like that of the microkernel. OS/400 users are familiar with messages. Application and operating system components in the AS/400 communicate using messages, and all work in the system is dispatched as a result of these communications. As with the implementation of a microkernel, the AS/400's tasking structure is implemented at the lowest level of the system. In the System/38 and the early AS/400, tasking was implemented in the HLIC. But in the RISC-based AS/400 systems, tasking is implemented in the SLIC for optimal performance. SLIC is not a microkernel, nor is it built on a microkernel. It does, however, share many of the same design philosophies.

Microkernels got their start in the mid-1980s, when Carnegie Mellon University developed the Mach microkernel. In recent years, just about every new operating system is based on a microkernel model. Although there is far more to a microkernel than just the message-based communications and dispatching mechanism, it is important to note that this mechanism, which all these new operating systems use, was pioneered in the System/38 and later used in the AS/400. For this reason, we want to start our study of process management at the bottom of the AS/400 system.

Starting at the Bottom

Earlier, we defined a process and said it was basically a unit of work in the system. A task is also a unit of work in the system, so in this respect a task is similar to a process. A process is a higher-level function in SLIC that is built on top of a task. There is a third, even higher-level, unit of work in OS/400, called a job. We will see how these three concepts of work on an AS/400 interrelate.

The names task and process came from two different System/38 development organizations. Engineering talked about tasks, and programming talked about processes. Many people thought that because of the different names, there must be fundamental differences between the two, but there were not.

In the early days of the System/38 development, we were trying to define the mechanism the operating system would use to control the flow of work and the allocation of resources within the system. This, after all, is the primary responsibility of any operating system, and we wanted to make sure we got it right. Operating systems in the early 1970s were just starting to incorporate the idea of a process as a unit of work in the system. We, too, thought this was a good idea for our operating system.

The processors in those days knew nothing about a process. They had evolved during the 1960s, but they only understood interrupts. An interrupt is a change in the flow of instruction execution caused by either an error detected while executing an instruction or something outside the running program. This latter cause is usually related to I/O. The processor initiates the I/O device operations, which then execute outside the processor. When an I/O operation completes, it needs some way to tell the processor, and an interrupt provides that mechanism.

An interrupt stops the running program and transfers control to an interrupt handler, which performs some appropriate action. When the interrupt handler finishes, it returns control to the interrupted program. The interrupt handler must restart the interrupted program in exactly the same state it was in when the interrupt occurred. This means restoring all the internal registers to their pre-interrupt state. Some processors provide multiple sets of registers, and when an interrupt occurs, the interrupt handler uses a different set of registers. Returning control to the interrupted program means switching back to the original set of registers.

Most interrupt schemes include the idea of priority. Priority provides a pecking order for interrupts, from most important to least important. When an interrupt occurs, the processor is only switched to a new program if that program has a higher priority than the running program. Most processors provide only a small number of interrupt priorities. To support processes, the operating system software has to take the interrupt mechanism and build processes on top.

In the 1970s, we were building a new microprogrammed processor for the System/38. We reasoned that if we could build a process structure right on top of the hardware, and eliminate some of the interrupt overhead, we would have a more efficient system. Even our I/O could use this process structure, without the need for a separate interrupt mechanism. This would also save circuits in the processor — something near and dear to engineering management.

In effect, engineering had signed up to create the process structure for the system and to write the microcode to support it. But explaining what we were doing to someone in engineering proved to be an interesting experience.

I vividly recall one such discussion with Ray Klotz, our engineering manager, and his staff. I was explaining how, with the new structure, we would not be limited to just a few interrupt levels. We could support hundreds of processes, and each could have a different priority level. Each I/O device could even have its own priority, if we chose, because our system would support multiple processes.

Ray interrupted and said, "You mean you're building a multiprocessor?"

"No," I replied, "we're building a system to support multiple processes, not multiple processors."

"What's the difference?"

"A process is just like a task," I answered. "We're building a system to support multiple tasks, not multiple hardware processors."

After a moment of silence Ray said, "Then why don't you just call them tasks?" From that day on, we did.

Task Dispatching in the AS/400

Associated with each task in the AS/400 is a control block in memory called a *task dispatching element* (TDE). A TDE is the fundamental data structure on which the tasking support is built. Because it exists below the MI, the TDE structure is not visible above the MI. This data structure is not a system object, but it is an important component of some system objects. Later in this chapter, we will examine an MI process and see how this system object incorporates a TDE. A TDE contains all the necessary information to control the execution of a task. A task is a program in execution, so the TDE has the responsibility to tie together the program and the status of the executing program.

The States of a Task

Any task in the system can be in one of four states. A state defines the eligibility of a task to run in the processor. Note that from a terminology standpoint a state can have more than one name. In this section, we will use the SLIC names for each state. The four states are

- Suspended — This is the state where a task starts or ends. In this state, a task is not able to run in the processor.
- Ready — This is the state of a task that is ready to run in the processor but is not yet running. Outside of SLIC, this state is also called ineligible, meaning some other task is running instead of this task.
- Running — This is the state of a running task. Outside of SLIC, it is also called the active state. In a single processor, only one task can be running at any instant of time.
- Wait — This is the state where the task is waiting for something, usually I/O. A task is not able to run when in this state.

Figure 9.1 shows the four states of a task, along with the transitions that can occur between the states.

Figure 9.1 States of a Task

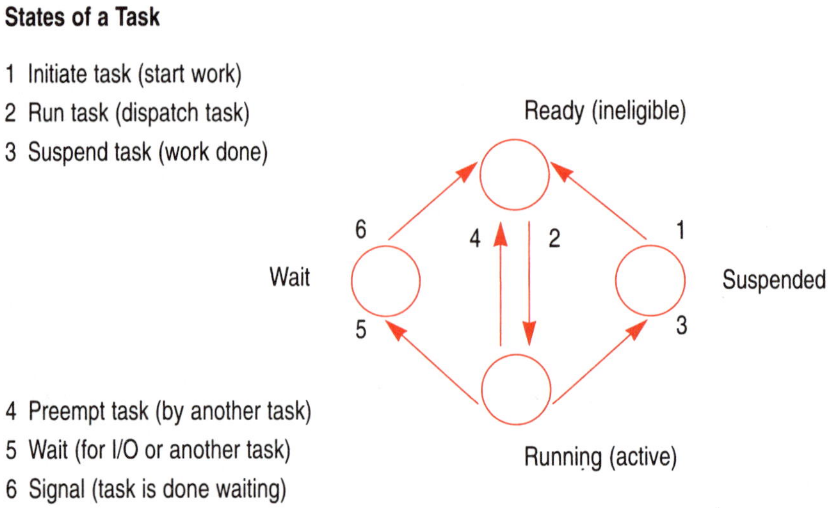

States of a Task

1 Initiate task (start work)
2 Run task (dispatch task)
3 Suspend task (work done)
4 Preempt task (by another task)
5 Wait (for I/O or another task)
6 Signal (task is done waiting)

With four states, 12 possible transitions can occur between two states if all are allowed. In an AS/400, only six transitions are allowed. They are

- Initiate Task (Suspended to Ready) — This transition occurs when work is started and a task moves to a state where it is ready to run.
- Run Task (Ready to Running) — This transition moves the task into the running (active) state and is usually called dispatching the task.
- Suspend Task (Running to Suspended) — When the work for a task is finished, the task moves to the suspended state.
- Preempt Task (Running to Ready) — When a task has not completed and is moved back to the ready state, it is said to be preempted. This move implies that there are other tasks in the system that are more important (higher priority) and can preempt a running task.
- Wait (Running to Wait) — If a running task initiates some operation that forces the task to wait for the operation to complete before it can continue, the task moves to the wait state. An I/O operation can force a task to wait.
- Signal (Wait to Ready) — If the operation a task is waiting for completes, the task moves from the wait state to the ready (ineligible) state.

Anyone who has used the Work with System Status (WRKSYSSTS) command will recognize some of these transitions. The WRKSYSSTS display shows rates of the following transitions: active to wait, active to ineligible, and wait to ineligible. These values are used when tuning the activity level in a storage pool. Later in this chapter, we will define activity levels and storage pools and show how they fit into the system.

The state in which a task exists is determined by the location of the TDE associated with the task. TDEs move about in the system — actually, they don't physically move, they logically move. All TDEs exist in the AS/400's memory. A TDE contains address fields that can link it to other data structures. When we talk about a TDE moving, we mean the addresses in the data structures are adjusted to logically move the TDE to another data structure. Inserting a TDE to a data structure is called *enqueuing*, and removing a TDE is called *dequeuing*. Enqueuing and dequeuing are the operations provided in the SLIC to link the addresses. These linking operations are very fast compared to physically moving the TDE.

Task Dispatching Queue

The TDEs for all tasks eligible to run in the processor at any given time are arranged in a data structure called a *task dispatching queue* (TDQ). A TDQ is implemented as a chained list in memory with the TDEs ordered in priority sequence, as shown in Figure 9.2. Each TDE contains a priority field

Figure 9.2 Task Dispatching Queue

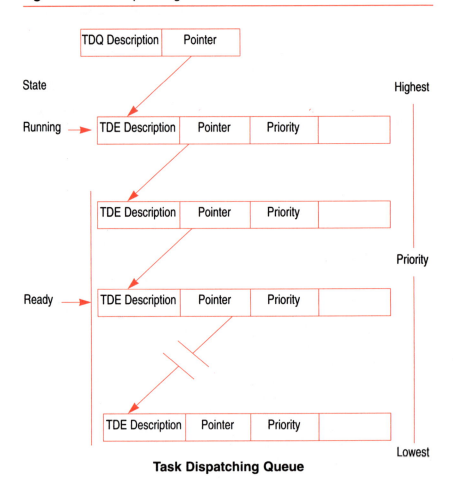

Task Dispatching Queue

that is used for this ordering. The TDE for the task with the highest priority is at the top in this ordering.

The task dispatcher implemented in SLIC selects the TDE with the highest priority (the one on the top of the list) and gives it control of the processor. In this way, the top TDE is the one associated with the currently running task in the processor. All other TDEs on the TDQ are associated with tasks that are in the ready state. The currently running task will continue to run until it has to give up control of the processor. Several events can cause this to happen. The running task may perform an operation that forces it to give up control. Waiting for an I/O operation is one example. When a task uses up its allocated time in the processor (called timeslice end), the task is also forced to give up control. The running task can be preempted by some higher-priority task, which is still another way that forces it to give up control. Whenever the running task gives up control, the next highest priority task on the TDQ gets control and becomes the running task. Thus, any TDE that is on the TDQ is by definition either in the running or the ready state.

Send/Receive Queues and Counters

The method used to synchronize the execution of tasks as well as to communicate between tasks is based on Dijkstra's semaphore.[2] In 1968, Dijkstra proposed a primitive function to synchronize the execution of processes in a multiprogramming operating system. Synchronization is the ability of one task to pause and wait until another task has performed an operation. A semaphore provides a mechanism to allow a task to wait.

[2] E.W. Dijkstra, "The Structure of 'THE' Multiprogramming System," *Communications of the ACM*, Vol. 11, No. 5, May 1968, pp. 341-346.

The original semaphore has a counter and a waiting list. Two operations (instructions) are defined. The "V" operator increments the value of the counter by one. The "P" operator tests the value of the counter; if the value is greater than zero, the P operator decrements the value of the counter by one and lets the next instruction in the instruction stream execute. If the counter value is not greater than zero, the P operator will wait until the value becomes greater than zero before it completes its operation and allows the next instruction to execute. The waiting comes about when the P operator is executed and the counter is not greater than zero. In this case, the task that executed the P operator waits until some other task increments the counter with a V operator. This allows tasks to be synchronized.

In many situations, it is desirable to exchange some information, or a message, as a part of this synchronization operation. The AS/400 defines a *send/receive queue* (SRQ) to support synchronization and message passing. An SRQ is a data structure in memory that is used as a "mailbox" for messages sent from one task to another.

When a running task executes a SEND MESSAGE operation, another data structure called a *send/receive message* (SRM) is enqueued to an SRQ associated with some other task. This SRQ is the mailbox for the other task. The SRM contains the message the running task wishes to send to the other task. When a running task wants to obtain a message from an SRQ (its mailbox), it does so by executing a RECEIVE MESSAGE operation. If no message is available, the task has the option to wait for the message. If the task chooses to wait, the TDE for the running task is dequeued from the TDQ and enqueued to a wait list that is part of each SRQ. The task dispatcher is then invoked to select the highest priority, ready task and make it the running task.

At some later time, another running task executes a SEND MESSAGE operation to the SRQ. If a TDE is waiting for the message, it is dequeued from the SRQ and enqueued on the TDQ in priority sequence. If the newly enqueued TDE has higher priority than the running TDE, the running task is preempted. If more than one TDE is waiting, a bit in the header of the SRQ indicates whether all waiters should be awakened or just the first one.

Any task whose TDE is enqueued to an SRQ is, by definition, in the wait state. Figure 9.3 shows the migration of TDEs and how the state of the task is determined by the location of its TDE.

Not shown in the figure are the other data structures that can have TDEs enqueued. One of these is the *send/receive counter* (SRC). An SRC has no message passing, so it is similar to the original semaphore. SLIC provides operations of SEND COUNT and RECEIVE COUNT to provide synchronization between tasks where no messages need to be exchanged.

Some readers who are familiar with the Send Program Message (SNDPGMMSG) and Receive Message (RCVMSG) commands at OS/400 may be wondering whether or not they are related to the operations used by the tasking structure in SLIC. The answer is, "Yes, there is a very close relationship." The exact format of SRMs, SRQs, and SRCs is designed for the tasking functions being performed, but the operations of enqueuing and dequeuing the messages are fundamentally the same throughout the system. SLIC is responsible for providing all these functions.

Figure 9.3 Task Dispatching Element Migration

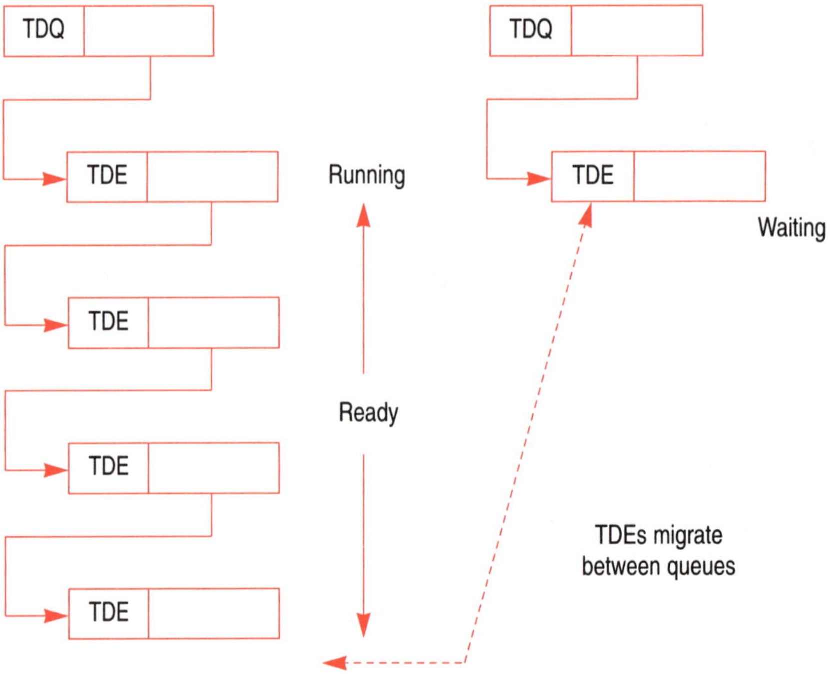

We have simplified the discussion of task dispatching in an AS/400 here to make it more understandable. Since the first System/38, numerous additions have been made to the tasking structure to satisfy the requirements for different application environments and system structures. For example, the priority of a task is not fixed. If a task is not getting enough processor time to make progress, or if a task has locked some resource in the system that a higher-priority task is waiting for, the priority of the task is temporarily increased.

Multiprocessor Considerations

The discussion in the preceding section assumed only a single processor and, therefore, only one running task. In contrast, a multiprocessor system potentially has many running tasks. The task dispatching mechanism includes the support for multiprocessors. Although much of this function was included in the original System/38, it was never used in that system. It wasn't until 1990 that multiprocessing was introduced and first used on the AS/400. Some of that original support for multiprocessing has still not been fully exploited in the AS/400, but it is available for future multiprocessor implementations.

Symmetric Multiprocessing

Earlier, we saw that a symmetric multiprocessor (SMP) system allows the operating system to run on any free processor or on all processors simultaneously, sharing the memory among them. This is exactly how n-way processing operates on an AS/400. Any component of the operating system, including the task dispatcher, can run on any or all processors in the system.

The task dispatcher in an n-way system provides automatic workload balancing among the processors without requiring software changes from a single processor design. Because the memory is shared, the task dispatcher running on any processor has access to all the queues, including the TDQ. The effects of the task dispatcher, however, are not limited to the processor on which it runs. The task dispatcher running on one processor can cause a task switch to occur on another processor.

With multiple processors, we have multiple running tasks — one for each processor. Simplistically, we would just dispatch the n top TDEs on the TDQ. These n tasks do have the highest priorities of the ready tasks. But while this simple approach seems to be the best choice, it often isn't.

Suppose we have two tasks, A and B, executing on processors 1 and 2 in a two-processor system. Suppose further that a waiting task C, with a higher priority than task A but lower than task B, comes out of the wait state. Its TDE will be enqueued on the TDQ just above the TDE for task A. The task dispatcher will cause a task switch to occur on processor 1 to make task C a running task. Now suppose task B on processor 2 either completes or goes into a wait state. Task A is the highest priority ready task and should be dispatched on processor 2 — but this may not be the best choice.

Depending on how long ago task A was preempted, we may or may not want to dispatch task A on processor 2. If the time was short, there are still instructions, and data still exist, in the cache of processor 1 for task A. Dispatching task A to processor 2 would mean the cache for processor 2 would have to be reloaded as cache misses occur, resulting in reduced performance for the task and the system. In this case, it may be better to dispatch a lower priority task on processor 2 and wait until processor 1 is available for task A.

What we have just described is *cache affinity*. A given task may have an affinity for a particular processor based on the contents of its cache. Task dispatching in a multiprocessor version of an AS/400 is based on a combination of priority, cache affinity, and another characteristic, *eligibility*. Eligibility can be used to restrict a task to a subset of the processors. Eligibility is never overridden by the task dispatcher. If all processors for which a task is eligible are running higher-priority tasks, the task is not dispatched.

A task is only dispatched if the processor for which it has cache affinity is available. An exception to this rule is made if *not* dispatching the task would result in a processor remaining idle or in an excessive number of higher-priority tasks on the TDQ being skipped. A skip threshold based on the number of processors is set by the SLIC for the system. If the number of tasks skipped reaches the threshold, affinity is ignored and the task is assigned to any processor for which it is eligible. If tasks are skipped and the end of the TDQ is reached before a task is assigned to each processor, the skip threshold is dynamically reduced until there are either no unassigned processors or no skipped tasks.

The three fields in the TDE that are used for multiprocessor task dispatching are

- Eligibility field — This field has one bit for every processor in the system. Setting a bit on in this field indicates that the task is eligible to run on the corresponding processor. If all bits are on, the task is eligible to run on any processor.
- Active field — This field has one bit for every processor in the system and indicates the processor on which the task is currently active. At most, one bit can be on if the task is running; otherwise, no bits are on.
- Affinity field — This field has one bit for every processor in the system and indicates the processor on which the task executed most recently.

In addition to the support for multiprocessors just described, the AS/400 can have multiple TDQs. This support was included in the original System/38 to enable dispatching from multiple queues, although it was not used for that purpose. As the number of processors increases to the point where a single TDQ becomes a bottleneck, the dispatching can be accomplished with multiple TDQs.

The current n-way processors use an SMP shared-memory model with all processors operating out of the same memory. In Chapter 12, we will look at other SMP models that will be used in future AS/400 systems. All of these are supported by the existing tasking structure.

Asymmetric Multiprocessing
Before leaving this section on multiprocessing, we want to look briefly at the topic of asymmetric multiprocessor (ASMP) systems. In an ASMP system, parts of an operating system, or even different operating systems, run on dedicated processors. The tasking structure in an AS/400 also supports this model of multiprocessing.[3] An early design for the System/38 implementation included multiple processors, each running a part of the operating system below the MI. The idea was to have one processor dedicated to the database management system, another dedicated to storage management, and so on. This ASMP design used the tasking structure to exchange messages between the processors and to dispatch work. This exact model of multiprocessing, where many operating system functions are split across multiple processors, was never used in the System/38. A version of this ASMP model, however, was introduced with the AS/400.

In Chapter 10, we will examine the AS/400's I/O structure, which was a major change from the original System/38 design. The AS/400 uses multiple processors to execute specific I/O operating system functions. A large system can have hundreds of these processors. We will see that each of these I/O processors has its own operating system. While most of these operating systems are designed specifically to support I/O functions, some of them are beginning to be more general purpose. This design allows other operating systems and the applications written for these operating systems to run under the covers of an AS/400. Thus, it will be possible to have multiples of these application engines in an AS/400 in addition to the main processors.

Now that we have covered the lowest level of task dispatching in an AS/400, we can begin to see how this function supports the higher concept of a process.

[3] We probably shouldn't talk about this as ASMP. Many "propeller heads" today believe this is old-fashioned technology. So in the following chapters, we will talk about these processors as coprocessors or application engines.

MI Processes

A process is a system object at the MI; it is called a process control space. Notice there is no equivalent OS/400 object, as we will see when we look at work management later in this chapter. The responsibility of an MI process is to tie together the resources needed to execute a program, or more accurately, the *invocation* of a program. Because programs are shared, multiple users can be executing the same program. Of course, each user has his or her own data that the program is using. Because programs need some place to temporarily store the information or the variables used during its execution, we need to provide a work area for each invocation of a program. This responsibility falls to the MI process.

Before we look at the structure of a process itself, we need to understand the types of storage a program in execution uses. The use of compilers and high-level languages significantly affects how programs execute, and a big factor is how the compiler allocates and addresses the program's variables. A high-level language often has some form of declaration statements to identify the type of variables and where the compiler should allocate space for these variables.

To understand what a process must support, we want to look at the three separate areas in which current high-level languages allocate their data. They are

- Static storage area — A compiler uses this type of storage to allocate global variables and constants for the program. The name *global* is used because any part of the program can access this storage area. For this reason, some systems call this area the global data area.

- Automatic storage stack — This area is used to allocate local variables. When a program executes a call instruction, the variables associated with the calling procedure must be saved somewhere so they can be restored on a return instruction. These variables are called *local*, because they only have meaning to the procedure that executed the call. Calls can be nested, meaning one procedure can call another, which can call another, and so on. This means the storage area must automatically grow and shrink on calls and returns, respectively. A *stack* is used for this automatic storage area. A stack has two parts. It has a contiguous block of memory containing the data, and it has a stack pointer telling where the top of the stack is located in memory. The bottom of the stack is at a fixed address in memory, and the stack pointer contains the high address. On a call, the address in the stack pointer is increased to provide enough storage for the local variables of the calling procedure. On a return, the address in the stack pointer is decreased by the amount of local variable space. In this way, the size of the stack grows and shrinks dynamically. In some systems, this storage area is called the dynamic storage area.

- Heap storage area — This area is used to allocate dynamic data that does not adhere to a stack structure. A stack is good for storing single variables (scalars) because all entries are the same, usually the size of a single register. A stack does not work well for variable length data, such as arrays of data elements. Data arrays can be stored in a heap. An array in a heap is accessed using an address that points to the beginning of the array, and then using offsets to that address.

Note that all three areas are referred to as storage areas, not memory areas. Any particular system may use a combination of registers, memory, and disk storage to implement these areas, hence the name storage.

Original Process Model

Like the original program model discussed in Chapter 3, the original process model was designed to support languages such as RPG, COBOL, and CL. The original model reflected a structure where each process was a single unit of work and the programs executed by the process tended not to be very modular.

A process is implemented as a system object at the MI. In addition to all the control information, the object either contains the storage areas or points to the storage areas the process uses. The three types of storage areas needed by a process were supported by the original process model as follows:

- Program Static Storage Area (PSSA) — A single copy of a static storage area existed for the entire process.

- Program Automatic Storage Area (PASA) — This area in the process object contained the call/return stack.

- Heap Storage — No support existed for heap storage in the original process model. Heap storage had to be managed outside the model separately by each language compiler.

Looking at the internals of the system object for an original MI process, which was also called a process control space, we would see two segments. The base segment contained much of the control information, along with the TDE for the process. The second segment was called the invocation work area (IWA) segment. The primary function of the IWA segment was to hold the call/return stack the process used.

This original process model served the types of applications written for the System/38 and early AS/400 very efficiently. However, the move to more block-structured languages and the desire to incorporate applications written to standards, as POSIX demonstrates, led to the development of the ILE process model.

ILE Process Model

The ILE process model was first introduced in the AS/400 at V2R3, along with the ILE program model and the ILE compilers. The original process model and the ILE process model co-existed in the AS/400 until the appearance of the RISC processors. The RISC processor systems only support the ILE program model and the ILE process model. (Both the ILE program and process models were created with the RISC processors in mind.)

In this and the following sections, we will look at the ILE process model in more detail. Before we do, we need to revisit the changes made on the AS/400 to support the ILE program model. The constructs used at the MI to support ILE programs are program activations, activation groups, procedure invocations, and a new procedure pointer.

In Chapter 3, we looked at the ILE compilers and program model. We saw that ILE changes the way programs are created, and we introduced the idea of a module. The module is the output of an ILE compiler, and a module can contain one or more procedures. The ILE binder packages these modules into programs and service programs. In this way, programs and service programs can contain one or more modules, and these modules in turn can contain one or more procedures. The two types of call instructions (CALLPGM and CALLBP) defined as part of the ILE are used to reference the programs and the procedures within the modules.

A program is an MI system object that is always called with an external call (CALLPGM) instruction at the MI. Similar to the older CALLX instruction, the CALLPGM instruction uses a system pointer to identify the program. The CALLPGM instruction *activates* the program. This activation operation completes the inter-program binding, as we described in Chapter 3. For example, if a program uses modules that are bound by reference, the links to the service program are resolved at the time the program is activated. Activating a program implicitly creates the activation groups, which provide the working storage for the program. The program activation operation will also initialize the static storage for the program.

A program contains one or more procedures. One of the procedures is designated as the program entry point at the time the program is created. Control is passed to this procedure by the CALLPGM instruction as a part of the program activation. This operation of passing control to a procedure is called a *procedure invocation*.

A CALLBP instruction is used to invoke any other procedures associated with the program. The CALLBP instruction uses a procedure pointer to identify the procedure being called. The procedure being called can either be in the program if it was bound by copy, or in a service program if it was bound by reference. Note that MI tracks call flow invocations by procedures, not by programs.

When an application program is first moved to a RISC processor, the original program is converted to an ILE program containing a single procedure. Thus, a converted original program, like any program with only one procedure, will always be called with a CALLPGM. If a program created with an ILE compiler has more than one procedure, the first procedure is called with a CALLPGM and subsequent procedures are called with CALLBP.

We also introduced activation groups in Chapter 3. Activation groups provide the storage resources for the program activations. Each activation group has its own static storage area, automatic storage stack, and heap storage area. An activation group is the working storage that is allocated to run one or more programs. Because only the ILE process model exists now with the RISC processors, this working storage is also designed to support all original processes, and it replaces the old PASA/PSSA storage areas.

An activation group is not an MI system object; it is part of an MI process object. Each MI process object contains two or more activation groups. One of the activation groups is used by the system. Each process object also contains at least one user activation group. When an original process created on an IMPI processor system is moved to a RISC processor system, that original process is transformed into an ILE process containing a single user activation group.

An activation group does more than just partition the storage used by a process. Each activation group has its own control information, which lets each activation have different protection states, file usage, and commitment control. This gives a great deal of flexibility for jobs above the MI.

All activation groups are named, either explicitly by the user or implicitly by the system. Programs and service programs can specify explicitly as part of the program object definition which named activation group they are to run in and can cause the activation group to be implicitly created under a job when the program object is called.

Inside an ILE Process

In this section, we will look inside the ILE process. The ILE process structure is complex and, like many other parts of the AS/400, has a set of names and acronyms that can make even a die-hard computer scientist beg for simplicity and common terminology. While it is not necessary to read this to understand how processes work on the AS/400, we are including this section for completeness. So for those masochists who need another dose of acronyms, read on.

ILE Process Structure

Let's get some of the acronyms out of the way first by defining the components that make up an ILE process.

- Process Control Block (PCB) — The PCB is contained in the system object that represents an MI process. Earlier we saw that this system object is called the process control space and, among other things, it contains the TDE for the process. The PCB also contains addresses of other components associated with the process, as we will shortly see.

- Process Activation Work Area (PAWA) — The PAWA is a heap used for allocation of runtime structures, such as the activation groups. There is one PAWA per process.

- Parent Activation Group (PAGP) — The PAGP is the root structure for the process substructure. It contains a list of all activation groups for the process. Contrary to what its name implies, a PAGP is not itself an activation group.

- Activation Group (ACTGRP) — We have already introduced activation groups. The ACTGRP provides the storage resources (stack, static, and heap) for program activations. The ACTGRP is like a mini-process.
- Tombstone Segments — These segments are used to construct process object pointers (POPs). POPs are "handles" to SLIC structures. A handle is used by many operating systems, including OS/2 and Apple Macintosh, as a way to indirectly point to a block of memory in a heap. Instead of giving direct addressability to the block, a handle points to a master pointer. The master pointer is typically in a fixed location and contains the address of the block. As these blocks are relocated in memory, only the address in the master pointer has to be changed. These segments are called "tombstone segments" because they do not give direct access to SLIC structures; that is, no way exists to get at the SLIC structures, even if the system security level allows access to these segments. The master pointer is in a memory area that can only be accessed by SLIC.
- Process Queue Space — Every process has one or more send/receive queues (SRQs) to hold messages, and these queues are contained in the process queue space.

Figure 9.4 shows how these components fit together to form the ILE process structure. Notice that the PAWA contains the *list* of all the activation groups (the PAGP), along with all the activation groups. The figure shows four activation groups, although as we saw earlier, the minimum number is two. The first ACTGRP is always the default activation group for the system and the second ACTGRP is always the default activation group for the user. We are now at a point where we can look inside an activation group.

ILE Activation Group

An activation group contains, or links to, several other components with strange names and acronyms. Let's start with a definition of these components.

- Program Activation Control Block (PACB) — A PACB is an addressing structure that is used during the execution of a program. It locates procedures and data that are bound to the program. There is one PACB per active program and each PACB contains one or more Module Binding Vectors (MBVs).
- Module Binding Vector (MBV) — The MBV is an addressing structure for a single module. It contains the runtime addresses of the data and procedures referenced by the module.
- Activation Group Directory (ActGrp Directory) — The ActGrp directory is a symbolic directory used for late binding between data and programs.

Figure 9.4 ILE Process Structure

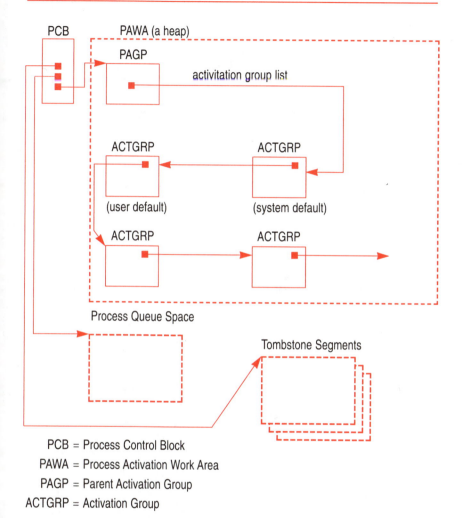

PCB = Process Control Block
PAWA = Process Activation Work Area
PAGP = Parent Activation Group
ACTGRP = Activation Group

- Procedure Reference Table (PRT) — The PRT segments contain the procedure entry points used by inter-activation group and procedure pointer calls. There is one PRT per activation group.
- Heap List and Heap Spaces — The heap list identifies the heap spaces associated with the activation group. A heap space consists of a control segment plus multiple data segments. Heaps for MI and SLIC use are managed by a heap manager in SLIC.
- Auto Storage Segments — These segments contain the stack used for automatic storage by the activation group.

- Static Storage Segments — The static storage for the activation group is contained in these segments.

Figure 9.5 shows how these components fit together to create an activation group. To summarize, we can say each process in the AS/400 has a PAWA. Within this PAWA is the PAGP and two or more ACTGRPs. Each ACTGRP has a PACB that contains multiple MBVs, an ACTGRP directory, a PRT, a heap list, one or more heap spaces, auto storage segments, and static storage segments. Now, isn't this perfectly clear?

Figure 9.5 ILE Activation Group

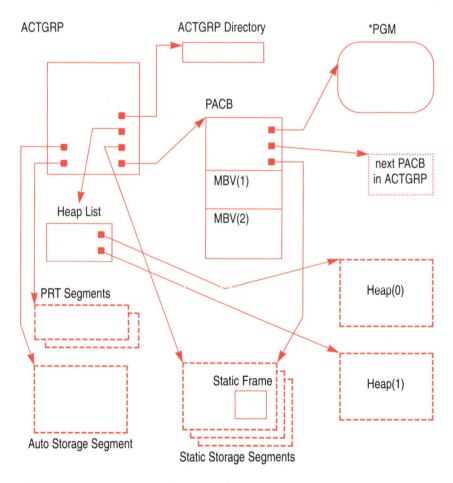

PACB = Program Activation Control Block
MBV = Module Binding Vector
PRT = Procedure Reference Table

Exceptions, Events, and Interrupts

When something doesn't conform to the general rule, we usually say it is an exception to the rule. Computer systems also take exception to the general rules of processing. In this section, we will look at how exceptions, events, and interrupts are handled in an AS/400.

At the hardware level, it is usual to talk about interrupts. As described earlier in this chapter, an interrupt is an occurrence, other than a branch, that changes the normal flow of instruction execution. The interrupt may be caused by the execution of an instruction or it may be caused by some action outside of the running program, such as the completion of an I/O operation. The PowerPC architecture defines a full interrupt mechanism to allow the processor to change state as a result of external signals, errors, or unusual conditions arising in the execution of instructions. We will see how this works later in this section.

Programs and processes at the MI know nothing about interrupts at the hardware level. However, an interrupt that occurs as a result of MI program execution must be reported at the MI. The SLIC is responsible for detecting, handling, and reporting these interrupts at the MI.

Exceptions and Events at the MI

MI distinguishes between an exception and an event. An exception is defined as either a machine-defined error detected during the execution of an instruction or a user-defined condition detected by a user program. An event, on the other hand, is defined as an activity that occurs during machine operation that may be of interest to machine users. Exceptions are synchronous, meaning they are caused by the execution of an instruction, while events are asynchronous, meaning they are caused by actions outside the currently executing instruction. In general, however, the two are very similar.

A couple of examples may be helpful. Suppose we have a program that attempts to divide a number by zero, an obvious error condition. This error will be reported as an exception when it is detected during the execution of the divide instruction. It is synchronous because the same error will occur at the same place in the program whenever the program is run (assuming the data values are always the same). Let's further suppose an I/O operation, such as reading a record from a disk, is executing while we are running our program. At some point, the I/O operation completes and this fact is reported. The mechanism used to report the I/O completion is an event, because it is caused by an action outside of the currently executing instruction. The event is asynchronous, meaning it is not tied to the execution of the running program and it can occur at any time.

Just as there are two types of exceptions at the MI, errors and user-defined conditions, there are two types of events. The two types of MI events are object-related events, such as a message limit being reached on a queue, and machine-related events, such as a specific time interval elapsing. An MI process can monitor the occurrence of a set of events and take action based on some or all of the events.

With the introduction of the ILE program and process models, some changes were made to the exception model. An exception at the MI is a formally architected process message. All process messages are retained in the process queue space, which is a part of the ILE process structure described in a previous section. Because the exception is reported as a message, a delay is possible between the signaling and the processing of the exception. So far, the characteristics of exception structure just described are the same for the original models and for the ILE models.

New for ILE is that the exception monitoring and handling now are explicitly controlled by the MI user. Exception monitors are used to detect the occurrence of particular exceptions. Instructions placed in the MI instruction stream enable and disable these exception monitors. Multiple monitors can be enabled at the same time. Each monitor has a priority, so exception searching and handling is based on priority when more than one monitor is enabled. Associated with each monitor is an exception handler routine. An exception handler is always an external ILE procedure.

SLIC supports both event and exception monitoring and handling. In Chapter 5, we saw that access to system objects was monitored by the machine. This capability, plus some special system linkage instructions inserted into the PowerPC instruction stream, can accomplish most of the event-monitoring function. Much of the exception-monitoring function is accomplished by the hardware and is reported to the SLIC exception-handling routines through the PowerPC interrupt mechanism. In the next section, we will look at the exception management component of SLIC.

SLIC Exception Management

Exception management in SLIC is primarily a routing function. The PowerPC interrupt mechanism starts the routing function whenever the hardware detects an interrupt. Once an exception occurs, all applicable SLIC exception handlers are given a chance to handle the exception. If the exception is handled, the process continues as if nothing happened. If the exception is not handled in the SLIC, the process is terminated and the exception is passed to the appropriate ILE exception handler.

Interrupts are classified by whether they are caused specifically by the execution of an instruction or by some other system event. The PowerPC architecture defines a total of 15 types of interrupts. Five of these interrupts are system-caused. They are

- System Reset — This interrupt occurs whenever the system is reset or powered on.
- Machine Check — A machine check interrupt reports hardware malfunctions.

- External — An external interrupt notifies the processor that some event outside the processor (e.g., I/O) needs attention.
- Performance Monitor — If the performance monitoring capability is enabled, this interrupt notifies the processor that some event being monitored has occurred.
- Decrementer — The decrementer is used for timing functions. This interrupt notifies the processor that some time interval has expired.

The instruction-caused interrupts are

- Data Storage — This interrupt indicates that an instruction has attempted a data storage access that cannot be performed. This type of interrupt is used to report an effective address that cannot be translated (a page fault), a storage protection violation, or an effective address overflow (EAO) exception.
- Instruction Storage — This interrupt is similar to the data storage interrupt, except it is caused by an attempt to fetch the next instruction to be executed.
- Direct-Store Error — This interrupt is also similar to the data storage interrupt, except it occurs when the access is made to a direct-store (DS) address. Note you cannot get a page fault on a DS address.
- Alignment — The alignment interrupt occurs when there is an attempt to access an operand that is supposed to be aligned on a memory boundary but isn't.
- Program — The program interrupt is used to report such things as the processor's attempt to execute a privileged instruction without authority to do so, or its attempt to execute an invalid op-code.
- Floating-Point Unavailable — This interrupt occurs when an attempt is made to execute a floating-point instruction and a bit in the MSR indicates that the processor cannot execute any floating-point instructions. The PowerPC architecture allows floating-point operations to be inhibited.
- Floating-Point Assist — This interrupt is used to allow software assistance for relatively infrequent and complex floating-point operations. The processor must recognize the floating-point instruction as one that is implemented in software, and generate this type of interrupt.
- Trace — The capability to do a single-step trace on all instructions or to trace all branches is enabled by bits having been set in the MSR. When these bits are set, a trace interrupt is generated after the successful execution of every instruction being traced.

- System Call — A System Call instruction, which we will describe in the next section, can be placed in the instruction stream. The execution of this instruction causes a system call interrupt to be generated.
- System Call Vectored — A System Call Vectored instruction, which we also describe in the next section, is similar to the System Call instruction, except that with the System Call Vectored instruction, control can be passed to any one of 128 routines.

SLIC provides separate routines, one to handle each type of interrupt. When the hardware detects an interrupt, control is passed to one of these First Level Exception Handlers (FLEHs). We discuss how the hardware passes control in the next section. The FLEHs handle many of the frequently expected exceptions. If one of these routines handles the exception, control is passed back to normal instruction processing. If the exception is instruction-caused and has not been handled, the FLEH passes control to the Second Level Exception Handler (SLEH).

The SLEH can handle some of the other expected but less frequent exceptions, such as a lock exception on a system object. It also is responsible for sorting out the exceptions that cannot be handled in the SLIC. If the unhandled exception occurred while the system was executing an instruction translated from the MI, the SLEH passes control to the MI exception generator. If the unhandled exception occurred while the system was executing an SLIC instruction, the SLEH passes control to the Third Level Exception Handler (TLEH).

The TLEH gets control when the exception occurred during the execution of an SLIC routine. The TLEH gets control from the SLEH, the machine check handler, if the machine check occurred during the execution of an SLIC routine, or during any other SLIC routine that has detected an exception. The TLEH first invokes the Component Specific Exception Handlers (CSEHs) that were set up by various SLIC components. After they finish, the CSEHs pass control back to the TLEH. The TLEH then determines what to do with the exception. If the exception occurred in an SLIC task that was running as part of an MI process, control is passed to the MI exception generator. If the exception occurred in an SLIC task that was not running as part of an MI process, the task is destroyed.

The CSEHs are defined by various SLIC components to free resources acquired while performing some operation, to clean up partial results of a failed operation, or to tolerate a failure in a particular code sequence. CSEHs are given control from the TLEH. The CSEHs to be executed for a particular task are determined by CSEH blocks that are chained to the TDE of the task. Each CSEH block contains the address of the CSEH routine, the definer's stack pointer, and any data needed by the CSEH routine. After all CSEHs for the task have been executed, control is passed back to the TLEH.

The MI exception generator prepares the data for the process message, performs some clean-up operations, and sends the message to the queue space of the appropriate MI process.

Hardware Context Switching

Because the exception routines just described may need access to privileged instructions at the PowerPC level, the interrupt mechanism must have the ability to switch the state of the processor when control is passed to one of these routines. We usually describe this action as switching the *context* of the processor. The context is defined as the state of the processor with regard to privilege, relocation, storage protection, 64-bit mode, C2 security, and so on.

In addition to just switching the context, the interrupt mechanism must perform context synchronization. Synchronization means the processor hardware must ensure that all instructions initiated before the interrupt will complete execution in the context in which they were initiated. Then the hardware must ensure that the instructions following the operation will be fetched and executed in the context established by the operation.

In Chapter 8, we looked at the Machine State Register (MSR) and the meaning of some of the bits in this register. The PowerPC architecture for the MSR defines several other bits, some of which were described in the preceding section. Because we have already covered the ones that are related to the topics we want to discuss, we will not discuss the remaining bits. What is important to understand is that the settings of all the bits in the MSR determine the context of the processor. The setting of these bits can be altered when a processor interrupt occurs.

The System Call (sc) instruction can be used to call an SLIC routine when it is necessary to change the context of the processor. This instruction can be used within translated MI programs to call upon the SLIC part of the operating system to perform some service. As we just saw, when the sc instruction is executed by the processor, a System Call interrupt is generated. Readers familiar with S/370 may recognize the sc instruction in the PowerPC architecture as being very similar to the Supervisor Call (SVC) instruction in the S/370 architecture. The execution of either of these instructions causes an interrupt to occur. The PowerPC architecture has its roots in the original 801 minicomputer, which was defined in the middle 1970s. The 801 architecture was heavily influenced by the mainframe architecture of the time, the S/370. In some sense, the MSR is analogous to the Program Status Word (PSW) of the S/370.

When any interrupt occurs, the PowerPC processor hardware first performs context synchronization to ensure the interrupt processing operation is not initiated until all instructions already in execution have completed to a point where they have reported all exceptions they will cause. Note that each interrupt has a priority, so if more than one interrupt is pending, the highest priority one is first selected. The effective address of the instruction that was executing when the interrupt occurred is then saved in a special 64-bit processor register, called the Machine Status Save/Restore Register 0 (SRR 0). In the case of a System Call interrupt, the effective address of the instruction following the sc instruction is stored in SRR 0. Next, selected bits from the current MSR are saved in another special 64-bit processor register, called the Machine Status Save/Restore Register 1 (SRR 1). Finally, still other bits in SRR 1 are loaded with information specific to the type of interrupt that occurred.

After saving the current machine status, the interrupt hardware causes some of the bits in the MSR to be altered. The new MSR bit settings are specifically defined by the architecture for each interrupt type. In particular, the relocation bits (MSRIR and MSRDR) are always turned off so the interrupt routines will use real addresses and never get a page fault. After modifying the MSR bits, the interrupt hardware then causes the next instruction to be fetched from an address that is a fixed offset from a base address. The PowerPC architecture also defines the specific offset to be used for each type of interrupt. Another bit in the MSR, called the interrupt prefix, selects one of two base addresses to be used.

The result of the hardware interrupt processing just described is to transfer control to the first instruction of one of the SLIC interrupt handlers described in the previous section. The context of the processor has also been switched before this routine gets control so, for example, privileged instructions can be executed in this routine.

When the interrupt handler routine is finished, it executes another special PowerPC instruction. This instruction, called Return From Interrupt (rfi), restores the processor to the state it had before the interrupt occurred. The selected bits in SRR 1 are first placed into the corresponding bits in the MSR. Then the next instruction is fetched, under control of the new MSR value, from the address in SRR 0. If this instruction enables any pending exceptions, the interrupt associated with the highest priority pending exception is generated before the first instruction in the context established by the completion of this rfi instruction.

The two PowerPC instructions just described, sc and rfi, allow the processor to call an interrupt handler when an interrupt occurs and to return to normal instruction processing when the interrupt has been handled. Within the AS/400, we wanted a similar mechanism to allow one SLIC routine to call another. For example, we wanted the FLEH to call the SLEH in a very efficient manner. To accomplish this, we defined two new instructions for the PowerPC architecture. They are called System Call Vectored (scv) and Return From System Call Vectored (rfscv).

The scv instruction is similar to the sc instruction, with a few important differences. Instead of transferring control to only one location, the scv instruction identifies one of 128 locations. A separate SLIC routine can begin at each of these 128 locations. Thus, the scv instruction can be used to efficiently pass control between SLIC routines. Another difference is the scv instruction does not modify the settings of the MSR bits. This means, for example, a called routine can use virtual addresses. With virtual addressing, SLIC routines can be written to be pageable. Still another difference is that the scv instruction does not use the SRR 0 and the SRR 1 registers to save the machine status. Instead, it uses two processor registers that can be accessed with non-privileged instructions. The rfscv instruction provides the return operation for the scv.

Work Management and OS/400 Jobs

The preceding sections show the difficulties of having a full-fledged process structure. A tremendous amount of functionality is provided with any modern process structure, but that functionality can also mean a tremendous amount of complexity if the user has to manage the structure. In keeping with the philosophies of technology independence and integration, the AS/400 manages this complex structure for the user through OS/400's work management component. A user deals with the definition of a job, which more closely matches a business application for the system. OS/400 and the underlying machine do the rest.

There is a downside to building a full job structure on top of the process model. There is much more flexibility if the characteristics of the process can be tuned to match the characteristics of any particular application; this tuning enables enhanced performance of an application that does not need all the function the job structure provides. A lightweight process, or a subprocess, which is usually called a *thread*, is becoming a fundamental building block for many new operating systems. Applications written to this model do not use a full-function job structure, and consequently they can achieve higher performance when it comes to switching between processes.

At this point it is important to note that, at the hardware level, the AS/400 has one of the most efficient tasking structures in the industry. In a commercial application, a large percentage of the processing, often as high as 80 percent or 90 percent, is performed in the operating system rather than in the application. The applications request services from the operating system instead of performing the services themselves. In an AS/400, those services are primarily performed in SLIC, and SLIC uses the highly efficient tasking structure. In a following section we will look at how the AS/400 is beginning to support the concept of a lightweight process to accommodate applications written for other operating systems.

Work Management Concepts

The management of the flow of work submitted to the AS/400 is provided by OS/400's work management component. A job is the unit of work submitted by the user. To review an earlier discussion, work management recognizes several types of jobs, including the traditional interactive and batch jobs.

The process discussed in the preceding sections describes the unit of work submitted by work management to the underlying machine. An MI process object has no counterpart in OS/400. A job is not an OS/400 object. Neither are routing steps or subsystems, which we will discuss shortly. Work management deals with processes directly. A job can be executed within a single process, or it can be executed within a series of processes whose initiation is managed by one or more controlling processes. From a user standpoint, each new process initiation on behalf of a job is called a *routing step*.

Work management views the total system as the hierarchy of domains shown in Figure 9.6. The lowest level in this hierarchy is the routing step. The next higher level is the job. A job is processed by one or more consecutive routing steps. Jobs are contained in *subsystems*, each of which contains similar types of jobs, such as all interactive jobs. Subsystems control certain resources of the system, as we will see shortly. Finally, the highest level in the hierarchy is the system itself. Associated with the system are certain system values and network attributes that are used for the entire system. An example would be the name of the system in a network of systems.

Figure 9.6 Work Management Concepts

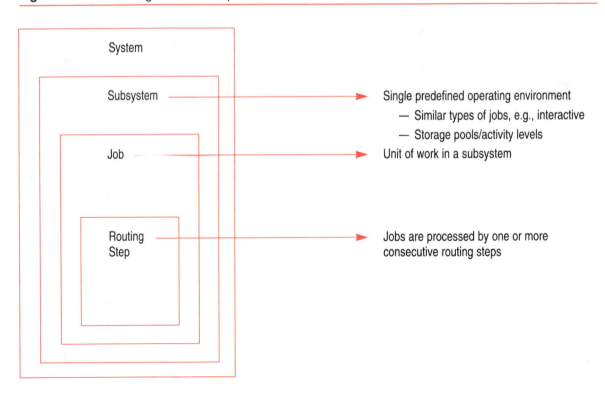

Subsystems

An AS/400 subsystem is a single, predefined operating environment. All the jobs in a subsystem should be of the same type (e.g., batch) and share certain system resources. Because the configuration of a subsystem and determining which jobs run in which subsystem are entirely under the control of each AS/400 installation, there is no guarantee all jobs in a subsystem are the same type. An OS/400 object, known as a subsystem description, is associated with each subsystem. The subsystem description contains general information about the resources allocated to the subsystem, and it points to other OS/400 objects that provide more information about the jobs in the subsystem. The OS/400 object types pointed to by a subsystem description include job descriptions, classes, and programs.

A job description is an OS/400 object that identifies attributes and resources associated with a job. Identified are such things as

- Default library list
- Job queue
- Routing data
- Default printer
- Output scheduling priority
- User profile

A class is an OS/400 object containing parameters that specify the runtime environment. Some of these parameters relate to the allocation of processor resources to the job. For example, there may be a limit to the number of processes in a class that can be concurrently eligible for execution. This arrangement provides a means to control the amount of interference among processes that compete for the same system resources. This limit, which is usually called the activity level, is associated with a *storage pool*.

A storage pool, not to be confused with an auxiliary storage pool, is a means of reserving a certain amount of main memory for a subsystem. Logically, the storage pool should be called a "memory pool"; but remember that IBM doesn't like to give human characteristics, such as memory, to its computers. Main memory can be divided into as many as 16 storage pools, one of which is always reserved for the machine. A storage pool is a quantity of memory from which the dynamic paging requirements of processes assigned to that storage pool are satisfied. For example, one storage pool could be defined for all interactive jobs and another for all batch jobs. This would ensure that a batch job could not steal a page frame from an interactive job and thus affect the response time for a particular interactive user. Batch jobs could only steal pages from other batch jobs in the batch storage pool. Storage pools are defined in the subsystem description.

The user of the system controls the pool sizes, the number of pools, and the activity levels. In this way, the system can be adjusted to achieve optimum performance for a given user workload. This adjustment can be made manually or automatically as the workload changes, through the use of various performance tuning tools available on the AS/400.

Original and New Job Structures

The introduction of the ILE process model described in previous sections also changed the structure of a job in the AS/400. We can see the differences by looking at the application resources available for the original job structures and the new job structures, and by noting how these resources can be used. In general, the application resources for a job include shared files, commitment control, and storage.

For the original job structure:

- Shared files are seen by all application programs in the job.
- External names are shared at the job level, not at the application level within a job.
- Commitment control is done for the entire job.
- Only one activation of a program is allowed in the job.
- Only one static storage area exists per job.
- Only one automatic storage area (stack) is allowed per job.
- Only one dynamic area exists for every language (no sharing).

For the new job structure, based on the ILE process model:

- Shared files can be seen by all application programs in the job, or each application can define its own file usage.
- External names are scoped to a single application, meaning each application in a job can have its own name space for externally defined variables.
- Commitment control can be done on a job basis, or each application can have its own commitment control in effect.
- Multiple activations of the same program are allowed with the job.
- Each application has its own storage areas and each is protected.
  — static storage
  — automatic storage (stack)
  — dynamic storage (heap)

With the new job structure, each job, similar to each process, has two or more activations. Each of these activations has its own storage packaging and protection state.

Processes, Tasks, Jobs, Activation Groups, and Threads

The AS/400 defines three levels of work, as we have seen. A *task* is the lowest level below the MI. A *process* exists at the MI and is built on top of the tasking structure in the SLIC. OS/400 supports a *job* as a unit of work for the system and the job is built on the MI process model. Most other operating systems deal directly with a process. OS/400 does not. In this respect a job in OS/400 is analogous to a process in some other operating systems.

The full-function job provides greater levels of resource sharing and security than does the process definition supported by some other operating systems; however, a full-function job takes a long time to create. Consequently, it is very appropriate to describe a job in the AS/400 as being a heavyweight.

The current trend in many newer operating systems, exemplified by the definition for POSIX, is to define a structure where a process can be quickly created, used, and then destroyed. To accomplish this requires a fairly lightweight process, and this trend has led to a new definition of a process in the industry.

These newer definitions of a process break a process into two separate components. The first component contains all the resources for a group of cooperating entities. The resources include the virtual memory, the communications ports, and the files that the operating system allocates to the process. Some systems even call this part of the process a task.

The second part of a process is the active execution environment, usually called a *thread*. A process can have one or more concurrently executing threads. The original definition limited a process to only one unit of execution. The newer definition allows multiple units of execution, the threads. A thread is a subprocess that has some of its own private resources as well as the shared resources of the process. Thus, a multithreaded process can have multiple units of execution sharing system resources.

Threads are important because they can exploit parallelism in certain types of applications. Different parts of the same application can run in parallel. Threads are particularly important in a distributed environment, and they are required for the implementation of the standard known as the Distributed Computing Environment (DCE).

Because we wanted the AS/400 to implement both DCE and the POSIX interface, we had to find some way to support POSIX threads. We considered two models. The first was to define multiple TDEs per process. Each activation group could have its own TDE and, therefore, be a separately dispatchable unit of work. Each activation group in a process then would be analogous to a thread. This model also fits reasonably close to the threads model used in the industry. Unfortunately, this model also required more changes to OS/400 than time permitted for us to achieve an implementation for V3R1. So we had to select a second, somewhat less optimum, model for the initial implementation.

We defined the concept of a shared activation group for the second model of threads. Multiple OS/400 jobs can share the same activation group. Thus, a thread by this definition is an OS/400 job that shares an activation group. A POSIX process can be thought of as all OS/400 jobs sharing an activation group. All threads in the POSIX process share the same static storage and heap, while each thread has its own automatic (stack) storage.

This definition of using an OS/400 job as a thread works, but it has one big drawback: The full-function OS/400 job takes a long time to create compared to the lightweight thread other systems use. To improve AS/400 performance, we created a standby pool of previously created jobs. When a thread needs to be quickly created, one of the jobs from this pool is used. Destroying a thread moves the job back to the standby pool.

Over time we expect that more and more applications will be written for the operating systems that support the POSIX model of threads. To run these applications most efficiently on an AS/400 without having a pool of jobs waiting, we will have to change the threads implementation to perhaps match the first model described.

Conclusions

Various operating systems implement processes in different ways. Each system decides how the processes should be structured, how they are protected, and how robust they will be. The AS/400 process model has proven itself to be an industrial-strength implementation, capable of handling business-critical applications. The very modern tasking structure on which everything else is built will allow this system's process and job models to evolve to handle the needs of its future application environments.

In the following chapter, we will look at the I/O system and see how it is evolving to meet the AS/400's future application environments. We will see how the tasking structure plays an important role in the I/O system, both now and in the future.

Chapter 10

The I/O System

The AS/400 I/O system rarely gets much publicity. On the one hand, Input/Output (I/O) in general *seems* to be a second-class citizen these days, with most of the attention focused on processor designs. We are rapidly approaching a time when machines from low-end PCs to the fastest supercomputers will be built from the same basic microprocessor technology, and its I/O capabilities may be the only feature that distinguishes one machine from another. So it can be argued, on the other hand, that I/O is the most important component in the system. After all, without I/O that high-performance processor would just sit there and chuckle to itself.

What is the I/O system and why is it so important? Loosely defined, the I/O system comprises the group of components, both hardware and software, that are responsible for processing input from and delivering output to a variety of devices attached to the system. Whenever you require any system resource — when you read from or write to a file, when you request some instructions of a program to execute, when you require any other system object, when you create or destroy an object, when you communicate with some device — and that resource has not already been brought into memory, the computer must go through the I/O system to retrieve or store, create or destroy the resource. As I said, without the I/O system not much would get done in the computer.

The AS/400 has never had industry-leading processor performance. Yet, it handily holds its own against other systems. More often than not, it can put another system with a higher performance processor to shame on almost any real-world benchmark. In fact, the AS/400's "secret weapon" to accomplish this feat is one of the most sophisticated and powerful I/O systems in the industry.

Many people have a vague idea about the way AS/400 I/O is structured; but beyond the fact that there are multiple IOPs, few people understand how it works. In this chapter, we will look at some aspects of the AS/400's

I/O system that are familiar, as well as many that are not so familiar. In keeping with our approach in other chapters, we will start by looking at the origins of this I/O system.

Historical Perspective

I/O devices are attached to a computer via an I/O bus. A bus is simply an electrical pathway between two hardware components. Typically, an I/O bus will have anywhere from 20 to 100 wires, some of which are used to transfer data and some of which are used to pass control information to and from the I/O device. An I/O device consists of two parts, one containing most of the electronics, called the I/O controller, and one containing the physical device itself, such as a disk drive. The job of an I/O controller is to control its device and to handle bus access for it. For example, when a program wants data from a disk, it gives a command to the disk controller, which then issues seeks and other commands to the drive.

In a simple computer such as a PC, a single bus exists to connect the processor, memory, and I/O controllers. The bus is used not only by the I/O controllers, but also by the processor for fetching instructions and data. When the processor and an I/O controller want to use the bus at the same time, a chip called the bus arbiter decides who goes next. Usually, the I/O controller is given preference because disks and other moving devices cannot be stopped, and forcing them to wait could result in lost data. When no I/O device is running, the processor is free to use all the bus cycles for itself. When an I/O device is running, however, that device will request and be granted the bus whenever it needs it. This process, called *cycle stealing*, slows down the computer.

The I/O structure just described for a PC is not acceptable for a larger computer that performs many I/O operations. Large systems usually need multiple buses, and some way to offload the processing from the main processor is also desirable. One approach is to use a channel, which is a specialized computer built alongside the main processor. The I/O buses are attached directly to the channel rather than to the processor.

A channel has it own instruction set designed specifically to communicate with the bus-attached I/O controllers and to transfer data between the I/O device and the memory. A channel receives programs (called channel programs) to run from the main processor. These channel programs can be run by the channel concurrently with other programs running in the main processor. Thus, there is little interference between the two processing units. When the channel is finished with its program, it interrupts the main processor to get more work.

The two basic types of channels are selector channels and multiplexer channels. A selector channel is designed to support high-speed devices, such as disks, and it can only handle the data transfer from one device at a time. On the other hand, a multiplexer channel can handle data transfers from multiple low-speed devices, such as terminals, by interleaving the data from each device on the bus. The amount of data interleaved for each device can be a single byte or a block of bytes. Multiplexer channels are classified as byte-multiplexer channels or block-multiplexer channels. A System/370 supported both of these channel types.

The System/38 had a channel similar in many ways to a System/370 channel. This channel was a throwback to the original design, where a group of engineers thought they were actually building a System/370. But unlike the System/370, which supported multiple selector and multiplexer channels, the System/38 only had one channel. For those readers who are purists, the System/38 channel could be described as a block-multiplexer channel, operating in a fixed-burst mode.

The I/O controllers used for the actual device control in the System/38 were fairly shallow, meaning most of the intelligence to perform I/O operations was back in the channel. The System/34 and the System/36, which had no channels, used intelligent processors to control their I/O devices. The System/34 used different I/O processor designs for different devices. The System/36 standardized on the CSP for most of its I/O processors. Thus, a System/36 could have a disk controller, a workstation controller, and a communications line controller, each with its own separate CSP. A large System/36 could have several of these CSPs used for I/O.

The AS/400 eliminated the channel of the System/38 and instead uses one or more I/O buses with intelligent processors attached. Most of the I/O processing is performed in these intelligent IOPs. This structure is different from either the System/36 or the System/38, although it is much closer to the System/36. Where this structure came from is the subject of the next section.

The Fort Knox Project

In the early 1980s, IBM management decided it had too many "midrange" systems. At the time five separate IBM systems were competing for the same customers. IBM made the decision in 1982 to converge all five of these systems into one. The project, called Fort Knox, was motivated not so much by a desire to produce a better system for customers as it was to reduce IBM development expenses. The fundamental idea of convergence was simple enough, but implementing the idea proved to be more of a challenge.

Not only were the five systems developed in different locations, but they also belonged to different divisions within IBM. To fix this situation, IBM decided to put all the locations and their systems into a single division. Rather than create a new division, IBM decided to put all the systems into the Systems Products Division (SPD).

IBM's Research Division convinced SPD management that a totally new system could be built to run all the existing operating systems, plus some new ones. The new processor they proposed to accomplish this feat was called

Iliad. Iliad was a version of the original 801 processor, and it was to be IBM's first RISC processor.

With the processor decision made, the developers in Boca Raton started a campaign to use the Series/1 I/O bus for the new Fort Knox system. The Series/1 was a very good device controller and its I/O bus design was one of the best. With a few modifications for anticipated future growth requirements, the Series/1 I/O bus was used in the Fort Knox systems. It was renamed, the SPD bus.

For Illiad's software, each location was to port its existing operating system to run on the Iliad processor. In this way, any customer could move all its applications to the Fort Knox system. Where needed, special assist hardware could be built alongside the processor to support unique features of the existing operating systems. Meanwhile, a new native operating system for Iliad was also to be built. To get Rochester to buy into the whole convergence idea, IBM gave our group the responsibility for the development of the new operating system.

As the various designers began to port their operating systems to the new Iliad processor, they began to identify changes to the Iliad design that were needed to support each operating system. IBM Research, which owned the Iliad design, steadfastly refused to make any changes to its processor architecture. Unable to get changes into the base processor, system designers began to add more function to the assist hardware. The special assist hardware grew and grew to accommodate the unique characteristics of the existing operating systems.

Before long, the assist hardware for each system took on a life of its own, to the point where each became a full-fledged processor. We called them co-processors, but they clearly had the ability to stand alone without the Iliad processor. Rochester developed both a System/36 and a System/38 co-processor while Endicott developed a System/370 co-processor.

Finally, the Fort Knox system structure had to be redefined. Instead of having multiple operating systems somehow running on the same processor, only the new native operating system would run on the Iliad processor. If one or more of the existing operating systems had to be included to run customer applications, each operating system would run on its own co-processor.

By 1985, it was clear that Fort Knox was a failure. After spending hundreds of millions of dollars, IBM canceled the whole fiasco. For a brief period, many at IBM thought the 9370 could be the organization's only midrange product. When IBM announced that system in 1987, it also placed some very unrealistic expectations upon it. The 9370 was a successful product in its own right, but it was not going to single-handedly take back the midrange market IBM had lost in the preceding five years.

It is somewhat ironic that the Endicott-developed models of the 9370 systems each contained a RISC processor. The operating system and the applications ran on the System/370 co-processor, while the Iliad processor was relegated to the role of a service processor. Because the Iliad processor in those systems did not play a significant role, the fact that it was a RISC design was never advertised.

The Silverlake Project
In 1985, Rochester's business was in shambles. The System/38 was seven years old and had been left to die a few years earlier. The System/36 still had a couple years left, but was quickly reaching the limits of its capability. Because we had neglected our products for so long, our competitors were attacking from every side and had already taken away most of our business. Our worldwide market share in midrange computers had plummeted from nearly 33 percent in the late 1970s to a mere 9 percent by 1985. Worse yet, we were still tied to SPD, whose management continued to believe the 9370 would solve all of IBM's midrange ills.

Finally, in late 1985, new management came to SPD in the form of Steven Schwartz. Shortly after Schwartz took over as our division president, a proposal for a new system emerged from Rochester. In the back rooms of the Rochester laboratory, a handful of developers built a demonstration of System/36 applications running on a System/38. For years we had known this was possible, but the former SPD management wanted to hear nothing about it. In December 1985, we showed it to Steve Schwartz. Two months later Schwartz approved the project and brought in Tom Furey as our laboratory director to make it happen. Twenty-eight months later the Silverlake project, as we called it, became the AS/400.

Contrary to some claims made at the announcement of the AS/400, we did not have time to develop a new system in only a little more than two years. We had to take what we had, repackage it, and add as much new function as we could. For our high-end 9406 models, we used the rack-mounted packaging developed for the 9370. We threw out the Iliad processor and only used the System/38 co-processors that we had already developed. For software, we used the entire System/38 operating system to which we added about three releases' worth of enhancements. Tom Furey brought in many of our own customers to directly help us decide exactly what enhancements should be added.

Our low end presented another problem. The Endicott rack-mounted packages were simply too expensive and difficult to build. We needed a new low end, easy-to-assemble package. Again, we had a group of very talented packaging and mechanical folks in Rochester. Led by people such as Art Reckinger and Zanti Squillace, this group had proposed a new, modular packaging design. One characteristic of their design was the use of aluminum "books" to hold the logic cards. Their design was not met with much enthusiasm early on. With Silverlake, they were given a chance to prove their new package in the low-end 9402 and 9404 models. Today, all AS/400s use their modular design and their book packages.

For the I/O, we had no time to make any changes. All models of the AS/400 used the SPD bus and the IOPs developed for the Fort Knox systems. With the Advanced Series and the new RISC processors the only remnant of Fort Knox is the SPD bus. Even the division after which it was named has disappeared. Fortunately for us, the SPD bus has proven itself to be a winner as we will see in the following sections.

Hardware I/O Structure

Figure 10.1 illustrates a logical view of the AS/400 hardware I/O structure. The system processors are attached to the main memory via the memory bus. Also attached to the memory are the service processor and the bus control units (BCUs). One BCU is associated with each SPD bus. Attached to the SPD buses are the I/O bus units (IOBUs). Finally, the IOBUs provide the interface to the I/O devices.

Figure 10.1 Hardware I/O Structure

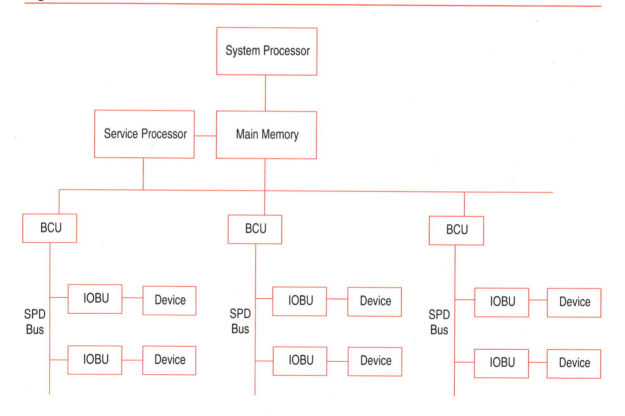

The logical structure just shown is more of a programming view of the I/O than it is a physical view of the hardware. This is a convenient way to see how I/O operates in an AS/400. The I/O commands for a particular device are sent by the system processor to the IOBU associated with the device over the appropriate SPD bus. Recall from Chapter 8 that the processor uses a direct-store address to uniquely identify the bus, the IOBU, and the device. The IOBU, as we will soon see, is made up of an IOP and the software that runs on the IOP. The IOBU receives the command, causes the device to perform the requested operation, and controls the data transfers to and from the main memory. When the I/O operation is completed, the IOBU responds back to the system processor with status information to tell whether or not the operation was successful. We will examine these operations in more detail in the following sections. First, let's look at the way these components are physically connected and some of their characteristics.

I/O Hardware Connections Using Fiber Optics

The system processors are connected to the main memory via the memory bus. Also attached to that memory bus is a local bus attachment card. The local bus attachment card contains the logic used to attach the first SPD bus. The local bus attachment card and the first SPD bus are packaged with the processing unit. This first SPD bus is often called a "copper" bus because it is packaged directly with the processing unit. This is the only SPD bus in the smaller models of the AS/400.

Larger models of the AS/400 can optionally have multiple SPD buses. A very large model can have up to 18 additional buses, for a maximum of 19 SPD buses on any single system. These additional SPD buses are connected via optical links, and they are often called "optical" buses. The local bus attachment card in the processing unit can optionally attach a multiplicity of optical link cards (OLCs) to support the additional SPD buses. Each OLC has two completely independent optical links and therefore can support two SPD buses.

Fiber-optic technology is used to attach the additional SPD buses. This technology is used to increase the I/O bandwidth and to allow increased distances between the processing unit and the I/O expansion units. The OLC, designed in Rochester, was first introduced on the AS/400 in 1991. The performance of this optical link has continued to increase; today, SPD buses transfer data at either 266 megabits per second or 1 gigabit per second (the higher rate is available only on the RISC models).

A remote bus attachment card is packaged in an I/O expansion unit. The remote attachment card contains one OLC and two BCUs. Each BCU attaches an SPD bus directly to one of the optical links on the OLC. The two BCUs are also interconnected to provide an alternative path between the BCU and an optical link. This alternative path provides redundancy in the fiber-optic I/O buses.

The SPD bus is composed of 36 lines that are used to transfer data (32 data bits and 4 parity bits), plus additional lines that are used to transfer control information. For a copper bus these lines can be thought of as physical wires. An optical bus serializes these data and control bits, but is functionally equivalent. Both addresses and data can be transmitted over the bus. The SPD bus operates asynchronously. To understand why an asynchronous bus was chosen, let's look at some characteristics of synchronous buses for comparison. A synchronous bus includes a clock in the control lines and a fixed protocol for communicating that is relative to the clock. A synchronous bus requires every device on the bus to run at the same clock rate, which usually means the devices must be in close proximity. This type of bus is fast and is used for the memory bus in an AS/400 between the processors and the main memory. Conversely, because an asynchronous bus is not clocked, it can accommodate a wide variety of devices and can be lengthened without worrying about clock skew or synchronization. This added flexibility is why the asynchronous SPD bus was selected for the AS/400.

To coordinate transmission of data between sender and receiver, an asynchronous bus, like the SPD bus, uses a handshaking protocol. A handshaking protocol requires that the sender and receiver proceed to the next step only after both agree. The separate control lines with the SPD bus implement this protocol. For example, the sender may put a read request on the control lines and an address on the data lines. These control signals are asserted until the receiver indicates the control lines have been seen by putting a signal on the acknowledge control line.

Attached to each SPD bus are at least two IOBUs. A maximum of 32 IOBUs can be attached to a single SPD bus. With multiple IOBUs attached to the bus, arbitration is needed if more than one unit wants to use the bus at the same time. A priority arbitration mechanism is used. Each IOBU is assigned a priority, and this priority is used to decide which IOBU can use the bus when two or more are contending for its use.

Both the main processor and the device controllers operate as IOBUs. The device controllers are implemented as IOPs that are used to perform the I/O device operations. These IOPs are microprocessors from various vendors, although most are Motorola microprocessors. Each IOP has its own memory and contains its own operating system. These special-purpose, real-time operating systems are designed primarily for I/O device control. The application running in the IOP is obviously tuned for the specific device interface, communications interface, or LAN interface that the IOP supports. From an I/O operational viewpoint, the IOP, including all its software, is considered to be an IOBU.

Before we leave this topic to continue with our I/O discussion, we should note that an IOP can be used for other functions than just device control. It should be obvious that an IOP is a full processor with its own operating system and application programs. It also has direct access, via the SPD bus, to the main memory and, through the bus, to the disk system of the AS/400. An IOP can, therefore, be used to run user applications. In the following chapter, we will look at the file-serving IOP (FSIOP) on the AS/400 and see how it is used as an application engine. This capability to run other operating systems and applications on an IOP will be heavily exploited in future AS/400s.

I/O Bus Operations

Each SPD bus has it own BCU. The BCU provides the master control over the bus operations. During normal operation, the BCU handles error recovery and retry. It also handles the arbitration when more than one IOBU tries to use the bus at the same time. Additionally, the BCU initializes the bus at IPL time.

At IPL time, the BCU assigns the logical addresses to the attached IOBUs. Note that this is done at every IPL. This means a new IOBU, possibly with a new device attached, can be plugged into an AS/400; and when the system is IPLed, the new IOBU is automatically configured into the AS/400. No other user intervention is required. This is equivalent to plug-and-play I/O in the PC world.

In addition to assigning logical addresses to the attached IOBUs at IPL time, the BCU assigns bus priority to each unit. It checks out each IOBU's ability to communicate over the bus and downloads the operational code to the memory of each IOP.

All communications during normal operations are between IOBUs. As stated earlier, the system processors function as IOBUs, as do all the IOPs. Information is always exchanged between the IOBU that originates the bus operation (called the master) and the IOBU selected by the originator (called the slave). All bus operations are between master and slave.

Information is transferred between IOBUs in the form of fixed-length messages or variable-length DMA operations. DMA, which is an acronym for direct memory access, is hardware that is added to many computer systems to allow block transfers of a number of words to or from the main memory without intervention by the processor. With DMA, an IOBU can directly access the main memory without going through the system processor.

We can define a bus operation as a momentary connection between two IOBUs. Each bus operation has two parts:

- The first part of the bus operation has a master select a slave. The master also determines the type and direction for the data transfer.

- The second part of the bus operation consists of from one to 16 data cycles, during which time the data is transferred. Note that 32 data bits are transferred per cycle on the SPD bus.

Two types of bus operations are supported in an AS/400: unit operations and storage operations. For a unit operation, a message is transferred from the master to the slave. The message is architected to always be 12 bytes in length. We will look at the format of these messages in a later section.

The storage operation enables DMA movement between an IOP memory and the system main memory. The movement is controlled by the master who establishes the connection and the direction of the transfer. The maximum number of bytes transferred during a single storage operation is 64 (16 data cycles, 4 bytes per cycle).

Both the system processor and the IOPs can perform either a master or a slave unit operation. The system processor can perform either a master or a slave storage operation. An IOP can only perform a master storage operation. Data can never be transferred from one IOP memory to another IOP memory, because no IOP can perform a slave storage operation. This means there is no peer-to-peer I/O in an AS/400. For example, data cannot be transferred directly from a disk IOP to a tape drive IOP without going through the system's main memory. But peer-to-peer I/O is important, so we are likely to see new IOPs in the future with this capability.

I/O Operations on the AS/400

Having examined the hardware I/O structure of the AS/400 we are ready to see how OS/400, SLIC, and the hardware all work together to perform an I/O operation for an application program. We will start by looking at the objects that are used to support I/O in the AS/400. Then we will look at the layered structure between OS/400, SLIC, and the hardware. Finally, we will put it all together by following an I/O operation from OS/400 all the way out to the IOP and back.

Objects to Support I/O

There are separate objects in OS/400 and at the MI for I/O, but they are closely related. Three system objects exist at the MI to support I/O; four similar objects exist in OS/400. The easiest way to think about these objects is to picture how a device can be attached to an AS/400.

A device can be attached directly to an IOP. We need to describe the characteristics of this device to the system, and we would use a system object to accomplish this. Remember that the MI is independent of the underlying hardware, including I/O device hardware; so we would want a logical description of the device rather than a physical description. In other words, we want to know that the particular unit is a printer, but we don't need to know what the printer data stream looks like for this device. We need to know this information down in the machine, but not at the MI. The system object used to describe a device at the MI is appropriately called a *logical unit description* (LUD). The equivalent OS/400 object is called a *device description* (DEVD).

Devices are not necessarily directly attached to an IOP. They may be attached to a controller which in turn is attached to an IOP. This controller may be able to attach many devices. The controller may attach all the same kind of device or different kinds. But the controller is generally specialized for a class of devices. Thus, we have communications controllers, disk controllers, printer controllers, and so on. The system object used to describe the particular controller at the MI is called a controller description (CD). Similarly, the equivalent OS/400 object is also called a *controller description* (CTLD).

Rather than just being locally attached to the system, devices and controllers may be remotely attached. Some sort of communications line or network is attached to the system with a controller or device at the other end. The system object used to describe the line or network at the MI is called a *network description* (ND). OS/400 recognizes both a line description (LIND) object and a network interface description (NETINTD) object.

OS/400 also looks at all I/O as source/sink devices. Recall that we don't let OS/400 know about disks. Above the MI, everything is treated as an object with memory inside those objects. An I/O device is either a source of information from outside the system or it is a sink for information being sent out of the system. A device is never used to store information in the system. Thus, all disk I/O is performed under the MI in SLIC.

The Components of I/O

It should come as no surprise that I/O, like almost everything else in the AS/400, has its own language and its own set of new acronyms. It is difficult to talk about I/O without using this language, so we might as well jump right in. Table 10.1 lists the acronyms we are about to use. This is the language of I/O.

The AS/400 I/O structure is shown in Figure 10.2. Shown is the structure from the MI down to the interprocess communications facility (IPCF) in SLIC.

Starting at the top of Figure 10.2, an MI process is shown to represent an example of a user application program running in the system. In Chapter 8, we defined a simple running example that we used to illustrate the single-level store implementation. Let's expand on that example to illustrate the AS/400's I/O operations. If you remember, we had an application program doing a sequential read to an indexed database file, which we said could be accomplished with either a high-level language READ or an SQL FETCH. Either of these instructions would result in a request for an I/O operation to fetch a record from the disk. To make this a little more interesting, suppose that, instead of fetching the record from a disk attached to our local system, we want to fetch the record from a remote system at the other end of a communications line using an SQL command to do so.

In Chapter 6, we saw that the SQL interface uses the Distributed Relational Database Architecture (DRDA) to access remote data. Before an SQL request is executed, our application program must execute an SQL CONNECT statement to identify the name of the remote database in a

Table 10.1 The Language of I/O

AMQ	Available Message Queue
BCT	Bus Control Table
BCU	Bus Control Unit
BTM	Bus Transport Mechanism
BUB	Bus Unit Block
BUM	Bus Unit Message
CAT	Control Address Table
CCB	Connection Control Block
CGCB	Connection Group Control Block
CID	Connection ID
FBR	Feedback Record
IOBU	I/O Bus Unit (IOP)
IORM	I/O Request Message
IPCF	Inter Process Communication Facility
MIRQ	MI Response Queue
RID	Request ID
RRCB	Request Response Control Block
SSD	Source Sink Data
SSR	Source Sink Request

relational database directory. After the communications link has been established between the systems, the SQL request can be sent to the remote system. The database manager on the remote system performs the SQL request and returns the records that satisfy the request to the local system.

Also in Chapter 6, we saw that it is possible to use the Distributed Data Management (DDM) architecture to access the remote database. With the DDM approach, the file processing is performed on the local system. DDM sends all records in the file back to the local system; whereas, with DRDA, only records that meet the selection criteria are sent back to the local system. For our example, we have elected to use the SQL interface, which means we must use DRDA. The processing will occur on the remote system and we will only see the results of that operation. Completing the SQL FETCH instruction requires four I/O operations, two on the local machine (one to send the SQL request, and the other to receive the response), and two corresponding operations on the remote machine.

Chapter 10 The I/O System **265**

Figure 10.2 AS/400 I/O Structure

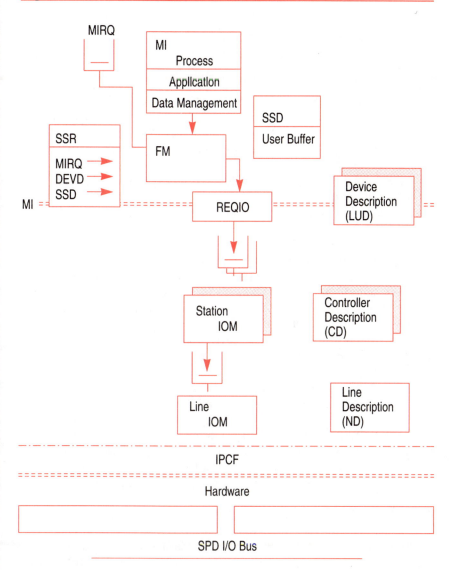

Communications in the AS/400 are layered — split between OS/400, SLIC, and the hardware. The four processing layers we will examine for our example are

- Application support
- Function manager

- Station IOM (input/output manager)
- Line IOM

We will cover the hardware layer in the next section.

Some application support for communications can run in OS/400. This support can be supplied either by the user or by IBM. The ability to plug in user-supplied communications support is provided through the use of APIs. Of course, not every application provides its own communications support, but the facilities are available to do so. In our example, the application support is supplied by the DRDA component of the AS/400 database support.

The function manager (FM) is a component in OS/400 that provides the interface between applications and the MI boundary. For each communications "transport" that exists in SLIC, there is usually a corresponding FM in OS/400. The FM handles the top layers of the communications protocol so that, for example, the presentation of data to the application is in the form the application expects.

In our example, we are going to use the FM for the communications support called advanced program-to-program communications (APPC). The first implementation of APPC appeared on the System/38 and provided the capability to have parallel sessions between systems, thereby allowing multiple applications in the separate systems to communicate concurrently. The communications protocol used for this was logical unit type 6.2 (LU 6.2). The logical unit provides the port for an application program to establish conversations and to send and receive data from a partner application in another system.

The AS/400 built upon this implementation with the development of advanced peer-to-peer networking (APPN) to meet the needs of distributed processing across both LANs and remote communications. APPN provides functions such as distributed directory searches of the network to locate any remote system requested by a local application. It will calculate the best route, if more than one exists, between the local system and the remote system based on the class of service the user has selected. Several enhancements have been made to this support over the last several releases of the AS/400, including automatic configuration when an incoming connection request is received from an unknown system directly connected on a LAN. Another enhancement is support for multiple network connectivity. The APPN support allows applications written for the APPC/LU 6.2 API to communicate with a remote application without modification when multiple systems are providing networking services.

The SQL CONNECT statement in our example identifies a device file to use for this I/O request. Let's assume that in our example the device used to connect the local AS/400 to the remote one is a modem (as opposed to an adapter connecting to a network). The DRDA support in the database passes control to the APPC FM. This FM is called to build the necessary

I/O structures and to create the I/O request. The FM issues the Request I/O (REQIO) instruction at the MI. This is an MI privileged instruction that cannot be issued by the application program. The REQIO instruction has associated with it a Source Sink Request (SSR), which contains

1. A pointer to the MI response queue (MIRQ), which will receive a message when the I/O operation is completed.
2. A pointer to the device descriptor (DEVD), which at the MI is called the LUD, used for the device.
3. A pointer to the source/sink data (SSD), which is a user buffer to store the data being transferred to or from the device. In our example this buffer will contain the SQL request we are sending to the remote system.

The I/O request in the form of a message is then sent to a queue below the MI belonging to the station IOM. The station IOM is a program in SLIC that receives requests from the FM to establish connections, sometimes called sessions, with remote systems, devices, or applications. The station IOM handles the middle layers of the communications protocol. These middle-layer functions include such things as path control and networking. Each type of communications path has a corresponding station IOM. There is, for example, a station IOM that supports peer-to-peer communications, as well as communications to a host system, such as a System/390. Still another station IOM allows the attachment of PCs running the LU 6.2 protocol. In our example, we want to establish a peer-to-peer connection with the remote system identified by the SQL CONNECT statement. We will, therefore use the station IOM for APPN. This APPN station IOM surrounds the request message with the control information needed to establish the remote session. It also provides the interface between the FM and the line IOM.

The station IOM uses the controller descriptor (CTLD), which at the MI is the CD, that exists for this particular connection. The CD is a configuration object that contains information about the remote system (remote system address, APPN control point name, and any other specific parameters that are required). Based on the description in the CD, the station IOM adds any commands or control characters to the I/O request needed to establish the remote system connection. When it is finished, the station IOM sends the I/O request to the queue belonging to the line IOM.

The line IOM implements the data link protocols. The line IOM provides a transparent interface to the station IOMs independent of the underlying data link protocol and network being used. For our example, we are going to use the synchronous data link communications (SDLC) protocol.

The line IOM manages the flow of data, and it identifies the physical connections to the line. It uses the line description (LIND), which is called the network descriptor (ND) at the MI, for the SDLC line and adds the necessary control characters to the request. The line IOM also provides the interface between the upper layers of the communications protocol and the hardware connection.

The I/O request is then sent to the interprocess communications facility (IPCF) in SLIC. IPCF is used for all devices; it communicates with the I/O hardware to send the request across an SPD bus to an IOP. IPCF uses the LUD (DEVD identified in the SSR) to determine that, in our example, we are using a modem. The modem is attached to the IOP, which in turn is attached to the physical communications line. Shortly, we will see exactly how these communications are accomplished; but first we need to look at the I/O control blocks that allow the SLIC to work with the hardware.

Figure 10.3 shows these I/O control blocks and how they are interconnected. These blocks contain all the information necessary for IPCF to

Figure 10.3 I/O Control Blocks

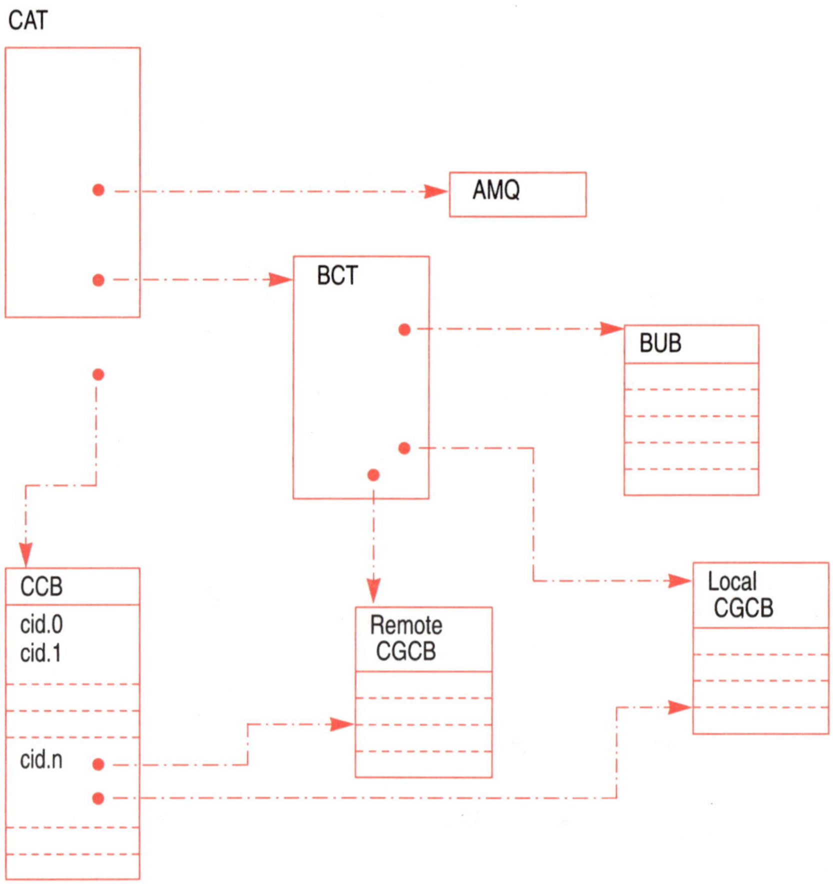

locate a device. This information is updated at IPL time when IOBU addresses are assigned. The information must be kept in memory tables where it is accessible to both hardware and software. Note that the arrows shown in Figure 10.3 indicate addresses, whereas the arrows in Figures 10.2 indicate control transfers.

The seven control blocks shown are

- Control address table (CAT) — The CAT is a system-wide table that contains the addresses of the major control blocks used by SLIC.
- Available message queue (AMQ) — The AMQ is pointed to by an address in the CAT. This is the queue with the blank messages that various SLIC components, including IPCF, can use.
- Bus control table (BCT) — There is one BCT for each SPD bus in the system. The BCT contains buffers, SRQs, and pointers to other control blocks.
- Bus unit block (BUB) — There is one BUB for each SPD bus in the system. The BUB contains information about the various bus units attached to the bus. The I/O request message is enqueued here while waiting for an I/O device operation to complete. Note that this BUB is not the same as the BUB (Bring Up Bind) that was used to measure progress of the SLIC implementation, which I described in Chapter 4. Perhaps I should say, "This BUB's not for you."
- Remote connection control block — One of these blocks exists for each SPD bus in the system. This control block is used to store device identifiers, status, and IOBU addresses for the remotely connected (not in the processor) IOBUs on the bus. There is one entry for every connection identifier assigned by an IOBU. A given IOBU may support multiple devices and can therefore have multiple connection identifiers.
- Local connection control block — One of these blocks exists for each SPD bus in the system. This control block is similar to the remote block, except this one contains information on the locally connected (with the processor) IOBUs.
- Connection control block (CCB) — There is one CCB for the entire system. The CCB contains the connection identifiers and routings for all SPD buses in the system. It also maintains linkage to the connection information kept for each individual bus in the connection control blocks.

Putting It All Together

We are now ready to complete the I/O example we started. To see how the entire I/O operation occurs, let's start over at the beginning where the application requested the I/O operation, and follow it through until the application is notified that the operation has completed.

270 Inside the AS/400

Figure 10.4 gives a slightly simplified version of Figure 10.2 that we will use for our example. This figure shows the operation down to the point that the operation start (OPSTART) message is sent across the SPD bus to the appropriate IOP.

At the MI, we have the REQIO instruction. Also shown is the SSD, the user buffer. To simplify our example, only one IOM is shown. As before, the I/O request is sent to the queue belonging to the IOM. When the IOM is finished, a send request is passed to IPCF. This is where we left our example previously.

IPCF creates two data structures to accomplish the I/O operation. The first is a message, called the I/O request message (IORM). This message will be used by IPCF to keep track of this particular request and who sent it. The second data structure is a request response control block (RRCB). This data structure is going to be used by the IOP to determine what operation is requested, where the data to be either read or written is located in main

Figure 10.4 I/O Operation (Start)

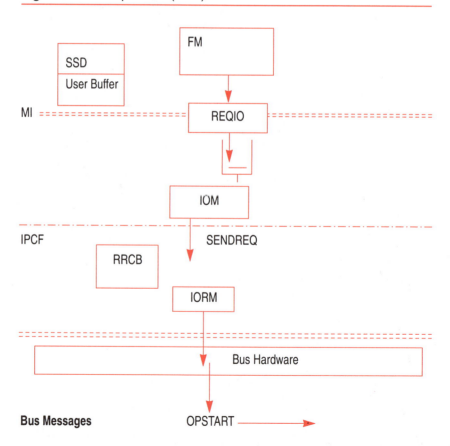

memory, and where the completion status is to be placed. This data structure contains information from the seven control blocks in Figure 10.3.

Figure 10.5 shows the format of the IORM and the RRCB. It also shows the format of the two SPD bus messages that are used to start and to end the I/O operation.

Figure 10.5 IPCF Data Structures

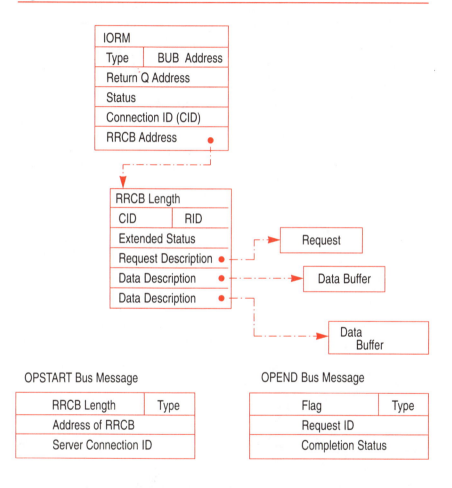

The IORM is a message used to identify who requested this I/O operation, or more accurately, who should be notified when the operation has completed. Fields in the message identify the type of message and the bus unit block address. This bus unit block address identifies the bus unit block, the BUB, for the SPD bus that has the IOP for the device to which we are sending the request. This message will be enqueued to the BUB identified while it is waiting for the I/O operation to complete. Enqueuing means the IPCF places an address in the BUB pointing back to the IORM. Only one IORM can be enqueued to a BUB at a time. This means there is only one I/O operation per SPD bus at a time.

Also included in the IORM is the address of the queue to which the message will be sent when the I/O operation is completed. This message queue is associated with the IOM that sent the request to IPCF. The status field in the IORM will be filled in before the message is sent to the IOM's queue to tell whether the operation finished correctly or there were problems.

The final two fields in the IORM are the connection identifier (CID) and the RRCB address. The CID is filled in by IPCF using the connection control blocks discussed in the last section. The CID uniquely identifies the device. IPCF gets the CID from the remote connection control block using information from the IORM. The RRCB address is the location in main memory where this control block can be found. Note that the memory addresses used in these blocks are real addresses, not virtual addresses.

The RRCB is a control block that the IOP uses to determine the details of the I/O request being sent. Unlike the control blocks established during IPL, the RRCB is a temporary control block that is created for each I/O request. An RRCB can be variable length, so the first field specifies the length of this block in memory. Following the length field are two fields that specify the CID (the same as in the IORM) and also a request identifier (RID) that can be used to track the various requests. Following these two fields is an extended status field. This field is used if the return status will not fit into the status field of the IORM.

The remaining fields in the RRCB are main memory addresses. The first is the address of the I/O request itself, followed by the addresses of one or more data buffers. The I/O request is the instruction to the modem; it is not our request for information from the remote computer system. That information is in the data buffers. The I/O request is not kept in the RRCB, because it can vary in length for different devices. The request is at a location in memory pointed to by this field. The data buffers pointed to by the following fields contain the data to be transferred to the device. For our example, the address given would be for the user buffer, the SSD, where our SQL request to the remote system is stored.

Figure 10.5 also shows the formats for two bus messages, OPSTART and OPEND. These are examples of the 12-byte messages sent across the SPD bus during the unit operation previously described. The first of these messages, the OPSTART, will be used to initiate the I/O operation in our example.

The OPSTART bus message contains four fields. The first field contains the length of the RRCB in memory. The second field identifies this as an OPSTART message. The address of the RRCB in memory occupies the third field. The last field contains the server connection identifier. The server here is an IOP, so for the bus message we need to identify the server. The server connection identifier is part of the CID. The full CID in the RRCB identifies the device.

To initiate the I/O operation, IPCF sends the OPSTART message across the appropriate SPD bus (using a unit operation) to the identified IOP (we are not at the modem yet). When the IOP receives the bus message, it knows there is work to perform. The IOP then initiates a storage operation across the SPD bus, and using DMA, fetches the entire RRCB into its own memory. Once the IOP has the RRCB, it again initiates a storage operation to fetch the request from its location in the main memory. Finally, because the operation calls for data (our SQL request to the remote computer) to go out to the device, the IOP fetches the data from the data buffers that contain our SQL FETCH request.

The IOP now instructs the modem to send our request across the communications line to the remote computer system. Data is transferred from the data buffers in main memory as requested. When the operation has completed with the remote system signaling it has received the transmission, the IOP creates an OPEND bus message. It then initiates a unit operation to send the OPEND message back to the IOBU, which is the system processor. Remember that both IOPs and the system processor act as IOBUs.

The OPEND bus message shown in Figure 10.5 contains four fields. The first field has various flag bits that give information about the operation and its completion. The type field (the second field) identifies this message as an OPEND. The third field contains the request identifier (RID) originally put into the RRCB by IPCF for tracking purposes. Finally, the fourth field contains the completion status. Based on certain flag settings, the completion status may instead be found in the extended status field of the RRCB.

Figure 10.6 shows the end of the I/O operation in our example. The receipt of the OPEND bus message means the IOP is finished processing the request. The I/O handler (not shown in Figure 10.6) dequeues the IORM that was enqueued to the BUB for the SPD bus that sent the OPEND message, updates the status field, and sends it to the IPCF router's queue.

The IPCF router examines the completion status, and assuming everything completed normally, sends a response message to the queue identified in the return queue address field of the IORM. The IOM that originated the I/O request performs any necessary cleanup and, again assuming that everything completed normally, sends a feedback record (FBR) to the MI response queue (MIRQ) that was identified in the original source sink request. This notifies the function manager that the first I/O operation has completed. At this point the FM is finished and can perform other operations. The application program that requested the SQL FETCH will wait until the remote system sends back the results of the database operation.

The I/O operation just described has sent our SQL request to the remote system. When the request arrives at the remote system, and after the remote modem has signaled the local system that the transmission was received, the

Figure 10.6 I/O Operation (End)

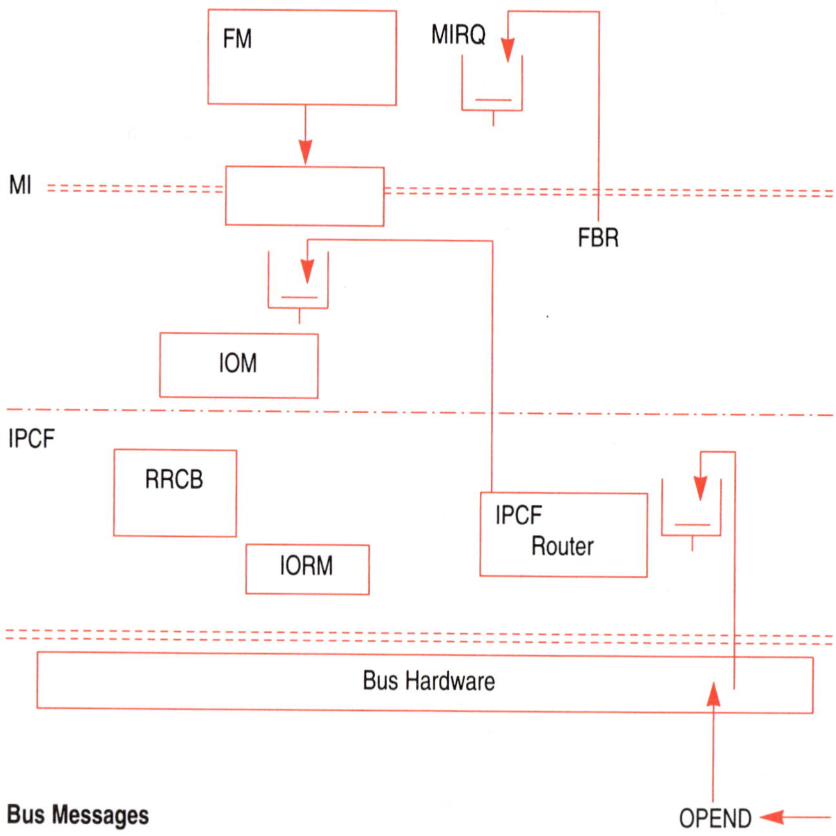

```
                    FM              MIRQ
                    ┌──────┐        ┌────┐
                    │      │        │    │
                    └──┬───┘        │    │
                       │            │    │
MI  ═══════════════════▼════════════│════│═══════
                    ┌──────┐        │    │
                    │      │        │    │       FBR
                    └──┬───┘        │    │
                       │            │    │
                    ┌──▼───┐        │    │
                    │ IOM  │        │    │
                    └──────┘        │    │
     ══════════════════════════════ │ ══ │ ══════
IPCF                                │    │
         ┌──────┐                   │    │
         │ RRCB │              ┌────▼─┐  │ ┌────┐
         └──────┘              │ IPCF │  │ │    │
                ┌──────┐       │Router│  │ │    │
                │ IORM │       └──────┘  │ │    │
                └──────┘                 │ │    │
     ════════════════════════════════════│═│════
                ┌──────────────────────┐ │ │
                │     Bus Hardware     │ │ │
                └──────────────────────┘ │ │
                                         │ │
Bus Messages                          OPEND ◄──
```

modem at the remote system causes the start of an I/O operation to receive it. At some time in the future, when the database on the remote system has finished executing our SQL request, the remote system will initiate an I/O operation to send the results back to us. In the local system, the IOP with the attached modem will receive data from the remote system and initiate another I/O operation. This time, the IOP will send the OPSTART to the main processor, which, as we saw earlier, can also perform all the IOBU functions necessary to complete an I/O operation. When MIRQ receives the completion (OPEND) message from the second local I/O operation, the function manager signals the application program that its I/O request (the SQL FETCH) has completed.

Before we leave this example, I should point out that when multiple systems are interconnected with OptiConnect for OS/400 instead of a communications line, there is far less time required to complete the I/O operation.

First, the connection between the systems is a high-speed, fiber-optic cable with a transfer rate of either 266 megabits per second or 1 gigabit per second. Second, the APPC and APPN communications protocols are replaced with a special device driver. This device driver doesn't have to perform the complex error checking that is required when we are exchanging data using a conventional communications line. Communications lines have inherently "noisy" electrical signals. Redundant information must be transmitted to provide for error checking and error correction. A fiber-optic cable transmits information using light, which is reasonably noise free. Thus, the device driver used for OptiConnect provides a more direct connection with less redundancy.

I should also point out that if the SQL request was for the local database, none of the operations involving the APPC FM, the APPN station IOM, or the SDLC line IOM that I just described would occur. Instead, the database support in the local system would handle the SQL FETCH just as I described in our example in Chapter 8 using the single-level store. Page faults that result in disk operations are handled by storage management working directly with IPCF.

Conclusions

The majority of the hardware and the operating system software on an AS/400 is dedicated to I/O, and this is not likely to change in the future. The rapidly increasing performance of processors continues to strain most I/O systems. The physical devices simply cannot improve in performance nearly as fast as processors. To keep up with the increasing demands of higher performance systems, more and more devices and the control of these devices will have to occur in parallel.

The AS/400, with its use of multiple buses and IOPs, is uniquely positioned in the industry to take advantage of the tremendous growth in both system capacity and performance that is anticipated to occur in the next few years. This use of programmable I/O processors and the capability to perform massive numbers of I/O operations will distinguish the AS/400 for many years to come.

It is interesting to note that the first system to use programmable I/O processors was the CDC 6600. CDC called its I/O processors peripheral processors. You may remember that the CDC 6600, designed by Seymore Cray, had the first general-purpose load/store processor to use pipelining. This design led to RISC processors. Perhaps this first supercomputer also knew something about I/O. Today's AS/400 certainly learned some lessons from it about building high-performance systems.

In the next chapter, we will look at how the many pieces we have already studied fit together to address the growing application environment known as client/server computing.

Chapter 11

Client/Server Computing

Business computing is going through a major revolution. To call it a revolution may seem overly dramatic, but the impact this change will have on the way we think about computer systems in our businesses will affect all of us. The revolution I am talking about is the move to client/server computing.

Two major factions are driving the move to client/server: end users and business executives. End users are the ones leading the move to client/server. End users like the distributed computing model with its PC-based graphical interface, in contrast to the time-shared, green-screen computing model they consider old-fashioned. Business executives like client/server computing because they see it as a catalyst to transform the business enterprise to operate more effectively.

The use of more and more PC LANs is also driving this phenomenon. A LAN is characterized as a communications network with a maximum distance of about one kilometer (about 0.6 miles for those of us not in the metric mindset). LANs provide an ideal way to connect workgroups of PC users in a single business location. PC workgroups need to communicate and share information. New client/server software for workgroup computing, usually called groupware, is becoming very attractive to many businesses. We will look at groupware later in this chapter.

Is client/server just a passing fad? Our industry is notorious for grabbing on to some new technology and proclaiming that the future has arrived. To be sure, client/server has become one of the most over-hyped terms in the industry, but it is for real.

By some estimates, there are more than 100 million PCs in the world, and the number grows daily. As PC users, most of us have come to look at computing from a client perspective. From this client-centric view of computing, the midrange and mainframe systems we use in our businesses become servers of the clients. This new computing paradigm is not likely to go away anytime soon.

As the computing paradigm is transforming, so too is the AS/400. The AS/400 has always been a strong application system, with more than 25,000 applications available from ISVs.[1] Many of these existing applications are rapidly evolving to work within the client/server model. New client/server applications are also being added at a rapid rate. Thousands of client/server applications now exist for the AS/400, and the number continues to grow.

In this chapter, we will look at how the AS/400 provides the server functions to meet the changing business environments of the 1990s. We will start by examining this new business computing model. We will then look at the family of client/server enablers and solutions the AS/400 provides to deliver the next generation in client/server computing. Finally, we will look at the role workgroup and object technologies play in this environment.

With the announcement of the AS/400 Advanced Series, IBM said these systems were designed to address the "next generation in business computing." Exactly what this means is the topic of our next section.

The Next Generation in Business Computing

Business computing models have changed over the past 30 years. A convenient way to talk about these changes is in terms of generations. We can identify four distinct generations:

- First Generation: Mainframe computing — Thirty years ago, business computing was characterized by a host-centered world. Companies such as IBM produced proprietary products, both hardware and software, that did the total computing for a business. This is often described as the "glass-house" model of computing, because the computer systems were often kept behind glass walls away from end users. This type of computing was usually batch, which also had the effect of isolating the system from the end user.

- Second Generation: Minicomputers — Primarily because of the arrogance of those who controlled the glass house and their inability to meet end-user requirements, many end users began to buy their own computers. During the 1970s, the cost of smaller computers had come down to the point where groups of users could buy their own computer. These small groups may have been separate businesses or departments within larger businesses, and this approach was sometimes called departmental computing or two-tier computing. (The term two-tier computing applied because mainframe computers were still used in the business.) Use of these minicomputers was mainly interactive, where many users could share the system at the same time. This movement had the effect of putting computers under the control of the end users,

---

[1] ISV software is extremely important for the AS/400. More that 80 percent of all AS/400s are sold with ISV software.

and of alienating those in the glass houses. The systems built in Rochester certainly prospered during this time period — and did put Rochester at odds with the mainframe mentality in IBM.

- Third Generation: Personal computers — PCs revolutionized business computing. Starting in the early 1980s, an end user could buy this technology directly for the first time. The PC was a dedicated computer, capable of running many applications the user needed. As prices came down, the need to get approval for the purchase of such a computer was handled lower in the organization. The result was that many businesses didn't even know how many PCs they had or how they were being used — in effect, there was an uncontrolled explosion of PCs, shrink-wrapped software, LANs, and workstations. PCs were primarily used for personal-productivity applications, while most mission-critical, business applications were still handled by mainframes and minicomputers. The mainframes and minicomputers did have the capability for attaching PCs, but the PCs were used primarily as terminals, rather than as peer computers.

- Fourth Generation: Client/server computing — For most businesses today, distributed computing is a way of life. Many businesses, especially larger businesses, have settled on a three-tiered infrastructure, where computing is distributed by function. The first tier comprises the enterprise production and database systems. A decision support system, which we will soon see is usually a separate system, may also be part of this tier. The second tier consists of the department or workgroup systems. Finally, the third tier includes the PCs, workstations, and terminals. The challenge with this architecture is how to make the distributed information and resources available to everyone who needs them, and to do so in an easy-to-use way that protects the business-critical nature of the information. Client/server computing holds the promise to bring together this new world of three-tiered, intelligent distributed computing in a form that does not compromise the goals of either the end users or the overall business.

Because there is no generally agreed-upon definition of client/server computing in the industry, I have the opportunity to take a stab at my own definition, which I will now do.

What Is Client/Server?

If we just look at the name, client/server, we can see that there are two separate entities — the client and the server — working together to accomplish some task. Client/server computing is a relationship between the separate machines: the server providing services and the client consuming those services. The key word to describe this relationship may be *interoperability*, which means two (or more) systems working together in a cooperative manner, such that they appear to the user to be a single system. An early name used to describe client/server computing was cooperative processing. However we choose to define client/server, we may be able to agree on some characteristics:

- In client/server computing, the intelligence is distributed across a network — it is not in a single location.
- Servers provide resources that are shared among many clients. These resources are both hardware and software.
- The location of the shared resources is transparent to end users. The resource may be on the same system as the client or on a different system elsewhere in the network.
- Clients always initiate the operations by requesting a service. A server waits for the requests from the clients.
- Clients and servers exchange information via messages. The connection between clients and servers is either a local or a remote communications network.
- The system is viewed from the perspective of the user. Earlier, I called this client-centric, but user-centric is probably a more descriptive term.

An evolution exists in client/server computing wherein clients and servers can each act as providers and consumers of services. We will discuss this distributed computing model (fifth generation?) more fully in Chapter 12, when we talk about futures. With the definition and characteristics we have just created, we can now look at the models of client/server computing.

Models of Client/Server Computing

Many different models of client/server computing exist. The idea of splitting an application across more than one system has been used since the introduction of the PC in the early 1980s. One way to classify client/server models is to look at how an application is split — what part of the application is on the client and what part is on the server. I prefer to classify client/server models based on the functions the server provides. With this view of client/server computing, we can identify five, and possibly more, server models.

The first server model is a *print and file server*. This usually is a single-server, multiple-client model, but it is also possible to have multiple servers. Here, a number of PCs (the clients) are attached to a LAN, which in turn is attached to a server. The server, which may be another PC, provides a printer that can be used by any of the attached clients and disk drives that can be accessed by any of the attached clients. Many PC users are not aware that the original PC was created in just such a LAN environment back in 1973.

The first PC, which served as a model for Apple's Macintosh and other computers that use Microsoft's Windows or IBM's OS/2, was developed at the Xerox Palo Alto Research Center in 1973. This machine, called Alto, integrated the I/O functions into the microcode of a 16-bit processor. It had a bit-mapped graphics display, a mouse (which had been invented earlier), and a removable cartridge disk. The Alto was connected to the first Ethernet network. It also supported the first-ever laser printer. When an Alto was configured as a print server, this laser printer was accessible over the Ethernet network. The single processor in the Alto drove the display, mouse, disks, and the network. In its spare time, it ran the user's program.

The file and print model of client/server just described is still the one used on many LANs. This model is very usable for many small workgroups, which explains its popularity. Larger organizations, however, generally need more sophisticated models of client/server computing.

The second server model is a *database server*. In this model, instead of an entire file being copied from one machine to another, a subset or a summary of the information stored in the file is sent in response to a query (typically in some standard format such as SQL). The DRDA example we used in Chapter 10 illustrated a similar type of operation where one AS/400 sent an SQL request to another AS/400. A PC client could make the same kind of SQL request to an AS/400 server. A database server also provides the foundation for a decision-support system such as many businesses use.

Business professionals often use a decision-support system to analyze data and create reports. This type of system provides the user with flexible views of the data, and with tools to manipulate and present the data in various report formats. A decision-support system is often used to answer what if questions. A variation of this decision-support system is an executive information system, which usually provides more information, as well as the relationships between the information.

Many businesses separate their operational databases from their decision-support database, which they often call an information database. Many reasons for this separation exist. For example, operational data needs to be current, while only a reasonably timely snapshot of the data is needed for a decision-support application. Operational data is usually associated with a single application, whereas decision-support data comes from multiple application sources. For these and many other reasons, the two types of databases are separated, and some form of automated update to allow current information from the operational database to be transferred to the information database is implemented. This process is sometimes just called data propagation, but usually some form of data synchronization is also required among the multiple application databases that are used to update the information database.

The idea of a separate information database for decision support is called data warehousing — IBM likes to call this information warehousing. An information warehouse in a client/server environment, therefore, is a repository of data for decision-support processing. We will discuss AS/400 information warehousing later in this chapter.

Another very popular application being used on the information databases in many businesses today is a data-mining application. With a decision-support application, you usually have to know the result ahead of time. That is, you want the application to construct a report based on some preconceived view of how the data are interrelated. If the assumed relationship is not true, a new request must be formulated. A data-mining application looks at all of the database and finds relationships that may not have been previously known. It is very important for businesses to understand these relationships, so they can modify their business processes and become more competitive. Data mining is, therefore, becoming a very useful tool.

A third model of a server is a *transaction server.* In this model, a client sends an SQL request to the server to invoke a remote procedure that runs on the server. The remote procedure on the server can be a sequence of SQL statements that work against the server's database, or it can be some other program that is resident on the server. This model is different from the database server, because the entire unit of execution (a sequence of SQL statements or a program) is performed on the server with no interactions with the client. This unit of execution is called a transaction, which accounts for this server's name. Many SQL databases provide facilities to support this model of client/server computing. For example, in Chapter 6 we looked at stored procedures. A stored procedure is one way for a client to invoke a remote procedure on the server.

A fourth model of server is a *groupware server.* A relatively new form of computing that has been enabled by the client/server technology is known as *groupware.* Groupware is built around the ideas of collaborative human activities — that is, people working together in a group to perform some business activities. Examples would be creating a document with multiple contributors, having a conference with participants in remote locations, or simply exchanging electronic mail (E-mail). Groupware has also been called collaborative computing and workgroup computing.

A groupware server has five fundamental components:

- Document management — Electronic imaging forms the basis for document management. Here, documents can be scanned into the system and stored in the electronic filing cabinet, which is likely to be some form of optical storage attached to the system. In general, documents can contain text, graphics, images, voice, and even video. These multimedia documents are managed by the groupware server — it can store, index, compress, retrieve, and move documents around to optimize cost/performance tradeoffs of various storage media. Clients can access the documents to review, annotate, change, print, or fax them.

- E-mail — A groupware server can act as an E-mail server. E-mail has been one of the fastest growing areas for many businesses because it provides an easy way for people to communicate, within a local organization or across the world. An E-mail server needs to provide support for the various PC-based mail systems (such as Lotus cc:Mail or Microsoft Mail). This function is usually accomplished through the support of industry-standard mail APIs, as we will see later in the chapter when we look at some specific support in the AS/400. An E-mail server also must provide gateways to the various mail systems a business needs to access.

- Conferencing — A rapidly growing area for many PC users is conferencing. Millions of people are beginning to use conferencing via electronic bulletin boards provided on CompuServe, Prodigy, America Online, and the Internet. These bulletin boards allow people to participate in ongoing group discussions any time they want. This type of conferencing could be called *asynchronous* conferencing, because people can join and leave any time. Another form of conferencing could be called *synchronous* conferencing. Here, participants interactively collaborate on a joint project in real time using instantly refreshed documents, electronic whiteboards, voice, and even video images of one another. These "electronic meetings" are also becoming popular with many businesses.

- Scheduling — Scheduling, or calendaring, as it is sometimes called, permits electronic scheduling of meetings as well as sharing calendars and "to-do" lists. The server's responsibility in this environment is to maintain the shared information, and it may even use functions such as database triggers to manage and schedule group activities.

- Workflow — Many businesses are looking at the technology known as workflow as a means to help them improve their responsiveness for various business processes. An example of a simple business process is receiving an order from a customer and fulfilling that order. Another example is the computer Help desk, where a fast and accurate response to a user's question is important to keep the business running efficiently. As businesses are "re-engineering" or redefining these business processes, many are starting to incorporate workflow ideas. Workflow technology can be used to automatically route work from one program to the next. Workflow defines the operations that must be performed at each step and what needs to be done when exceptions occur. Workflow started in the world of computer-aided manufacturing (CAM) to optimize and automate the flow of work in a manufacturing facility. Workflow is now being applied to many other parts of a business, such as an office environment with lots of "paper processes." For example, an insurance company office has to process insurance claims for customers. Like a manufacturing line, this claims process has many steps with many people involved; the difference is that the claims process is handled with paper moving between the people. As this paper becomes an electronic image, a computer can handle the movement of documents from one process step to another automatically. In such a system, the server receives requests and events from the clients and interprets them according to the rules of the user-defined workflow. The server then routes the work to the people who can act on it. The server also tracks the progress to make sure the work gets done by the right people.

A groupware server combines all five of these components to provide a synergistic environment. For example, when the workflow component determines that some additional person needs to be brought into the loop for a particular process, it can use the E-mail component to notify that person.

In the industry today, Lotus Notes is probably the premier client/server groupware product. Making the AS/400 into a Lotus Notes server is but one of the things we are doing to transform the AS/400 into a groupware server.

A fifth and final model of server we are going to consider is an *object server*. The idea here is that objects exist in both the clients and the server. An application is then a set of objects, some in the client and some in the server, that can communicate. The client invokes a method that is supported by a server object class — recall that in Chapter 4 we discussed objects, object classes, instances, methods, and the relationships between them. In Chapter 4, we were talking about everything being in a single system. Now we are splitting the application across the client and the server, so we need a means of communication between them. Client objects communicate with server objects using an object request broker (ORB). An ORB locates an instance of the server object class, invokes the requested method, and returns the results to the client object. Later in this chapter, we will see how the AS/400 uses an ORB based on the Common Object Request Broker Architecture (CORBA) to support distributed objects.

In the preceding paragraphs, we have discussed the five models of servers as if these were separate servers each interfacing to the clients. They, of course, do not need to be separate servers; any combination or all of them can exist in the same system. To fully participate in the client/server world, a system must implement all five of these servers. For the remainder of the chapter, we are going to look at how the AS/400 integrates the support for all five of these servers.

No matter which model or what combination of the five models is used, a successful client/server implementation is one that can be integrated with existing applications. It permits the use of existing business infrastructures while providing the means to migrate to new business models as needed. This is the vision of the AS/400 for client/server computing.

Transformation of the AS/400

Before we look at the AS/400 in a client/server environment, there is a question we need to address. How can a second-generation minicomputer, such as the original AS/400, transform itself into a fourth-generation server?

Most of the minicomputers of the 1980s, such as Digital's VAX or HP's 3000 series, are for all practical purposes disappearing, being replaced with Unix-based servers from these same computer manufacturers.

One of the obvious reasons the AS/400 has been able to evolve from a host-centric system to a distributed client/server system is its architecture. As we have seen, whole new environments can be added at the MI, and even fundamental structures such as the program and process models can be changed, without disrupting existing applications. Customers can add applications in the new environment, if they wish to do so, at their own pace. This is a powerful capability, but it doesn't fully explain the AS/400 transformation.

From the early 1980s, Rochester recognized the need to provide the capability in its computers to support large distributed systems. The System/36 added extensive communications support for a distributed systems environment, and many customers installed large distributed System/36 networks. In fact, some of the largest System/36 networks had thousands of systems.

The System/38 was not as strong as the System/36 when it came to supporting large distributed networks, but it did have an internal design geared toward a network. The System/38's original structure was designed to support multiple processors, each running a part of the operating system. Its message-based dispatching structure made such a design possible. Inheriting this ability to internally split an "application" among processors from the System/38 gives the AS/400 some unique capabilities to provide server functions. With its many processors — main processors and IOPs — the AS/400 has been described as "a network in a box."

Rochester developers were also heavily involved in defining some of the distributed system architectures. A good example is the Distributed Data Management (DDM) architecture, which was developed there. As we saw earlier, an application program can work transparently with a file on a remote system using DDM.

As far back as 1983, Rochester systems were attaching PCs. A product called PC Support was first introduced on the System/36 in that year. Originally, PC Support was intended to simply allow the PC to emulate a 5250 workstation. Over time, the system and its applications began to exploit the inherent value of having an intelligent client attached.

Very early, Rochester people recognized the potential the AS/400 had in a distributed client/server environment. Individuals such as Gene Jurrens, who led the DDM architecture effort in Rochester, and Dick Kiscaden,[2] who led the strategy for distributed computing and PC attachment, had a great deal of experience working with customers who wanted to do this kind of distributed computing. They joined forces with others who shared their vision and began to show developers how the AS/400 could be transformed. The AS/400 soon was delivering client/server products and server systems to satisfy the growing customer requirements.

[2] Dick and I first worked together back in 1969. We were trying to build a high-level machine that directly executed an RPG-like language. Dick wrote the microcode for our prototype. That project, which we called LINUS, was a precursor for the high-level machine interface proposed for the System/38, and it demonstrated that such a system was possible.

The two major products to support client/server computing on the AS/400 are called Client Access for OS/400 and the File Server I/O Processor. In addition, there are special server models of the AS/400 that are specifically targeted at the emerging server market. In the following sections, we will look at the functions these products and systems provide.

Client Access for OS/400

We introduced Client Access for OS/400 briefly in Chapter 5. Client Access was announced in 1994 as the replacement to IBM's PC Support/400 product. Although PC Support/400 was a very successful product, installed on nearly 80 percent of all AS/400s, after 11 years it needed to be restructured. In short, we needed to infuse new technology into this product.

Client Access is a family of products to support various clients. The original PC Support/400 clients (DOS, DOS with Extended Memory, and 16-bit OS/2) are supported, as are new clients (Windows 3.1 and 32-bit OS/2). The new support for OS/2, called Client Access Optimized for OS/2, is implemented using the same object-oriented technology that is used for the SLIC. With this new modular, object-oriented technology, other optimized clients can easily be added without the need to wait for a major AS/400 product release. Support for additional new clients, such as Windows 95, AIX, Apple, or Taligent, will be shipped when the new software is ready. Each Client Access product is a single integrated package that includes

- Connectivity support with protocol independence
- 5250 emulation support
- Print services
- Mail and office services
- Security
- System management
- Database access
- Application programming interfaces

We will look briefly at some of these functions in the following sections.

5250 Emulation

Client Access is far more than just an emulator for 5250 workstations, but an emulator is still part of the integrated package. A 5250 emulator makes a PC look like a 5250 workstation. Specifically, it supports the 5250 "data stream." A data stream includes all the control characters that allow the display to send information to and from an application running on the AS/400. Many applications written for the AS/400 expect to see the 5250 data stream, and they will not work properly if it is changed. Because the 5250 terminal and its datastream are so important to many of our customers, the AS/400 will continue to support these terminals and this datastream. With more and more customers attaching PCs to their AS/400s, 5250 emulation through Client Access is rapidly becoming the norm for 5250 support. Three emulators are available, depending on the operating system the client uses.

Workstation Function (WSF) is the emulator for DOS. WSF supports multiple sessions from a single PC over a variety of physical connections and using any one of several data-link protocols. WSF has been updated to support the latest PCs, printers, and adapters.

RUMBA for OS/400 is an emulator for Windows and OS/2. The RUMBA product has been optionally available for several years and is now an integrated part of the Client Access family. RUMBA provides a graphical user interface (GUI) emulator that can support up to 32 display and printer sessions. This product includes support that can constantly and automatically update a windowed application, such as a spreadsheet, as the data in an AS/400 changes.

PC 5250 is another emulator for Windows and OS/2 clients. This emulator has the same look and feel as another emulator for 3270 workstations, called PC 3270. PC 5250 will be attractive to customers who frequently use both 5250 and 3270 emulation. PC 5250 also has extensive double-byte-character-set (DBCS) functionality to support certain national languages.

Print Serving

The AS/400's print-serving functions allow a PC user easy access to any printer in the network. It doesn't matter whether the printer is directly attached to the AS/400, to another PC, or at the end of a communications line across the country. If the AS/400 knows the printer exists, the PC user can get to it. A print-distribution facility even allows PC printouts to be routed to other PC printers anywhere in the network. A new Host Print Transform function is a collection of print drivers that lets the AS/400, instead of the PC operating system, control the printer. This function currently supports more than 120 different printers from several major manufacturers.

Mail/Office Offerings

Client Access provides two types of mail and office offerings. The first is a host-centric offering that will support both terminals (non-programmable) and PCs. OfficeVision for OS/400 is an example of such an offering. The second is a PC-centric offering that supports PCs only. An example of this second type of electronic mail (E-Mail) is Lotus Notes.

Today standard APIs are being defined to provide interoperability between the different E-Mail products. The emerging standards are Vendor Independent Messaging (VIM) and Messaging Application Programming Interface (MAPI) for Microsoft Windows. Lotus Notes uses VIM, while other products, such as Microsoft Word and WordPerfect, use MAPI. Client Access supports both of these APIs.

Through Client Access, PC users can have a PC mail solution or a host solution. In addition to OfficeVision, AnyMail for OS/400, a new option for the AS/400, is available that provides services such as a distribution engine, a directory, and a message store. Any of the PC E-Mail products can access AnyMail services and have access to the entire network.

Still another offering called Ultimedia Mail for OS/400 provides multimedia and E-Mail solutions to PC users. Users can create, send, and receive a variety of media types (text, image, audio, simple video, and so on) over existing communications connections. This product is intended to support existing cc:Mail and Microsoft Mail clients, as well as mail gateways to interoperate with existing mail servers.

Data Serving

In a client/server environment, data on the AS/400 can be viewed and accessed in two different ways: as a database and as a file. Client Access provides both database serving and file serving.

The access structure for database serving is library/file/member (record) as we saw in the database chapter. The database contains records. The ability to query, add, delete, and update can be done by record or by file. The AS/400 provides a GUI database access and a file transfer as the primary user interfaces to the database. There are also several programming interfaces to the database, which we will cover in the next section.

Internally, data in the AS/400 database can be stored in different encodings, as we will soon see; but it is primarily stored in a form called the Extended Binary Coded Decimal Interchange Code (EBCDIC). This is different from the internal form used in PCs, called the American Standard Code for Information Interchange (ASCII). The two forms were defined by separate organizations back in the 1950s to represent alphanumeric characters (letters and numbers). They both started out as 6-bit codes, meaning they could each represent $2^6 = 64$ characters. Over time, each evolved to its present 8-bit form that now can represent 256 characters.

It is hard to say which form of data encoding is better, because the assignment of meaning to each of the 256 combinations found in 8 bits is arbitrary for both forms.[3] It is, however, difficult to switch a computer system from one form to the other, because both application and operating system software can be dependent on the particular encoding of the data. For example, in Chapter 6 we looked at the binary radix tree used for indexes in the AS/400. Recall from the example we used to construct the binary radix tree that the structure was dependent on the bit configurations used in the key fields. If we were to switch from EBCDIC to ASCII, the structure of the tree would change, and any software that was dependent on the original structure may no longer work properly.

Neither EBCDIC nor ASCII supports national languages, such as Japanese Kanji, that require more than 256 characters. A double-byte code is

---

[3] A nice feature of EBCDIC is that there are no known viruses. Even if a PC virus is brought into an AS/400 in a PC ASCII file, it cannot contaminate AS/400 data.

required for these languages. The answer to all these inconsistencies may lie with the American National Standards Institute (ANSI) standard encoding called Unicode. In V3R1, the AS/400 took the first step toward the implementation of Unicode by encoding names in some of the integrated file system with this multi-byte encoding scheme. With V3R6, the support was expanded to allow database files to store data encoded in Unicode. Until there is widespread acceptance of Unicode, the AS/400 and other systems will have to live with multiple encodings of data and continue to provide conversions from one to another.

File serving is usually associated with PC data. The structure for accessing a PC file is directory\subdirectory\file. The files contain byte stream data and are stored internally in a system object called a byte stream space. These files are stored in ASCII, the form used for PC applications. Applications can get, put, and delete data in these files.

Several options are available on the AS/400 for storing and accessing data. In Chapter 5, we discussed the various ways to access data through libraries, shared folders, and the integrated file system. We saw how the integrated file system provides the many ways in which the file system can be accessed from an application either on the AS/400 or on the client. Not only can the data be accessed, but through the use of generic commands the data also can be moved between file systems. The available commands are copy (CPY), move (MOV), save (SAV), restore (RST), and delete (DLT). For example, when data is moved between an AS/400 file and a PC file, the EBCDIC-ASCII conversion is done automatically.

Client Management

The value of integration in the AS/400 is well recognized. As a part of this total system integration philosophy, the AS/400 has always had very robust systems management, service, and support capabilities — the AS/400 has always been very good at taking care of itself.

A very large — and expensive — problem many businesses face is the cost of managing their PCs. This is usually a hidden cost, because in many businesses the users manage their own PCs. In other cases, where there are questions about whether or not the users have the skills necessary to install, configure, or change applications on their PCs, businesses may choose to employ a separate support staff.

Systems management on an AS/400, in general, is under the umbrella of AS/400 SystemView, which supports six types of systems management functions. These are

- Business management — This support includes inventory management, security management, and financial management.

- Change management — This support includes planning, scheduling, distributing, applying, and tracking changes to the information system.

- Configuration management — This support includes managing the physical and logical properties of resources, such as connections.
- Operations management — This support includes managing the system and resources to support the information-processing workloads.
- Performance management — This support includes capacity planning, performance data collection, and resource tuning.
- Problem management — This support includes detecting, analyzing, correcting, and tracking incidents and problems in systems management.

Client Access provides several functions to work with AS/400 SystemView for client management. One of those functions, called PC Update, can be used to apply fixes and new releases of code with no user intervention. Entry and exit programs are supported so that an application can perform clean-up steps, such as deleting unnecessary files. Another function, called the System Administrator, lets an administrator create configuration files for all PC users and create install diskettes for PC users.

Many PC hardware and software products are beginning to use an industry-standard interface, called the Desktop Management Interface (DMI). The hardware and software products can use this interface to report information. The Client Access support for optimized clients will report such things as software installed on the PC and software errors. A Simple Network Management Protocol (SNMP) agent takes any of the DMI messages and passes them up to the AS/400 system management products. The AS/400 Electronic Customer Support (ECS) can be used to order and deliver fixes back to the PC in response to known problems that may occur.

Several other IBM products enhance client management. One of them, ManageWare for OS/400, simplifies the tracking and use of PC licensed software. Used with Client Access, ManageWare simplifies the distribution of updates to PC users and maintains information about where and when packages were distributed.

AdStar Distributed Storage Manager for OS/400 (ADSM) provides client or server archive, back-up, and recovery of data. ADSM uses a graphical interface to automate and schedule these operations. The scheduling can be based on time or on some other policy.

Still another product, LANRES for OS/400, provides configuration administration for Novell servers from the AS/400. LANRES provides disk serving, two-way print serving, and data distribution. LANRES adds server-to-server management options to the total system. Another product, called NetWare for SAA, provides a direct communications link between a Novell NetWare server and an AS/400. NetWare for SAA can be used in conjunction with Client Access to provide access to the AS/400.

Programming Interfaces

One of the most important aspects of Client Access is the tremendous number of industry-standard programming interfaces it supports. The reason for all these APIs, of course, is to make it easy for application developers to write client/server applications and to access AS/400 resources. A complete list reads like alphabet soup. Rather than just list them, let's look at some of the more significant APIs and standards.

DB2 for OS/400 Database Interfaces

Database Access GUI provides a window into the AS/400 database using a visual point-and-click interface. This interface makes it easy to get DB2 for OS/400 data into a Windows or OS/2 application such as Microsoft Word or Lotus 1-2-3. The visual interface allows a user to quickly build and execute queries so that data can be analyzed using one of these PC applications. All the while, DB2 for OS/400 maintains the security and integrity of the business data. This interface can also be combined with other PC-based graphical tools, such as Microsoft Visual Basic or Powersoft Powerbuilder, to create applications which need access to the server database.

The File Transfer function provides both a command interface and a GUI for transferring data between a PC and the AS/400. PC data in many different formats can be stored in a byte stream file in the AS/400. When transferring to the PC, the fine-transfer function enables a single transfer request to select and join up to 32 files. These transfers can also use all the capabilities of DRDA such as stored procedures, rules, and triggers.

Portable database interfaces are provided to allow interaction with other databases. Because almost every PC database uses a slightly different data-access method, Microsoft identified a set of SQL commands for use in Windows. Many database providers now use this standard, called Open DataBase Connectivity (ODBC). Client Access implements the full ODBC Level 2 set of calls for Windows 3.1 and the optimized clients.

Still another portable database interface is Apple's Database Access Language (DAL). DAL can be used to access DB2 for OS/400, although it is currently supported outside of Client Access. As IBM adds new support for Apple clients, this interface will become part of Client Access.

As described in Chapter 6, the AS/400 supplies the industry standard database access language, SQL. SQL allows consistent data access across heterogeneous systems and is the best interface for direct manipulation and query of database information. Client Access provides support for remote SQL and SQL extensions for its clients.

Remote SQL lets PC applications issue SQL commands to be executed on the AS/400. Full SQL capability is included for such functions as SELECT, INSERT, DELETE, COMMIT, and ROLLBACK. Also included are several other functions — for example, to permit block fetch and field-level transformations.

Several SQL extensions are included for the optimized clients. A dynamic SQL feature allows users to construct queries to DB2 for OS/400 as needed. Static SQL allows a set of predefined queries to be built for an end user. Functions are also available to bundle ODBC statements together to improve database performance. The OS/400 call-level interface and access to stored procedures with the SQL CALL statement are also provided. Clients can change the AS/400 server library list, create source physical files, and use the native database copy file functions.

Support for distributed databases through DRDA is provided to let a client use the AS/400 as a gateway to other databases that support DRDA. The optimized clients support DRDA Level 2, while the original and Windows clients support DRDA Level 1.

You can use the File Transfer API to access DB2 for OS/400 files from PC applications. SQL-like statements can select file, records, and fields. This API can be used to do such things as load a PC database from an AS/400 or upload daily transaction files to a master file.

The Hierarchical File System API allows the AS/400 to use file systems that contain PC files. Applications can be written in any AS/400 high-level language to use file system functions, similar to those file system functions used in Unix and OS/2, to work with directories and files.

Application Interfaces

Another important class of APIs enables applications on the client and on the server to work closely together. Most of these interfaces are designed for programmers who are familiar with programming on the AS/400. We will look at a few of these interfaces in this section.

Queues are heavily used in the AS/400 to communicate from one program to another (we certainly saw this was true in the I/O chapter). An OS/400 object called a *data queue* is frequently used by programmers as a simple method to pass information from one program to another. The Data Queues Program-to-Program API allows the same sort of programming style to be used between host and PC applications. The advantage of this style of programming is particularly evident if host applications and PC applications are written in different languages. For example, the host application may be written in RPG and the PC application may be written in a PC language such as C++. Even though the languages may not work together directly, having come from different vendors, the data queue is there to take the input from one program and pass it on to the other.

One such application that is built with data queues is GroupShare for OS/400. This is an integrated workgroup application that lets a group of workers share information and communicate through client workstations attached to an AS/400. Two of GroupShare's more useful functions are ClipQ and Chat. ClipQ is similar to putting something on the clipboard in Windows, except an AS/400 queue is used with ClipQ. Someone else can take the information off the queue and insert it into an application. Chat allows interactive conversation among workgroup members.

Another set of APIs provides different kinds of remote program calls. The Distributed Program Call permits an AS/400 activity to be started from the PC. Control Language (CL) commands can be submitted to let a user start an AS/400 application from a PC. This call is interactive, meaning it waits for a completion response from the AS/400 program. Another command, called Submit Remote Command, can be used for non-interactive programs. Run Remote Command starts a PC command from the AS/400 and does not require an active 5250 session on the receiving PC; this only works with optimized clients. Another similar command for other clients, called Start PC Command, does require an active 5250 session.

Program-to-Program Communications
The Windows 3.1 and the Optimized clients have implemented the Multi-protocol Transport Networking (MPTN) architecture and use IBM AnyNet functions. This combination allows users to get all the same functions in the same manner no matter what underlying network transport layer is used. There is no difference, whether a client is attached via a System Network Architecture (SNA) network, the traditional IBM network, or a Transmission Control Protocol/Internet Protocol (TPC/IP) — the wide-area network used by popular Unix networks. This network protocol independence makes it easier to write or buy applications. Applications can be written to a variety of APIs, including Common Programming Interface for Communications (CPI-C), Advanced Program-to-Program Communications (APPC), and Sockets.

CPI-C and APPC are programming interfaces for applications intended to run on SNA networks. Sockets is a programming interface for applications intended to run on TPC/IP networks. Thanks to AnyNet, applications written to these interfaces can run on either network. Finally, these protocols can be used across a variety of connections, such as Token-Ring, Ethernet, asynchronous, twinaxial, and others.

Messaging Interfaces
Messaging is the way people communicate over the network. The messaging interfaces form the basis for most mail solutions. We have already seen the three main mail interfaces Client Access supports. VIM is the messaging interface that many PC E-Mail products support, MAPI is the mail/messaging interface defined by Microsoft for its Windows environment, and Ultimedia Mail is IBM's new multimedia mail product.

Multimedia Enablers
The use of multimedia in daily business applications is becoming commonplace. Client Access enables multimedia through the Ultimedia System

Facilities for OS/400 (USF). USF permits multimedia to be added to both existing and new applications. It provides a set of APIs and a GUI to create, store, and manage multimedia objects.

The OS/400 Ultimedia System Facilities APIs use standard interfaces that are callable from high-level languages (COBOL, RPG, and C) used in the AS/400. The Client Ultimedia APIs are callable from programs written in C and are available in the Windows 3.1 and the optimized clients. Object handlers are available to capture and play back video objects, audio objects, and images. An object manager is available to query a multimedia object repository, and to browse, create, copy (and so on) the multimedia objects.

Several multimedia "snap-in" products also exist that can be added to the AS/400. Ultimedia Builder for OS/400 provides a means to create multimedia presentations and applications. Perfect Image for OS/400 is an image enhancement program that allows a user to edit, capture, and enhance images. Both of these products run on an OS/2 client.

Ultimedia Conferencing for OS/400 lets users work together in multimedia conferencing mode even if they are thousands of miles apart. All participants see the same window on the workstation screen. Image, video, graphics, and text can be displayed in the window, and high-quality audio can be shared between workstations. Person-to-Person (P2P) can be used in combination with Ultimedia Conferencing to provide a chalkboard that can be used interactively between participants. These last two multimedia products run on both OS/2 and Windows clients.

Client Access for OS/400 is a significant product for the AS/400 and more than one million copies were purchased in just its first year of availability. Client Access provides the support for the AS/400 to perform many of the functions we discussed in the early part of this chapter. Client Access lets the AS/400 act as a file and print server, a transaction server, a database server, and a groupware server, although some functions outside of Client Access are needed for full groupware support. In the following sections, we will see how the remaining groupware and object-server support are provided in the AS/400.

File Server I/O Processor

The File Server I/O Processor (FSIOP)[4] is the first of the application engines to be introduced in the AS/400. In Chapter 10, we saw how an IOP with its specifically designed, real-time operating system can perform device control functions. Device control was the original intended use for the IOPs, but it is not the only use. Because all IOPs are intelligent processors and can support different functions and even different operating systems, it was only a matter of time until one or more of these IOPs was used to run other types of applications. In the last few years, we introduced special-function IOPs on the AS/400, which provide more than just device support. Examples of the special functions these IOPs perform include RAID-5, fax, wireless network,

[4] In some places, such as the U.K., this is sometimes called the "fizzy op."

and AppleTalk support. A natural extension was to use IOPs to perform still other types of applications, including server applications. The first of these server applications running on an IOP was announced in 1994 as the FSIOP. The type of application that can be run on an IOP is not limited to just server applications; we will call these IOPs by the more general name, application engines. In the next chapter, we will look at some of the future plans for these application engines. In this section, we will look at the current support for the FSIOP.

The file-serving function is obviously an important one for client/server computing. In the industry, a couple of major PC server applications are dedicated to performing this function very efficiently. One is Novell's Netware; another is OS/2 LAN Server. Earlier in this chapter, we talked about NetWare for SAA and LANRES, which allow an AS/400 to interconnect and even manage the attached PC servers running either of these file-server products.

There are still some disadvantages to having a separate PC file server. The PC file server has to have its own disk drives. If the data in this server is critical business data, the customer will no doubt want to take some precautions to protect that data. The AS/400 can automatically back up the data in case something should happen to the disk drives in the server, but even that may not be enough. Many customers want a high-availability disk system to protect the data and to ensure that the business is not disrupted if a disk fails. Disk mirroring and RAID disk technologies are available for PC servers. Then there is the question of security. Here again, software packages exist that can be added to the server to provide various levels of security.

The problem here is the duplication of resources. If the AS/400 already implements disk mirroring or RAID technology, it may make sense to use the disk devices in the AS/400. The same is true for security — it doesn't make sense to purchase something the AS/400 already has. An obvious answer is to put the PC under the covers of the AS/400 and give it access to the AS/400 resources, and that is exactly what the FSIOP does.

The FSIOP is a double-wide card that plugs directly into the AS/400. The card contains an Intel processor and its memory. Other I/O devices, including disks, are shared with the AS/400. This card supports one or two LAN ports with up to 255 users per port. Either Token Ring or Ethernet LANs can be attached, and more than one of these file server cards can be attached to the AS/400.

OS/2 is used as the operating system for this application engine, although the customer never sees or has to deal with this operating system. The AS/400 manages all the interactions with the OS/2 operating system; the customer only sees the server application. The first file-server application announced was LAN Server/400. Later, NetWare/400 was added.

The benefits of this file server under the covers are many. First, the PC file-serving operations are offloaded to a dedicated processor to improve performance. Without the need for a separate hardware system, the customer has a single-server environment. The AS/400 provides the integrated security, integrity, and administration functions for the file server. For example, one of the supported file systems in the integrated file system is called QLANSrv. This is the file system used by the file server. Data can be moved to and from the other file systems with some simple commands. In addition, the file server has access to all the devices on the AS/400.

The FSIOP and the LAN Server software may also provide a cost savings for AS/400 users. A file server cost comparison was reported in the June 27, 1995, issue of *PC Magazine*, showing the FSIOP solution to be less expensive than PC servers from four major vendors (Compaq, Digital, HP, and IBM).[5] The comparison looked at hardware and software costs for configurations that would support 100 users on the server. The people cost to manage the servers, which is a real strength of the AS/400, was not considered. Of course, it was assumed you already have an AS/400.

The LAN Server software is a tightly integrated package. OS/2 and OS/2 LAN Server code is delivered on an AS/400 tape, and both are installed using the standard AS/400 licensed program installation.

In 1995, support for both Novell NetWare and Lotus Notes on the FSIOP was announced. A different software packaging strategy is used in these server and workgroup applications for the FSIOP. First, the OS/2 code required to run the FSIOP is separated from the server or workgroup application. This allows the FSIOP to run as a communications adapter without support for file serving. The second part of the new strategy is to enable standard versions of server and workgroup applications to be loaded without modification into the FSIOP. The base enablement for these applications runs the server or workgroup application as if it were on a PC server. The value added by the AS/400 is hardware integration and support for AS/400 disk and back-up devices. A third part of the new strategy is to provide enhanced integration packages, which add value for the AS/400 over a PC-based server. For example, Novell NetWare files with the enhanced integration feature will become a part of the AS/400 integrated file system. For Lotus Notes, the enhanced integration feature will integrate Notes Mail with AnyMail for OS/400 and OfficeVision for OS/400.

AS/400 Advanced Server Models

We knew early on that it was possible for us to transform the AS/400 into a world-class server. We had an architecture that allowed us to move into a full server environment without walking away from our traditional customers, most of whom were still using the AS/400 as a host-centric system. Our customers told us they wanted to evolve to client/server computing, but they didn't want to disrupt their business to do so. This was not a problem for the AS/400. We did, however, have an image problem with much of the industry — actually, because of a real problem among other vendors.

[5] *PC Magazine*, Vol. 14, No. 12, June 27, 1995.

Most other minicomputer vendors had also decided to become server vendors, but they had a problem. Their existing minicomputers could not be transformed into servers and had to be abandoned. Just about every one of these vendors replaced their host-based systems with a new system, which usually ran a Unix operating system. These vendors told their customers that if they wanted to move to client/server computing, they would have to walk away from their existing systems and move to the new system. This usually meant they would also have to convert or rebuy all their applications to use the new system.

Consequently, the computer industry would not believe we could turn an existing AS/400 into a server; so we decided to create some new server models to show we were serious about this market. This was not totally a marketing ploy, but it did give us the chance to optimize these models for better cost/performance on a server workload.

In September 1993, we introduced three server models (100, 135, and 140) as part of the original AS/400 family. The AS/400 Advanced Server models were announced in May 1994; there were two models (20S and 30S) originally in this server family, which covered the middle to the low end of the AS/400 market. In June 1995, we announced three new server models (40S, 50S, and 53S) to cover the complete AS/400 range. We needed to optimize the performance of these servers for three functions:

- Database serving
- Communications serving
- Batch processing

All these functions are more compute-intensive than is interactive processing. For a given server model, we needed more performance than the equivalent traditional model used for interactive processing. To accomplish this, we took some of the higher-performance processors out of the larger traditional models and repackaged them into the smaller server models. For example, we took the processor from our large rack-mounted F70 model in 1993 and packaged either one or two of these processors in our smaller deskside package to create the server models 135 and 140. We also ensured that these models had sufficient memory, disk capacity, and LAN connections to support the large processors in a server environment.

The higher-performance processors greatly improve the performance of server applications over the equivalent traditional models. Also improved is the performance for network, database, file serving, and compiling operations. Because the server models are not intended for interactive computing, the performance of traditional interactive applications, such as those using 5250 workstations, is de-tuned on these server models. The number of interactive workstations that can be attached to a server model is also restricted.

Customers who have both interactive and client/server applications can achieve the same level of server performance as the server models by using a traditional model with one of the higher-performance processors. The traditional models have no restrictions for either interactive or server applications. The server models are special-purpose systems designed to improve server performance at a lower cost. For a client/server workload, the cost of a server model for a given level of performance will be lower than the cost of a traditional model.

A server model with an FSIOP used for file serving has shown the ability to outperform either Unix or PC-based servers in a client/server environment. The benchmark used to measure server performance was designed for a workgroup environment that has a combination of on-line transaction processing (OLTP), decision support systems (DSS), and PC file serving over the LAN. This benchmark, which is available from a consultant for anyone to run, has been recognized as one which will provide substantial value to IS (information system) decision makers responsible for acquiring a new generation of servers.[6]

[6] "Client/Server Benchmarks: IBM Sets the Standard," *Aberdeen Group Technology Viewpoint*, Volume 7, Number 9, December 9, 1994.

Application Enabling for Client/Server

Early in this chapter, I noted that thousands of existing AS/400 applications have already been converted to a client/server model. Many new applications are also being written. In this section, we will briefly examine the application development support that you can use to develop client/server applications for the AS/400. Several of the new tools are specifically for object-oriented programming, but we will hold off that discussion until the next section, where we will consider how objects fit into the client/server environment.

Client/server development tools for the AS/400 come from many different software vendors. A few years ago, Rochester created the AS/400 Client Series, which is a collection of software products recommended by IBM for use in the AS/400 client/server environment. We can't list every available product in this series, but we can talk about the types of tools, together with a few examples.

Application development tools can be either host-based products, which run on the AS/400, or PC-based products, which run on a PC. In recent years, there has been a growing movement to application development tools that are PC-based. The reason for this is three-fold. First, the PC's graphical interface provides a visual development environment. With a visual programming environment, the programmer selects interface components from a palette of parts and connects them. The parts may represent a database, a communications link, or any of several entities needed by the application. The programmer can review the interface as it is being built. When the programmer is satisfied with the interface, the connecting code is automatically generated.

A second reason to use a PC-based development tool is to provide an easy way to split an application between the client and the server. Finally, by using a PC-based development tool, we can share the same application development tools across multiple systems. For example, by using cross-compilers, we can target an application developed on a PC to more than one host platform. A couple examples of the newer tools in the AS/400 Client Series will illustrate this type of application development tool:

- VisualGen — This OS/2-based application development tool from IBM can be used to develop applications that run in a variety of workstation and host environments. Client, server, and single-system applications can be defined, tested, and generated in the same development environment.
- Obsydian — This application development environment from Synon Corporation uses model-based business abstractions along with the software reuse principles of object orientation to improve the quality and productivity of software development.
- LANSA/CS400 — Aspect Computing provides this cross-platform tool to develop applications for AS/400 LANSA/Server, which helps to connect AS/400s to PC networks and provides access to the AS/400 database.
- GUIdelines — JBA International provides this GUI development tool to interactively design and implement GUI client/server applications. GUIdelines Server-Logic allows a developer to write application code on the client and translate it into RPG for compilation on the AS/400. GUIdelines Object allows the developer to design and implement GUI object-enabled applications.
- SequeLink — This product from TechGnosis provides client/server data access to a wide range of databases, including Sybase, Informix, and DB/2 for OS/400. SequeLink Client supports various clients and SequeLink Server provides a GUI front-end to AS/400 applications.

Two other PC-based application development products are available from IBM for non-object-oriented AS/400 languages. They are the CoOperative Development Environment/400 (CODE/400) and Visual RPG (VRPG). CODE/400 provides edit, compile, and debug facilities for AS/400 applications, as well as the ability to generate database description files. CODE/400 supports ILE RPG, ILE COBOL, and ILE CL. VRPG contains a GUI builder with an integrated RPG development environment. VRPG also provides a conversion function to assist developers in updating existing RPG applications by converting AS/400 user interface objects to GUI. Both of these application development products run on an OS/2 workstation.

A host-based package of development tools is also available for the AS/400. This package is called the Application Development ToolSet for OS/400 (ADTS), and it provides several of the basic development tools we have seen in earlier chapters. This collection of tools, well known to most

AS/400 developers, includes Source Entry Utility (SEU), Screen Design Aid (SDA), and Data File Utility (DFU). These tools work with the ILE compilers — ILE RPG, ILE COBOL, ILE C, and ILE CL — which are themselves host-based.

Client/server development tools are designed to split the application between the client and the server. Different tools, however, split the workload differently. Some tools, such as PowerBuilder, SQLWindows, and Visual Basic, are PC-centric tools. With these tools, most of the processing takes place on the client. Other tools, such as VRPG, GUI/400, and Synon/CSG, are host-centric. These tools use the PC, but the majority of the work is done on the host server. Some of the newer tools, such as Progress, LANSA, Guidelines, Synon/Obsydian, and VisualAge, split the workload more evenly between the client and the server.

We are now ready to look at the newest application development environment, the object-oriented environment. Objects, especially distributed objects in a client/server environment, are beginning to take over the application development world. This is our next topic.

Distributed Objects in a Client/Server Environment

Throughout this book, we have talked about object technology and the role it has played in the AS/400. Within the industry, object technology is being heralded by some as the cure for every programming ill. Whether or not this is true remains to be seen, but there is no doubt that object technology will play a significant role for every major vendor. There are certainly pockets of object technologies in use today. Still, debates on when object technology will be in widespread use continue. Many believe it will not happen until the end of the decade. However, tools and products have to be prepared now if this is going to happen.

The AS/400 vision for object technology is a distributed one, like the distributed client/server environment we have been discussing. This leads us to a computing model based on distributed objects. Because the systems (hardware and operating systems) used in a distributed environment often come from different vendors, it is important that the object technology be based on industry standards.

As we described earlier, there is no consensus on which language is best for OO programming. This means the AS/400 must support more than one OO language. It also means that any object model must be language independent. The language-independent object model used in the AS/400 is called the System Object Model (SOM). This object model will be used across all IBM operating system platforms and is based on industry standards. The industry standards for objects are being led by the Object Management Group (OMG) and its open, cross-platform Common Object Request Broker Architecture (CORBA) specification. SOM is OMG CORBA-compliant. Before we talk about this object model, let's look at the languages and development tools that are supported for writing applications.

Application Development Environments

The AS/400 provides application development environments for the two dominant OO languages (C++ and Smalltalk). As the various fourth-generation languages (4GLs) and Computer Aided Software Engineering (CASE) tools adopt object technologies, they also will be used to develop application solutions. The requirement is to provide integrated environments for the development, runtime, and management of distributed client/server applications. Of course, all these environments must be SOM enabled.

The C++ application development environment for the AS/400 is provided by VisualAge C++ for OS/400. This product replaces the older C Set ++ product. VisualAge C++ is designed to enable the development of cross-platform applications using the C++ language. The set of tools includes

- A visual programming environment

- VisualAge C++ cross-compiler — This C++ cross-compiler runs on an OS/2 workstation and generates C++ modules to run on an AS/400. The C++ cross-compiler is part of the ILE compiler family and supports access to programs written in other AS/400 languages. This compiler will enhance the development of client/server applications by taking advantage of existing AS/400 applications. The VisualAge C++ product also contains the C++ compiler for OS/2 to allow the creation of programs to run on OS/2 only, AS/400 only, or split between the two systems.

- Class libraries — This product includes two class libraries: the C++ Base Class Library and the AS/400 Access Class Library. The Base Class Library allows the manipulation of objects, and the AS/400 Access Class Library allows the part of the application running on OS/2 to access the AS/400 as a server.

- Productivity tools — Programmer productivity tools, such as a source editor and a class browser (which allows you to navigate through the class methods), are provided with the VisualAge C++ product.

VisualAge for OS/400 provides the Smalltalk development environment for the AS/400. A product called ENVY/400 was the first Smalltalk-based environment for the AS/400. Many people feel that Smalltalk is a better OO language than is C++. Envy/400 is an integrated team-development environment, meaning several developers can work on an application at the same time. ENVY/400 includes the ability to manage the entire software product lifecycle using version control, library, and change-management functions. ENVY/400 has been a successful product for the AS/400 and has now been converged into the VisualAge family of products. Both VisualAge and VisualAge C++ products are fully integrated, team-programming environments for the development of client/server applications.

VisualAge, like VisualAge C++, offers code reuse of programs written in non-object-oriented languages, such as COBOL and C. It also provides access to the many communications protocols we have already discussed. Both local and remote database support, as well as multimedia support, are also included in VisualAge. The platforms supported are OS/2, Windows, and OS/400.

IBM Smalltalk is the language in which VisualAge was developed. It is a standards-based language that is SOM enabled. Smalltalk is a pure OO language, as opposed to C++, which can be used simply as a better C language. Because of this, some developers prefer to work directly in the Smalltalk language, instead of using it as part of the VisualAge environment. For this reason, Smalltalk is offered as a separate product.

SOM and DSOM

Class libraries defined in C++ or Smalltalk are language dependent and in general cannot be used with other languages, because too much implementation detail is exposed in the binary interface. This has been a major problem with C++; and many argue that with regard to packaging and distribution of binary modules, C++ is a giant step backwards. For example, when the C++ class library is updated or changed, the client programs typically have to be recompiled to accommodate the changes. This is definitely not technology independence.

SOM was created to provide a language-neutral object model. Objects defined in SOM's interface definition language (IDL) can be used by OO and non-OO languages alike. For AS/400 application developers, IDL can be thought of as the DDS for objects. SOM reduces or eliminates the need to recompile applications when class libraries are changed. SOM employs a runtime engine to enable objects to bind dynamically while preserving the flow of inheritance across object boundaries. An application can use SOM objects that were not known at compile time.

SOM objects can be distributed across a network through the use of Distributed SOM (DSOM). DSOM allows application programs to access objects across address spaces. This is an extension to SOM that makes the SOM object's location transparent to the client. The objects themselves do not move. They are used in place. DSOM uses function shipping, not data shipping.

One of the major differentiations of the AS/400 RISC models is the support for SOM in the operating system, and the introduction with V3R6 of SOMobjects. SOMobjects provides the runtime support for SOM and DSOM in the AS/400. SOMobjects is not available on the AS/400's IMPI models, because SOMobjects uses the object-oriented support found only in the SLIC. SOMobjects allows portability of classes across the various systems that support SOM.

SOMobjects also includes a variety of *frameworks*. The reuse of objects can be accomplished through the use of class libraries, as we just saw. Another similar approach to sharing objects is through the use of frameworks. A *framework* is a collection of objects to provide a common solution to a particular problem. A class library is more general purpose, not necessarily designed for a particular problem.

Certainly the most important framework included in SOMobjects is the DSOM framework, which can be used to write applications based on distributed objects. The DSOM framework allows a program in one system to execute a method on an object in a remote system. When a program creates an instance of an object, that object can be on a remote system. The DSOM framework recognizes the object is remote and starts a conversation with the DSOM framework at the remote site. The remote-site DSOM framework will create the actual instance of the object, while the local DSOM framework will create a shadow of the object, called a *proxy*. The program talks to the proxy, and the local DSOM framework will take care of routing requests to the real object at the remote site. This process is transparent to the users. The DSOM framework will create the proxy object and start the conversation with the remote site automatically at runtime. The DSOM framework requires TCP/IP to activate its conversation. Information about the location of the various objects and the structure of the objects is stored in two databases, called the Information Repository and the Interface Repository. These databases are automatically updated as the objects are created.

The implementation of SOM on the AS/400 goes one step further than the implementations in other systems and supports the idea of persistence. We discussed persistence in Chapter 8 when we looked at the single-level store. In other systems, the lifetime of objects corresponds to the duration of the job that created them. This limitation causes problems if you want to share objects across different jobs. Other systems have implemented various solutions; for example, there is a Persistence framework on OS/2 and AIX. These solutions still require the programmer to manage the object persistence by ensuring that the object contents are periodically made permanent on disk, which can require a significant programming effort. The AS/400 doesn't use the Persistence framework.

Instead, the AS/400 uses its single-level store to support persistent SOM objects, with no involvement from the programmer. When you create an instance of a SOM object, you specify whether or not it is to be a *protected object* — a protected object is a persistent object. Protected objects are encapsulated and exist alongside the OS/400 objects we have already discussed. When a protected object is created, it is put into an IFS directory, similar to the way an OS/400 object is created into an AS/400 library. Protected objects have names and can be shared, saved, or restored just like any OS/400 object can using OS/400 commands. At the MI, these objects are implemented as byte space objects. Thus, security for protected objects is through system pointers and the authority component in SLIC. For compatibility reasons, SOMobjects also supports unprotected SOM objects.

So far, we have talked only about the runtime environment for SOM and DSOM on the AS/400 (called SOMobjects for OS/400). Developing SOM-based applications for the AS/400 requires the use of the SOMobjects Developer Toolkit for OS/400, which includes the SOM compiler for the AS/400. The toolkit is an OS/2-based object that can produce the appropriate binding files for creating SOM classes and SOM-based applications. Both ILE C and VisualAge C++ for OS/400 are supported.

Implementations for SOM and DSOM are either available or planned for OS/2, AIX, Windows, and MVS. Additionally, IBM, HP, and SunSoft have jointly announced they will use DSOM to interoperate with similar products from HP and SunSoft. With a common object model on multiple platforms, applications developed to SOMobjects for OS/400 will run on multiple platforms.

Application and System Frameworks

Frameworks can be classified as either application or system. We just looked at some system frameworks that are part of SOMobjects for OS/400. Application frameworks will come from IBM and business partners. Some will be cross-industry, usable for any business. An example of a cross-industry framework would be one that contains basic financial management objects. Most any business could use such a framework. Other frameworks will be vertical, meaning they are designed for a specific business or industry. An example of a vertical framework could be one that contains objects specifically for the banking industry. Because the core technologies for objects is the same across all IBM platforms, business partners can participate in a wider set of markets.

System frameworks will be developed to support traditional operating system functions in an object environment. Examples of this kind are a framework to support save/restore functions and a framework to manage communications across platforms.

Application Environments

Two additional topics relate to emerging object-oriented application environments. They are OpenDoc and Taligent.

OpenDoc

OpenDoc is Apple's architecture for object-oriented compound documents. Apple, along with IBM, Novell, Sun, Xerox, Oracle, and Taligent — collectively known as the Component Integration Laboratories (CIL) — is pursuing this architecture to simplify the creation of documents that include text, charts, tables, spreadsheets, graphics, images, video, and sound. These parts can be combined to form multimedia documents. Other parts will be available from IBM and others to provide access to AS/400 resources, such as a database file. End users will be able to "cut and paste" or "drag and drop" these parts to create an OpenDoc document.

The basic technologies in OpenDoc are the Bento storage mechanism (named after the Japanese plates with compartments for different foods) and a scripting technology that borrows heavily from AppleScript and SOM's IDL. In a Bento document, each object has a persistent ID that moves with it from system to system. This allows storing and tracking of multiple revisions of each object. If a document has several drafts, only the incremental changes need to be stored. Because the Bento system can be shared safely among multiple users with this revision control, it lends itself to collaborative applications where users share documents and parts. Underlying OpenDoc is the SOM. This makes OpenDoc language independent.

Microsoft's OLE provides an equivalent function for compound documents. Apple plans to make OpenDoc compatible with OLE. The idea is to wrap OLE with a layer of message-translation software. This OpenDoc container would see an embedded OLE object as an OpenDoc object, and the OLE object would see its container as an OLE container. The reverse translation is also possible, where OpenDoc objects function in OLE containers. Companies such as WordPerfect are working on the translation layers.

Taligent

IBM and Apple originally formed Taligent to create an advanced operating environment. HP later became a partner in the joint venture. The new environment will provide a portable application system with new development tools. The technologies developed by Taligent will be brought to the market by the three partners. The AS/400 will be one of the systems to receive these technologies.

The Taligent environment is being built on an OO operating system base, using SOM, and it makes extensive use of frameworks. At the base are the system frameworks, both support and domain frameworks. On top of this are the application frameworks. A major part of the Taligent environment is the new user interface called Taligent's People, Places & Things. This highly graphical user interface on the Taligent client workstation is designed to provide a more intuitive user experience than the user interfaces provided by Windows, OS/2, or Apple Macintosh. For example, a "business card," which is used to represent a person in the Taligent interface, can be dragged to an icon representing an electronic conference, and the person represented by the card will be connected to the conference.

First to be put on the AS/400 is the support for Taligent clients. Taligent application components will be able to access AS/400 data and services within the Taligent frameworks APIs. There will be no need to use remote procedure calls, remote commands, data queues, or any other procedural APIs. AS/400 mail services can be used to deliver a Taligent compound document from one Taligent user to another. In addition, some of the Taligent classes that support server applications will be implemented directly on the AS/400.

WebConnection for OS/400

Our final topic in this chapter is the AS/400 in the world of network-centric computing. With network-centric computing — which may well represent the future of client/server computing — everyone can access and distribute information, applications, and services provided by the network. Today, many companies are looking to exploit the Internet and to enable new ways of doing business, including electronic marketing. WebConnection for OS/400 allows the AS/400 to become a data repository and data server on the Internet. WebConnection for OS/400 provides several functions for V3R1 and V3R6:

- World Wide Web Hypertext Transport Protocol (HTTP) Server — The HTTP server provides a mechanism whereby the AS/400 can be a data repository for a business on the World Wide Web. This allows customers around the world to access the AS/400 across the Internet using any web browser software. Today, most PC operating systems provide such a browser. Local access is also available on a LAN via TCP/IP.

- Logging of World Wide Web Server access — This function allows AS/400 customers to track who is accessing their servers and what parts are being accessed most frequently.

- Access to AS/400 applications via a Hypertext Mark-up Language (HTML) device driver — With this enhancement, natively developed applications on the AS/400 can utilize web browsers as clients. The web browsers can be attached locally or, via Internet, attached anywhere in the world. This means AS/400 users can develop Internet applications using their favorite native application development environment.

- Serial Line Internet Protocol (SLIP) asynchronous communications connections — This function allows inexpensive access to the World Wide Web and the Internet.

- Anonymous FTP support — This support provides access to a restricted area of data on the AS/400. The public can access this area without either a password or user identification.

In addition to the features supported by WebConnection for OS/400, the AS/400 itself has several advantages over other systems by which a business can be attached to the Internet. The AS/400's integrated database prevents unauthorized access to data — security authorization and auditing are pervasive in the system. The system's object-based structure also prevents program objects from being altered — viruses are not easily introduced into the system. In short, the AS/400 is well positioned to exploit the Internet and the new business opportunities the Internet provides.

Conclusions

Some readers may have considered this chapter to be "acronym heaven" or "acronym hell," depending upon their viewpoint. The purpose was not to list as many acronyms as possible, but to show the broad range of support the AS/400 provides for the five types of servers we discussed earlier in this chapter. Much of the support complies with industry standards, which over the years have created this mountain of acronyms.

Some industry consultants simply use the list of acronyms supported by a system to measure the goodness of one system when compared to another. What they miss is how well the system integrates these standards. Remember: A successful client/server model is one that can be integrated with existing applications. It permits the use of existing business infrastructures while providing the means to migrate to new business models as needed. A long list of acronyms does not necessarily do this. The AS/400's value will continue to be its integrated nature, for client/server applications or for anything else.

Chapter 12

The Future of the AS/400

In the past 30 years, more information has been produced than in the previous 5,000 years. That amount of information continues to double every five years.[1] During the same 30-year period, the density of a single computer chip used to process and store that information doubled every year, while its performance doubled every 18 months.

To put this into perspective, suppose the automobile industry had made the same progress in the past 30 years. If so, you would be able to buy a new Porsche for about $2. It would go faster than the speed of sound and could travel over 1,000 miles on less than an ounce of gasoline. Make mine a red one.

In this chapter, we will do a little speculation on the future of the AS/400 and what we might expect in the next five years. As with any speculation on the future, there is no guarantee that anything we predict will come true — but, it is fun to do. So fasten your seat belt; our new Porsche is rapidly approaching the speed of sound as we drive toward the possible future.

Future Processor Technologies

Cobra and Muskie are not general-purpose PowerPC processors. These first 64-bit RISC processors are used exclusively in the AS/400, including the AS/400 Advanced 36. Neither will be used in any other IBM system, nor will they be sold for use in non-IBM systems through the Somerset Design Center established by IBM and Motorola.

The reason for this, as we saw back in Chapter 2, is because these two processor designs only implement the tags-active mode. Other operating systems that have been ported to PowerPC need the tags-inactive mode. The only way another operating system, such as the SSP, can run on one of these processors is under the control of the SLIC, which provides the underlying

[1] **Quantifying information is no trivial problem. We could use information theory and the mathematical expression to calculate the "entropy" or randomness that exists in all information being transmitted in the world — the lower the entropy, the higher the information content. If we can show how much the entropy has gone down over some period of time, we could calculate how much the information content of the world has increased. I prefer the less scientific method of estimating the amount of junk mail I receive today compared to what I received five years ago. Richard Saul Wurman, in his book, *Information Anxiety*, did a little more thorough research and estimated that information has doubled in the last 30 years and is now doubling every 5 years. His estimates are good enough for me.**

support for the other operating system. Part of that support is the I/O. These early AS/400 processors only implement the AS/400 SPD bus I/O structure, so SLIC needs to provide the interface to this I/O structure.

The decision to build processors to be used only in the AS/400 was made because IBM has no other operating systems that today can take advantage of a 64-bit RISC processor. Even outside IBM, the number of 64-bit operating systems can be counted on one hand, and a 32-bit processor will satisfy the needs of the industry for several years to come. A second reason these RISC processors do not implement the tags-inactive mode is because we have no plans to run another operating system on the AS/400 without the SLIC.

Like everything else, this situation can change. In the future, processors used in the AS/400 likely will implement both the tags-active and the tags-inactive mode. They will also support industry standard I/O interfaces as well as the SPD I/O interface. These processors will then be able to run OS/400 or any other PowerPC operating system. Let's look briefly at how this might happen.

For the next few years, there are not likely to be any new 64-bit operating systems. New operating systems take many years to develop and mature. Besides the AS/400, a couple other 64-bit operating systems currently exist, including a Unix operating system from Digital, but they are not yet major players in the industry. Some popular 32-bit operating systems will begin to migrate to 64 bits; but this too, will take time. Oh, there will be more systems using 64-bit RISC processors, and they may even advertise that they have 64-bit operating systems; but, in reality, most will use only 32 bits of the processor hardware. Therefore, the processors built for the AS/400 over the next couple years will be *exclusively* for the AS/400.

Sometime in 1998, we anticipate seeing the first of the 32-bit operating systems reaching 64 bits. There may then be a need in IBM and in the general industry for 64-bit RISC processors that are optimized for commercial processing. The AS/400 processors around this time will likely implement both tags-active and tags-inactive modes to allow their use in other systems with other operating systems. They will also support the industry standard I/O, as we will shortly see. These same processors could also be used by non-IBM systems and could be sold through the alliance with Motorola.

Anticipating a convergence of hardware technologies within the next few years, IBM formed a new division in 1994. This division, called the System Technology and Architecture Division (STAD), has the responsibility to develop and implement common hardware technology for IBM server products. This group is working on common subsystem components such as memory subsystems, processor complex designs, I/O, and system packaging. The processor designers in Rochester and Endicott who developed the Cobra and Muskie processors were assigned to the new division. Other hardware designers from Austin and Poughkeepsie are also part of STAD.

In the following sections, we will look at a possible road map for the AS/400 processors through the end of the decade.

AS/400 RISC Processor Road Map

Multiple versions of the Cobra and Muskie processors are used in the AS/400 models announced in 1995, as we detailed in Chapter 2. The low-end models in the AS/400 product line use the Cobra-CR processor running at 50 MHz. The middle of the product line uses Cobra-4 running at 50MHz and 77 MHz. The high-end models of the AS/400 use the Muskie processors running at 125 MHz and 154 MHz. These high-end models can have one, two, or four of the Muskie processors.

The design of the Cobra processor, in particular, is such that higher-speed versions can be created as they are needed. To meet the performance requirements for the AS/400 low-end and middle models, probably through 1997, various implementations of the Cobra processors can be used. This is not so for the high end of the line.

Rochester has publicly stated that the goal for the high end of the AS/400 line is to increase the overall system performance by five times over a three-year time period. To accomplish this requires an average of 70 percent system performance improvement per year. The use of RISC technology will go a long way toward helping Rochester accomplish this goal. Of course, processor performance is but one element of system performance. Total system performance depends on processor, memory, and I/O performance, as well as on the bandwidth between these elements.

Assuming a balanced approach, where the performance of each element is increased to achieve the overall system performance, we need to increase the performance of the high-end processor itself. There is some capability to increase the speed of a Muskie processor in 1996. For example, the 6.5 nanosecond cycle time (giving 154 MHz) can likely be reduced to somewhere in the range of 5 to 6 nanoseconds. Beyond that, it is not possible to achieve a large speed-up each year in a single processor. To reach the stated performance goal, we will need multiprocessors beyond the current four-way designs. Recall that the Muskie processors are implemented with BiCMOS technology. BiCMOS is fast, but hot. Going to a six-way or an eight-way in the current physical packages is not an option.

This means we need a new high-end processor design for 1997. Endicott was given the responsibility for developing this processor. The design team in Endicott likes to name their processors after snakes, or so most people think. Actually, the names are of high-performance American sports cars, such as the original Ford Cobra.

Like the Cobra processor, the new high-end Endicott processor will be a single-chip design implemented in CMOS technology. Unlike Cobra, it will be multiprocessor enabled to let it be used in n-way configurations. AS/400 models will be available in 2-way, 4-way, 6-way, and 8-way configurations using this new processor. The possibility exists of going beyond 8-way, perhaps as high as 12- or even 16-way configurations.

Like Cobra, this new Endicott processor will be exclusively for the AS/400 and will only implement the tags-active mode. Some changes, however, will be made to the processor memory bus. This bus, which connects the processors and the main memory, is the same one used for other PowerPC processors. The advantage of this bus, which is sometimes called the 6xx bus, is that it will allow the attachment of other processor complexes and different I/O buses.

A separate bus, which is actually a loop, supports the Scalable Coherent Interface Link (SCIL) protocol and is connected to the 6xx bus with a new SCIL chip. One of the SCIL chips and SCIL loops would be used to attach other processor complexes. Another SCIL chip and loop would be used to attach the I/O buses. The SCIL protocol is based on the IEEE SCI standard modified by IBM to achieve the required data integrity for commercial customers. The SCIL protocol is an asynchronous, duplex, point-to-point connection.

Two implementations of the SCIL architecture exist. One implementation, called SCIL:SM (SM is for shared memory), can transfer one gigabyte (8 gigabits) per second and is intended to interconnect the processor complexes. Note that the transfer rate of this bus is eight times that of the fastest optical SPD bus. We will see how the SCIL:SM bus can be used to interconnect processor complexes in a later section. The other implementation, called SCIL:IO, is for connecting I/O buses and can transfer data at 250 megabytes (2 gigabits) per second. The bus control unit for each I/O bus in the system is attached to the SCIL:IO loop.

One of the I/O buses that will be supported on this new Endicott processor is, of course, the SPD bus. Existing AS/400 devices will attach directly to a multiplicity of these buses just as they do today. In addition, the industry-standard, high-performance peripheral component interconnect (PCI) buses will be supported. This means that devices designed to the PCI interface can be attached to an AS/400. In a later section of this chapter, we will discuss the future plans for I/O on the AS/400.

Earlier, we said that we anticipate the need for a PowerPC processor with both tags-active and tags-inactive capability sometime in 1998. The processor design group in Austin is developing this processor. IBM's intention is to replace the entire AS/400 processor line with this new design. In Chapter 2, we saw that the original design for the high-end processor in the 1996-97 time frame was called Belatrix, named after a star in the constellation Orion. That single design, which was to satisfy both NIC and commercial requirements, was overly ambitious for the schedule and was canceled. The new converged design has a more realistic schedule.

This new AS/400 processor will also be based on a single-chip CMOS design. The processor will be able to run at different speeds to make up the implementations within the total family of processors. All these processors will implement both the tags-active and tags-inactive modes to enable any PowerPC operating system. The new processor will also support the PCI interface, so this processor can be sold outside IBM for use in non-IBM systems. This is the first processor that will not be exclusive to the AS/400.

The RISC processor technology described in this section will take the AS/400 through 1998 and even beyond. Several other PowerPC processors are being designed by the Somerset Design Center that are targeted for specific environments, not related to the AS/400. In the following section, we will look at a possible processor design that is beyond RISC and that could form the basis for AS/400 processors after about 1998.

Beyond RISC

Late in 1993, HP held a meeting for computer industry analysts. The company had just spent about one million dollars to license the work of a now-defunct computer company called Multiflow Computers. Multiflow had expertise in Very Long Instruction Word (VLIW) hardware technology and something called trace compiler technology. We will explain both of these technologies later. HP announced that these technologies would be the basis for the successor to their PA-RISC architecture. Their engineers talked about the proposed PA-9000 processor, which they said would be available at the end of the decade and which would use the new technologies.

Joel Birnbaum, head of Hewlett-Packard Laboratories (remember, he was the one who managed the 801 project before going to HP to lead the PA-RISC design), commented on the announcement. He said their experiments indicated that VLIW will be a superior target for binary translation of the PA-RISC instructions. He seemed to indicate that HP planned to do some sort of on-the-fly translation to migrate customers from PA-RISC. There were also hints that those technologies could support other processor architectures as well. These hints confused many in the industry. What was HP up to?

A few months later, HP and Intel, in a joint announcement, cleared up the mystery. They were merging their respective HP-PA and x86 architectures by the end of the decade. The resulting microprocessor, which the press quickly dubbed the P86, is to implement a 64-bit architecture and what HP has described as super-parallelism. Super-parallelism is based on the VLIW technology. The companies stated that the new architecture would also be binary compatible with both predecessors.

Many industry analysts thought the HP/Intel announcement was made five years before the delivery of any products to try to hold off the onslaught of the PowerPC RISC processors, which will surely have an impact on the fortunes of both companies. In any event, the announcements sent many experts in the computer field back to their textbooks to understand what this arcane VLIW technology was all about.

VLIW is a technology that has the potential to reverse the trend of RISC processors towards more on-chip complexity. Earlier, we called these processors Brainiacs because of this added complexity. Simpler designs, such as the Speed Demons, can spin faster and achieve higher MHz ratings. VLIW pushes the complexity back to the compilers.

The problem with RISC processors, and the reason for all the complex hardware, is the difficulty with keeping the pipelines full. We saw that most RISC designs have the ability to dispatch only a small number of instructions, say three or four, in a single cycle. This limits the amount of instruction parallelism we can get in a single processor to the number of instructions that can be dispatched. If I can only dispatch a maximum of four instructions per cycle, the maximum parallelism I can ever achieve is four times and, due to dependencies between instructions as well as branches, the average parallelism is likely to be around two times or even less on some real-world workload.

As an example, let's look at the Muskie processor. In Chapter 2, we saw that for every cycle this processor can fetch eight instructions from its instruction cache — the Muskie's instruction cache is 32 bytes wide and each PowerPC instruction occupies four bytes. Yet this processor can dispatch only four instructions in a single cycle. Why can't it dispatch all eight of the instructions it can fetch in a single cycle?

The answer to this question has to do with the limitations of a RISC processor. First, a RISC processor usually doesn't have enough independent functional units to allow eight instructions to run in parallel — this is a hardware technology limitation. The second limitation is that there is not enough time in a cycle to analyze eight instructions, determine which functional units are not busy, and send each of the eight instructions to the appropriate functional unit. Taking enough time to do all of this would slow down the cycle time and reduce the processor performance. The third limitation is the compiler's inability to package eight independent instructions that can be dispatched each and every cycle.

Remember that the first RISC processor (the 801) was designed in the mid-1970s, and it could only fetch and dispatch one instruction per cycle. Most of the RISC processors of the 1980s used this same design. It wasn't until 1990 that the first superscalar RISC processor with its multiple functional units appeared in the RS/6000. This superscalar design recognized that compilers had become more sophisticated in their ability to schedule multiple instructions for multiple functional units, so the hardware was built to fetch and dispatch multiple instructions per cycle. A VLIW design takes this to the next logical step.

Hardware technologies have continued to advance so that soon even a single-chip processor will be able to have lots of independent functional units; processors with 16 or more functional units will be possible in the next few years. Compiler technology has also improved to the point that more instruction parallelism can be recognized and more independent functional units can be scheduled. This ability to schedule more instructions would be useless if the processor hardware could only dispatch a few instructions per cycle, as does a RISC processor. To solve this problem, a VLIW design takes the dispatching function away from the processor hardware.

Rather than having the processor hardware analyze each instruction in the instruction stream and then dispatch the instructions one at a time to the functional units, as a RISC processor does, the VLIW compiler creates a separate instruction for each functional unit for each cycle. For example, if we have 16 functional units, the compiler will create 16 instructions for each processor cycle. Each cycle, the VLIW processor will fetch from its instruction cache all 16 instructions; but unlike a RISC processor, which has to analyze which functional unit can take which instruction, the VLIW processor simply sends each instruction to its corresponding functional unit. The first instruction is sent to the first functional unit, the second instruction is sent to the second functional unit, and so on. Of course, if the compiler has no work for some functional unit during a given cycle, it still has to create a no-operation instruction for that unit. Because there is no thinking on the part of the VLIW processor, the cycle time of a VLIW processor can be shorter than that of an equivalent RISC processor built from the same hardware technology. This shorter cycle time, plus the increased instruction-level parallelism that can be achieved with more usable functional units, gives a VLIW design a performance advantage over the RISC design.

"Why is it called a VLIW processor?" you might ask. Well, the compiler packages all those independent instructions for each cycle into one *very long instruction word* — hence, the VLIW name. The processor fetches one of these very long words from its instruction cache each cycle. Let's see, if we have 16 instructions, each of which is four bytes long, we have a 64-byte- (512 bit) long instruction word. That certainly qualifies as a very long instruction word.

The back end of the compiler (which is similar to the AS/400's translator) for a VLIW processor has the ultimate responsibility to find enough useful work for the processor to do each cycle and to create the instructions to perform that work. HP representatives said at the time of their announcement that they were hoping to get from 4 to 20 useful instructions executed per cycle, which would produce throughputs in the giga-instruction-per-second range.

Some of the industry experts wondered at the time whether HP and Intel had just pulled off the technology coup of the century and had indeed found the successor to RISC technology. Obviously, they speculated, the two companies would make it impossible for anyone else to build P86-compatible processors by surrounding their VLIW design with patents.

In Rochester, the news was met with a great deal of glee. What no one else in the industry knew is that a VLIW design effort had been underway in the Rochester laboratory for more than five years. Furthermore, the major VLIW patents in the last few years all belong to the folks in Rochester. The HP/Intel announcement indicated there were still some inventions required to make their design work. We in Rochester chuckled at the thought that HP might be counting on the use of our VLIW patents.

The Challenge of VLIW Technology
VLIW technology has not been very aggressively pursued in the computer industry because many people questioned its applicability to commercial processing. While this technology offers some great potential performance gains, it also has several problems that must be overcome.

The biggest problem with the VLIW approach is that the back end of the compiler needs to be intimately tied to the hardware. To schedule an instruction for each functional unit in the processor, the compiler needs to know exactly what units are present on the chip and how they relate to one another. This makes it difficult, if not impossible, to use the same compiler output on different chip implementations, because there is no binary compatibility.

To solve this problem, HP, in its original announcement, said it was looking at three alternatives. The first was on-the-fly translation, where the output from a compiler (maybe the intermediate code out of the front end of the compiler) would be translated into the machine code as it is loaded into the processor to execute. The idea is that different chip implementations could be built and the compiled code would be optimized dynamically.

This is similar to the approach Intel uses in its P6 processor, where the x86 instructions are converted on-the-fly to a sequence of RISC-like instructions right on the chip. Intel calls these RISC-like instructions micro-ops and describes this technique as dynamic execution. The core of the P6 processor then takes these micro-ops and executes them in a pipelined implementation that looks just like a RISC processor.

Intel is not the first to do this. NexGen, another x86 chip maker, was the first to introduce this idea in its Nx586. NexGen calls its internal instructions RISC86 instructions. AMD's K5, another x86 chip, is similar with its use of R-ops. Cyrix's M1 does not use the same approach, but it does use other RISC techniques to achieve similar efficiencies.

This dynamic execution approach works for a RISC processor, as these several vendors' products demonstrate, but it likely will not work well for a VLIW processor. The reason has to do with the amount of parallelism in the instruction stream.

A RISC processor looks at the next three to six instructions in the instruction stream and dispatches them to as many functional units in the processor as are available. The RISC compilers are responsible for scheduling independent instructions in that instruction stream, so as many as possible can be dispatched by the processor each cycle. The back end of the compiler takes the intermediate text and generates the binary-level machine instructions. To schedule these instructions for the processor usually requires examining the generated instructions from a range of intermediate text to find enough independent ones to schedule.

In a VLIW machine, the number of functional units increases dramatically to achieve more parallelism. A number from 16 to 32 functional units is not unreasonable in the near term, with even larger numbers possible later on. To schedule instructions for this kind of machine requires the back end of the compiler to examine a much larger range of intermediate instructions. The compiler may have to look at the generated code from hundreds or even thousands of intermediate instructions to find 16 to 32 independent binary-level instructions to be dispatched each cycle. The dynamic, on-the-fly approach looks at only one intermediate instruction at a time. The chances of this approach working efficiently are slim.

HP recognized the on-the-fly approach might be a problem, so it announced it was considering other approaches. One is a compiler that produces two binary outputs, conventional PA-RISC and VLIW. This presumably would mean existing HP customers would only have to recompile all their applications to move to the new architecture. Just because this has never before been accomplished in the computer industry is no reason to dismiss it. However, it is highly unlikely that a single compiler could generate optimized code for two such different architectures. The second approach HP said it is considering is to run PA-RISC binaries through a software translator to produce the VLIW instructions. The obvious reason HP is looking at all these alternatives is to ease its user's migration to the new architecture. What is also obvious is that the company doesn't yet have a solution.

Of course, if HP had a technology-independent architecture instead of a processor-centric architecture like PA-RISC is, all of these problems would simply go away. The AS/400 is pursuing VLIW because there is no problem upgrading customers to any new processor technology.

History of Long Instruction Word Machines in Rochester

The interest in long instruction word machines started in the early 1980s in Rochester. At that time, we established an advanced technology organization in the Rochester laboratory to investigate new technologies that we might someday use in our future systems. My role in that organization was to manage the systems group.

In some respects the advanced technology organization was a sanctioned skunkworks that reported to the laboratory director. We even located in a different building, separate from the laboratory, so no one quite knew what we were doing. This was the time of the Fort Knox development in Rochester, and we needed a group of dedicated people to work on new technologies for our existing systems if Fort Knox failed.

We had no trouble attracting good people to this organization, including architects such as Dick Bains and Roy Hoffman from the System/38 and Dick Mustain from the System/36. We were a group of nonbelievers when it came to Fort Knox, so this was an opportunity to show what could be accomplished with our existing systems. As a result, we had several leading-edge technology projects underway. Many of the advanced technologies that later appeared in the AS/400 came from this group. Examples of these include image, neural networks, telephony, and fax technologies. Others will appear in the future.

In the systems group, we concentrated on high-performance computing and parallel processing, mostly with the System/38. We were convinced that some day we would build very high-end models of a System/38 and we wanted to be ready for that day. One of the areas, led by Roy Hoffman, was the exploration of co-processors. The idea was to add special-purpose processors to the System/38 to efficiently execute applications for which the System/38 was not well suited. One of the co-processors we attached to a System/38 was a high-performance, floating-point engine. In a later section, we will look at the future AS/400 plans for co-processors, which we now call application engines.

The idea in an advanced technology area is not necessarily to do the actual design to be shipped to customers, but to demonstrate that the ideas are sound and the design can be built. And, the best way to demonstrate an idea is to build a working prototype. As long as we were at it, we decided for the floating-point project to go all out and build a System/38 with the performance of a supercomputer. Our internal goal was to demonstrate applications with heavy floating-point usage running on our prototype that would outperform a System/390 with its vector feature.

Floating Point Systems (FPS) in 1975 introduced the AP-120B, which was the first member of FPS's array processor family. This array processor was primarily used in signal processing. In 1980, the FPS-164 was introduced to extend the AP architecture into large-scale scientific processing. Array processors operate on ordered sets of data, usually vectors or matrices. The FPS-164 was a full 64-bit processor designed for this type of scientific computing. It could hold its own against any of the supercomputers of the day, including the Crays.

The FPS processor was not a stand-alone system. It would always be attached to some other host computer system. We thought this would make a great co-processor for a System/38, so we bought an FPS-164 and attached it to a System/38. We also began to track down commercial applications that needed high-performance, floating-point computations. We wanted to show that this type of computing could be used for more than just scientific computing. We found several applications; the ones that held the most promise came from the banking and securities industries.

The FPS-164 was not exactly a small system. Physically, this co-processor was much bigger than the System/38. It also had a few environmental requirements that the System/38 didn't need, such as lots of cold air. We built a special room with a raised floor and some of the biggest air conditioners our maintenance people had ever installed in such a room. The fans in the FPS box drew cool air from under the floor. When we turned the unit on, it sounded like a very noisy hovercraft was in the room with us. When it was off, it was too cold for any of us to work in the room. For a computing engine, however, the FPS-164 was really fast.

FPS had plans to bring out newer technology versions of the FPS-164 that would operate in an office environment and easily fit along side of the System/38. But we never had a chance to add one of these to the System/38, because the Fort Knox project was canceled and we needed to put all of our energies into Silverlake. We did learn several things from this work that will find their way into future AS/400s. Two of those are co-processors and VLIW.

The FPS systems were among the first long instruction word machines containing multiple operations per instruction. The machine had 10 functional units and each unit needed its own subinstruction every cycle. The long instruction word had separate subinstructions for each of the 10 functional units. A complete vector loop was possible in a single instruction.

Instead of using an optimizing compiler to create the long instruction words, the machine provided assembly language libraries so it could be used efficiently. The host computer would handle the program logic and call out the long instruction word routines to be run on the FPS machine. There were similarities between this type of programming and wide-word microcode such as the HMC used in the System/38. Although our HMC instructions did not have as many bits as the long instruction word in the FPS, each HMC instruction did start multiple functions in the System/38 processor. For a time, we looked at how we could incorporate some of the techniques used to dispatch the multiple functional units into our HMC.

At about the same time, a group of researchers at Yale University proposed creating a machine with a very wide instruction (512 bits), and they named this type of machine a VLIW. The code was generated for this machine with a technique called trace scheduling. This software approach analyzes a routine to find the most likely sequence of operations, called a trace, and then compacts this sequence into a small number of wide instructions. This technique had originally been developed to generate horizontal microcode, such as the HMC. The machine from Multiflow Computers commercialized the ideas developed at Yale, but Multiflow Computers eventually failed due to a lack of financial backing.

Rochester continued to have an interest in VLIW machines in the late 1980s, especially as this technology related to the HMC. After the AS/400 was announced, work started on the processor design for the next generation of systems. VLIW was a part of that design.

VLIW for AS/400

One of the leaders of the VLIW effort that began in Rochester several years ago was Dave Luick. Dave was one of our original processor designers who first led the design of the System/38 Model 7 processor, and he has been involved with every one since that time. He was always one to push the limits of high-performance processor technology and was very interested in how some of the VLIW techniques could be applied to the HMC. The C-RISC processor, discussed in Chapter 2, was being designed as the processor for the Advanced Series before we adopted the PowerPC technology. C-RISC had some RISC capabilities, but it also had an HMC with many characteristics of a VLIW machine, thanks to Dave and others who shared the same vision for processor design.

Dave was a member of our 10-person team in 1991 that was to evaluate the use of PowerPC processors for the AS/400. After we decided to go with the PowerPC technology, he and others turned their attention to building a PowerPC-compatible VLIW machine. Because VLIW is so very dependent on compiler technology, this team immediately formed a joint effort with IBM Research. In Research, a group of people was working on VLIW, but this group needed a platform that could use this technology. Most systems have great difficulty adopting such a new technology without creating a negative impact on their customer base. But the AS/400's technology independence makes that a non-issue. AS/400 and VLIW may be the perfect combination for everyone.

The VLIW work in Rochester has shown that this technology has tremendous potential to increase the AS/400 processor performance. First, the processor cycle times can be decreased because of the simpler structure — it is more like a Speed Demon design. For a given technology, processor chips that run at twice the speed of a standard PowerPC are possible. Second, it is possible to achieve far more parallelism than with a RISC design. Instead of only 5 or 6 pipelines, 16 or even more are achievable on a single chip in the next couple of years.

To illustrate, suppose we build a single-chip CMOS processor with a speed of 154 MHz, the same speed as a Muskie. Now suppose we build a VLIW processor using the same CMOS technology. We would have a single-chip processor running at 308 MHz. Common wisdom says our VLIW processor would be twice as fast as our RISC processor because of the faster cycle time. Performance work done in Rochester shows that our VLIW processor design is more like 12 times faster than the RISC processor on a commercial workload. Furthermore, the Rochester VLIW design is fully PowerPC compatible and could possibly be shipped in an AS/400 as early as 1998. Maybe we will even sell some of them to HP.

So far, we have only talked about single processors and how they might be incorporated into the AS/400. Today, we support n-way processing with up to four processors. In the next section, we will look at how n-way processing will likely evolve over the next few years.

The Future of Multiprocessor Systems

In the computer industry today, most vendors are shipping systems that contain multiple processors. The way in which these processors are interconnected determines the type of applications that can be efficiently run and how easy it is to move an application designed for a single processor to a multiple processor configuration.

The usual reason for having multiple processors is to have scalability of systems for performance reasons. The two ways to classify these machines are to group them into either multicomputer clusters or symmetric multiprocessing (SMP). Another reason for having multiple processors is to provide computing facilities not available in the main processor. This usually takes the form of a co-processor or an accelerator, and it is sometimes called asymmetric multiprocessing (ASMP). For our purposes, we are going to hold off a discussion of ASMP until we get to the subject of application engines.

Multicomputer Clusters

A multicomputer cluster is composed of multiple nodes typically interconnected through the use of a LAN or a WAN. Each node can have one or more processors and can be packaged in separate physical boxes. An example of a multicomputer cluster is OptiConnect for OS/400, which we discussed in Chapter 6.

Multicomputer clusters have several common characteristics. Each node in the cluster runs its own operating system and can address only the memory contained in the node itself. All sharing between nodes is accomplished by passing messages in the software. The nodes in the cluster are connected via an I/O link, typically a high-speed LAN.

The structure just described does not present to the user the image of a single system. The user still sees and manages multiple systems. Partitioning the workload, security management, and maintenance must be handled for each computer in the cluster. Efforts are underway in the industry to create a cluster with a single-system image, but so far there are none.

Multicomputer clusters are also called *loosely coupled* systems. A loosely coupled system works very well where applications can be split into separate pieces with little or no sharing between the pieces. Another way to look at this is to recognize that each processor has its own physical and virtual memory. From a memory perspective, there is no sharing of memory. Any sharing is done in the secondary storage system. If one job needs to communicate or share data with another job in a different node, it does so by sending messages across the network. For this reason, this type of system has also been called a message-passing model.

There are variations on this message-passing model. Suppose we put several processors in a single box and replace the I/O connection (LAN or WAN) with a high-performance switch. Doing this could greatly increase the bandwidth and reduce the time it takes to pass messages. We would still not, however, have a single-system image, so applications still have to be split, with sharing done outside of the memory. The IBM RS/6000 SP, which we first described in Chapter 2, is a good example of this message-passing type of system.

Symmetric Multiprocessing

We introduced the SMP class of machines in Chapter 9 while discussing process management considerations for multiprocessing. To recap, all processors in the SMP machine have identical capabilities. A process can be executed on any processor. Other characteristics of this class of machine include a single address space with shared main memory, a single I/O subsystem shared by all processors, and one copy of the operating system, which is executed by all processors. This class of machine presents a single-system image to the user.

Within the SMP classification are two types of architectures, based on the way they share main memory. The two types have the generic names uniform memory access (UMA) and non-uniform memory access (NUMA). Both these types will play an important role in the future of the AS/400. Let's look at the characteristics of each.

All processors in a UMA system are connected to a shared main memory via a single memory bus or memory switch. This single connection means it will take the same amount of time for any processor to get to any main memory location. This is why it is called uniform memory access. N-way processing in the AS/400 is a UMA system. Although UMA is a more descriptive name for this type of system, in the industry it is more commonly called a *tightly coupled* system.

This type of system has advantages over the loosely coupled model. Any processor can directly access any part of the main memory and all applications can share all instructions and data. This means there is no impact on applications. An application designed for a single processor system will, in general, see better performance when run on a tightly coupled system with no changes to the application. This is not so for a loosely coupled system where the application must be restructured to run on the separate processors.

The disadvantage of a tightly coupled system is the number of processors that can be supported is much smaller than for the loosely coupled model. The bottleneck is the single main memory interface. As more processors are added, there is more memory contention. The resulting improvement in system performance is lessened with each new processor. At some point, adding another processor results in the memory interface being unable to support the demands of another processor; and there is no gain in system performance.

With today's processor and memory technologies, a reasonable upper limit is eight processors sharing a common memory. The AS/400 will implement 6-way and 8-way multiprocessing with up to 16 of the new Endicott processors. As mentioned earlier, we are considering tightly coupled AS/400 systems with up to 12 of the Endicott processors. There is work going on in IBM to create high-speed switches between processors and memories to enable tightly coupled systems with many more processors. While we expect to see from 8 to 16 processors connected by such switches in the next few years, we are nowhere near having hundreds of processors in a tightly coupled system.

Another way to look at loosely and tightly coupled systems is in terms of the time required to access a shared piece of data. A loosely coupled system can send a request to another processor for the data, or the information to be shared can be in the file system. In either case, the time required is in the millisecond range. A tightly coupled system has direct access to all data in memory, so the time required is in the nanosecond range. Perhaps there is something in between that can combine the best of both worlds and still achieve a sharing of data in the microsecond range? There is, and it is called a *firmly coupled* system.[2]

Firmly Coupled Multiprocessing

Commercial applications share data, as we have seen on numerous occasions in the previous chapters. A tightly coupled system, with total memory sharing, is ideally suited for commercial applications. Some special-purpose commercial applications, such as database queries or compiles that can be split to work on separate sets of data, work well for loosely coupled systems. Many technical computing applications, which by their very nature tend to be repetitive and to share little, can also exploit a loosely coupled system.

A loosely coupled system has the advantage that more processors can be added and the performance can improve linearly. As we just saw, the number of processors in a tightly coupled system is limited. We wanted to grow the number of processors in an AS/400, but we didn't know how best to do it.

It was then that a group of people led by Dick Booth in Rochester had an idea. Dick for a time had taken an assignment to work on multiprocessors at IBM Research. While he was there, an idea for a system design that was between loosely and tightly coupled systems emerged. He believed the idea would work for the AS/400 and brought it back to Rochester.

Dick convinced others that this was a good idea, and together the members of this small group began to sell their idea. They established a joint project with IBM Research in 1991 and started work on a prototype system. Like most new ideas, this one was met with some skepticism. The group persisted.

[2] The firmly coupled name was selected because this type of system fits somewhere between tightly coupled and loosely coupled systems. The name *snuggly coupled* was briefly considered, but it didn't seem macho enough for a high-powered computer system.

They finished the prototype and demonstrated that the idea did indeed work. Slowly, the technical community began to come around. Firmly coupled systems, as this group called them, will likely be part of the AS/400's future. Others in IBM are just beginning to recognize the value of this approach for use in other systems.

A firmly coupled system is a specific architecture in the NUMA classification of SMP machines. Instead of having a single shared main memory, as the UMA class does, the NUMA class partitions the shared memory among the processors. A simple way to think about this is to picture a piece of the shared memory packaged with each processor in the system and a high-speed global interconnection between the shared memory pieces. Each processor has its own local memory bus connected to its piece of the shared main memory, but any processor can access any location in the shared memory across the global interconnection. The difference is the time required for the access. Local accesses will be faster than global accesses. This is why this class of machine is described as a non-uniform access machine.

Other than the access-time differences, this is an SMP machine. The shared-memory bottleneck has been moved from the single-memory interconnection to the global interconnection. This type of system works well if most of the memory accesses are local and just a small percentage of the accesses go across the global interconnection. In the industry, this type of machine has commonly been called a distributed shared-memory machine.

The firmly coupled system is a distributed shared-memory machine designed specifically for the AS/400. The single, real main-memory address space is distributed across the entire machine with each node assigned a range of the real address space. Each node can be a single processor or an n-way processor. Because this is a shared-memory system, any application or operating system software that runs on an n-way runs on a firmly coupled system with no changes required.

The difference between an n-way and a firmly coupled system is that performance of the firmly coupled system is very dependent on the memory reference patterns. A *local* memory reference uses a real main memory address contained in the same node. A *non-local* memory reference uses a real main memory address contained in some other node. If memory reference patterns are randomly distributed across the nodes, the global interconnection will become the bottleneck. To prevent this, the memory reference pattern must be managed such that the majority of references are local. The design point of the AS/400 is to have a non-local memory access be approximately four times slower than a local memory access. To achieve good system throughput, the design goal is to have 90 percent local and 10 percent non-local memory accesses.

The initial implementation of a firmly coupled system will have up to four nodes of 8-way processors, for a total of 32 processors. For this system, a global interconnection loop that supports the SCIL:SM protocol was selected.

Earlier, we saw that the SCIL:SM loop can support a transfer rate of 1 gigabyte per second over a copper bus. Work is underway to replace the copper media with parallel fiber optics. Each 8-way processor node has its own cache memories, so the only traffic over the global bus is for cache misses to a non-local memory.

The reason for pursuing high-performance uniprocessors, such as the VLIW machines, and high-performance multiprocessors, such as the SMP machines, is sometimes questioned. Why does the AS/400 need both? The answer is because they address different performance needs. The faster a uniprocessor runs, the better the response time will be for users of the system.

SMP technology, either n-way or firmly coupled systems, achieves greater throughput for a system. The unit of dispatchable work for these SMP systems is relatively large (a few hundred thousand instructions). As a result, adding more processors increases the number of jobs that can be run or the number of users that can be supported, but it does not reduce the response time for any one user.

The AS/400 will continue to pursue both. To satisfy higher throughput requirements, we will use SMP technologies. To satisfy lower response-time requirements, we will use faster uniprocessors. Combining the two technologies into a single AS/400 system should provide some impressive machines.

Let's see, 32 high-performance 64-bit PowerPC RISC processors should certainly be able to run the payroll program — or just about anything else an AS/400 customer wants to run. If that isn't enough, we can always add more nodes or wait for the VLIW processors. These processor technologies should keep us until the year 2000.

The Future of AS/400 I/O

The higher-performance processors for future AS/400 systems are pretty worthless if we can't feed enough data into the processors to keep them busy. In this section, we will look at where we are going with IOPs, I/O buses, and even some high-performance devices.

Future IOP Technology

In Chapter 10 we saw how the IOPs are attached to an AS/400. The largest current system (530 or 53S) can have 19 SPD buses with 238 IOPs attached. This is for a single node system. With a four-node, firmly coupled system these numbers will become 76 SPD buses and 942 IOPs. More nodes can be added if needed.

The current IOPs are mostly Motorola microprocessors. Each has its own memory and runs a special-purpose, real-time operating system. New IOPs will use PowerPC processors. They will be from the standard 32-bit family of PowerPC processors built in Burlington. Over time, all IOPs will move to this processor technology.

The real-time operating systems running on the current IOPs have been updated many times over the last several years, just as any other operating system has been. So there can be different versions running on different IOPs in the same AS/400. The latest version of this operating system has been ported to the PowerPC processors. At some time in the future, we may develop a new real-time operating system for the PowerPC processors that will be microkernel based. Part of the reason we may want to do this is to make this software more portable, allowing it to run on other microprocessor implementations.

With the PowerPC processors, the IOPs will also have the capability to run other operating systems. These co-processors will also play a major role in future AS/400s, as we will see shortly.

The use of the 6xx bus and the attachment of the SCIL I/O loops to our processors in 1997 and beyond gives us the chance to attach different types of I/O devices. In addition to the devices attached to the SPD bus, we will attach devices to the PCI bus. The PCI bus interface is rapidly becoming the standard for attaching devices to PCs. Supporting this bus on the AS/400 will allow the attachment of any of these devices in the future. Who knows? We may even be able to attach a Sound Blaster card to the AS/400.

Existing SPD I/O devices continue to improve with time; and new devices, either SPD or PCI bus attached, will be added to the AS/400. New networks, such as the Asynchronous Transfer Mode (ATM) networks,[3] are being attached to provide speeds up to 1,000 times faster than the physical links in common use today. All these are important, but from a system performance perspective, the most important devices are the disk drives. We need to look at the future of these devices.

[3] At the June, 1995, AS/400 announcement, a statement of direction on ATM support was made and a prototype of the ATM I/O card was shown to the press. Sharp-eyed reporters noted the I/O card contained a PowerPC 603 processor and a PCI bus interface.

Disk Arrays

Individual disk devices are getting faster, but at nowhere near the rate needed to keep up with processor technology. Besides, they are mechanical devices, which means it is far more difficult to increase their speed. Rather than just depending on performance improvements in the devices themselves, we need to use these devices in different configurations.

Several vendors have recently announced the technique of *striping* data across an array of multiple disks. They are presenting this as a major breakthrough to increase system performance. This technique of striping data across multiple disks first appeared on a commercial system in the System/38. As we previously saw, in a System/38 or an AS/400 application, several system objects are used. We decided for performance reasons to distribute the various objects across multiple disks so that they could be accessed in parallel. Data striping has been used on System/38 and AS/400 systems ever since.

The technique just described improves the AS/400 system performance when more than one object needs to be read or written. If, however, we want to improve the performance of an access to a single record, this striping technique does nothing to help. A variation of the data striping technique that can achieve a performance improvement for individual records is to spin of all the disks in the array synchronously. This means that the arms on all disks are always over the same track, and sector 0 on every disk rotates under the head at exactly the same time. This synchronization now allows single records to be spread across all the disks in the array, thereby improving the performance for all individual data transfers.

To see how this works, imagine we have an array of four disks spinning synchronously. Assuming we have enough device controllers and data paths, we could write parts of a single record to each disk in parallel. One fourth of the total record would be written to the first disk; another fourth of the same record would be written to the second disk; and so on. The entire record could be written to the four disks in one fourth the amount of time it would take to write the record to a single disk. The same is true when we go to read the record.

From a system perspective, this array would appear to be a single disk with a single arm, but it would have a transfer rate that is four times that of any single disk in the array. This is analogous to increasing the rotational speed of the disk by a factor of four times; something that may not be physically possible.

This technique of synchronizing the spinning disks in an array has been used for years by supercomputers to achieve high-performance transfers of data in and out of the systems. The downside of this approach is that the array appears to the system to only have a single arm. As the cost of these disk arrays comes down, so that many of them can be attached to a system, this may be a way to improve system performance without having to wait for mechanical performance improvements.

In Chapter 8, we saw that one of the advantages of the single-level store was that no application or operating system software above the MI even knows about disk drives. Part of the reason for hiding the disks was the thought that someday this mechanical technology would be replaced by something else. Semiconductor disks (large semiconductor memories with battery backup) may provide one such possibility, but there are others.[4]

Let's now turn our attention to some of the software technologies that will take the AS/400 into the future.

Future AS/400 Software Technologies

Applications, applications, applications. That's what the AS/400 is all about. It would be wonderful if every possible application could run on any system, but that is not reality. Many AS/400 customers want to run applications that are written for another system, or more specifically, for another operating system. To do so today means having to deal with and support different operating systems, usually on different hardware platforms.

[4] In the past few years, I have jokingly proposed using some unusual new memory technologies, such as fungus memories, in future AS/400s. A recent article in *Science* magazine proposed the use of the protein bacteriorhodopsin as a memory technology. This protein can be formed into cubes and accessed a plane at a time. Different colors of light drive the protein through a three-phase structural cycle. These cycles can be used as states in the memory.

Businesses need the applications that run on these systems, and so they put up with the added expenses of managing the multiple systems. If a single system could manage all this by providing a single-system image without requiring customer involvement with the multiple operating systems, then the overall cost of doing business could be reduced. The AS/400's Advanced Application Architecture makes this possible. In the following sections, we will look at the technologies that will enable this on the AS/400 and the approaches we will likely use to add the new applications.

Microkernels

In Chapter 4, we briefly introduced the notion of a microkernel and how we incorporated similar technologies in SLIC to support the System/36 personality. In this section, we will look at how the microkernel technology might be used in the future.

A microkernel is a small operating-system core that handles the lowest-level functions in the system. The reason for using a microkernel is to provide the foundation for building a portable operating system. Other operating system functions would be built in a modular fashion using some high-level language or even object technology to run on top of the microkernel. With such a structure, moving the operating system to another processor should only involve porting the microkernel. Of course, a 32-bit microkernel will still only run on 32-bit hardware.

As we discussed earlier, the development of the Mach microkernel began in 1985 at Carnegie Mellon University (CMU). The first implementation was running on a Digital VAX minicomputer in the spring of 1986. Shortly after that, an implementation for the IBM PC RT was started. IBM was interested in the idea of a future microkernel-based operating system, and worked with the Open Software Foundation (OSF) to extend the Mach 3.0 microkernel to support parallel processing and real-time operations. This extended microkernel is called the IBM Microkernel.

Several vendors have announced other microkernel-based operating systems. Microsoft's Windows NT, for example, is microkernel based. Other microkernel-based operating systems from vendors such as Apple, Novell, Sun, OSF, Next, and Taligent are either available or being developed.

With the microkernel technology, the computer industry had the opportunity to achieve a level of commonality across all operating systems. If the major vendors could agree on a single version of a microkernel, all operating systems could run on the same base. Once the common microkernel had been ported to a given hardware platform, all of the operating systems would be immediately available. The ability to share system software outside of the microkernel would also be easy to do. An ISV developing a system software component, such as a database, would immediately be able to deliver that component on all the operating systems.

As with so many standards, however, this was not to be. The big battle in the industry is not whether to build a microkernel-based operating system, but how to build the microkernel and what functions belong inside or outside of this kernel. The result is almost as many microkernels as there are microkernel-based operating systems; some have commonalities that can be exploited, but most do not.

For some idea of the differences, consider where device drivers should be placed. IBM says they should be outside of the microkernel so others could easily build new ones. OSF says device drivers belong in the microkernel. Microsoft says they should run in the microkernel's address space, but only use limited functions in the microkernel.

Some of these decisions depend on whether the particular microkernel is to be used for multiple operating systems, or just to port a single operating system to multiple hardware platforms. These different objectives lead to different microkernel tradeoffs.

For example, IBM's implementation, which is designed to support multiple operating systems, locates the scheduling policy outside of the microkernel. Only the process dispatch is in the microkernel. This separates policy from implementation and allows different operating systems to choose their own policy while still using the same microkernel. This is important, because different systems are designed to support different application environments. An optimum scheduling policy for a multiuser commercial system is very different from one designed for a single-user workstation. This is again a recognition that one size does not fit all.

Workplace Technologies

Within IBM, a project was undertaken in 1993 to use common software components, including the microkernel, across IBM's major operating systems. It was announced that the three operating systems that would eventually use the PowerPC processors (OS/2, AIX, and OS/400) would share all these technologies. The mainframe operating system (MVS) would share some technologies, but not the microkernel.

The project, called Workplace, was intended to provide a very efficient way for IBM to share software technologies across its operating systems. Unfortunately, Workplace was very misunderstood in much of the industry. Some people thought this was IBM's attempt to converge the three operating systems into a single new operating system, called Workplace OS. To them, it looked like a reincarnation of Fort Knox, and they questioned why it would work now when it had failed in the past.

Others in the industry focused on the possibility of running multiple operating systems on the same hardware. They envisioned a system concurrently running OS/400, AIX, and OS/2 personalities. Many of them wondered how a customer would deal with this multiple-headed monster. The subject of dominant personalities was a topic of many conversations.

The real intention of Workplace was none of the above. The idea behind it was to allow sharing of common software technologies and components across IBM's operating systems. A new operating system component could be written once and then would be available for use in any of the operating systems. Each operating system would continue to maintain its unique design point and select only those components that made sense for that design point. For example, a single-user OS/2 operating system has very different requirements than do multiuser operating systems such as OS/400 and AIX. All components could not be shared, but many could; and that was the value of Workplace.

To accomplish this sharing of software technologies, a new organization was announced in mid-1994. The new organization was made a part of the Personal Systems Products (PSP) division and was managed by Dave Schleicher, the former head of AS/400 development in Rochester. Some of our development programmers from Rochester, as well as programmers from Austin and Boca Raton, were assigned to work in this new organization.

The early work on the IBM microkernel was to support the 32-bit, single-user OS/2 client operating system. This original microkernel would not support either OS/400 or AIX environments without significant enhancements. The responsibility for extending the microkernel so that it could be used for something other than a client operating system was begun. The PSP group in Rochester was given this responsibility to extend the microkernel to a full 64-bit implementation.

There was absolutely no way to have a 64-bit, multiuser microkernel ready for the announcement of the RISC-based AS/400s. We had been working on SLIC two years and knew we would drastically delay the project if we even tried to switch to a microkernel base at this late date. We had already incorporated some of the same technologies used in a microkernel, like a message-based dispatcher, so we knew we had a chance to add more later.

When the 64-bit, multiuser microkernel would be available, we intended to put it into the AS/400. We thought about how to do this and quickly decided the best way was to put the microkernel alongside SLIC. Rather than attempt to put one kernel on top of another, we would have two kernels linked together running on the same hardware. The PSP group in Rochester began to develop the hooks needed for the two operating system kernels to coexist and to share some of the same functions. For example, they were able to share a single dispatching function that could dispatch work on either the SLIC or the microkernel side.

The original vision for Workplace was significantly scaled back later in 1994 because of the overall expense of the project and IBM management's unwillingness to fund the total project. OS/2 continued to use the microkernel as the base for its new PowerPC implementation, but AIX opted out because of the expense involved to move to a new microkernel base. In Rochester, PSP developers continued to work on the 64-bit version of the microkernel for use in future server versions of OS/2. Because many of the hooks into SLIC had already been defined, there was still the capability to put the microkernel on the AS/400 and share some software technologies and components with OS/2.

The possibility of sometime in the future sharing some software technologies and components with OS/2 running on the same processor as OS/400 is but one way of bringing new applications to the AS/400. Another is through the use of application engines.

Application Engines

The AS/400 has never had a shortage of processors. In addition to the main processors, up to 238 IOPs can be attached, and these numbers will grow dramatically in the next couple of years. With all of these processors moving to PowerPC technology, we have some exciting possibilities. Why not use some of those PowerPC-based IOPs to run user applications?

In the early 1980s, we started to work on a co-processor approach to bring new applications to our systems, as we described earlier in this chapter. We learned a great deal about how best to do this. Based on some of those early experiences, work was started around 1990 to add a RISC co-processor to the AS/400. Not surprisingly, Roy Hoffman led this work. He proposed to incorporate a POWER processor from the RS/6000 into the AS/400 and to run the AIX operating system on that processor. Unix applications could then run directly on this co-processor. A prototype showed that this approach was feasible. We were just starting to develop our own RISC processor at the time and decided we were not ready to divert development funds to make the co-processor approach a reality. A couple years later, however, we were ready.

Our first venture into using co-processors as application engines was with the FSIOP discussed in Chapter 11. We started with a double-wide I/O card that could support one or two LAN ports. Normally, we would package a standard IOP and its memory on such a card. That standard IOP would run the special-purpose, real-time operating system used for normal I/O operations. This time, we replaced the standard IOP and its memory with a 66 MHz Intel 486 processor and its memory. Instead of using the IOP operating system, we put OS/2 on the Intel processor.

We now had a processor and an operating system capable of managing the LANs that were attached to the card. But then, the standard IOP and its operating system can do that. What is different with the Intel processor and OS/2 is that we can now run the actual user application in this processor. There is no need to run the application back in the main processor and then to communicate with the IOP to get to clients on the LAN. This ability to offload the application to an outboard processor can greatly enhance the system performance, as has been demonstrated with various server benchmarks using the FSIOP.

Keep in mind that the AS/400 is a server, so we are interested in server, not client, applications for our application engines. We originally selected PC file-server applications. The first one announced was LAN Server for OS/400 followed by Novell NetWare. Because many of our customers wanted to use Lotus Notes in their businesses, we added the support to let the FSIOP be a Notes server. This was a good beginning, but it was only a beginning.

For our application engine hardware, our design allows the processor and memory technologies to be upgraded. Higher performance Intel 486, Pentium, or even P6 processors can be added with little effort. Shortly, we will include the PowerPC processors. Again, various versions and performance levels of the PowerPC processors can be used. Our current intention is to only use the 32-bit implementations, although there is no reason 64-bit versions couldn't be used at some time in the future.

We will certainly continue to support OS/2 on both the Intel and PowerPC versions of the application engines. OS/2 is a good operating system, and we do get a great price on it. There are, however, server applications we want in the AS/400 that do not run on OS/2. No problem. We will just use another operating system that does support these applications. The advantage of using the PowerPC processors for our application engines is that so many operating systems, and therefore so many applications, are available.

At last count there were about nine operating systems that had either ported to the PowerPC processors or were planning to port. Besides OS/400, SSP, and OS/2, some of the other operating systems that will run on PowerPC processors include AIX, Microsoft's Windows NT, Sun's Solaris, and Apple Macintosh. We will not likely use every one of them for our application engines, but we will incorporate those that support the applications our customers want. AIX is a pretty good bet to support Unix applications, and Windows NT is a possibility. Any number of these application engines can be plugged into the AS/400, each running the same or different applications, and possibly even different operating systems.

The AS/400 in the 21st Century

Speculating on what the computer industry will be like five or more years in the future is a bit like guessing who will win the Super Bowl in the year 2000. Most everyone has an opinion and is usually willing to share that opinion. But aside from collecting a bunch of opinions, this speculation doesn't offer much of value. But as long as we are at it, we might as well offer an opinion on the computer industry after the year 2000. (Oh, before we start... That Super Bowl will be won by the Minnesota Vikings. On the thirtieth anniversary of their first Super Bowl meeting, they will defeat the Kansas City Chiefs by a score of 17 to 10.)

Technologies

To no one's surprise, technology will continue to march on. The performance of microprocessors will continue to double every 18 months, and the costs will continue to come down. By the year 2000, the cost/performance of microprocessors should be about 15 times better than today. This improvement should make the cost of compute-intensive technologies such as OO and multimedia very affordable.

The speed and the cost of high-bandwidth communications will also continue to improve. Newer communications technologies such as ATM, fiber optics, and satellite will be far more widespread, enabling the use of even more distributed applications. Wireless communications, both local and wide area, will see major improvements in cost and performance, which in turn will further accelerate the use of mobile computing.

Some of the new identification and location technologies will enable new ways to perform traditional types of applications in several industries. New low-cost identification and transponder devices will change the way an application like inventory control is done. Location via Global Positioning Satellite (GPS) will also change the way a distribution application is done. Imagine what it will be like to have your computer able to continuously monitor exactly where every shipment is anywhere in the world.

As previously noted, the amount of information in the world is doubling every five years. By the year 2000, we will be inundated with data in all forms. The key functions our systems will need at that time will be data management, security, data distribution, and data synchronization. Newer functions like data mining (sifting through large amounts of data to find patterns or similarities) and data filtration (sorting data via a user-defined filter to find only the information that is important to the user) will also become important.

Operating system technology will be slow to evolve. A new operating system takes from five to eight years to develop and then another couple to mature. The investment in applications for current operating systems also hinders the development of new ones. By the year 2000, we should expect to still be living with today's operating systems. There will be enhancements to some of them, and others will go away, but the fundamental structure of the operating systems we will be using will be unchanged.

Increases in performance and bandwidth will enable simpler, more humanly accessible interfaces such as speech and handwriting. This will greatly increase the number of people who will become computer users. There is even hope for those whose VCRs are still flashing 12:00 a.m.

The use of all these technologies will change somewhat. Although use will vary based on cultural and geographic differences, by the year 2000 there will be a blurring of the boundaries between working in the office, working at home, working on the road, personal management, learning, and recreation. A synergy between entertainment, communications, computer, and consumer markets will rapidly evolve. The computer game Doom will finally run natively on the AS/400.

Client/Server
The client/server trend will continue. The number of nodes in a network will increase as businesses move away from a host-centric environment. As the client hardware becomes even more robust, client software will become more like a version of the server software that is optimized for the desktop. The client-to-server relationship will evolve to a distributed peer-to-peer model. Operating systems that are optimized for a distributed client/server model today will have the best chance for success in this era.

As today's desktop goes mobile, there will be additional demands placed on tomorrow's servers. Because of the range and capacity of both radio and infrared communications, there will be more times when the user is not connected. The server will have to act on the user's behalf in these times. The model in which the server just stores requests for the user and then presents them when the user reconnects will not be acceptable. The server will have to act upon those requests for the user. Many of us have had the experience of signing onto the system and finding hundreds of notes and messages waiting for us to process. Letting the server handle most of these notes and messages for us may actually make it pleasant to use electronic mail once again.

With the tremendous increase in information that will be available to each and every one of us, the term information overload will take on new meaning. The server of the future will have to help us by providing intelligent filtering of all that information. The server will present only the information a user needs to see.

With the capability for information access from anywhere and the massive amounts of information available, it will become increasingly more difficult to remain workstation-centric with only local files. A PC LAN not attached to a wider network will likely go the way of the typewriter. The network does become the system, and high-function servers such as the AS/400 will make it all possible.

Application Development
The underlying technology for application development will be OO. The OO technologies have already demonstrated the potential to greatly increase development productivity, and new applications will be developed by them. Traditional procedural programs will continue to be enhanced until they are redesigned or totally replaced. This process will take many years.

The biggest problem with OO is the skill level required. As a result, application development and customization will take place on many levels, with a range of skills required. For example, only a relatively small group of professionals who create operating systems and application development tools will use the native OO languages such as C++ (otherwise known as the double-edged razor blade). Solution providers and ISVs will likely use customizable frameworks and reusable components. Semiprofessional solution providers will use visual component interconnection, while casual users will use human-centered interfaces and self-learning tools.

OO technology provides us with a new paradigm for application development. 1996 has been called the breakout year for object technology. By sometime in 1998, the Object Management Group (OMG) predicts that half of all businesses will have adopted OO technologies for new applications. By 2000, that number will reach 80 percent of all businesses. Only time will tell how quickly this OO adoption actually happens. The direction, however, seems clear to most in the industry.

Conclusions

We began Chapter 1 by discussing how quickly today's technologies become discardable and the impact this is having on today's businesses. The future hardware and software technologies described in this chapter will only accelerate this trend. All of these technologies will come and go. Some of them will have value for customers, giving them a competitive advantage in their business. Once this value is recognized, these technologies will be incorporated into computer systems from all vendors. Over time, even newer technologies will displace them.

Just as technologies come and go, so do computer systems and computer companies. This is especially true if a given computer system or company is tied to a technology that is either no longer of value to businesses or is commonplace in the market. History illustrates very clearly how true this is.

Imagine for a moment it is the early 1980s. We have a business and are going to purchase a midrange commercial computer to run our business. Further, pretend that Rochester never got into the computer business back in 1969. Maybe IBM caught on to Rochester's plan to build a new line of incompatible computers back in the 1960s and said No. Whatever the reason, assume for the purposes of our little saga that we have no Rochester systems to consider for our selection of a business computer. The hot technology of the day is office systems. Most vendors have separate data processing and office systems. One of the first vendors to integrate these two systems is Wang Computers. In the early 1980s, Wang is the leader in office systems. This technology is obviously important to our imaginary business, and so we purchase one of these office systems from Wang. Others in the computer industry also quickly recognize the value of office systems technologies, and soon this technology begins to appear in other midrange systems.

Now assume it is the late 1980s, and our business has decided to upgrade our technology with the purchase a new midrange computer system. By this time, the minicomputer vendors, who started in the technical computing arena, have strong offerings in the commercial world. Lead by systems such as Digital's VAX, they now include most of the technologies businesses want. Digital, for example, has a software offering it calls All-in-One, which provides all the office functions most businesses want. We decide to replace the Wang system with a Digital VAX.

Pretend now we are in the early 1990s. Businesses have become concerned that they are being tied into proprietary computer systems such as Digital's VAX. They are seeing the disruptions caused in their business when they change systems every couple of years. Openness and standards are the hot topics. The most open system is considered to be a Unix system. Vendors who had moved away from their proprietary systems, such as HP, are touting the advantages of Unix. Many businesses believe they can easily move between different systems and different vendors if they just adopt Unix. The appeal is strong, so we decide to go through the last system conversion we will ever have to do. We decide to replace our Digital VAX with an HP-9000.

It is now the mid-1990s. Most every computer vendor has adopted open standards. The Unix systems have not delivered on their promise to move easily between systems, and they are more expensive to own than businesses originally thought. The hot topic is client/server computing. Some businesses have tried to replace their midrange systems with PC LANs, but that usually only works for very small businesses. Large, multiprocessor PC servers seem to be the answer. Also, we have discovered that proprietary operating systems, such as Microsoft's Windows NT, can be every bit as open as a Unix system. As a result, Unix popularity in the commercial market is fading. We want the latest technology in our business, so one more time we bite the bullet and replace our HP-9000 with a Compaq Proliant server running Windows NT.

Time marches on and we have now reached the late 1990s. The PC world has been far more expensive than we expected. Applications from various vendors don't seem to work together any better than they did in the past. Even the anticipated cost reductions have not materialized because we need to upgrade our hardware and software every six months, just to stay current. At last, the development of new technologies has allowed the creation of an entirely new concept in computer systems that finally solves all of our business problems. This for sure will be the last time we need to convert to a new system. We throw out our Compaq server and install the new VR2000 computer from Virtual Reality Corporation. As their slogan says, "If it seems too good to be real, it probably isn't."

Our saga ends here because no one knows whether the next hot system will be the VR2000 or something else. The only thing we can be certain about is that there will be one. We can also be certain that the latest system will not solve every business problem, any more than its predecessors have, and moving to it will again cause a major disruption in our imaginary business.

Why do businesses continue to play musical chairs with their computer systems? It certainly keeps a lot of people employed, but is it worthwhile? No business, not even an imaginary one, wants to fall behind and lose its competitive edge. This helps to explain why so many businesses are constantly searching for a new system to lead them into the future. Their attitude is best explained in the words of former Vice President Dan Quayle, "It's a question of whether we're going to go forward into the future, or past to the back."

Fortunately, in the real world, there was another family of systems available to provide a competitive advantage to our imaginary business without causing major expenses and disruptions. Perhaps this explains why more than 650,000 commercial systems from Rochester were installed in businesses worldwide during the past 15 years. No one else even comes close.

Returning one last time to the message we started with in Chapter 1, the staying power of any computer system and its ability to protect the investment of its customers is still the most important consideration when you are purchasing a business computer. The reason the AS/400 is the most successful multiuser business computer ever made is because it meets the needs of businesses and it has staying power. The fact that it accomplishes all this with the most sophisticated architecture and the latest technologies beneath its covers doesn't hurt.

Index

16-byte pointers, 39, 40
077 Numeric Collator, 11-12
188 Collator, 12
801 processor, 23
5250 workstation, 285
   emulation, 286-287
9370 systems, 256

A

A10 (Cobra) processor, 35, 46-47, 88
   clock rates, 47
   Cobra-4, 46
   Cobra-CR, 46, 311
   design, 311
   design objective, 46
   implementations, 46
   instructions, 46
   See also Processors
A30 (Muskie) processor, 42-46, 311
   BiCMOS, 43
   characteristics, 45-46
   error-correction codes, 45
   implementations, 42
   instruction cache, 314
   processor block diagram, 43
   See also Processors
Abbreviated virtual page number
   (AVPN), 210
Abstraction, 3
Access group
   defined, 217
   segments, 217-218
Activation Group (ACTGRP), 238
Activation groups, 236-237
   defined, 57
   function of, 237
   ILE, 238-240
   MI process objects, 237
   names, 237
   shared, 252
Address space, 107-108
   virtual, 179
Address translation, 202-215
   overview, 204
   steps, 206
   with tags active, 205
   types of, 202
   virtual-to-real, 207-215
Address(es)
   direct-store, 183, 204, 205
   effective, 179-180, 198, 202-215
   MI pointer, 199
   permanent, 201
   running out of, 200-201
   size, 178
   temporary, 201
   virtual, 181-183, 202, 210
Addressing
   capability-based, 101-102
   extended (XA), 197
   segment-relative, 179, 186
   See also Address(es)
AdStar Distributed Storage Manager
   for OS/400 (ADSM), 290
Advanced 36, 16, 85-88
   operating system, 88
Advanced Application Architecture,
   1-20

defined, 10
Advanced peer-to-peer networking (APPN), 266
Advanced program-to-program communications (APPC), 266, 293
Advanced Series, 1, 19, 21, 189, 278
  See also AS/400
Advanced Server models, 296-298
  with FSIOP, 298
  types of, 297
  See also AS/400
Alto, 280-281
Amazon, 32
American National Standards Institute (ANSI), 289
American Standard Code for Information Interchange (ASCII), 288
Anonymous FTP support, 306
ANSI standard, 289
AnyMail for OS/400, 288
API-centric architectures, 8-9
Apple Computer, 21-22
  Database Access Language (DAL), 291
Application development, 334-335
Application Development ToolSet for OS/400 (ADTS), 299
Application engines, 331-332
Application environments, 304-306
  development, 301-302
  OpenDoc, 304-305
  Taligent, 305-306
Application programming interfaces (APIs), 8
  MI instructions, 50
  POSIX, 8-9
Architecture(s), MI, 50-51
  API-centric, 8-9
Array(s), 326-327
  data striping and, 326-327
  in heaps, 234
  synchronously spinning disks and, 327
Artificial intelligence (AI) algorithm, 137
AS/400, 294-296
  48-bit address, 178
  65-bit processor, 40-41
  A10 (Cobra) processor, 35, 46-47, 88, 311

A30 (Muskie) processor, 42-46, 311, 314
address size, 178
address space, 107-108
Advanced Series, 1, 19, 21, 189, 278
Advanced Server models, 296-298
architecture definition, XX-XXI
CISC, 30
classification, 7-10
client/server computing products, 286-296
commercial RISC processor, 29-31
computer, 2, 5
DDM, 138
decimal support instructions, 41
defined, 2
DRDA, 138
Electronic Customer Support (ECS), 290
evolution of, 284-286
File Transfer function, 291
future of, 309-337
future processors, 310
high-level machine, 9-10
illustrated, 17
IMPI, 30
in 21st century, 332-335
instruction set, 3, 4
Intel x86, 3
integration, 75-89
introduction of, XX
I/O
  future of, 325-327
  operations, 262-275
  structure, 42
  system, 253-275
language compilers, 53-58
management team, XXIII-XXIV
merging of System/36 and System/38 and, 16
microcode, 81
naming of, 18-19
operating system, 77
  function split, 79
"pimp" bit, 41
POWER, 27
PowerPC, 28, 31-33, 36-38, 39-41, 245
  processors, 42-47
  union, XX-XXI
print-serving functions, 287
processor-centric, 8

processor implementations, 42-47
registers and, 6
RISC processor road map, 311-313
security implementation, 158
SMP and, 45
software technologies, 327-332
subsystems, 249-250
success of, XX
System View, 289-290
tags-active mode, 41, 42
tags-inactive mode, 42
tasking structure, 222-233
technical development team, XXI-XXIII
technology-independent architecture, 1-2
total, 2-3
VLIW processors for, 320-321
See also Advanced Application Architecture; Client Access for OS/400; File Server I/O Processor; OS/400
ASCII, 288
Assembler, 3
  using, 6
Assembly language, 3
  operating systems and, 5-6
Associated space, 109
Asymmetric multiprocessing (ASMP), 321
  tasks and, 233
  See also Multiprocessing
Authority
  add, 165
  ALL, 165
  authorization list management, 165
  CHANGE, 165
  delete, 165
  EXCLUDE, 165
  grouping, 166-168
  list example, 167
  object existence, 164
  object management, 164
  object operations, 164
  program adaption of, 166
  public, 168
  read, 165
  search algorithm, 168-169
  search order, 168
  special, 165-166
    all object, 165

job control, 166
save system, 166
security administrator, 165
service, 166
spool control, 166
update, 165
USE, 165
user, 101
See also Security; User profiles
Authorization. *See* Authority
Automatic storage stack, 234
Auxiliary storage directories, 218-219
Auxiliary storage pools (ASPs), 215-216
  defined, 215, 216
  management, 216
  system, 216

B

Bains, Dick, XXI-XXII, 83, 122, 318
Base segment, 109, 113, 115
  binary radix tree, 144
  data space, 143
  data-space indexes, 143-144
  See also Segments
BASIC, 4
Belatrix, 33-34, 312
Berg, Bill, 32, 35, 81-83
BiCMOS (Bipolar-CMOS), 43
Binaries, 5
Binary digits, 3
Binary numbers, 3
Binary radix trees, 149-155
  building, 150-151
    illustrated, 152
  characteristics, 152-153
  defined, 149
  entry insertion, 153
  entry removal, 154
  example illustration, 153
  finding entries in, 152
  implementation of, 154
  internals of, 154-155
  key fields, 150-151
  layers, 149
  node location, finding, 154
  partitioning scheme, 154-155
  root node, 152, 155
  subdividing, 154
  terminal nodes, 149, 151
  test nodes, 149, 151
  using, 152-153

See also Machine indexes
Binary searches, 148-149
  algorithm, 149
  examples, 148-149
  explained, 148
  See also Machine indexes
Binding
  early, 56
  late, 56
Birnbaum, Joel, 27, 313
Booth, Dick, 323
Bound-by-copy calls, 57
Bound-by-reference calls, 57
Bring, 145
Bring up Binds (BUBs), 84
Buffers
  segment lookaside (SLB), 183
  translation lookaside (TLB), 183, 212
Bus. *See* I/O, bus; SPD bus(es)
Bus control units (BCUs), 258
  function of, 261
Business computing, 277-278
  generations of, 278-279
Business Partners, 88

C

C++ language, 83, 301, 302
C2 level security, 162
C language, 4, 7, 83, 84
C/400 language, 54
Cache
  affinity, 232
  memory, 187
CALLB instruction, 57
CALLBP instruction, 236
CALLPGM instruction, 57, 236
Calls
  bound procedure, 57
  bound-by-copy, 57
  bound-by-reference, 57
  external, 56
  program, 57
  static, 57
  See also CALLB instruction;
    CALLBP instruction; CALLPGM
    instruction
Capability-based addressing, 101-102
CDC 6600, 25-26, 275
  I/O processors, 275
Channels, 254-255
  multiplexer, 254-255

selector, 254
System/38, 255
Charge-coupled devices, 216
CHGQRYA (Change Query Attributes)
  command, 140
Chili pepper system, XXVII-XXVIII
Class libraries, 82
Classes, 82
  defined, 249
  user, 163-164
Clear request, 184
Client Access for OS/400, 98, 286-294
  5250 emulation, 286-287
  ADSM and, 290
  AnyMail for OS/400, 288
  AS/400 System View, 289-290
  client management, 289-290
  data serving, 288-289
  E-Mail product APIs, 287
  LANRES for OS/400 and, 290
  ManageWare for OS/400 and, 290
  NetWare for SAA and, 290
  OfficeVision for OS/400, 287
  PC 5250, 287
  PC Update, 290
  PC-centric offering, 287
  print serving, 287
  programming interfaces, 291-293
    application, 292-293
    DB2 for OS/400 database, 291-292
  program-to-program communi-
    cations, 293-294
  RUMBA for OS/400, 287
  Ultimedia Mail for OS/400, 288
  Ultimedia System Facilities for
    OS/400 (USF), 293-294
  Workstation Function (WSF), 287
  See also Client/server computing
Client management, 289-290
Client/server computing, 30, 277-307
  AS/400 supportive products, 286-296
  characteristics, 280
  Client Access for OS/400, 286-294
  database server, 281-282
  defined, 279-280
  distributed objects in, 300-306
  File Server I/O Processor, 294-296
  fourth-generation computing, 279
  groupware server, 282-284
  interoperability, 279-280
  models, 280-284

Index **343**

move to, 277
object server, 284
print and file server, 280-281
transaction server, 282
trends, 334
Client/server development tools, 298-300
CMOS (Complementary Metal Oxide Silicon), 43
COBOL, 4
    MOVE statement, 72
Cobra processor. *See* A10 (Cobra) processor
Cobra-Lite processor, 88
Cocke, John, 23, 26-27
Codd, E.F., 122
Command interpreters, 4
Commit block, 147
    adding objects to, 147
    removing objects from, 147
COMMIT operation, 133
Commitment control, 132-133
    defined, 133
    in SLIC, 147
Common intermediate form, 52-53
Common Object Request Broker Architecture (CORBA), 284, 300
Common Programming Interface for Communications (CPI-C), 293
Common Use Back End 1 (CUBE-1), 54-55
Common Use Back End 3 (CUBE-3), 57
Compilers, 4
    AS/400 language, 53-58
    back end, 52
    common intermediate form, 52-53
    CUBE-1, 55
    CUBE-3, 57
    extended program model, 55
    front end, 52
    ILE program model, 57-58
    multiple passes, 52
    optimizing, structure of, 52
    pass, 51
    pipelined processors and, 26
    PL/MP, 83
    structure, 51-52
    W-code, 57, 78
Complex instruction set computers (CISC), 1
    architectures, 30

processors, 1-2
Component Integration Laboratories (CIL), 304
Component Specific Exception Handlers (CSEHs), 244
Computer Aided Software Engineering (CASE) tools, 301
Computer(s)
    architecture, 2, 5
    components, 3
    digital, 3
    instructions, 3
    minicomputers, 278-279, 285
    PCs, 5, 98-99, 279
    processor, 3
    registers, 6
    time-sharing, 11
    See also specific computers
Conferencing, 283
Context switching, 245-247
Control Store Processor (CSP), 87
Controller description (CTLD), 263, 267
CoOperative Development Environment/400 (CODE/400), 299
Coprocessors, 256, 319
Corrigan, Mike, 32
Cray, Seymour, 23, 25, 30
C-RISC processor, 31, 320
    shipping, 34
    See also RISC processors
CRTDUPOBJ (Create Duplicate Object) command, 146
CRTLF (Create Logical File) command, 125
CRTPF (Create Physical File) command, 125, 126
Cursors, 144-145
    activating, 145-146
    deactivating, 145-146
    defined, 144
    finding, 181
    permanent, 146
    scrollable, 144
    segments, 145
    sequential file, 144
    SQL, 144
    temporary, 146
    See also Data spaces
Cyclic redundancy check (CRC), 194

D

Dahl, Steve, 85
DASD (direct access storage device), 171
   See also Disks
Data
   independence, 128-130
   integrity, 131-133
   recovery, 131-133
   security, 130
   serving, 288-289
   sharing, 130
   user's path to, 145-146
Data Description Specification (DDS), 123
data dictionary, 127-128
   file creation, 125-128
   interface, 123
   logical file, 124
   physical file, 124
Data dictionary, 127-128
   defined, 127
   purpose, 127-128
Data File Utility (DFU), 300
Data pointer, 105
Data queues, 292
Data spaces, 142-143
   finding, 181
   See also Cursors
Data striping, 326
Database Access GUI, 291
Database Access Language (DAL), 291
Database management system (DBMS), 123
   functions, 125
Database server, 281-282
Database(s)
   distributed, 137-138
   function implementation, 141-147
   gateways to, 138-140
   index, 121
   join operation, 122
   key values, 121
   objects, 142-145
      cursors, 144-145
      data spaces, 142-143
      data-space indexes, 143-144
   operations, 124-141
   order operation, 122
   performance enhancements, 137
   record keys, 120
   relational
      defined, 122
      evolution of, 120-122
      selection operation, 122
   See also DB2 for OS/400
DataPropagator for OS/400, 138-139
Datasets, 92
Data-space indexes, 143-144
   arranging, 143
   base segment, 143-144
DB2 for OS/400, 119-155
   database interfaces, 291-292
   Database Manager, 123
   DDS interface, 124
   DDS language, 123
   file access, 292
   naming of, 119
   performance prediction, 137
   predictive query governor, 137-140
   SQL interface, 124
   SQL statement translation, 123
   See also Database(s)
Decimal support instructions, 41
Decision support systems (DSS), 298
Dequeuing, 227
Desktop Management Interface (DMI), 290
Device description (DEVD), 262, 267
Digital Equipment Corporation (Digital)
   All-in-One, 336
   Alpha architecture, 2, 7, 8
   Open VMS, 7
   VAX, 336
Directories
   auxiliary storage, 218-219
   free space, 219
   permanent, 219
Direct-store address, 183, 204, 205
Discovision, XXIV
Disk arrays. *See* Array(s)
Disk management, 215-219
   access group segments, 217-218
   ASPs, 215-216
   auxiliary storage directories, 218-219
   disk extents, 217
   storage segments, 216-217
Disk(s)
   extents, 217
   high-availability systems, 134-136
   magnetic, 194

mirroring, 135
  pointers on, 194-195
  redundant, 135
  replacing, 216
  tags on, 194-195
  See also Disk management
Distributed Computing Environment (DCE), 251
Distributed Data Management (DDM)
  architecture, 138, 285
    file processing, 264
    OptiConnect for OS/400, 139
Distributed Database Directory, 138
Distributed Database Driver Manager, 138
Distributed databases, 137-138
Distributed Program Call, 293
Distributed Relational Database Architecture (DRDA), 138, 263-264
Distributed SOM (DSOM), 302-304
  defined, 302
  framework, 303
  See also System Object Model (SOM)
DMA operations, 261
  storage, 262
Document management, 282
Drums, 175
  defined, 175
DSPJOBQ (Display Job Queue) command, 93
DSPOUTQ (Display Output Queue) command, 93

E

Early binding, 56
EBCDIC, 288
Effective address, 179-180
  32-bit, 180
  defined, 179
  overflow (EAO), 198
  range, 202
  translation, 202-215
  types of, 202
  See also Address(es)
Effective segment identifier (ESID), 207
Eligibility, 232
E-mail, 282-283
Emulation, 4
Emulator, 76

Encapsulated Program Architecture (EPA) header, 108-109, 113-115
  address fields, 115
  contents, 113-115
  damage attribute, 114
  location, 109
  object identification fields, 115
  space attributes, 115
Encapsulation, 51
  defined, 82
Endicott processor, 311-312
Enqueuing, 227
Enterprise System/9000 (ES/9000), 19
Error detection, 192
Error-correcting code (ECC), 191
Events, 241-242
  asynchronous, 241
  defined, 241
  types of, 241-242
  See also Exceptions
Exception(s), 241-245
  defined, 241
  handlers, 244
  MI generator, 245
  SLIC management, 242-245
  synchronous, 241
  types of, 241
  See also Events
Exchange operation, 184
Exclusive or (XOR) operation, 135
  result, 135
EXPLAIN command, 137
Extended addressing (XA), 197
Extended Binary Coded Decimal Interchange Code. *See* EBCDIC
Extended Program Model (EPM), 54
  OPM and, 55
External file description, 128

F

Fess, Ron, 169
Fiber optics, 259, 333
  I/O connections using, 259-261
  transmission with, 275
File Level Exception Handlers (FLEHs), 244
File Server I/O Processor (FSIOP), 261, 294-296
  Advanced Server models with, 298
  support on, 296
  See also I/O processors (IOPs)

File serving, 289
Firmly coupled multiprocessing, 323-325
    defined, 324
    n-way system vs., 324
Floating Point Systems (FPS), 318-319
    processor, 318
Floating-Point Unit (FPU), 44
    instructions, 44
Fort Knox project, XIX, 255-257
FORTRAN, 4
Fourth generation languages (4GLs), 301
FPS-164, 318-319
Frameworks, 303
    application, 304
    system, 304
Function manager (FM), 266
Furey, Tom, XXV, 122, 257

G

Gebhardt, Carl, XXV-XXVI
Gerstner, Lou, 21
Global Positioning Satellite (GPS), 333
Group profiles, 167
GroupShare, 292-293
Groupware, 282
Groupware server, 282-284
    conferencing, 283
    document management, 282
    E-mail, 282-283
    Lotus Notes and, 284
    scheduling, 283
    workflow, 283-284
    See also Client/server computing; Servers
GUIdelines, 299

H

Haines, Malcolm, XXVII
Hardware
    changes, 6-7
    context switching, 245-247
Hashing, 208-210
    defined, 208-209
    Sears, 209
Headers, 108-115
    contents of, 110-115
    customized, 109
    EPA, 108-109, 113-115
    segment, 108, 111-113
Heap storage area, 234

Hennessy, John, 27
Henry, Glenn, XXIV, 93
Hewlett Packard (HP)
    HP-9000, 336
    Intel alliance, 22
    PA-RISC, 38
    Precision Architecture (PA), 2, 8
High-availability disk systems, 134-136
High-level machine architecture, 9-10
High-level programming language (HLL), 4
Hoffman, Roy, XXI, XXII-XXIV, 222, 318, 331
Horizontal Licensed Internal Code (HLIC), 81
Horizontal Microcode (HMC), 80
    See also Microcode
Host Print Transform function, 287
Howard, Phil, 154
Hypertext Mark-up Language (HTML), 306
Hypertext Transport Protocol (HTTP), 306
Hz, 38

I

I/O
    AS/400, future of, 325-327
    bus, 254
        control units (IOBUs), 258-259
        operations, 261-262
        Series/1, 256
        SPD. *See* SPD bus(es)
    components of, 263-269
    control blocks, 268-269
        illustrated, 268
        list of, 269
    controllers, 254, 255
    devices, 254
    handler, 273
    hardware connections using fiber optics, 259-261
    importance of, 253
    language of, 264
    memory-mapped, 205
    objects to support, 262-263
    operations, 262-275
        end of, 274
        full occurrence of, 269-275
        start of, 270
    request message (IORM)

address queue, 272
connection identifier (CID), 272
defined, 270
enqueued, 272
format, 271
function of, 271
RRCB address, 272
status field, 272
See also Request response control block (RRCB)
structure, 42
hardware, 258-262
illustrated, 265
PC, 254
processing layers, 265-266
subsystems, 8
system, 253-275
history of, 254-258
I/O processors (IOPs), 140, 260
file serving (FSIOP), 261, 294-296
future technology, 325-326
intelligent, 255
IOBU and, 260
modems and, 268
Motorola, 325
standard, 331
system processor and, 262
See also I/O; Processors
IBM 801, 23, 26-27
uses, 27
IBM
Motorola/Apple Computer agreement, XX, 21-22
System Products Division (SPD), 255, 257
Yorktown Research Laboratory, 26
See also Rochester
IMPI (Internal Microprogrammed Interface), 29-31
architecture, 30
code creation, 53-54
instruction set, 63
instructions, 194
op-codes, 63
Indexes
data-space, 143-144
defined, 147
independent, 147
machine, 147-155
Information Management System (IMS), 123

Inheritance, 82
Initial program load (IPL)
access path rebuilding during, 132
long, times, 132, 172
temporary objects and, 105, 106, 199
Inside the AS/400
chili pepper system, XXVII-XXVIII
how to read, XXVII-XXVIII
reason for, XXV-XXVI
Instruction pointer, 105
Instruction set architecture, 3, 4, 51
IMPI, 63
MI, 51, 53
PowerPC, 36, 51
Instructions
ACTIVATE CURSOR, 145
Add Numeric (ADDN), 67, 70
optional forms of, 72
Branch (B), 71
CALLB, 57
CALLBP, 236
CALLPGM, 57, 236
COMMIT, 147
CPYBLAP, 71-72
CREATE, 105, 109-110
Create Object, 92
Create Program, 61-62
DEACTIVATE CURSOR, 145
DECOMMIT, 147
FETCH, 264, 273, 275
Request I/O (REQIO), 267, 270
RESOLVE, 102
Return From Interrupt (rfi), 246
Return From System Call Vectored (rfscv), 246
Supervisor Call (SVC), 245
System Call (sc), 245
System Call Vectored (scv), 246-247
Integrated database. *See* DB2 for OS/400
Integrated file system, 98-101
illustrated, 100
naming convention, 99
QFileSvr.400, 99
QLANSrv, 99
QOpenSys, 99
QOPT, 99
QPWXCWN, 99
user-defined structure, 99
Integrated Language Environment (ILE), 56

activation group, 238-240
   components, 238-240
   illustrated, 240
  binder, 236
  MI support of, 235
  modules, 56
  process model, 235-237
   job structure based on, 250
  processes, 237-240
   components of, 237-238
   illustrated structure, 239
  program model compilers, 57-58
Integration, 75-89
  lack of flexibility and, 76
  MI and, 75-76
  operating system, 77-79
Integrity, referential, 134
Intel
  HP alliance, 22
  microprocessor, 21
  x86 architecture, 3, 49
Interactive SQL, 123
Interpretation, 4
Interprocess communications facility (IPCF), 268
  data structures, 271
  router, 273
Interrupt handler, 225
Interrupts, 241
  classification of, 242
  defined, 224
  function of, 224-225
  instruction-caused, 243-244
  overhead, 225
  PowerPC architecture, 241
  priority, 225
  system-caused, 242-243
  See also Events; Exceptions
Inverted page table, 208
Invocation work area (IWA), 235
IRP (Intermediate Representation of a Program), 53
  code conversion, 53

J

Job(s)
  activation groups and, 252
  defined, 224
  description, 249
  full-function, 251
  structures, 250

  work management and, 247-251
  See also Objects
Jones, Chris, 35, 83
Journaling, 131-132
  SLIC, 146-147
  See also Recovery
Journal(s)
  data segment, 147
  defined, 131
  entries, 131
  ports, 146
  space object, 146
  spaces, 146
  uses, 131
Jurrens, Gene, 285

K

Kempke, William, 222
Kernel, 78
  performance sensitivity of, 83
  SLIC technologies, 84-85
  See also Microkernels
Kiscaden, Dick, 285
Klotz, Ray, XXIII-XXIV, 196, 225
Kuehler, Jack, 31-32

L

LANRES for OS/400, 290, 295
LANSA/CS400, 299
Late binding, 56
Libraries, 96-97
  organization of, 96
  OS/400 structure, 97, 99
  See also specific libraries
Licensed internal code (LIC), 77-79
  components, 78
  defined, 77
  function split, 79
  See also OS/400; System Licensed Internal Code (SLIC)
Limited-capability users, 159-160
Logical files, 124
  creating, 126-127
  data record, 127
  defined, 126
  file attributes, 127
  file description, 127
  format, 128
  join, 127
  multiple-format, 126, 129
  structure, 126-127

See also Physical files
Logical unit description (LUD), 262
Loosely coupled parallel database, 141
Loosely coupled systems, 321-322, 323
Lotus Notes, 294
    FSIOP support, 296
Luick, Dave, 320

M

Mach microkernel, 84, 224, 328
Machine indexes, 147-155
    characteristics, 148
    defined, 147
    uses, 147-148
    See also Binary radix trees
Machine interface. *See* MI
Machine Product (MP), 80
Machine space pointer, 105
Machine State Register (MSR), 202-203
    64-bit mode bit, 203
    bits list, 203
    C2 security bit, 203
    data relocate bit, 203
    instruction relocate bit, 203
    key value computation, 214
    PowerPC architecture for, 245
    problem state bit, 203-204
    user state bit, 204
    See also Registers
Machine Status Save/Restore Register.
    See SRR (0 and 1)
Magnetic bubbles, 216
Main Store Control Unit (MSCU) chip, 44
Main Store Processor (MSP), 87
Mainframe computing, 278
Mainframe operating system (MVS), 329
Management team, XXIII-XXVII
ManageWare for OS/400, 290
Massachusetts Institute of Technology (MIT), 10
Materialization, 63
    definition table (MDT), 115
McCullough, John W., 222
Memory
    access modes, 212-214
        G (Guarded Storage) bit, 213
        I (Caching Inhibited) bit, 213
        M (Memory Coherence) bit, 213
        mode-control bits, 212
        W (Write Through) bit, 213
    cache, 187
    local reference, 324
    model characteristics, 202
    non-local reference, 324
    page frames, 182
    physical main, 108
    segmented, 107-108
    tables, 186, 208
    tags, 39
    virtual, 107
    words, 191
        32-bit, 192
        64-bit, 192
        parity bit, 192
Memory-mapped I/O, 205
Messaging Application Programming
    Interface (MAPI), 287
Messaging interfaces, 293
Methods, 82
MHz, 38, 188
MI, 9, 49-73
    APIs, 50
    architecture
        components, 50
        overview, 50-51
    AS/400, illustrated, 61
    boundary, 10, 50
        object, 51
    characteristics, 59-60
    conventional, 60
    exception generator, 245
    ILE support and, 235
    instruction set, 51, 53
    instructions, 51
        branch conditions and, 69
        call, 56
        compare, 69
        computational, 68
        examples, 70-72
        execution, 51, 70
        formats, 67
        intermediate form, 53
        op-codes, 59
        physical structures and, 59
    integration and, 75-76
    LUD, 267
    machine independence and, 76
    object view, 181
    op-code, 68
        bit assignments, 69

extender, 68-70
operands, 50
pointer address, 199
PowerPC, 34
processes, 233-240
programs, 60-64
    creating, 61-62
    destroying, 62
    materialization and observability, 62-64
response queue (MIRQ), 267, 273
Technology Independent Emulation Interface, 87
See also System objects
Microcode, 79-81
    AS/400, 81
    defined, 79
    Horizontal Microcode (HMC), 80
    operating system functions in, 86
    System/38, 80
    Vertical Microcode (VMC), 80
Microkernels, 84-85, 328-329
    32-bit, 85
    defined, 222, 328
    history of, 224
    horizontal structure, 223
    Mach, 84, 224, 328
    message-passing communications structure, 222
    personalities, 84
    technologies, 222-224, 328
    uses, 328
Microprocessors, 21
Microprogramming, 4
Microsoft
    OLE, 305
    Structured Query Language (SQL), 120
    Windows NT, 7, 120, 187, 328
Million floating-point operations per second (MFLOPS), 42
Million instructions per second (MIPS), 42, 188
Minicomputers, 278-279
    replacement of, 285
    See also Computer(s)
Mirroring, 135
Modules, 56
Motorola, 21-22
    88110, 38
Multicomputer clusters, 321-322

MULTICS, 11
Multiflow Computers, 313
Multimedia enablers, 293-294
Multiplexer channels, 254-255
Multiprocessing, 231-233
    asymmetric, 233, 321
    firmly coupled, 323-325
    future of, 321-325
    loosely coupled, 321-322, 323
    multicomputer clusters and, 321-322
    symmetric, 45, 140, 231-233, 321, 322-323
    tightly coupled, 322-323
Multi-protocol Transport Networking (MPTN), 293
Multisegment objects, 109-110
    defined, 109
    illustrated, 110
Muskie processor. *See* A30 (Muskie) processor
Mustain, Dick, 85, 318

N

National language support, 136-137
NetWare for SAA, 290, 295
Network description (ND), 263
Network interface description (NETINTD), 263
NexGen, Nx586, 316
Non-uniform memory access (NUMA), 322
Novell NetWare, 296
Numerically intensive computing (NIC), 33, 36

O

Object authority. *See* Authority
Object definition table (ODT), 65
    defined, 107
    Direction Vector (ODV), 65, 66
    Entry String (OES), 65
    instructions and, 66
Object locks, 105
Object Management Group (OMG), 300, 335
Object request broker (ORB), 284
Object server, 284
Object-based languages, 91
Object-oriented (OO) programming, 82
    application development and, 334-335

languages, 91
progress measurement, 84
Objects, 82, 91-117
   accessing, 101-105
   attributes of, 114
   authorization of, 164-165
   commit block, adding/removing, 147
   CPF, 93
   creating, 109-110
      illustrated, 111
   damage to, 114
   database, 142-145
   defined, 92
   distributed, in client/server environment, 300-306
   examples of, 115-117
   finding, 96-101, 181
   identification of, 115
   journal space, 146
   MI view, 181
   multisegment, 109-110
   naming, 93-94
   OS/400, 94-96, 249
      database file, 96
      library, 96-97
      list of, 94
      one-to-one mapping, 93
      user profile, 162-166
   pageable, 185
   permanent, 178, 218
   persistence of, 106
   program, 106-107
   protected, 303-304
   reasons for using, 92
   supporting I/O, 262-263
   system, 60
      associated space, 109
      authorization of, 105
      characteristics, 105-106
      creation of, 61
      customized header, 109
      data space, 96
      data space index, 95
      destroying, 62
      EPA header, 108-109
      functional portion, 102-103
      illustrated, 104
      list of, 95
      names of, 105
      restricting access to, 169
      segment header, 108
      space portion, 103
      structure of, 108-109
      temporary, 105, 106
   temporary, 105, 106, 199, 217, 218
   uses of, 117
   virtual address of, 181-182
Observability, 64
Obsydian, 299
On-line transaction processing (OLTP), 298
OO technology, 83, 84
   See also Object-oriented (OO) programming
OpenDoc, 304-305
Operating system
   Advanced 36, 88
   component functions, 77
   defined, 77
   function split, 79
   functions in microcode, 86
   future technology, 333
   integrated, 77-79
   security, 161-162
   virtual memory and, 188
   See also OS/400; Unix operating system
Operation codes (op-codes), 59, 68
   IMPI, 63
   MI, 68
      bit assignment, 69
      extender, 68-70
OPNQRYF (Open Query File) command, 145
Optical link cards (OLCs), 259
OptiConnect for OS/400, 139-140
   DDM and, 139
   multiple system connections with, 274
Original Program Model (OPM), 53
   block-structured languages and, 55
   instructions, 65
OS/2 operating system, 295
   LAN Server code, 296
OS/400, 77
   Distributed Database Directory, 138
   function manager (FM), 266
   function split, 79
   functions, 78
   library structure, 97, 99
   object types, 93
   objects, 93, 94-96, 249

database file, 96
library, 96-97
list of, 94
one-to-one mapping, 93
user profile, 162-166
V3R1, 20
work management component, 221, 247-251
See also Licensed internal code (LIC)
Overhead
process switch, 176-177
two-level store, 177-178
Overlays, 176
OVRDBF (Override Database File) command, 145

P

P operator, 229
Page number
real (RPN), 207
table, inverted, 208
virtual (VPN), 207
Page table, 187, 207
entries (PTEs), 209-212
bits, 211-212
format, 211
length of, 210
page-protection (PP) bits, 214
entry group (PTEG), 209
Page(s)
512-byte, 195
access allowed, 214
clearing, 185
from data segment, 191
frames, 182
removing, 185
searching for, 212
pinned, 184
from pointer segment, 191
protection, 214-215
virtual, I/O, 185
Parallel databases, 140-141
loosely coupled, 141
SMP, 140
See also Database(s)
Parent Activation Group (PAGP), 237
PA-RISC architecture, 313
Pascal, 54
Password security, 159-160
Patterson, David, 27
PC 5250, 287

PC Support, 98, 285, 286
PC Update, 290
PCs, 279
directory, 99
file names, 99
file storage, 98
processors, 5
See also Computer(s)
Perfect Image for OS/400, 294
Personal Systems Products (PSP) division, 330
Physical files, 124
creating, 125-126
data part, 126
defined, 125
file attributes, 126
file description, 126
structure of, 128
triggers in, 133-134
See also Logical files
Pipelining, 26-27
defined, 23
PL/MP, 83
compiler, 83
Pointers, MI, 199
16-byte, 196
128-bit, 219
counterfeiting and, 194
data, 105
hardware protection for, 191-193
inside, 195-201
instruction, 105
machine space, 105
on disk, 194-195
procedure, 105
process object (POPs), 238
protecting, 185
resolved, 195-196
segment, 191
space, 62, 104
stack, 234
structure, 190
system, 62, 101-103
in system object, 190
system state and, 101
Polymorphism, 82
Porting, 81
POSIX
APIs, 8-9, 251
process, 252
threads, 251

POWER2 processor, 33
POWER3 processor, 33
POWER (Performance Optimization
  With Enhanced RISC) architecture,
  27, 331
PowerPC, 34
  32-bit mode, 33, 36
  64-bit versions, 33, 36
  alliance, XX
  architecture, 28, 31-33, 36-38
    design, 36
    extended, 32
    extensions, 39-41
    for MSR, 245
    virtual addresses and, 210
  AS instructions, 41-42
  AS processors, 42-47
  AS/400 union, XX-XXI
  at the MI, 34
  code expansion, 37
  compound instructions, 36
  direct-store addresses, 204
  evolution of, 23-28
  historical background, 22
  instruction set, 36, 51
  Optimized, 39
  PowerPC 604, 50
  PowerPC 630, 33-34
  processors, 22, 332
    64-bit high performance, 28
    low-power, 28
    operating systems and, 332
    single-chip, 28
  registers, 36
  technology, 21-47
    AS/400, 31-35
  virtual memory and, 180-181
  See also RISC
Predictive query governor, 137-139
Print and file server, 280-281
Print-serving functions, 287
Procedure invocation, 236
Procedure pointer, 105
Procedures
  defined, 56
  stored, 136
Process access group (PAG), 200
Process Activation Work Area
  (PAWA), 237
Process control block (PCB), 146, 237
Process control space, 233

segments, 235
Process management, 221-252
  defined, 221
  See also System Licensed Internal
    Code (SLIC)
Process model, 235-237
  ILE, 235-237
  original, 235
Process object pointers (POPs), 238
Process Queue Space, 238
Process switch, 176
  overhead, 176-177
  performance, 190
  use of, 189-190
  virtual memory and, 188
Processes, MI, 233-240
  defined, 224
  ILE, 237-240
  multithreaded, 251
  POSIX, 252
  suspended, 221
Processing Unit (PU) chip, 44
Processor-centric architectures, 8
Processors, 3
  A10, 46-47
  A30, 42-46
  32-bit, 6-7
  64-bit, 7, 310
  801, 23
  AS/400 future, 310
  CISC, 1-2
  Cobra, 35, 46-47, 88, 311
  Cobra-Lite, 88
  Control Store (CS), 87
  C-RISC, 31, 34
  cycle time, 23
  Endicott, 311-312
  FPS, 318
  input/output (IOPs), 140
  interrupt priorities of, 225
  Main Store (MSP), 87
  Muskie, 42-46, 311, 314
  PC, 5
  peripheral, 275
  pipeline scaler, 24
  POWER2, 33
  POWER3, 33
  POWER, 331
  PowerPC, 22, 28, 332
  RISC, 1-2, 21, 27, 30
  single-chip, 43

354 Inside the AS/400

System/32, 87
VLIW, 313-321
See also I/O processors (IOPs)
Program objects, 106-107
Program Resolution Monitor (PRM), 53
Program template, 62
   inside, 65-72
   memory conservation and, 67
   syntax check, 62
Programs
   adaption of, 166
   defined, 56
   finding, 181
   independence, 128-130
   materialized, 63
   MI, 60-64
      creating, 61-62
      destroying, 62
      materialization and observability, 62-64
   service, 56-57
Program-to-program communications, 293-294
Protected objects, 303-304
Protection key processing, 214-215
Punched-card machines, 11-13
PWRDWNSYS (Power Down System) command, 165

Q

QAUDJRL system value, 158
   auditing capabilities, 162
QDLS, 99, 100
QFileSvr.400, 99
QLANSrv, 99
QMAXSIGN system value, 159
QOpenSys, 99
QOPT, 99
QPWXCWN, 99
QSECURITY system value, 158
   valid values, 159
QSYS library, 97, 99, 100
Query Manager, 123
Query optimizer, 137
Queues, 292-293
   data, 292

R

Real page number (RPN), 207
Reckinger, Art, 257
Recovery
   backward, 132
   data, 131-133
   forward, 131
   See also Journaling
Reduced instruction set computer. *See* RISC
Redundant arrays of inexpensive disks (RAID), 135
Referential integrity, 134
Registers, 6
   MSR, 202
   PowerPC, 36
   segment, 179, 186
   SID, 197
   SLB, 186
   tag, 195
   TLB, 187
Relational database. *See* Database
Relative address, 144, 150
Report Program Generator. *See* RPG
Request response control block (RRCB)
   address, 272
   defined, 270
   format, 271
   function of, 272
   length field, 272
   main memory addresses, 272
   request identifier (RID), 272
   See also I/O, request message (IORM)
Resolved pointers, 195-196
   functions, 195
   parts of, 196
   See also Pointers
Resource security, 160-161
Revolutions per minute (RPM), 38
RISC, 1
   advantages, 22
   AS/400s, 9-10
   beyond, 313-321
   code expansion, 37
   load-and-store string instructions, 37
   See also PowerPC
RISC processors, 1-2, 21
   32-bit, 30
   801, 314
   AS/400, 29-31
      road map, 311-313
   compiler optimization, 27
   C-RISC, 31, 34, 320

superscalar, 27
See also Processors; RISC
RISC System/6000 (RS/6000), 22, 33
   Scalable POWERparallel
      (RS/6000 SP), 33
Rochester
   1962 summer job, XVII
   1968 job with IBM, XVIII
   Development Laboratory, 12
   development organizations, 174
   history of, XXV-XXVI
   long instruction word machines in, 317-320
   management team, XXIII-XXVI
   punch-card machines, 11-13
   single-level store in, 173-175
   skunkworks, 86
   technical development team, XXI-XXIII
   unit record system, 13
   Wells Department Store, 174-175
   See also IBM
ROLLBACK operation, 133
ROMP (Research/Office Products Microprocessor), 27
Rounding, 68
Routing step, 248
RPG, 4, 14
   creation of, 13-14
   indicators, 70
   MOVEL command, 72
   programming in, 14
   RPG II, 14
   visual (VRPG), 299
RS/6000. *See* RISC System/6000 (RS/6000)
Rubin, Richard, 172
RUMBA for OS/400, 287

S

Scalable Coherent Interface Link (SCIL), 312
Scan function, 121
Scheduling, 283
Schleicher, Dave, 330
Schmidt, Bob, 86
Schwartz, Steve, 19, 257
Screen Design Aid (SDA), 300
Second Level Exception Handlers (SLEH), 244
Security, 157-169

AS/400 implementation, 158
C2 level, 162
data, 130
function location of, 78
importance of, 169
integrated, 157-158
no, 159
operating system, 161-162
password, 159-160
physical, 159
resource, 160-161
system levels, 158-162
system values, 158-159
System/38, 160
See also Authority
Security Administrator user class, 164
Security Officer user class, 164
Segment header, 108, 111-113
   contents, 111
   flag bits, 112
   See also Segments
Segment identifier (SID), 197
   effective (ESID), 207
   extender, 198-199
   registers, 197
   temporary, 201
   virtual, 207
   wrap problem, 201
   See also Segments
Segment lookaside buffer (SLB), 183
   registers, 186
Segment registers, 179, 186
Segment tables, 180, 186
   performance degradation and, 187
Segmented, 107-108
Segment-relative addressing, 179, 186
Segments, 107-108
   64-kilobyte, 200
   access group, 217-218
   base, 109, 113, 115, 143-144
   composition of, 108
   cursor, 145
   defined, 107
   journal data, 147
   MDT, 115
   pointer, 191
   secondary, 109
   storage, 216-217
Selector channels, 254
Send/receive counter (SRC), 230
Send/receive message (SRM), 229, 230

Send/receive queue (SRQ), 229-231
　defined, 229
　format, 230
SequeLink, 299
Serial Line Internet Protocol (SLIP), 306
Servers
　database, 281-282
　groupware, 282-284
　object, 284
　print and file, 280-281
　transaction, 282
　See also Client/server computing
Service programs, 56-57
Shared folders, 98
Silverlake project, XX, 18, 257-258
Simple Network Management Protocol (SNMP), 290
Single-level store, 60, 171-219
　address translation, 202-215
　advantages of, 190
　bytes addressed by 64 bits, 172-173
　defined, 171, 176
　disadvantages of, 178, 190
　disk management, 215-219
　displaying characteristics of, 172
　long IPL times and, 171, 172
　overview, 181-186
　performance implications, 186-190
　pointers, 195-201
　in Rochester, 173-175
　segments, 180-181
　sharing and, 190
　space and, 172
　See also Virtual memory
Single-processor unit, 43
　chip make-up, 44
Skunkworks, 86
Sloan, Jim, 122
Smalltalk, 301, 302
Software
　application, 5
　AS/400, future technologies, 327-332
　design, 5-7
　system, 5
Solie, Darryl, 32
SOMobjects Developer Toolkit for OS/400, 304
Source Entry Utility (SEU), 300
Source Sink Request (SSR), 267
Source/sink data (SSD), 267

Space, 60
　address, 107-108, 179
　associated, 109
　attributes, 115
　data, 142-143
　journal, 146
　single-level store and, 172
Space pointer, 62, 104
　machine, 105
　See also Pointers
SPD bus(es), 256, 258-261
　asynchronous, 260
　copper, 260
　lines, 260
　messages, 271, 274
　　format, 274
　　OPEND, 273, 274
　　OPSTART, 272-273
　operations, 261-262
　optical, 260
　priority, 261
　remote attachment, 259
　synchronous, 260
　units (IOBUs), 258-259, 260
　　information exchange, 261
　　in operation occurrence, 269
　See also I/O, bus
Special authority. *See* Authority
SQL Development Kit, 123
Squillace, Zanti, 257
SRR (0 and 1), 246
Stack(s), 234
　pointer, 234
Static storage area, 234
Storage areas, 234-235
　automatic stack, 234
　heap, 234
　process model, 235
　static, 234
Storage management. *See* Single-level store
Storage pools, 249-250
　defined, 249
Storage segments, 216-217
Stored procedures, 136
　accessing, 136
Structured Query Language (SQL), 123
　CALL statement, 136, 292
　CREATE TABLE statement, 125, 127
　CREATE VIEW statement, 127

cursor, 144
Remote SQL, 291
standardization, 123
Static SQL, 292
system-wide catalog, 128
tables, 124
    creating, 125-126
views, 124
    creating, 126-127
Subsystem(s), 249-250
    descriptions, 249
Sun, SuperSPARC, 38
Supercomputers, 23, 25
Superior, 18, 19, 34
    as AS/400 Advanced Series, 19
Superscalar machines, 27
Supervisor Call (SVC) interface, 87
Symmetric multiprocessing (SMP), 45, 231-233, 321, 322-323
    architecture types, 322
    NUMA classification, 324
    parallel database, 140
    tasks and, 231-233
    technology, 325
    upper limit, 323
    See also Multiprocessing
Synchronous data link communications (SDLC) protocol, 267
System Application Architecture (SAA), 19
System Licensed Internal Code (SLIC), 81-86
    commitment control in, 147
    database maximum sizes, 142
    defined, 81
    development environment, 83-84
    exception management, 242-245
    journaling, 146-147
    kernel technologies, 84-85
    object management component, 101
    See also Licensed internal code (LIC)
System Network Architecture (SNA), 293
System Object Model (SOM), 300
    application development, 304
    distributed (DSOM), 302-304
    implementation, 303
    interface definition language (IDL), 302
    objects, 303
System objects, 60

    associated space, 109
    authorization of, 105
    characteristics, 105-106
    creation of, 61
    customized header, 109
    data space, 95
    data space index, 95
    destroying, 62
    EPA header, 108-109
    functional portion, 102-103
    illustrated, 104
    inside, 107-117
    list of, 95
    names of, 105
    restricting access to, 169
    segment header, 108
    space portion, 103
    structure of, 108-109
    temporary, 105, 106
    See also Objects
System Operator user class, 164
System pointers, 62, 101-103
    capability, 101
    contents, 101
    resolving, 102
    unresolved, 102
    user authority, 101
    See also Pointers
System Programmer user class, 164
System security levels, 158-162
    level 10, 159
    level 20, 159-160
    level 30, 160-161
    level 40, 161-162
    level 50, 162
    See also Security
System state, 101, 161
System Support Program (SSP), 87
System Technology and Architecture Division (STAD), 310
System/3, XVIII-XIX
    announcement of, 14-15
    development organization, 173
    illustrated, 17
    integrity problems, 92
    Model 2, 15
    single-byte op-code, 92
    success of, 15
System/32, XVIII-XIX, 15
    illustrated, 17
    microprogrammed processor, 86

processor, 87
System/34, XVIII-XIX, 15
　illustrated, 17
　interactive system, 121
System/36, XIX, 15-16
　Advanced, 16, 85-88
　illustrated, 17
　user interface, 17
System/38, XIX-XX, 15-16
　application development
　　environment, 17
　architecture, 15
　channel, 255
　DDS interface, 123
　engineering organization, 173
　error-correction code bits, 40
　Horizontal Microcode (HMC), 80
　illustrated, 17
　microcode, 80
　security, 160
　small models of, XX
　tag bit, 39
　Vertical Microcode (VMC), 80
　Wells building and, 174-175
System/360, 12, 14
System/370, XXI
System/R, 122-123
System-Managed Access Path
　Protection (SMAPP), 132
System-wide catalog, 128

T

Tables
　memory, 186, 207
　page, 187, 207, 208
　segment, 180, 186, 187
Tag bits, 39-40
　AS/400, 40
　Load and Verify Tags (lvt), 199
　Load Multiple Doubleword (lmd), 195
　Load Quadword (lq), 193
　pointer modification and, 193
　Store Quadword (stq), 193
　System/38, 39
Tag(s)
　address translation with, 205
　instructions, 193
　on disk, 194-195
　register, 195
　See also Tag bits

Tags-active mode, 41, 42, 193-194
Tags-inactive mode, 42
Taligent, 305-306
Tashjian, Harry, XXIII-XXIV
Task dispatching element (TDE), 225-226
　contents, 226, 227
　defined, 225
　function of, 226
　inserting in data structure, 227
　migration, 230
　movement of, 227
　multiple, per process, 251
　multiprocessor fields, 232
　on TDQ, 228-229
　removing from data structure, 227
Task dispatching queue (TDQ), 227-229
　defined, 227
　illustrated, 228
Tasking structure, 222-233
　implementation, 224
　message-based, 223
　multiprocessing model, 233
　See also Process management;
　　Task(s)
Task(s), 225
　asymmetric multiprocessing and, 231-233
　defined, 224
　dispatching, 225-231
　priority, 231
　states, 226-227
　　illustrated, 226
　　list of, 226
　　transitions, 227
　symmetric multiprocessing and, 231-233
　See also Task dispatching element (TDE)
Taylor, Perry, 122
TDE. *See* Task dispatching element (TDE)
TDQ. *See* Task dispatching queue (TDQ)
Technology Independent Emulation Interface, 87
Technology Independent Machine Interface. *See* MI
Third Level Exception Handlers (TLEH), 244

Threads
  defined, 247, 251
  importance of, 251
  POSIX, 251
Tightly coupled system, 322-323
Timesharing, 11, 221
  defined, 176
  virtual memory for, 176-177
Timing sequence, 23
  example, 24
Tomashek, Mike, 35, 81, 83
Tombstone Segments, 238
Transaction Processing Council, 188-189
Transaction server, 282
Translation look-aside buffer (TLB), 183
  registers, 187
  searching, 212
  size of, 212
Translator, 53
Transmission Control Protocol/Internet Protocol (TCP/IP), 293
Triggers, 133-134
  adding, 134
  defined, 133
  event, 133
  in physical files, 133-134
  program, 134
  removing, 134
  See also Physical files
Turner, Rick, 188, 222

U

Ultimedia
  Builder for OS/400, 294
  Conferencing for OS/400, 294
  Mail for OS/400, 288
  System Facilities for OS/400 (USF), 293-294
Unicode format, 99-100
  V3R1 and, 136
  V3R6 and, 100-101, 136-137
Uniform memory access (UMA), 322
Unix operating system, 8-9, 11, 188
  component interaction of, 222-223
  disadvantages of, 223
  file structure, 99
  layering approach, 223
  See also Operating system
User authority, 101
User classes, 163-164
  defined, 163
  list of, 164
User profiles
  capability definitions, 163
  defined, 62, 162
  group profiles, 167
  lists, 164
  See also Authority
Users
  capabilities of, 163
  limited-capability, 149

V

V1R3, security, 161
V2R3, security, 162
V3R1, 20
  database enhancements, 120
  integrated file system, 98-101
  Single UNIX Specification API, 72
  Unicode format and, 136
V3R6, 20
  Unicode format and, 100-101, 136-137
V operator, 229
Vendor Independent Messaging (VIM), 287
Vertical Licensed Internal Code (VLIC), 81
Vertical Microcode (VMC), 80, 197
  address problem, 198
  memory management component, 200
  See also Microcode
Very Long Instruction Word. *See* VLIW processor
Virtual address
  48-bit, 182
  of objects, 181-182
  PowerPC architecture and, 210
  range, 202
  space, 179
  translation, 183, 207-215
Virtual memory, 107, 175-181
  file system and, 177
  for timesharing, 176-177
  history of, 175-176
  manager, 177
  operating systems and, 188
  persistent, 178-181
  PowerPC and, 180-181
  process switches and, 188
  single-level, 177-178

See also Single-level store
Virtual page number (VPN), 207
    abbreviated (AVPN), 210
Virtual segment identifier (VSID), 207
Visionary leaders, XXI
Visual RPG (VRPG), 299
VisualAge C++ for OS/400, 301-302
VisualAge for OS/400, 301-302
VisualGen, 299
VLIW processors, 313-321
    compiler and, 315
    cycle time, 315
    design effort, 315-316
    drawback, 316
    for AS/400, 320-321
    instructions, 317
    name of, 315
    parallelism, 316-317
    technology, 314, 316-317
    See also Processors

W

W-code, 57, 78
WebConnection for OS/400, 306-307
    functions, 306
Windows NT. *See* Microsoft, Windows NT
Work management
    concepts, 247-248
    hierarchy of domains, 248
    OS/400 jobs and, 247-251
    unit of work submitted by, 248
Workflow, 283-284
Workplace technologies, 329-331
    defined, 329
Workstation Function (WSF), 287
Workstation User user class, 164
Wottreng, Andy, 32
WRKSYSSTS (Work with System Status) command, 227
    display, 172, 184, 227

X

XOR operation. *See* Exclusive or (XOR) operation

Also Published by *NEWS/400*

APPLICATION DEVELOPER'S HANDBOOK FOR THE AS/400
Edited by Mike Otey, a **NEWS/400** *technical editor*
Explains how to effectively use the AS/400 to build reliable, flexible, and efficient business applications. Contains RPG/400 and CL coding examples and tips, and provides both step-by-step instructions and handy reference material. Includes diskette. 768 pages, 48 chapters.

C FOR RPG PROGRAMMERS
By Jennifer Hamilton, a **NEWS/400** *author*
Written from the perspective of an RPG programmer, this book includes side-by-side coding examples written in both C and RPG to aid comprehension and understanding, clear identification of unique C constructs, and a comparison of RPG op-codes to equivalent C concepts. Includes many tips and examples covering the use of C/400. 292 pages, 23 chapters.

COMMON-SENSE C
Advice and warnings for C and C++ programmers
By Paul Conte, a **NEWS/400** *technical editor*
C programming language has its risks; this book shows how C programmers get themselves into trouble, includes tips to help you avoid C's pitfalls, and suggests how to manage C and C++ application development. 100 pages, 9 chapters.

CONTROL LANGUAGE PROGRAMMING FOR THE AS/400
By Bryan Meyers and Dan Riehl, **NEWS/400** *technical editors*
This comprehensive CL programming textbook offers students up-to-the-minute knowledge of the skills they will need in today's MIS environment. Progresses methodically from CL basics to more complex processes and concepts, guiding readers toward a professional grasp of CL programming techniques and style. 512 pages, 25 chapters.

DDS PROGRAMMING FOR DISPLAY & PRINTER FILES
By James Coolbaugh
Offers a thorough, straightforward explanation of how to use Data Description Specifications (DDS) to program display files and printer files. Covers basic to complex tasks using DDS functions. The author uses DDS programming examples for CL and RPG extensively throughout the book, and you can put these examples to use immediately. Focuses on topics such as general screen presentations, the A specification, defining data on the screen, record-format and field definitions, defining data fields, using indicators, data and text attributes, cursor and keyboard control, editing data, validity checking, response keywords, and function keys. A complimentary diskette includes all the source code presented in the book. 446 pages, 13 chapters.

DESKTOP GUIDE TO CL PROGRAMMING
By Bryan Meyers, a **NEWS/400** *technical editor*
This first book of the **NEWS/400** *Technical Reference Series* is packed with easy-to-find notes, short explanations, practical tips, answers to most of your everyday questions about CL, and CL code segments you can use in your own CL programming. Complete "short reference" lists every command and explains the most-often-used ones, along with names of the files they use and the MONMSG messages to use with them. On-line Windows Help diskette available. 205 pages, 36 chapters.

DESKTOP GUIDE TO AS/400 PROGRAMMERS' TOOLS
By Dan Riehl, a **NEWS/400** *technical editor*

This second book of the **NEWS/400** *Technical Reference Series* gives you the "how-to" behind all the tools included in *Application Development ToolSet/400* (ADTS/400), IBM's Licensed Program Product for Version 3 of OS/400; includes Source Entry Utility (SEU), Programming Development Manager (PDM), Screen Design Aid (SDA), Report Layout Utility (RLU), File Compare/Merge Utility (FCMU) — *new in V3R1*, and Interactive Source Debugger — *new in V3R1*. Highlights topics and functions specific to Version 3 of OS/400. On-line Windows Help diskette available. 266 pages, 30 chapters.

DESKTOP GUIDE TO THE S/36
By Mel Beckman, Gary Kratzer, and Roger Pence, **NEWS/400** *technical editors*

This definitive S/36 survival manual includes practical techniques to supercharge your S/36, including ready-to-use information for maximum system performance tuning, effective application development, and smart Disk Data Management. Includes a review of two popular Unix-based S/36 work-alike migration alternatives. Diskette contains ready-to-run utilities to help you save machine time and implement power programming techniques such as External Program Calls. 387 pages, 21 chapters.

IMPLEMENTING AS/400 SECURITY, SECOND EDITION
A practical guide to implementing, evaluating, and auditing your AS/400 security strategy
By Wayne Madden, a **NEWS/400** *technical editor*

Concise and practical, this second edition brings together in one place the fundamental AS/400 security tools and experience-based recommendations that you need and also includes specifics on the latest security enhancements available in OS/400 Version 3 Release 1. Completely updated from the first edition, this is the only source for the latest information about how to protect your system against attack from its increasing exposure to hackers. 389 pages, 16 chapters.

AN INTRODUCTION TO COMMUNICATIONS FOR THE AS/400
By Ruggero Adinolfi; Technical editor, John Enck, a **NEWS/400** *technical editor*

This guide to basic communications concepts and how they operate on the IBM AS/400 outlines the rich mix of communications capabilities designed into the AS/400 and relates them to the concepts that underlie the various network environments. 183 pages, 13 chapters.

JIM SLOAN'S CL TIPS & TECHNIQUES
By Jim Sloan, developer of QUSRTOOL's TAA Tools

Written for those who understand CL, this book draws from Jim Sloan's knowledge and experience as a developer for the S/38 and the AS/400, and his creation of QUSRTOOL's TAA tools, to give you tips that can help you write better CL programs and become more productive. Includes more than 200 field-tested techniques, plus exercises to help you understand and apply many of the techniques presented. 564 pages, 30 chapters.

MASTERING THE AS/400
A practical, hands-on guide
By Jerry Fottral

This introductory textbook to AS/400 concepts and facilities has a utilitarian approach that stresses student participation. A natural prerequisite to programming and database management courses, it emphasizes mastery of system/user interface, member-object-library relationship, utilization of CL commands, and basic database and program development utilities. Also includes labs focusing on essential topics such as printer spooling; library lists; creating and maintaining physical files; using logical files; using CL and DDS; working in the PDM environment; and using SEU, DFU, Query, and SDA. 484 pages, 12 chapters.